Library of
Davidson College

THE ETERNAL TORAH

PART TWO

A New Commentary Utilizing Ancient and
Modern Sources in a Grammatical, Historical
and Traditional Explanation of the Text

THE ETERNAL TORAH

PART TWO

JOSHUA · JUDGES
SAMUEL ONE · SAMUEL TWO

Compiled and Edited by
DAVID LIEBERMAN

Published by
TWIN PINES PRESS
River Vale, New Jersey

Distributed by KTAV Publishing House, Inc.
New York City

Copyright © 1983 by David Lieberman

First Edition

All rights reserved. No part of this book may be
reprinted without written permission of the publisher.
Manufactured in the United States of America.

Library of Congress Cataloging in Publication Data
(Revised for pt. 2)

Lieberman, David, 1900-
    The Eternal Torah.

   Vol. 2 lacks subtitle.
   Vol. 2 distributed by Ktav Pub. House, New York.
   Contents: [1. without special title] — pt. 2. Joshua,
Judges, Samuel One, Samuel Two.
   1. Bible.   O.T.—Commentaries.   I. Title.
BS1225.3.L53   222′.107   78-65572
ISBN 0-9609840-1-1 (v. 2)

DEDICATION

To the memory of my sainted parents, Elimelech Daniel and Myndel Lieberman, in gratitude for my sacred heritage.

To my beloved Sophie for a life of devotion.

To our children, grandchildren and great-grandchildren, whose devotion to living by the guidelines of our Torah and to Eretz Yisrael have created a *reach nichoach*, contentment in our lives.

And...to our cherished Oren Jechiel ז״ל

ACKNOWLEDGEMENTS

The greater our accomplishments, the longer grows the list of our indebtedness to those who help us along the way:

The sages, scholars, and teachers, who paved my path with their wisdom and knowledge, and the inspiration to explain the Eternal Torah to my generation;

My wife, Sophie, for her patience and encouragement while I labored in the vineyard of the Eternal. Her diligence in proofreading the manuscript and the galleys was invaluable to the completion of this work;

My beloved brother, Abraham Lieberman, for his skillful design of the cover;

Mr. Joseph Weiss and Mr. Jacob Weiss of Star Composition Service for their dedication and cooperation in transforming words into type;

Mr. Alvin Schultzberg of The Town House Press, for his expertize and guidance in helping in the creation of this addition to the understanding of the House of Israel's sacred literature.

D.L.

TABLE OF CONTENTS

The Book of Joshua 1
   Contents and Synopsis 2
   Introduction 7
   Preface 15
   The Book of Joshua 16
   Addendum 70

The Book of Judges 79
   Contents and Synopsis 80
   Introduction 89
   The Book of Judges 91

The Book of Samuel One 173
   Contents and Synopsis 174
   Introduction 182
   The Book of Samuel One 186
   Addendum 278

The Book of Samuel Two 279
   Contents and Synopsis 280
   Preface 284
   The Book of Samuel Two 285

THE ETERNAL TORAH

JOSHUA
YEHOSHUA

TABLE OF CONTENTS: JOSHUA

THIS TABLE OF CONTENTS FOR THE BOOK OF JOSHUA, has been written with the intent that it can also be used as a synopsis to summarize the whole Book of Joshua.

CHAPTER 1
Pages 16.17

Joshua is inspired to assume the leadership of Israel upon the demise of Moses. He implements the long conceived plan for the conquest of the Holyland. He instructs his officers to mobilize Israel's army. The tribes of Reuben, Gad and Manasseh pledge their allegiance to Joshua's leadership.

CHAPTER 2
Pages 17.20

Joshua dispatches scouts to establish the mood of the inhabitants of Jericho, to discover their military preparations for the long anticipated invasion. Rahab's cooperation with Israel's scouts and their reciprocal pledge to evacuate her and her immediate family to safety.

CHAPTER 3, 4
Pages 20.24

Joshua's detailed plan to cross the Jordan River. The details for the line of march for the kohanim, the officers and Israel's army. Anticipating the success of his plans, he plans to establish an historic monument to this event. He is resolved to commemorate Israel's arrival in the Holyland by building a monument from the stones removed from the river-bed at their first campsite at Gilgal.

CHAPTER 5
Pages 24.26

Israel's successful crossing without incident, the establishment of the Mishkan at Gilgal inspired the local communities to recognize Israel's presence as a fait accompli. They agreed to barter their newly harvested crops, as Israel anticipated their needs for the observance of the Passover and the Omer. At this point Joshua challenged the multitude that were not circumcised in the desert, to courageously submit to circumcision. Israel's dedication gave Joshua the confidence to visualize his success in the planned invasion of Jericho (vs. 13.15).

CHAPTER 6
Pages 26.28

Joshua is inspired by the Eternal's messenger that he will succeed. In gratitude he zealously exceeds Torah law by issuing an order that every material object captured in Jericho become dedicated to the House of God. Joshua implemented the messengers inspiration in order to create consternation in the city of Jericho by marching around the wall of the city for seven consecutive days before he attacked. Joshua orders the scouts to redeem their pledge to Rahab and escort her to safety before they attack.

CHAPTER 7
Pages 28.30

Achan's contemptuous act and Joshua's overconfidence leads to the loss of 36 men in the preliminary battle of Ai (Joshua 7:6.13). Joshua's investigation, trial and execution of Achan.

TABLE OF CONTENTS: JOSHUA

CHAPTER 8
Pages 31.33
Joshua recognized his error and set into motion a strategy which took into consideration every contingency in the battle of Ai. Prodded by his guilt, Joshua led his army to take his objective which became the turning point in Israel's campaign to recapture the Holyland. Vs. 30.35, the writing of Mishneh Torah and the ceremony upon Mount Gerizim and Mount Ebal, were performed and recorded in chapter 24.

CHAPTER 9
Pages 33.36
The tyrants of the northern territory in the Holyland, lying west of the Jordan River, formed a coalition in order to check Israel's progress. The Gibeonites responded to this action by an effort to secure a treaty with Israel.

CHAPTER 10
Pages 36.40
To counter the Gibeonite peace treaty with Israel, Adoni Zedek, the king of Jerusalem, initiated an alliance with the surrounding local municipalities which included Hoham the king of Hebron, Piram, king of Jarmuth, Japhia, king of Lachish and Debir, king of Eglon. The Gibeonites learn of the alliance and appeal to Joshua for help. Joshua honored his treaty and responded; resulting in the conquest of southern Canaan. Vs. 12.14, contain Joshua's inspired command, "Sun stand still upon Gibeon." Horma, the king of Gezer, came to the assist of Lachish and was defeated. Joshua's victory resulted in the conquest of the Judean Hills, the Negeb area included the *haashedoth* the lowlands. The victory resulted in containing all the territory from Kadesh-barnea, in the east, to the border of Gaza, in the west. Included were the communities from Goshen in Judah to Gibeon v.41.

CHAPTER 11
Pages 40.42
Jabin, king of Hazor formed an alliance with the kings occupying the Galillee, northeast of the Lebanon mountains and the plain below the Chinnereth. V.19, these tyrants were bent upon not permitting any of the communities in their area from accepting Joshua's offer for peace (Deut. 20:10). This chapter concludes the military conquest of Canaan and lists in vs.16.23, all the communities conquered in the campaign.

CHAPTER 12
Pages 43.44
Vs.1.6, list territory conquered in Moses' lifetime, east of the Jordan River. Vs.7.24, list the names of kings and the territories conquered by Joshua west of the Jordan River.

CHAPTER 13
Pages 44.47
Joshua is determined to officially divide the land among the tribes, that they assume the responsibility for governing in their territories and its development. With this in mind Trans-Jordan was surveyed and divided vs.15.23, to Reuben. Vs.24.28, to Gad and vs.29.33, to Manasseh.

TABLE OF CONTENTS: JOSHUA

CHAPTER 14
Pages 47.48

Vs.1.5, exposes Joshua's desire to modify Jacob's admonition in (Gen.49:5.7) in order to deal reasonably with the tribe of Levi. Vs.6.15, Caleb reminds Joshua of Moses' promise to him in (Num.14:24, Deut.1:34.36) that he will receive Hebron.

CHAPTER 15
Pages 48.49

Caleb and Joshua are the only survivors of the generation present at the Exodus. Therefore the division of the Holyland began with the tribe of Judah. Vs.1.12, establish the boundary lines for the tribe of Judah. Vs.13.19, specify the towns deeded in this territory to Caleb and Othniel. Vs.20.23, name all the towns included in Judah's territory.

CHAPTER 16
Pages 49.50

The second lot was drawn by Ephraim. Vs.1.10, establish the boundary lines of Ephraim's territory. Some of their land areas were in the boundary lines of Manasseh.

CHAPTER 17
Pages 50.51

The third lot went to the tribe of Manasseh. Since the families of Machir, Novach and Jair had already received their allotment east of the Jordan River in Trans-Jordania. the other families of Manasseh that consisted of Abiezer, Helek, Azriel, Shechem, Hepher and Shemida, received their allotted territory beginning with the western shore of the Jordan River. The tribe of Manasseh therefore had land on both sides of the Jordan River. Vs.3.6, list the five sons of Manasseh and Zelaphchad's five daughters. Joshua now honored Moses' decree given in (Num. 27:1.11) by giving them 10 portions of land, thereby establishing a daughter's equal rights. Vs.7.11 establish the boundary lines of this allotment which included Beth-shean and its surrounding towns, Ibleam and its surrounding towns, Dor and its surrounding towns, En-dor and its surrounding towns, Taanach and its surrounding towns and Megiddo and its surrounding towns. This territory comprised three regions because it was contiguous to Ephraim, Asher and Issachar. Vs.12.13, exposes the disunity in the ranks of Israel. Though Manasseh and Ephraim represented the largest tribes in Israel, they could not unite to enforce their conditions upon the indigenous inhabitants now living in these communities. Vs.14.18, Manasseh's expanding needs plus its inability to occupy its allotted territory, demands that Joshua allot them additional land. Joshua challenged their ability to expand only by their own initiative.

CHAPTER 18
Pages 51.53

Joshua calls an assembly at Shiloh to deal conclusively with the seven tribes who have failed to occupy their allotted territory which he has succeeded in conquering. The tribe of Simeon has been integrated with the tribe of Judah. Dan is

TABLE OF CONTENTS: JOSHUA

	hampered by the Philistine occupation. Dan, Zebulun, Issachar, Asher and Naphtali have been transients because of their maritime interests with Phoenicia. (See The Eternal Torah p.553). Benjamin has dissipated its strength (Gen.49:27, see T.E.T.) Joshua demands they survey their allotted territories, divide it among themselves in accord with their needs and natural abilities. Vs.11.28, reports the results in their survey and the establishment of Benjamin's territorial boundaries.
CHAPTER 19 Pages 53.56	Vs..1.9, establish Simeon's inherited territory. Vs.10.16, records the boundaries of Zebulun's allotted territory. Vs.17.23, establish the legal boundary lines for Issachar. Vs.24.31, record the boundary lines for the territory of Asher. Vs.32.39, record the allotted territory for the tribe of Naphtali. Vs.40.48, the last one to be assigned was the tribe of Dan. This conforms with Moses' evaluation given in (Deut. 33:22) see The Eternal Torah. Though these verses establish their territorial boundaries, they never occupied this territory. Vs.49.50, Joshua requested and received Timnath-serach in the territory of Ephraim. He developed it and lived there to the end of his lifetime. V.51, concludes for the record the division of the Holyland. The titles were confirmed and recorded by Joshua, Eleazar the priest and the Nesiim-tribal leaders. The record was filed in the Mishkan to confirm the legal titles of each respective tribe.
CHAPTER 20 Pages 56.57	Joshua established the Cities of Refuge.
CHAPTER 21 Pages 57.59	Joshua recorded the allotment of the Levitical cities within the respective tribal territories, in accord with Torah law (Num. 35:1.8).
CHAPTER 22 Pages 59.61	Joshua expresses Israel's gratitude to the tribes of Reuben, Gad, Manasseh for having fulfilled their promise made in (Num.32:). Joshua discharged them from their oath and gave them permission to return to their homes and families in Trans-Jordan. Vs.9.12, Reuben, Gad and Manasseh, build an altar to express their gratitude for having been granted the ability to resume their normal lives. Vs.13.34, Phinehas and the Nesiim, are satisfied with their sincerity and dedication.
CHAPTER 23 Pages 61.63	Joshua's farewell address to the Elders, the leaders and the Judges.

TABLE OF CONTENTS: JOSHUA

CHAPTER 24 Vs.1.13, Joshua called an assembly at Shechem of all the
Pages 63.69 families of Israel, including women and children, to deliver a
major address. He reviewed Israel's past history. Vs.14.28,
record Joshua's challenge for rededication to the basic
principles set down in the Eternal's Torah. Joshua recorded
their oath and annexed the record in the Book of Joshua to be
identified as part of the Torah Covenant. On this note of
unity he discharged them. Vs. 29, 31, record the death and
burial of Joshua. V. 32, records the reinterment of the body of
Joseph. V. 33, records the death of Eleazer and his burial.

Introduction.. Pages 7.14

Preface.. Page 15

Joshua... Pages 16.69

Addendum.. Pages 70.77

Abbreviations
The Eternal Torah..T.E.T.
Jewish Calendar...J.C.
Before Common Era..BCE.
After Common Era..ACE.

INTRODUCTION TO THE BOOK OF JOSHUA

Joshua addressed Israel at the close of his life in the name of Adonai, the Eternal God of history. Like his master and teacher Moses, Joshua pleaded that Israel ever be mindful of the reason for its being. He challenged Israel to look back into pre-historic times. "Observe the generations of man in the process of evolution. Observe closely and meditate over the lives of the pre-diluvian generations (Gen.6:1.8). Research and study the history of Israel's genealogy (Gen.11:10.32). Ask your parents to enlighten you about your roots, the original and modest beginnings of your forefathers, from Noah to the present generation. Look into your Torah and study the historic development of all humanity. Observe the division of their territories, the establishment of their boundaries (Gen.10:1.32, 13:15.16, 15:18.21). Perceive for yourselves from the record in the Book of Genesis, that even at this early point in human history, the odds were overwhelmingly stacked against the descendants of Shem-Semites. Comprehend the direction of the Eternal in the evolution of history, as He designated Israel's future territory. He observed the inhumanities of man to man and the destructiveness of man to his ecology recorded in (Gen.10:8.10). Abraham's awareness of the fate which awaits Sodom, his genuine concern for their fate recorded in (Gen.18:17.33). This gave the Eternal God of history the proof of a human being concerned with the welfare of mankind. In (Gen.18:19) the Eternal recognized the genetic umbilical cord from which civilization shall evolve."

Nothing grows in a vacuum. Everything that occurs in evolution is the result of cause and effect. Let us therefore look back into history in order to evaluate the process of evolution. We who live in the 20th century ACE, have the archaeological evidence going back to the 8th millenium, the neolithic period, the beginning of the agricultural revolution. All the evidence suggests a common culture had created this development. The city of Ur, in Chaldea has surrendered its past human record into the 5th millenium. The evidence found there enriches our knowledge of the past as it reveals and exhibits the origin of western Asiatic culture at the dawn of history. These searches have established the settlers here at al-Ubaid, were agricultural Semites. We also learn that the Sumerian Semites who later settled in Mesopotamia had borrowed their agricultural and technical terminology.

Civilization began in Mesopotamia about the 4th millenium. The early settlers were Semites from the Persian Gulf, those later called Hebrews from the Arabian desert, the Semitic groups from the Syrian desert, the Semitic Elamites, from the Iranian highlands (Gen.10:22). Sumer-Shinar-Mesopotamia became the name of their land and Aramaic was their language. Though the evidence establishes writing as a pre-Sumerian invention, it is here that it reached its full development. It was here in Mesopotamia, that the "urban revolution" unfolded. It was here that bronze metallurgy and monumental architecture were exploited.

The very first city to be built was Eridu-Irad (Gen.4:17.18). This is confirmed by archaeological excavations. This city became a port of entry for seaborne

INTRODUCTION: JOSHUA

immigration and commerce. The evidence discovered confirms the devastating effect of the flood reported in (Gen.6:7:8:9:). History testifies it took about 200 years from about 3100-2900 BCE. for mankind to recover from its destruction. From 2900-2700, this period is called the Early Bronze Age-The Golden Era. For during this period great libraries were organized, academies were established to teach the new advancements in writing and language. The writing of literature flourished and it is most interesting that the names of each author appeared on their manuscripts.

The early Semites living in Babylonia-Mesopotamia were astrologers. From their speculation came astronomy, the calendar, medicine, grammar, mathematics, lexicography, history and philosophy.

Astronomy had its origin in everyday life. The Semitic tribesmen avoiding the scorching sun, traveled mostly at night. Like mariners they learned to identify the stars and the major planets. This enabled them to compute the time of day and night, the days of the month, the seasons of the year. Recognizing the wonderment of the heavens, the Semites worshipped them as gods. Their principal deities were; the moon, the sun and the five large planets. They divided the year into 12 months of 30 days each, they then harmonized the calendar to conform to the Solar Cycle of 365 days.

When the Semites were the dominant population in the Old Period of Babylonia, both geometry and arithmetic had reached the standards later acquired in Europe by Euclid and Pythagoris. This information was vital for construction purposes. The need to transport material from where it was abundant to Mesopotamia where it was in short supply. This was the creative inspiration that demanded weights and measures and maritime information, the knowledge how to take water from the rivers, to where it was needed for irrigation. This created the demand for the ration of "pi". This was also vital for cylindrical vessels and other objects. They developed the skills to deal with fractions and decimals and the ability to express the power of numbers.

Another Semitic development in the Near East, the term law became inseparable from the term justice. Excavations by Rawlinson in Nineveh, discovered the library of Ashurbanipal, the last of the Assyrian kings in 668-625 BCE. here were found the records of the flood (Gen.6:9.22,7:8) and a multitude of literary works recorded on clay tablets. Unfortunately when they were gathered they were shoveled in heaps and thereby much of the continuity was lost. It was from these records that much lexicographic material were discovered.

The incident reported in (Gen.10:8.10, 11:1.9) terminated the Golden Era when man lived peacefully in harmony with nature. Nimrod of Hamitic birth invaded Mesopotamia to build an empire. It was here that he organized a dictatorship and ruled over the capitals of southern Mesopotamia, Babylon, Uruk-Erech and Akkad. (Gen.10:11.12) reports that Ashur the son of Shem (Gen.10:22) resenting the oppressive methods of Nimrod, removed himself to the north of Babylonia

INTRODUCTION: JOSHUA

and built the cities of Nineveh, Rehovot-Ir, Callah and Resen. In contrast to Nimrod's fortified cities, Ashur built open cities with public roads leading to and from his cities.

Pieced together from the thousands of clay tablets found in Mesopotamia, are the chronicles inscribed upon them recapturing for history the past record of mankind. Among these inscriptions were found the King List, recording the names of the rulers that governed Mesopotamia from the post dilluvian period to the ascension of Hammurapi-Hammurabi, in 1794 BCE. From this list of 23 different rulers, we learn, that the first city to rise after the "Flood" was the dynasty of Kish. Toward the end of the list we learn of the rise of Sargon I, a Semitic ruler who founded the city of Akkad. This became the center for the development of the Semitic speech. Sargon ruled for 55 years in the 24th century BCE. It was during his reign that he consolidated the empire of Kish, Akkad, Uruk and Ur. From these chronicles we learn of man's pantheon of gods: Shemesh, the sun god, Bel-Merodech, became the national god. Disclosed in these chronicles are the rise and fall of new gods as man reaches for the source of his creation. Sargon was succeeded by his sons who ruled for 24 years and then followed by his grandson Naram-Sin, who consolidated the empire to reach its highest point during his 56 years of leadership. He called it Babylonia. From this high point in their development, the barbaric hordes from the north that were normally held at bay by the Sargonic kings, took advantage during the political turmoil as Shar-kali-sharri, the son of Naram-Sin was assasinated. This obscure horde destroyed Sargon's Akkadian empire and for 40 years they succeeded to remain as the rulers. With their ascension to power began the competition and the expansion of the Early Dynastic period II. This became known as the "Heroic Age" which lasted from 2500 to 2300 BCE. Temples were built to appease the ever growing pantheon of gods. During this period the priestly influence in the temples directed the political and economic affairs of Mesopotamia. The effect of this setback in Mesopotamia was felt in Egypt as the Old Kingdom of the Pyramid Age came to an end. It is important to note that while in the Old Kingdom of Egypt, the king was worshipped as a god, in the Sumer-league of Sargonic Semitic government, they formed a primitive democracy at Nippur called a divine assembly. It was this assembly that chose the leaders who ruled the city states, in the name of the god Enlil-El. The Semitic influence is also felt in 2630 BCE. in the city of Ur, led by Urukagina as the first social reformer, he declared freedom for all its citizens.

The years of 2300-2100, BCE. were years of assimilation. The barbaric hordes that destroyed the Sargonic empire took their places in their new society. They developed new skills and acquired a sense of literacy. The number of documents recovered at Ur and Mari by archaeologists in our generation attest to the advancement of the written word. From these finds we can reconstruct the development of writing. From the crude pictographic script which began in 3000 BCE. the Semitic peoples developed a flexible phonetic syllabary script adaptable

INTRODUCTION: JOSHUA

to every form of writing. Textbooks were created, vocabulary was developed and schools established to teach the new developments. Reading the Book of Genesis, there are many words that echo this whole development.

Many of the laws later developed and inscribed in the Torah, were incubated and born here. The biblical Sumer is Shinar-Babylonia-Mesopotamia Chaldea. The early occupants and the source of all the above described developments are the *anshe Hashem* (Gen.6:4). This is the source from which Egypt acquired its civilization. The rest of Africa was almost completely isolated from Egypt's advancement. The Semitic language cross pollinated the Egyptian language to enrich its usage and its ability to record its history.

2100-1800 BCE. were years of movement. The nomadic Semitic Amurru, whose home was in the area bounded by the Euphrates River in the east and the Mediterranean Sea in the west migrated toward Mesopotamia, to take advantage of the developments going on there. The term Amorites is used to describe all the Semitic tribes that came from the west. It was also used to describe those that came from southern Mesopotamia prior to 2000 BCE. This was also true at Mari, Babylon and Ashur about 1830 BCE. These wide ranging people, who spoke a common language were called Amorites. This was the beginning of Canaanite-Hebrew or Aramaic. The bulk of these Amorites came from the Syrian desert and scattered over Syrio-Palestine and Mesopotamia. The bulk of this emigration was centered at Mari. They adopted the Sumero-Akkadian or Syrio-Canaanite culture. Over the centuries this became the Canaanite-West Semitic dialect. Only the Sumero-Akkadians called them Amorites.

The Bible calls the indigenous natives who occupied Canaan, Amorites, they were composed of various ethnic groups: Hittites, Perizzites, Girgashites, Jebusites, Hivites, Horites. These groups were the result of constant invasions of Hammitic stock from Africa and Indo-Europeans from the west and the north. These various ethnic groups made up the Canaanite population prior to and at the time of the conquest of Canaan by Joshua. They are described by an ancient Sumerian Religious Text. "The weapon is his companion. He knows no submission. He eats uncooked flesh. He owns no house in his life-time. He does not bury his dead companion." The rift between these two cultures resulted in constant warfare as they jockeyed for position and fractured every effort to form a government. These ethnic groups were governed by sheikhs or elders. There is no link between the Hebrew usage of Emori-Amori and the Sumero-Akkadian Amurru, which ceased to be used 1000 years before Israel arrived in the Holyland.

Civilization is indebted to Berosos, a Babylonian priest, who lived in the third century BCE., for having compiled most of the historic records recorded in this introduction. It is Berosos that brought to light a copy of The King List, which begins with the reign of Hammurabi in 1794 BCE. Included in the list are the Dynasties that ruled Babylonia until the Persian conquest in 539 BCE. Consistent

INTRODUCTION: JOSHUA

with all Semitic historic records they have served humanity well. Their authenticity has withstood the vicissitudes of time. Though Berosos inspired Manetho, his contemporary in Egypt to record the ancient Egyptian history, the obstacles created by the Egyptian kings who destroyed the records of the kings they succeeded faulted the efforts of Manetho. For the proofs of this statement, see Addendum at the end of the Book of Joshua.

When the first wave of Semitic nomads entered Mesopotamia in 2900 BCE. they succeeded under the kings of Kish and Akkad to become full citizens and partners in the Sumero-Akkadian civilization as it developed. However, when the second wave infiltrated into Mesopotamia in the 21st century BCE. they spoke Babylonian in the south and Assyrian in the north. Therefore, the 19th century can be characterized as the political fragmentation by the Amorites from west-Canaan. The Fertile Crescent, nestling the territory between the Mediterranean in the west and the Euphrates in the east was firmly in the hands of the Amorite rulers between 1813-1783 BCE. Upon this scene entered Hammurabi in 1794-1750 BCE. Under his leadership he reunited Mesopotamia. Though this reunification lasted but 58 years, his enduring legacy lies in the legal, literary and artistic realm. Hammurabi preserved and cannonized the best in centuries of tradition and human development. Many of these legal formulations are paralleled in the Books of Exodus and Deuteronomy.

This is an important moment in history to recognize the great developments which originated in this small corner of the planet Earth. Every future development in science and industry, in religion and philosophy began here. Here originated wheat, millet, barley and the domestication of cattle, sheep, and goats. Their breeding goes back to prerecorded history. The Code of Hammurabi's Law was found at Susa in 1902 ACE.

Barbarism and tyranny are ever present to extinguish the light of human progress. Eight years after Hammurabi's death, the Kassites-Kashites, Indo-European barbarians from the north conspired with the alien forces in Babylonia and overthrew the existing government to found a new dynasty which lasted from 1780-1204 BCE. For 576 years they occupied the mountains north of Elam. They are the Cossaens in Ptolomie's time. They were the neighbors of the Medes. They are the Sussians in Aeschylus's time (525-468 BCE.).

Canaan was never a state in ancient history. It was destined to centuries of vassalage under the aegis of the surrounding colossuses. Only a people united in its idealism could unite this territory, its hills, gorges and mountainous promontories. It is limited by the number of rivers and the number of perennial streams. These factors set limits on agriculture. Most of the Canaanite cities were Semitic into the Neolithic period. Semitic penetration into Canaan goes back to the fourth and third millenium. Ugarit was dominantly Semitic. Their lexicon identifies a close affinity to the Akkadian speech. Inscriptions found upon shards and figurines in 1900 ACE., indicate a second wave of newly arrived immigrants

INTRODUCTION: JOSHUA

from the Syrio-Arabian desert. These Semites were called Amorites because of their language, which was identical with earlier Semites who inhabited Canaan even before the fourth millenium. Not until the 14th century BCE. would the Semitic Hebrew spoken in Canaan distinguish itself from the Aramaic spoken in Babylonia-Mesopotamia. Late in the 13th and 12th century BCE. in the process of evolution was another related dialect in contrast to Hebrew introduced in the western Mediterranean, which became Punic Phoenician. Canaanite early Semitic settlers of the third millenium had close contacts with Egypt until 1740 BCE. They had close ties with the Hyksos 1670-1570 BCE. Thutmosis III, 1504-1450 BCE. consolidated his hold upon Canaan until it became a Hittite vassal state. (Tel el-Amarna letters)

Seti I, and Rameses II, 1318-1234, reconquered Canaan until it was invaded by the Sea Peoples at the end of the 13th century BCE. The coming of these invaders from the Aegean Sea area, thrust an identity upon the indigenous Aramean-Amorite-Semites, as they had never known before. The 13th century BCE. revolutionary effect was as mighty as an earthquake. The Seapeoples came into conflict with the Egyptians, the Hittites divided Phoenicia and Syria into two spheres of influence. The Philistines defeated the Sidonians on the Mediterranean Coast and Ugarit and Arvad were completely destroyed. Tyre rose from the ashes at the end of the 13th century BCE. From this point to the reign of Hiram as king of Phoenicia, there was a lapse of 240 years. Joshua and the Israelites were poised at this very point in time in Trans-Jordania, for the historic conquest of the Promised Land.

The Hittite invaders originally came from Boghazkov, 100 miles east of Ankara. They were Indo-Europeans, who invaded the territory bounded by the Black Sea in the north and the Mediterranean in the south. Here they ruled in the second millenium. They adopted the Hattic language. Their king was Labarna. In the 19th and 18th centuries the Hattic princes ruled Anatolia.

For centuries the Assyrian traders criss-crossed the highlands of Anatolia. By 1740 BCE. the Hittites destroyed the trade centers, forged a new kingdom with Assyria, destroyed the Hammurabic kingdom at Carchemish and won control of the Euphrates River. Babylon was sacked. This put an end to the first dynasty of Babylon. The Hittite invasion was followed by the Sealand invasion and then by the Kassites. This barbaric transition brought on a full century 1600-1500 BCE. of darkness upon a civilization that was literate and kept abundant records from the 4th millenium.

North of Mesopotamia lay the Mittani Empire It was ruled by indo-Aryans. Their western branch at this point in time were invading India, who had commercial, religious and artistic connections with Sumer and Babylon. The Mittani's, the Hittites, the Kassites, the Sodgians, the Medes, the Persians, were indo-European and Aryan stock that invaded India at about the same time as Babylon was invaded. With these invaders came the brutality which created the

INTRODUCTION: JOSHUA

outcast stystem with slavery and bestiality. From this system grew the 40 million untouchables in India into modern history. To offset all this bestiality there entered the Habiru in the 16th and 15th century BCE. Amorite Semitic stock unwilling to submit to their non-Semitic conquerors. They were not organized on ethnic lines but as a social entity.

In 1365-1330, BCE. Assyria emerged under the rulership of Ashur-uballit, after a long succession of foreign masters: Akkad, Ur, Eshnunna, Shubat-Enlil and Wasukuna. Ashur had a long and consistent continuity going back to its founder recorded in (Gen.10:11). With the end of Mittanian power, the disengagement of Egypt in the Amarna period, Ashur-Ubalit challenged the Kassites who usurped their Babylonian traditions. Tikulti-Ninurta, in 1244-1208 BCE., defeated the Babylonians. The timing of his effort was wrong. The sack of Troy in about 1250 BCE., and the subsequent fall of Mycenean cities on the Greek mainland unleashed a new flood of refugees to Asia Minor. These Seapeoples did not come by boat. They came by foot along the shoreland and invaded every piece of land wherever they could settle. They engraved their presence across every Mediterranean littoral and island: Cilicia, Philistia-Gerar, Palestine, Sicily, Trurua, Sardinia. The indigenous settlers fled in the opposite direction. The Hurrians of Silecia fled to Hittite Anatolia. This marked the end of the Hittite Empire, as these refugees invaded the Mittani north of Syria. The Canaanites were displaced by the Philistines, who encountered the Israelites coming from Trans-Jordania. In a century the Near-East was turned upside-down as Israel, a social entity composed of people dedicated to introduce a new world order based upon moral, ethical and spiritual values appeared on the scene. (See Addendum in Book of Joshua for the cause of this upheaval). To complete the demographic picture, the Dorians, the Acheans, conquered Crete and the Aegean Sea in about 1400 BCE. They opened the shipping lanes to commerce (In 1950 BCE., the Phoenicians were already using these lanes as far west as Spain). All this new development freed commerce from the robber polluted highways.

The Five Books of Moses are the Source in which have been stored and collected every human endeavor by the Semitic branch of the human family for the development of a new world order. The Torah is essentially the Eternal God's Masterplan for a civilized human being inspired to create a "Messianic" age for all humanity. The Torah is a Universal Document. It establishes the importance of every human being that he become a member of a social entity dedicated to live by its Moral, Ethical and Spiritual values. With the information in this introduction we gain a birdseye view of the ancient world with its barbaric dictatorial governments and its debauched societies. We have also observed the marvelous development of human ingenuity, striving to create its needs. With this historic background, we can better understand Israel's invasion of the Holyland. The conquest of the Holyland is a challenge to the Israelites to become a model state for all of humanity. On the other hand humanity can only earn the

INTRODUCTION: JOSHUA

right to call itself civilized when it embraces the values inscribed in the Eternal God's Masterplan.

David Lieberman

In grateful gratitude to the Eternal, my God, for the opportunity to put into writing the accumulative effect of my studies and experiences gathered over 60 years of toiling in the vineyard of the Eternal God. May my thoughts inspire my generation which has much to its credit to scan these pages to recognize our blessings and correct our failures.

Kislev 18th 5741

PREFACE TO THE BOOK OF JOSHUA

Joshua inscribed Israel's testimonial oath given in the 12th century BCE., in the Book of Joshua 22:22.29,24:16.18,25. He annexed it to the Book of Deuteronomy, as a part of Sefer Torath Elohim, This oath is the force that binds every future generation to uphold the teachings inscribed in The Book of Divine Instruction.

Described in its teachings are the sensory impulses, the spiritual essence of the genetic demand of the Zelem Elohim, the built in gyroscope that determines human equilibrium. The Books of the Prophets are the human record of the metaphysical demand of self examination in our daily lives, the crucible of evolution. Highlighted in its pages are the moral values which cannot be inherited; they must be acquired in the biological process as we refine our physical desires-wants, to become our spiritual needs. The chemical compounds of our diet, our sexual desires, the environment of our homes, our personal and family lifestyle are transmitted by our genes in the process of procreation to strike cosmic roots in the continuity of life. From these roots the immortality of the human soul is assured. The Book of Joshua records the world that man creates for himself, while ignoring the real world, the New World Order striving to be born.

Peering through the telescope of history, 20th century civilization must conclude the distance it shall yet have to travel before it can claim for itself, its dedication to the ideals described in The Book of Divine Instruction. The route begins with ridding our psyche of all illusions. We can then reach for the ideal disciplines inscribed in Sefer Torath Elohim, as we refine our values, that the World is a Divine manifestation of all its parts. That every human experience must be inspired, directed and disciplined by the soul's impulses striving to encourage us to refine the quality of our dreams. Human responses to the Eternal's inspiration either speed or retard the progress of evolution.

Fortunate is the human being who inherits perfect good health in their genetic inheritance, then reenforces the prenatal and post-natal environment with moral, ethical and spiritual values to enhance the quality of daily living. Genes are our inheritance, from which evolve strategies for behavior and the quality of life. Mating selectively is to maximize our fitness, to immortalize our excellence.

David Lieberman

JOSHUA CHAPTER I

Vs. 1.4 During the 30 day mourning period for Moses, Joshua reviewed the teachings of his master Moses. He was inspired by his faith in the Eternal God, through the teachings and guidance he received during these past 40 years of dedicated service in the presence of Moses. When this 30 day period was ended Joshua revitalized Israel's plan of action to cross the Jordan River. He reviewed this plan with the Elders and once again confirmed the traditional concept of the territory which they may subdue as recorded in (Num. 34:1.15). This land has been in the possession of the descendants of Shem, from the beginning of human history. This conforms with God's promise to Abraham, Isaac and Jacob in (Gen. 12:1.3, 13:14.18, 15:1,21, 17:1.14, 22:1.18, 26:2.5, 28:11.22, 35:9.15, 46:1.4). This is confirmed by the historical facts as established in the introduction to the book of Joshua.

Vs. 5.7 "Be vigorous and courageous in your efforts. Only then shall no one challenge your leadership. The Eternal God of history will inspire you even as He did your great master Moses. Permit no obstacle to weaken your resolution to accomplish the goal I have set before you. I shall never forsake you. You shall indeed be My instrument through whose efforts the people of Israel shall inherit the Promised Land, which I have bequeathed to their forefathers Abraham, Isaac and Jacob. Your progress and your success are conditioned upon your determination. Inspire Israel to observe and to fulfill the disciplines inscribed in the Torah as set forth and taught by My faithful servant Moses. In your effort to fulfill My commandments, be not overzealous to exceed the purpose and intent of My law. Nor may you veer to the left to modify My laws, that they lose My direction and My aim in the process of the evolution of My people Israel."

Vs. 8.9 "Permit not expediency to detour you from the disciplines inscribed in this Blueprint for living the good life. Inspire Israel to meditate upon its teachings both day and night, that they too become inspired to observe these guidelines for the evolution of civilization. For only then will they prosper as individuals and as a nation. *"Halo tziviticha"* I have engraved into the lifeline of mankind's genes the conscious demand to observe My Natural Law, My Moral Law and My Ethical Law. Be vigorous and resolute in your efforts to inspire Israel to heed My guidelines inscribed in the Torah. Become not dismayed nor apprehensive when you falter. (Gen. 6.3) I shall ever be with you to guide you *"ki imcha Adonai Elohecha"* the Eternal's demand is ever in the soul of man demanding righteous living in his everyday existence." God's Presence is ever with us, prodding us on to succeed in all our activities, even in our moments of relaxation. (Gen. 18:19) He ever insists that our thoughts and intentions shall ever be pure, honest and just.

Vs. 10.11 Joshua issued the command to Israel's officers, that they issue his call to duty for all the men eligible for military service. They are to issue instructions for the preparation of all vital necessities including implements of war. For three days hence they shall cross the

JOSHUA CHAPTER 1

Jordan River. Joshua's emphasis is upon their psychological preparedness. *"Chazak veematz"* be fearless as you face the enemy without and be resolved to succeed as you face the enemy within, who ever demands self preservation. Your resolution must be equal to the task that confronts you in order to receive your reward, the inheritance promised to your forefathers.

Vs. 12.15 Joshua addressed the leaders of the tribes of Reuben, Gad and the leaders of the three families of Manasseh, Machir, Jair and Nobach, who had chosen to remain in Trans-Jordania. Joshua reminded them of their vow taken during the lifetime of Moses (Num. 32: Deut. 3:12.22). "You are now to mobilize all the men in your respective tribes capable of bearing arms. In accord with your vow made to Moses, you are to remain on the western side of the Jordan River until the conquest of the Promised Land has been completed. When your brethren shall have secured their portion of the land and you will have helped them become settled in their inherited portion, even as you have already become settled in your chosen portion in Trans-Jordan, only then will you be able to return to your homes. You shall then return to your homes and families secure in your moral and legal right to possess it. I, Eleazar and the Elders shall then discharge you from the oath taken before Moses in my presence."

Vs. 16.18 The reply of Reuben, Gad and Manasseh was spontaneous. "Every demand you shall make of us we shall fulfill. Wherever you shall command us to go, we shall heed your instructions. We dedicate ourselves to your leadership, even as we recognized Moses' authority in choosing you as his successor (Deut. 31:7). We pray the Eternal God, shall bless the labor of your authority, even as He did Moses. Any man in Israel, that shall challenge your leadership shall be guilty of treason. We urge you to be vigorous and resolute in your leadership. We pray, that you succeed in your goal."

JOSHUA CHAPTER 2

V .1 Jericho was considered the key to Israel's entry into Canaan. Israel's camp at this moment was Abel-hashitim on the eastern bank of the Jordan River. Jericho is about 20 kilometers from the western bank of the Jordan River. It is a four hour walk from the western shore of the river. Joshua sent two scouts, who were *heresh* disguised as potter merchants hawking their wares. Their secret mission was to ascertain the mood and the morale of the people of Jericho. They succeeded in entering the city gates and planned to spend the night at this inn, in the hope they may eavesdrop on the conversation of the day's happenings.

Vs. 2.3 Though their disguise seemed genuine, their choice as reputable merchants going to the inn of Rahab cast suspicion upon their mission. This fact was reported to the king of

JOSHUA CHAPTER 2

Jericho. For four decades the inhabitants of Canaan have lived with the fear of Israel's conquest. (Israel's tradition was well known to the inhabitants of Canaan. Most of them were descendants of Shem, though they had become assimilitated with the nomadic people from the north. Only the immediate descendants of Abraham and those who became converts to his concept of Monotheism as recorded in (Gen. 12:5), joined Israel when they left Egypt with the Exodus. The Torah records a multitude who were in Egypt were permitted to become converts and joined Israel upon their Manifest Destiny to become an Israelite nation. These numbers swelled the ranks of those recorded in (Ex. 12:37.38). This new wave of Semites are now about to thrust a new identity upon the indigenous Semitic inhabitants of Canaan. An identity which was in the process of evolution from the time of Shem). It was therefore reported to the king of Jericho, that two Israelite spies checked into Rahab's inn this evening, in order to reconnoiter and survey the city. The king therefore demanded that Rahab turn over the spies to the authorities to establish their identity.

Vs. 4.5 Rahab became aware that her guests were reported to the authorities. She therefore anticipated that she would be challenged with housing spies. She therefore hid them *vatizpeno* she hid each one separately. When questioned about these strangers seen at her inn, she admitted there were two strangers here this evening. "I do not know their nationality and therefore I cannot help you identify them. However, I did observe them leaving here as the city gates were about to close. I therefore do not know their destination. I would suggest that you pursue them at once, you may succeed in overtaking them before nightfall"

Vs. 6.7 The text establishes the reason the officers of the king could not find the strangers. Rahab hid them among the flax stalks which were being dried in the sun upon the roof of her inn. Anticipating that these strangers were Israeli spies, the officers pursued them in the direction of the Jordan River, toward the fords which were crossable. The text confirms the closing of the city gates, that no one may enter or leave until the investigation is completed.

Vs. 8.11 Having dispatched the officers in search of the scouts, Rahab went up to her visitors and engaged them in conversation. She exposed her fears and the fears of the people of Jericho. "For decades we have anticipated the conquest of Canaan. The surrounding countryside stands in awe as we analyze the magnitude of the miracles performed by your Eternal God. How, He dried up the Reed Sea when you left Egypt. We have had time to review the meaning of your victory over Sihon and Og, the Amorite kings in Trans-Jordan. These crushing facts destroyed our spirit of resistance. It dissolved our hope for mounting a defense. Your victories have overwhelmed us." Rahab gives voice to her monotheistic convictions as she confirms the existing gap between the Canaanite idolatrous faith and the God of Israel, Whose Natural Law governs the universe.

JOSHUA CHAPTER 2

Vs. 12.13 "I request that you take an oath, that you will demonstrate your convictions by an act of truth, *rachmanut* mercy, by which your Eternal God is identified. I recognize Him as the Director of human history. I now request that you reciprocate the kindness which I have shown you by saving you from the tyrants of Jericho. Your oath shall confirm your intentions to extend this kindness to save me, my father, mother, my brothers and sisters and all the immediate members of my family. Swear that you will make every effort to save us when you invade Jericho."

V. 14 "We the scouts of Israel, recognize our debt to you for saving our lives. We are grateful to you for your act of kindness which endangered your own life. For this sign of *emet* truth, we promise to save your life. We further promise to reciprocate your *hesed* kindness, by endangering our lives in order to save the lives of your immediate family. We have but one reservation, that this arrangement between us shall not be publicized and enlarged to include others."

Vs. 15.16 Rahab lowered the scouts by a rope attached to the window of her house which was built into the wall surrounding the city of Jericho. She directed them to head for the hills and to hide there for about three days in order to avoid the officers who were in the process of a thorough search for the spies.

Vs. 17.22 The scouts once again qualify the conditions of their oath. "When we shall invade the city of Jericho, you are to secure this very scarlet rope by which you are now making it possible for us to leave your home, to this very window. You are to assemble into your home the immediate members of your family whom we agreed to save. Should any of them venture outside, they shall bear their own guilt. We further qualify that you may not publicize the contents of our conversation nor may you disclose our presence. Should you fail to adhere to any of these conditions, we shall consider ourselves free from the oath we have taken in v. 14." Rahab confirmed their conditions as she bade them farewell and Godspeed your mission. She then secured the scarlet rope to the window in accord with their instructions. The scouts headed for the hills in accord with Rahab's advice and waited for about three days. This was to give them the assurance that the officers had returned from their search. Since they were but a few hours away from Abel-hashitim, their timing would conform with the three days established in v. 1:11, for the breaking of camp.

Vs. 23.24 *Vayashuvu* the scouts designated a point from which they could observe the very ford by which they intended to cross. From this point they ventured forth and returned to it until they felt assured that all was clear for their safe crossing. *Vayerdu* only then did they come down from the hill to the specific ford by which they planned to cross the Jordan River. *Vayavru* they then walked to Abel-hashitim. Vayavou they

JOSHUA CHAPTER 2

reported directly to Joshua in great detail and summed up for Joshua their conclusions. From the exactness of their language we conclude the trustworthiness of their perceptions derived from their conversation with Rahab. Though their mission was to concentrate upon Jericho and its environs, their report included the state of mind of all the inhabitants of Canaan. "They have resigned even before we attack them. This conforms with God's promise in (Ex. 15:15)."

JOSHUA CHAPTER 3

V. 1   The scouts arrived at Rahab's inn in the evening of the 6th day of Nisan. They returned to Joshua in the evening of the 9th day of Nisan. They gave their report that very evening when all was in readiness for the final order to march. Joshua issued the order that very evening to break camp at dawn of the 9th day of Nisan. They marched that very day to the banks of the Jordan River and spent the night there.

Vs. 2.4   At this point the officers who gave the original order to mobilize instructed the army in the following procedure: "When the Kohanim-Leviim start their march with the Ark, containing the Torah, the Law of the Eternal our God, you shall wait until they have advanced about 2000 cubits (1 kilometer and 200 meters). You shall then fall in line. Be sure to maintain this distance as you march. Do not shorten this gap. For the bearers of the Ark shall lead us to inspire us upon our mission."

Vs. 5.8   Joshua addressed the army of Israel and gave the order of *hitkadashu* in the evening of the 10th day of Nisan. They were to purify themselves, (Deut. 23:10.15) both physically and psychologically in anticipation of the Eternal's Presence. "For tomorrow you shall become witnesses to the effect of the Eternal's Natural Law." The miraculous timing is to conform with the demands of God's natural law. (v. 7, should follow v. 5). Though Joshua had first hand knowledge how the Jordan River functioned in past history, he had no knowledge of its effect upon the crossing of so vast a multitude at a given period of time. He was present at the crossing of the Reed Sea. He was a living witness to the Eternal's perfect timing. It was the explosion of the Island of Santorini and the collapse of the Island of Thera, which created the great geological drama and the *tsunamis* which devastated the Nile Delta, as the Israelites were performing their exodus from Egypt. The side effect of this upheavel in the Aegean Sea created the Pillar of Fire and the Pillar of Cloud described in (Ex. 13:20.22). (See Addendum pp. 70.77). Joshua is inspired at this very moment and confident the Eternal's promise given in (Joshua 1:1.9) will certainly come to pass. Without this miracle at the beginning of his leadership, Joshua has no standing with Israel. He therefore looked back to Moses' experience when Israel stood on the shores of the Reed Sea (Ex. 14:13.16). V.8, "Give your command to the Kohanim-Leviim. Proceed to the shore of the Jordan." V.6, it is the Kohanim-Leviim, the spiritual leaders of the

JOSHUA CHAPTER 3

people, who must take the first step into the River, to prove their faith in God's direction in history.

Vs. 9.10 Joshua is anxious to convey to Israel the inspiration he received in v. 7. "You are about to witness the effect of God's presence in your midst as He creates the momentum to inspire you to recognize His Eternal truth, that you will succeed in displacing *hakenaani* the Philistines whose homeland is in the *Aegean Sealands, the Hittites*, whose homeland is Anatolia, the Perizzites and Girgashites are Indo-Europeans from the west and the north. The Jebusites are Hivites and considered Hamitics from Africa. The Amorites referred to here were originally Semites who assimilated with the above mentioned peoples who invaded the Holyland to displace the indigenous inhabitants who were Semites. It is these usurpers that the Eternal shall dispossess in accord with His direction in history (Ex. 23:27.33)."

Vs. 11.13 "This Ark, which symbolically represents the covenant made with Israel, by *Adon kal haaretz* the Master of the universe. It is He that designated this land to become your inheritance in perpetuity. None may ever usurp it from your possession. Title shall ever remain in your name. To confirm this everlasting truth to you and to stimulate your faith in your Manifest Destiny, this Ark which represents the very Presence of the Eternal God in the history and evolution of man, shall lead the way for you, to give you the inspiration and the faith for your future." (As a father holding the hand of his infant child, the Eternal is striving to create the courage in Israel's ranks to march into history fearlessly and take possession of a piece of destined land reserved for it from the beginning of time). V.12, Joshua, now asked each tribe to choose one man who shall be ready to be programmed, to perform the *mitzvah* described in (Joshua 4:1.3). V.13, Joshua continued with his inspiration to breathe courage and hope into the ranks of Israel and to teach them the importance of timing. He is describing the extraordinary event which should convince them of God's Presence, "When the Kohanim, who shall be carrying the Ark of the Eternal, (the Master of the Universe) enter into the river Jordan, at that very moment the waters normally flowing from upstream shall cease flowing as if cut off from their source, where it shall accumulate and pile up."

Vs. 14.17 These verses describe the event as it unfolded. When the Israelites were ordered to leave their campground and fall into line, the Kohanim had already reached the shores of the Jordan River. The text reminds us that this was the 10th day of Nisan, that the spring tides were functioning normally by a constantly rising tide. Yet the river piled up from Adamah, fifteen miles north of Jericho. Adamah is on the western bank of the Jordan River and Zaretan is on the eastern bank of the Jordan about 12 miles further north. The tide which had already passed the area where the Kohanim stood continued to flow southward toward the Dead Sea. *Hachen* Here

JOSHUA CHAPTER 3

stood the Kohanim and Leviim urging on the multitude of Israel to cross the dry river in confidence.

We in the 20th century can now review this miracle in light of history which was not available to Joshua. Since human experience goes back to recorded history in the third millenium some of this knowledge was available to Joshua. Josephus reports that in 68 ACE., in one of the wars fought by the Israelites, they retreated from Bethennabris across the Jordan River fords, while crossing they were caught by a sudden rise in the river tide. In 1267 ACE. the Jordan ceased flowing for eight hours. In 1546 ACE. the Jordan ceased flowing for two whole days. In 1927 ACE. it ceased flowing for 21½ hours. In all of these instances, it was the result of earthquakes of various proportions which caused the high banks to collapse, resulting in blocking the river bed which stopped the normal flow of water going southward to the Dead Sea. The Jordan originates in the Lebanon mountains.

JOSHUA CHAPTER 4

Vs. 1.11   In vs.1.3, Joshua details and reviews with the men chosen in (Joshua 3:12) that they shall pick stones from the area in the river bed where the Kohanim and the Ark stood *"hachen"* to impart courage and inspiration to the multitude as they crossed over to the western shore of the Jordan River. These stones were to be carried by these 12 men, chosen to represent their respective tribes. They were to carry these stones until they arrive at their first camping ground that very evening. Joshua's plan was to camp at Gilgal, yet he has reservations because prudence teaches he must first be able to overcome all the physical probabilities before he reaches his goal. Man must place his faith in God first, yet plan ahead that he will overcome all contingencies until he reaches his goal.

In vs.4.5, Joshua issued the order to these 12 men to enter the river bed and begin removing the stones from the area where the Kohanim were standing.

In vs.6.7, Joshua states that these stones shall become a memorial for history, confirming to future generations Israel's experience this day when the Jordan River harmonized with the Eternal's direction in history. (Ex. 13:8.14) is the source of Joshua's inspiration for v.6, to teach every future generation preparedness. *Kriat yam suf* every day in the life of individuals or nations is filled with hazardous experiences which we must overcome. Man has been endowed with the *Zelem Elohim* a capacity for intelligence. Added to this biological truth is the reality that the Eternal God broadcasts His inspiration, to heed the disciplines inscribed in the Torah, to help us overcome every obstacle that faces us.

V.7, Joshua emphasizes the importance of keeping alive the experience of this day in the memory of every future generation.

V.8, confirms for the historical record that these 12 men chosen to create this memorial, did succeed in performing their mission after all the Israelites crossed over to the west bank of the Jordan River.

JOSHUA CHAPTER 4

V.9, indicates another group of men chosen at random from those crossing, they were instructed to build a large mound of stones to mark the very spot in the River bed where the Kohanim stood.

V.10, *Vayemaharu* is very instructive. Though Joshua's great faith in this natural phenomenon had come to pass, he ever remembered the laws under which the River Jordan functioned. This river could at any moment resume its normal flow and could possibly equal the experience reported by Josephus in 68 ACE. when hundreds of Israeli soldiers were drowned because they ignored this fact. Going back to the time of the Exodus, the Egyptians knew the natural law by which the Reed Sea functioned. They met their fate described in (Ex. 14:26.31) because their egos ignored the facts. V.11, confirms the successful crossing of the Jordan River and the resumption of Israel's march to their first camping ground in Canaan. Once again the Kohanim resumed their leading position in the march to show Israel the way and to constantly build their morale.

Vs. 12.14 Though bolstered by the miracle which Israel had just experienced, Joshua never lost track of the realities of warfare.
He is now in territory which has many unknown factors. As Israel's leader he must be sure of his weaknesses and his strengths, Joshua therefore examines the essence which motivates the vitality of his army. He recognizes the complete unity in the ranks of Israel and acknowledges his debt to the tribes of Reuben, Gad and Manasseh for having mobilized 40,000 men prepared to carry out their pledge to Moses. Their dedication and pledge made in (Joshua 1:16.18) validated Joshua's stature in the perception of the people of Israel. They equated and acknowledged their reverence for Moses in history, it has now transferred itself to Joshua.

Vs. 15.19 (These verses should follow v.10). Vs. 15.16. Joshua's intelligence is inspired to inform the Kohanim to come up out of the river bed. In v.17, Joshua issued his order. V.18, informs us that soon after the Kohanim set foot upon the western shore of the Jordan, the river resumed its normal flow, the tide rose to the height of its banks and resumed its normal flow downstream toward the Dead Sea. Vs. 11.14, belong here as the natural sequence of the narrative. V.19, confirms for the record of history that this day when Israel crossed the River Jordan into Canaan was the 10th day of Nisan. In v.3, of this chapter Joshua had reservations about the success of the operation and if there would be any delay could he reach Gilgal. He now informs us that Israel did camp in Gilgal as planned which is at the most easterly edge of the city of Jericho.

Vs. 20.24 Joshua built an historic monument with the stones removed from the Jordan River, recorded in v.8, of this chapter. The intent is to ever keep this important event fresh in the minds of all future generations. It was not a memorial to God. This was forbidden in (Deut. 16:22). This accords with the explanation given by Abrabanel. The book of Joshua was written in his time by the Kohanim and Leviim (Baba Bathra 14b).

JOSHUA CHAPTER 4

In the lifetime of Samuel it was updated by him to confirm the historicity of this event in his generation. In vs.23.24, Joshua has reference to other great moments in Jewish history recorded in (Ex. 13:9,14:31,15:16, Deut. 7:19, 34:12). The effectiveness of this historic monument is reported in (Sotah 34a,b). History reports that this monument was seen during the Byzantian period in the 5th century. The intent and purpose of this monument is to serve as a reminder to all of mankind, that nature ever performs in harmony with the Eternal God's direction. The tremendous power of natural phenomena must ever be present in the calculations of mankind. *Yirah* the awe of God is a constant demand programmed into the genes of humanity. It is the ultimate goal for men and women. When we bypass our reverence for God the Master of the universe, we short circuit our lives. Our conduct implements and sets into motion catastrophic moments in history which challenge humanity to become reverend.

JOSHUA CHAPTER 5

V. 1 *Kishemoa* when the inhabitants of the Promised Land heard that Israel succeeded to cross the Jordan, they now fully grasped the meaning of the Exodus. Every progressive step made by Israel during the past 40 years sent fear into the hearts of the Amorites. It was these despotic kings that hired the Amalekites to attack Israel soon after the Exodus (17:8.16, Gen. 36:12). 38 years later (Num. 14:25,45) the Amalekites were hired to annihilate Israel. (Num. 21:1.3,21.24,33, 22:23:24:25) are ongoing examples of the animosity of these (Semitic) political entities. The descendants of Seir-Esau, Amon and Moab-Lot (Gen. 19:30.38,33:15.16) are well aware that Israel will not attack them (Deut. 2:1.9) for the Torah recognized their territorial rites.

Almost a century before the conquest of Canaan, Rameses II, of Egypt, engaged in combat with the Hittites for the possession of the Mediterranean coast which Egypt held until the Sea People conquered it in (1318-1234 BCE.). This territory later became known as Philistia and Phoenicia. While Egypt was locked in battle with the Hittites, Sihon and Og, who were Semitic Amurru living in the area which later became known as Syria, took advantage of the situation and possessed the territory of Trans-Jordan. It was these Amurru, who refused their kin the Israelites to pass through it in order to take possession of the Promised Land. It is most important to research the above historical facts in order to understand the measures Israel will have to take when it locks in combat with people who have failed in basic humanitarian principles recorded in (Deut. 23:3.7, 20:10.11). Israel has been programmed to introduce a new plateau of civilization for all its inhabitants. It has come prepared to offer peace to those that desire it and no quarter to those who will oppose the principles of progressive evolution.

Vayimas levavam every arrogant hope of the inhabitants of Canaan was dissolved in the ego of their hearts. Israel's challenge that they surrender their pantheon of gods, liquidated their ability to defend themselves. It was this fear

JOSHUA CHAPTER 5

which completely disarmed the Canaanites and restrained them from uniting against Israel.

Vs. 2.8   At this moment in Israel's history, the multitudes that made up the nation recognized that the greatness of Moses had indeed passed on to Joshua when their great teacher and leader ordained him in (Num. 27:15.23, Deut. 31:3.8, 23). At this inspiring moment when the greatness of Moses and Joshua fused to inspire all of Israel to dedicate themselves to the conquest of their Manifest Destiny, Joshua issued the command for the circumcision of all those that were born after they left Mount Sinai. (Because of the hazards existing in their years of travel in the desert, this procedure was bypassed. All those born in Egypt, including those that joined Israel as proselytes were circumcised at Mount Sinai). Only Joshua and Caleb survived the original generation that left Egypt. This voluntary and courageous act of faith is the inspiration that continues to inspire the Nation of Israel to ever strive to become a light unto the nations of the world (Is. 42:6.7). V.6 Joshua reminded this generation, had their parents not challenged their Manifest Destiny, they too would of had the privilege of entering the Promised Land (Num. 14:22.24,28.31). V.8 with utmost faith in the Eternal's protective custody, all those that were circumcised remained inactive until they recuperated from their surgery. They remembered being told by their parents of the fear created by the plagues which terrorized Egypt (Ex. 11:6.7). Israel's capability to cross the Jordan River and to settle permanently in Gilgal, had paralyzed the defense of the Canaanites.

Vs. 9.12   Joshua commended Israel upon their courageous act of faith as they fearlessly observed the *mitzvah* of *milah*. No more can the Egyptians taunt you that you have forsaken the Covenant of Abraham (Gen. 17:9.14). To commemorate Israel's resolution to remain freemen in a sea of slavery, Joshua named this area Gilgal. *Ki galoti cherpat Mizraim*. Another condition vital for the observance of the festival of Passover has now been met as described in (Ex. 16:35, Deut. 12:8.14, Lev. 23:14). They set up the Mishkan-Tabernacle, in their first campsite in the Promised Land. They once again observed the Passover which was suspended during their 39 years of wandering in the desert. They were able to purchase food from the new crops in the plains of Jericho. They offered the Omer on the second day of Passover, because they no longer received fresh Mannah and had consumed their last supply. From now on Israel will create its own supply of food or purchase it from the natives in Canaan.

Vs. 13.15   Five days have passed in the recovery of those circumcised. All of Israel have observed the offering of the Pascal Lamb in the Mishkan. Joshua is utilizing this period in planning his next step in the conquest of Canaan. While contemplating and evaluating all the unknown factors of this forthcoming campaign, Joshua perceived a prophetic vision. Standing before him he visualized a man with a sword drawn for action.

JOSHUA CHAPTER 5

As a soldier he challenged his perceptive image to identify himself as friend or foe. "I am neither is the reply. I am the representative of the Eternal God of history. I have come in His behalf to fulfill His promise given in (Ex. 23:20, 33:2,11) to Moses." Joshua bowed to acknowledge his attentiveness to the message. "Before I continue, you must first remove your sandals from your feet for this is hallowed ground." Joshua recognized the source of his experience (Ex. 3:5.10) is repeating itself in history as confirmation of his potential success. Joshua gratefully conformed to the request of his Host.

JOSHUA CHAPTER 6

V. 1 Joshua awaits the inspiration and instructions from the Eternal's Host. He mustered his own experience from (Ex. 14:13.15, Deut. 1:29.31) and evaluated the meaning of Jericho's curfew. None are permitted to enter or leave the city.

Vs. 2.5 The Eternal's inspiration reassured Joshua that he shall succeed in conquering Jericho, her king and its mighty warriors. You are to pursue the following strategy: "Circle the city of Jericho once each day for six days. Seven Kohanim with a shofar in hand shall lead the Ark and the army of soldiers while blowing their rams horns periodically to inspire the men in their march. On the seventh day you shall circle the city seven times and the Kohanim shall blow their rams horns continually. At the end of the seventh round the Kohanim shall blow the long blast of the shofar. This shall be the signal for every man in the army to issue their war cry. The vibrations of their voices shall cause the wall to sink into the ground enabling the soldiers to enter the city in battle formation."

Vs. 6.9 Joshua now activated the inspiration he received in vs. 2.5. First he addressed the Kohanim and instructed them in the use of their rams horns. They are to blow their horns periodically to inspire the soldiers who shall be following them. He now addressed the officers of the army. "The order of the march shall be as follows: First will come the *hechalutz* the soldiers representing the tribes of Reuben, Gad and Manasseh, they shall be followed by the Kohanim, then will follow the soldiers representing the other tribes behind the Ark. Following them shall come *hameasef* the tribe of Dan, who ever formed the rear guard (Num. 10:25, 32:17.32), while the Kohanim continued to blow their rams horns."

Vs. 10.14 Joshua reenforced the original orders given by the officers. He personally explained the importance of his strategy, which is keyed to their co-operation. "You are not to shout any orders nor shall you permit yourselves even a whisper. Not a single sound shall be uttered from your lips. Not until I issue the order for you to let yourselves be heard, you are to refrain from issuing a single sound." Having finalized the orders and explained the strategy upon which the success of this operation

JOSHUA CHAPTER 6

depended, they left camp to initiate the encircling of the wall of Jericho. Having accomplished this first step safely, they returned to spend the night in camp at Gilgal. Vs. 12.14, restates the procedure outlined in vs. 6.11, which was followed for six consecutive days. Each day they returned to camp and spent the night at Gilgal, to start afresh the next morning.

Vs. 15.16   On the seventh day they rose at dawn in anticipation of the action they were to face. However, they followed the same procedure as in the previous six days, they left *baboker* three hours after sunrise v.12. On the seventh day they encircled the city seven times. V.16, while the Kohanim continued to blow their rams horns and the army was completing the seventh round, Joshua addressed the army, "That at the end of this round, when the Kohanim shall receive my command, they will blow the *terua gedola* the long blast of the shofar. This will be your signal to shout in unison, to express your potential success of conquering the city of Jericho." Joshua never revealed to any one that the wall of the city would collapse.

Vs. 17.19   Joshua continued to address the army before they completed the seventh round with new instructions for the conquest of Jericho. "This city and everything in it shall be destroyed completely. The example we shall establish here shall convey our message to the other inhabitants of Canaan. As stated in (Gen. 15:16.21) these peoples-nations have had the opportunity during these past four generations to correct their way of life. They have ignored all the moral indicators. Everything in it shall be put to flames. No individual may benefit from it in any material way. There is but one exception. We must recognize the oath taken by our scouts when they reconnoitered the city of Jericho (Joshua 2:9.21). We are honor bound to save the lives of Rahab and her immediate family and their personal possessions. Only these are excluded from the ban." The basis for Joshua's ban is recorded in (Ex. 22:19, Lev. 27:28). However, Joshua in his great effort to express his dedication exceeded the instructions given in the law of the Torah. He spelled out in great detail to every soldier the force of his ban. "All silver, gold, copper or iron, no matter in what shape or form are included in the ban. Everything found there shall be sanctified to the cause of God, dedicated to the evolution of man. Any individual who may be tempted to enhance his personal desire will endanger the lives of the whole camp of Israel (Gen. 34:30)."

Vs. 20.23   When Joshua issued his instructions in v.17, he immediately dispatched the two scouts to Rahab's inn, to save her and the immediate members of her family in accord with their oath taken in (Joshua 2:12.21, Lev. 19:12, Num. 30:3). They succeeded in their mission and carried them to safety outside their camp at Gilgal. There they would remain until they would conform with the details of purification as proselytes. They may have become subject to the law given in (Num. 31:19) for exposure with the dead in the environs of Jericho. Having completed his instructions, Joshua gave the order for the blowing of the *truah gedolah* the long blast of the

JOSHUA CHAPTER 6

shofar and the collective shouting in unison. The effect of the tremendous vibrations miraculously caused the walls of Jericho to collapse (Joshua 6:5). There is ample archaeological evidence that these walls had been destroyed many times in the past two millenia. Archaelogists lay special emphasis upon the devastation of the many barbarian invasions from the north during the 14th and 13th centuries BCE. As sections of the wall collapsed the army proceeded to lay the city waste in accord with Joshua's instructions in v.21.

Vs. 24.27   Confirms the rehabilitation of Rahab and all the members of her immediate family. In consideration for her heroic act they were extended citizenship in Israel. The city was put to the torch and all its contents were destroyed by fire. Only objects of silver, gold, copper and iron were classified as *herem* excluded from personal usage, to be designated as assets belonging to the nation. Its use must be authorized by the functioning authority of the Mishkan. Joshua again exceeded the law of *herem* as stated in the Torah (Ex. 22:19, Lev. 27:28, Num. 21:2.3, Deut. 7:26,20:17.18). Joshua placed a curse upon any one who will rebuild the city of Jericho. "May that individual lose his first born son when he lays its foundation. May he lose his youngest son when he succeeds to build the city gates." This curse became effective in the time of Ahab (1 Kings 16:34). Joshua's challenge to the rest of Canaan stands. They can accept the conditions laid down in (Deut. 20:10.18) which offers them a new beginning upon a new plateau of civilization, to begin by observing the Seven Laws of Noah (Gen. 9:1.2). Joshua's fearless challenge struck terror in the hearts of the Canaanites. Israel recognized Joshua's leadership ability on a par with his master Moses (Joshua 1:5.9, Deut. 2:25).

JOSHUA CHAPTER 7

Vs. 1.5   The text charges all of Israel with the trespass of Joshua's invocation of the law of *herem* which actually was chargeable to one man Achan, the son of Karmi, the son of Zabdi, the son of Zerach, the son of Judah (Gen. 38:30). Though Achan singlehanded had violated Joshua's ban, all of Israel became chargeable for his misdeed. It is this single act of an individual that was responsible for the lives of 36 men, which in and of itself is a great tragedy but the greater calamity was its effect upon the strident morale of Israel as they individually felt the pangs of a guilty conscience. Their *Zelem Elohim* grasped the effect of the wrath of the Eternal. Under these circumstances, Joshua had dispatched scouts to reconnoiter the city of Ai, known in Abraham's time (Gen. 12:8). Ai is 15 miles from Jericho. The initial climb is 1500 feet, it then rises for another 1700 feet in gradual steps. V.3, the scouts still riding on the successes of the past, report back to Joshua that this operation can be handled by one to three thousand men. Joshua's confidence reflected the optimism of his officers. He therefore permitted them to handle the whole operation by themselves. From the start the operation was doomed because the high ground favored the army of Ai. The city of Ai anticipated the action and

JOSHUA CHAPTER 7

from the start Ai was on the offensive. The attack was so sudden that it turned into a rout. When Israel went up the mountain it chose the best path. The sudden attack and the pursuit down the mountainside deprived them of any choice as they landed in a most hazardous area *shevarim* strewn with shards of broken stone or marble. Israel returned to camp and lost 36 men in this tragic action. This defeat was the result of overconfidence. They did not take into consideration the terrain, nor did they take into consideration the tremendous advantage which this mountain offered the army of Ai. The effect of this defeat destroyed the morale of Israel's invincibility. When Joshua ordered the battle of Ai, he was unaware of the desecration by Achan. The effect of this misdeed kindled the wrath of the Eternal (Num. 14:9). He has removed Israel's halo of invincibility.

Vs. 6.9 In great distress Joshua rended his clothing and secluded himself in the Tabernacle to meditate and pray. He was joined by the Elders of Israel and together they prostrated themselves in accord with the precedents established in (Gen. 37:29.34, Ex. 32:11, Num. 14:6.9). In great distress Joshua vented his feelings. "Woe has befallen us, Master of the Universe. You are indeed the Eternal God of justice and history. Would it not have been better for us to remain in Trans-Jordania? How can I reconcile our present position with Your promise made to my master Moses (Ex. 23:27.28)? Where is Your Divine protection which enabled us to cross the Jordan river and to sack the city of Jericho? Israel's defeat at Ai, will demonstrate to the Canaanites that the Eternal has reversed His promise, that Israel will ever remain in God's custody. When this defeat becomes known to the rest of the Amorites, they shall unite to destroy the very name of Israel. Where is Your promise, Eternal God of history and justice?"

Vs. 10.13 The Eternal addressed Joshua, *kum lach*, "Stand up and assume your responsibilities in this whole fiasco (Num. 27:16.20, Deut. 3:28, 31:23, Joshua 1:7). It was your responsibility to lead Israel in battle and not to delegate your authority to subordinates. You had no authority to enlarge upon My law, in placing a ban upon the booty of Jericho. It is your fanatic zeal which brought about this untenable situation, *(kum lach*, Ex. 14:15). This is no time for prayer, this is a time for action to discover the guilty one who challenged your authority, which I uphold in ordering the ban. He who took the consecrated property also became guilty of theft and concealment, he also implicated others who failed to report the desecration. I have removed My inspiration-My guidance from Israel, for they have desecrated their *Zelem Elohim* their intelligence which is rooted in My moral and ethical law. To reinstate My guidance, you must eradicate the existing condition. *Kum kadesh et haam* there can be no sanctification in Israel before you remove the evil force of a guilty conscience. Superficial, physical purification is but a symbol to confirm inner peace. *Veamarta alehem* issue a command for an investigation to discover the guilty ones who desecrated the law of *herem*. *Lo tuchal lakum lifne oyvecha* with a neurosis of guilt, you shall lack the courage vital to overcome your enemies (Ex. 33:16, 34:10. I Sam. 13:13.14)."

JOSHUA CHAPTER 7

Vs. 14.15   Contain the detailed procedure for the investigation. Each tribal leader was to approach the Ark and testify that his tribe was not involved in taking anything from the consecrated booty from the city of Jericho. When the evidence will point to a specific tribe, only then shall the investigation be narrowed to a specific family. Only then shall the search begin for the individual guilty of desecrating the consecrated objects. When the guilt will have been established, the law in (Lev. 27:29) shall be activated. The severity of this punishment is to serve as an object lesson for the future.

Vs. 16.26   The investigation began that very morning and though the evidence indicated the tribe of Judah, the culprit made no effort to confess his guilt. Even after the search pointed directly to Achan, Joshua anticipated Achan's objections to the method of the investigation. Joshua pleaded with Achan, "My son express your recognition and reverence for the Eternal God of Israel and confess before the Ark of the Covenant exactly what you did. Do not withhold any details in your confession." V. 20, "it is true I committed a grave sin *vechazot vechazot* not only at Jericho but also in the battle of Sihon and Og during the lifetime of Moses. In the last two instances I involved no one but myself and satisfied my conscience that I would be judged in accord with (Deut. 29:28) after I shall have completed my earthly existence. At Jericho I implicated not only myself but my family when I took a Babylonian garment, 200 shekels of silver and a wedge of gold worth 50 shekels. I then dug a hole in the middle of my tent and hid the *herem* objects until such time that I could retrieve them." Joshua dispatched messengers to retrieve the *herem* from Achan's tent. Joshua now ordered Achan, his family, his livestock and all his personal possessions to proceed to the valley of Achor (so named to commemorate this incident). In the presence of all the community, Joshua challenged Achan. "Was it necessary for you to embarrass the members of your family and to create tragedy in the ranks of Israel at a most critical moment in Israel's history? *Yaakarchah Adonai* may the Eternal evaluate the merit of your confession and punish you for the moral depravity of your lifetime. (Deut. 29:28) may you recognize *haniglot* the fairness of our evaluation of the exposed evidence as you are to become an object lesson to those present here and to those that shall succeed us in history." Achan was stoned and all his material possessions were destroyed by fire. The mound was then enlarged to be identified in history as the valley of Achor. Joshua and the elders are satisfied that their extreme action of this day shall be in the spirit of (Deut. 13:18) to win for Israel the *rachamim* so vital in restoring *Vayashav Adonai mecharon apo* the Eternal's favor in the daily lives of Israel.

JOSHUA CHAPTER 8

Vs. 1.9   Joshua is inspired by the Eternal to once again take the offensive. "Be not dismayed by your recent setback in the ranks of Israel and have no fear for the action which faces you. Plan an action which will involve the whole army of Israel. You will then succeed in doing to Ai, what you did to Jericho. However, place no ban upon the booty of the city. Do not restrain your soldiers from any incentive which will challenge them to win the battle of Ai. Destroy the city of Ai, even as you did to Jericho. Plan an ambush, to take advantage of their exposed tactic when Israel's army was routed." Vs. 3.9 are Joshua's plan of action. He dispatched an army of 30,000 men that very evening to secretly establish their position in the rear of the city. Joshua and another 30,000 men will feign a frontal attack in the hope that they will be pursued as before. He shall then pretend a rout in order to draw the army of Ai out of their city. When this condition shall become a reality, the army in ambush shall spring into action to occupy the city and to destroy it by putting it to the torch. V. 9 confirms the completion of the first stage of Joshua's plan as the first army reached their planned position midway between Beth-El (which is west of Ai) and Ai. Joshua and his second army spent the night fully mobilized on the outskirts of Gilgal.

Vs. 10.14   Joshua rose early the next morning to inspect his forces. He is mindful of the rebuke he received in (Joshua 7:10:13) he invited the Elders to join him as he led the army into battle. V.11, Joshua led his men up the first 1500 feet of the mountain to the plain before him. Since the city of Ai stood 1700 feet above this plain, it would appear from the top of the hill that Joshua's position was separated by this valley. Here the army made its camp in a northerly position from the city of Ai. V.12, indicates Joshua's extra precautions as he set up another ambush of about 5000 men west of the city of Ai between Beth-El and Ai. V.13, that very night Joshua led his forces from their northerly position to give the impression that he was going to attack frontally. He therefore proceeded across the valley to give the impression he is going to rise the next 1700 feet to attack the city of Ai. He also signaled the ambush to close the gap between him and their forces. V.14, confirms that Joshua succeeded in exposing his vulnerable position to the enemy. At dawn of the next morning the army of Ai left the environs of their city to attack Israel's army in the valley, they were unaware of the major force waiting to attack them in the rear of the city.

Vs. 15.23   Joshua and his men feigned a rout as they headed for the desert of Beth Aven, which leads deeper into the valley. The army of Ai now called out the reserve which stood by in the city in order to increase the force of its pursuit army. This action literally emptied the city of any protective force. V.17, we learn that Beth-El joined the tumult at this point and completely evacuated their city. Vs. 18.19, Joshua is inspired by the Eternal to recognize that this is the moment to issue the order for the smaller ambush to enter the city and set it on fire. This also was the signal for the larger

JOSHUA CHAPTER 8

force to enter the fray. V.20, confirms the turning point of the war as the army of Ai observed their city in flames they lost their intiative for the war. V.21, Joshua recognized this moment to reverse his strategy from defense to attack as the major ambush swung into action. V.22, the pincer action of three major forces locking in combat encircled those who evacuated the city and all the military forces of Ai, this was the moment for Joshua to deliver the coup de grace, the mortal blow to the bewildered enemy. V.23, the king of Ai was captured and delivered to Joshua.

Vs. 24.29   Records the complete destruction of the city of Ai, including those that remained in the city, those that were scattered in the field of battle and those that pursued Israel into the desert of Beth Aven. The text records a loss of about 12,000 lives. Only the livestock and the chattels that survived the fire were retrieved as booty and distributed among the soldiers in accord with V.2. V.28, the text reports the complete destruction of Ai, that it remained a *tel olam ad hayom hazeh* mound of destruction to this day. When the prophet Samuel finalized the writing of the book of Joshua, the city of Ai was not yet rebuilt. This territory (Ai) became part of the inheritance of the tribe of Benjamin. It was then rebuilt by them. (Ezra 2:28) reports that when the Israelites returned from Babylon in 538 BCE. the city was renamed Ayah and is so recorded in (I Chronicles 7:28). V.29, the king of Ai was hung on a gibbet. (San. 46a) Describes the law given in (Deut. 21:22.23) that no living tree may be used for this purpose. It must be a stump of wood specifically adopted for this purpose. Hanging on a gibbet is rooted in ancient history, to remove the body and be buried at sunset was a Torah innovation, introduced to express reverence for a human life created in the image of God. Once an individual has paid the penalty for a misdeed to society, it becomes obligated to show reverence for his humanity. Modern man may call this procedure primitive. However, examine the ancient record given in (II Sam. 21:) this happened 300 years later in the time of David. Though an example of justice was intended, the Gibeonites followed their ancient procedure by permitting the bodies to hang, to decay and contaminate the environment by putrefaction. The evolution of the Torah law is highlighted in (Ezekiel 39:12) 600 years later in 620-570 BCE.

Vs. 30.35   These five verses belong at the end of the book of Joshua. Ai, is geographically about 20 hours walking distance from Shechem (60 miles). Chronologically this procedure took place at the time, when Joshua divided the land among the tribes of Israel. Initially this should have been a separate chapter. Because it involves the implementation of five mitzvot-commandments: (1-Ex.20:25, 2-Deut.27:28:29:30:3, 11:26.32) the writing of Mishneh Torah. 3-It was to be recited on Mount Gerizim and Mount Ebal. 4-It involved the offering of sacrifices. 5-The recitation of the admonitions. The time frame for the fulfilment of these mitzvot was after the building of the Mishkan in Shiloh. This did not happen until 14 years after the land was conquered and divided. There is an opinion that the Gilgal where Israel camped

JOSHUA CHAPTER 8

was close to Shechem. Eloneh Moreh is defined in Deut. 11:30, which conforms with Abraham's description in Gen. 12:6.8, Abraham's *az yivneh* indicates his celebration for accomplishing the first part of his mission. Therefore, Joshua initiated and fulfilled the described mitzvot at the end of his leadership.

V.33.35 the text details the participants in these ceremonies included: the Elders, the officers, the judges on one side of the Ark, the Kohanim and the Leviim, who carried the Ark, on the other side. The division of the tribes followed the procedures prescribed in (Deut. 27:12.14). The procedure for the celebration carried the seal of The Great Liberator Moses, for it included all women and children and every proselyte that voluntarily agreed to live by the law of the Torah. The text is emphatic upon the equal rights of all, both native born Israelites and proselytes shall ever be equal before the law. The equality was demonstrated by the division of the numbers who converted to Israel into these groupings. Joshua included in his readings Deut. 29:9 through chapter 30:. This accords with the opinions of Abarbanel-Radak-Kimchi. Joshua inaugurated this ceremony for the first time in Israel's history.

JOSHUA CHAPTER 9

After the destruction of the city of Ai, Joshua issued a declaration to all the inhabitants of Canaan. To make sure that his intentions were absolutely clear, he defined the areas in detail. This conformed with the details outlined in (Num. 34:), and included the land mass cradled between the Mediterranean Sea in the west and the Euphrates in the east. It included all the mountainous areas as far north as the Lebanon Mountains. (This territory was occupied by the Semitic descendants of Shem going back to the 3rd and 2nd millenium. This was the territory known in history as the Fertile Crescent. Every civilized development originated in this area including writing. When the barbarians, the Indo-Europeans, the Indo-Aryans and the Sea Peoples invaded Canaan, most of the descendants of Shem lost their identity, either by assimilation or by death. The Israelites now striving to retake their Promised Land are either the descendants of Abraham or those who became proselytes over the centuries before the Exodus and the multitudes that joined Israel at the time of the Exodus. From (Joshua 8:34.35) we learn of a new wave of proselytes who accepted Israel's values. It could be possible that some of them were descendants of Shem).

Vs. 1.2 The text enumerates the nations who now occupy this territory which were identified in (Gen. 15:18.21). Comparing these two lists, we find the Girgashites missing. They had migrated to North Africa. Joshua makes it emphatically clear to these nation-peoples, that he considers them usurpers of their heritage. Their effort to unite as allies for war, Israel will meet their force with greater force. In accord with (Deut. 20:10.18) Joshua qualified his declaration by offering them peace if they agree to live by the Seven Laws of Noah. 1. Courts of Justice; 2. Prohibition of blasphemy; 3. Abolition of idolatry; 4. Prohibition of incest; 5. Prohibition of murder; 6. Prohibition of robbery; 7. Cutting flesh from a living animal. Should

JOSHUA CHAPTER 9

they commit themselves to these conditions, they can work cooperatively to conform with (Ex. 23:28.33).

Vs. 3.5 The citizens of Gibeon, decided to ignore the initiative of their leaders to form an alliance to defeat Israel. V.4, *bearmah* they devised a plan to send messengers to Israel for the purpose of negotiating a treaty. They are knowledgeable that Israel is morally bound by Torah law from entering into any treaty with those designated in (Gen. 15:18.21).

They are desirous of establishing the evidence that they come from a great distance which lies outside of this ban. To give credence to their statements their clothes were to demonstrate the arduous journey, their torn shoes were the result of their difficult journey. Their sacks were worn, their wine bottles decayed and tied where they split open to keep them from leaking. Their bread and other provisions were stale, dry and moldy. Gibeon was but 10 kilometers northwest of Jerusalem, in the valley of Aijalon.

Vs. 6.15 The messengers made their presentation to Joshua and the Elders. Though one of the Elders challenged their nationality rather superficially, they were overcome by the perfect camouflage of the messengers. Israel's leaders accepted their story as truth. Vs. 9.11, having succeeded with their proof, they enlarged upon the length of their journey. "Despite the long distance that separated us, we are knowledgeable of your great victories of Sihon and Og, in Trans-Jordania. We know about the great miracles performed by your God at the time of your Exodus from Egypt. Vs. 12.14, this bread was still warm when we placed it into our sacks when we started upon our journey, it is now as you observe dry and moldy. These wine bottles were brand new when we filled them, they are now all cracked. Our clothes have rotted from the arduous wear and tear and the atmospheric conditions." The Elders sampled their provisions to convince themselves that their story is in fact true. However, history must challenge the naivete of Joshua and the Elders. *veet pi Adonai lo shaalu* Rashi ... puts this experience in its proper perspective when he says in modern idiom, "they swallowed the bait with hook line and sinker, *shetzidum befihem.*" They should have verified the elementary facts of all the details. This is the full meaning *veet pi Adonai lo shaalu.* Joshua and the Elders made peace with them and secured it by a covenant in the form of a mutual defense treaty. (II Sam.21:) establishes the historic record that 300 years later the treaty was still honored.

Vs. 16.19 Three days after the covenant was concluded it became known that the Gibeonite ambassadors had publicized among their neighbors the wisdom of their initiative. Israel sent messengers to confirm the details of the publicity. They then confirmed the full implications of their Elders blunder. Gibeon, Chephirah, Beeroth and Kiriat-jearim, were part of the Holyland, which they are obliged to conquer as the legal inheritance of the tribe of Benjamin. The Gibeonite territory was strategically located to control access to Jerusalem. The Gibeonites were Hivites. When the officers of the army

JOSHUA CHAPTER 9

established these facts *vayilonu kal haedah al hanesiim* they took their leaders to task. The Nesiim admitted their error in not verifying the facts. They admit their anguish because under the law of the Torah (Ex. 20:7) in whose name the Nesiim took their oath, it will have to be honored as it was confirmed by the name of the Eternal God of Israel. Looking at the book of Joshua objectively, we find many important communities as Bethel and Michmash and many others west of Ai were bypassed militarily. The initiative taken and described in the above verses how Gibeon made peace with Israel is but an example, a vehicle to inform us that many communities accepted Joshua's challenge in vs. 1.2. Ideally this was and continues to be the goal of the Torah. This too was the motivation of communities that controlled many subsidiary cities to live in peace with Israel, to avoid fighting for its life. Archaeological facts confirm for history that Israel did not have to fight for every inch of its territory. Many of the inhabitants known under various nationalistic names and characteristics are remnants of the descendants of Shem that assimiliated with their conquerors and survived to make peace with Israel. Ethnically this was not difficult for them.

Vs. 20.23   The Nesiim appeased the anger of the whole community by designating the Gibeonites for the remainder of their natural lives to serve individually the whole community of Israel as hewers of wood and carriers of water. V.22, Joshua sent for the original ambassadors that represented Gibeon when he made a treaty with them. "Why was it necessary to use deceit in order to obtain our guarantee to live in peace with you? It should have been emphatically clear to you that your deception would soon be discovered, that your residence is right here in our very midst. We took our oath in good faith to extend our concept of moral and ethical justice to protect your lives and wellbeing. We shall honor our oath, to permit you to live in our midst. However, you have brought a curse upon your peace of mind. To designate you as second class citizens is not in keeping with Torah principles. It shall disturb our peace of mind as well, as we designate you in perpetuity to serve the servile needs of our people. It is from your ranks that we shall draft the *Nethinim* (as if you are captives of war) to serve in every humble capacity in the house of our God." Though the term *Nethinim* goes back to the antiquity of Ugarit, it is from this tradition that Joshua enlarged upon the penalty of the Gibeonites, who were to serve as uncircumsized temple personnel.

Vs. 24.27   The representatives of Gibeon stood their ground as they replied to Joshua's rebuke. "It has been known to us from the time of the Exodus, that you will indeed inherit the Promised Land. We knew of your intention not to take hostages (Deut. 20:10.18). For decades we analyzed your reasons to destroy every handicap that would retard your goal, to introduce a new world order into our midst. This challenge struck terror into our hearts. Our leaders were seeking millitary alliances for war to stop you even before you got started. Those of us desiring to live in peace were anxious for a peaceful solution. Basically, our great desire is to live in peace

JOSHUA CHAPTER 9

though initiated and inspired by deception. We surrender our lives to you, with utmost faith *katov* that you will treat us with kindness and consideration. *vechayashar beenechah* since your Torah strives to teach you to pursue justice, you will judge us with mercy." V.26, Joshua was sympathetic to their plea, he concurred with the verdict of the Nesiim in v.21, *yichu ken* he protected them from the wrath of the mob who wanted to kill them.

V.27, Joshua was justified by law to designate the Gibeonites as hewers of wood and drawers of water for the whole community of Israel, prior to the division of the land *kal haedah* was considered a military camp. When the land was divided and Israel settled in their own communities, they would be legally obligated to serve only the Central Sanctuary wherever the nation would designate it's proper location. In David's time they were designated as *Nethinim* to assist the Leviim. *Eved* in the Torah and in all sacred literature must be translated as a day worker. It can never deny any human being in Israel his or her human rights. Though their menial designation was considered a penalty, they were to be compensated as day laborers. The Mishkan was first established in Gilgal. It was then moved to Shiloh. In the time of David and Solomon it was established in Gibeon (IChronicles, 21:29, I Kings 3:4).

JOSHUA CHAPTER 10

Vs. 1.2   This is the first time in the Bible, that the name Jerusalem appears in the text. Adoni Zedek, who now rules in Jerusalem is an Amorite. Malki Zedek, who ruled here in Abraham's lifetime as the High Priest of El Elyon (Gen. 14:18) was a descendant of Shem. (See commentary in Eternal Torah, for historic background of traditions and meaning for honoring covenants-contracts-treaties made in everyday human relations (Gen.18:19, 21:22.34, 25:1.18, 26:12.33, Deut. 2:4.7,9.10,11.12, 22.25) originating with Shem and upheld and honored by its descendants throughout centuries of changing waves of barbarism, invasion, the consistent efforts by the descendants of Abraham was to introduce civilization to all of humanity. Adoni Zedek fully grasps the meaning of Israel's presence in Canaan. They have come to call these barbarians to the bar of justice (Gen. 15:16), to account for the atrocities of the past four centuries. They have had an opportunity to accept the Seven Laws of Noah, which has been known for about 800 years. All Joshua is now doing, is placing immediate emphasis on his demand on an *Either, Or* basis (Joshua 9:1.2). The Amorites-Canaanite people now ruling the territory in various forms are fearful of losing their godlike mastership over the slaves-villeins-settlers, who have never received citizenship, though they contribute to the economy of the community. They have no human rights or protection under the law. They are subjects-chattels, to be dealt with at will by their masters. V.2, Adoni Zedek recognized the full impact of the revolt initiated by the Elders of Gibeon, who rule by the consent of the governed. Should other communities accept Israel's challenge, Israel can win the fight without even a war. Ancient Gibeon has been established by archaeologists as el Jib, it was located eight miles

JOSHUA CHAPTER 10

north of Jerusalem. Its city was surrounded by a wall 10 feet thick broadened at the base to 26 feet. Its three contributary cities were all located high in the hills surrounding Jerusalem. Chephirah survives in Khirbet Kefirah, south of el Jib. Beeroth is believed to be Nebi Samwil. Kiriath-Jearim, is two miles south of Chephirah, high in the hills, it controls the present road from Jerusalem to Jaffa. History reminds us that it was a forest town a wooded area in the ancient past (not as Israel inherited it in the 20th century). El Jib is but an example of their advanced knowledge of deep round pools cut out of the rock formations with steps leading down to the pool for communal use. From the details establishing the mentality of the Gibeonites and their secure geographic position, we can reconstruct the many communities that made peace with Israel, recognizing the advantages it could bring them. Considering that Joshua chose the city of Ai for its example to the Amorites and not Gibeon, enlarges our respect for Joshua and Israel's knowledge of the important details.

Vs. 3.6 Adoni Zedek, issued a call to arms. He appealed to Hoham the king of Hebron, Piram the king of Jarmut, Jafia the king of Lachish and Devir the king of Eglon. "Let us initiate a joint effort to punish the Gibeonites for their surrender to Israel." The above enumerated kings heeded Adoni Zedek's call to arms as they felt threatened by the Gibeonites who lived in the very center of their territory the Judean Hills, which became the allotment of the tribe of Judah. V.6, Gibeon informed Joshua of the immediate threat, that Jerusalem, Hebron, Lachish, Jarmut and Eglon were mobilizing for war against them. *Al teref yadcha meavdecha*, "Do not begrudge us your help because of our deceitful diplomacy." *Aleh elenu meherah*, "Come to our assistance at once." *Vehoshia lanu veazrenu*, "We will be grateful for any aid you will give us in order to save us from the combined forces of the Amorites living in this hilly territory."

Vs. 7.11 Joshua's spontaneous response to Gibeon's call reenforced the justice and the success of his mission. In v.8, the Eternal encouraged Joshua to carry forth his plan of attack fearlessly. "I recognize your intent is to act justly in war as in peace, you therefore have no reason to fear your enemies." *Lo yaamod ish mipanecha*, "Not one of your adversaries individually nor their whole force collectively will dare challenge your authority when its goal is *Zedek*-righteousness." In v.5, the allies mobilized their forces in Jerusalem which is midway between Gilgal and Gibeon. They then proceeded to establish themselves before the walls of Gibeon for attack. V.9, reflects the effect of the Eternal's confirmation of his cause in v.8. Joshua pressed his army to hasten with their march. He marched them all that night in the hope that he arrives at the outskirts of Gibeon before the offensive is started by the allied troops. V.10, *pitom* Joshua's sudden appearence upon the horizon with his mighty force *vayehumem* confounded the allies. *Vayehumem Adonai* the Eternal confounded the enemy because Joshua recognized his moral duty in v.7. When Joshua activated his mission, the Eternal assured him that he was doing the right

JOSHUA CHAPTER 10

thing *Tzedek tzedek tirdof* in pursuing justice. The surprise of Joshua's initiative confounded the enemy at the very outskirts of Gibeon. They never entered the city nor did they succeed to batter its mighty walls. Joshua turned the battle from an offensive action to a rout as they panicked and fled through Beth-Horon, modern Ramlah. V.11, Israel's stampede gave the allies no choice but to take the narrow road from upper Beth-Horon to lower Beth-Horon. Only a single file could minipulate this path either going up or down. The *avanim gedolot* are meteorities which killed more of the enemy than in the military action of the combined forces. There is ample evidence of these meteorites to this day. (Deut. 2:15, Ex. 23:27) The invincibility of Israel's forces are tied to the ongoing challenge of Israel's dedication to (Lev. 26:3.13). Both sides of this equation must balance at all times. In (Sanhedrin 32b) this road is described about 1000 years later as incapable of carrying two camels abreast of each other. The term *Hishlich* instead of *himtir* also defines and confirms the physical nature of meteorites. In (Eziekeil 13:11.13, 38:22) the text describes the nature of hailstones.

Vs. 12.15   Joshua is overwhelmed by the phenomenon of his victory in territory which is treacherous geographically. It offers hazards at every step of the way. He recognized the *Etzba Elohim* the finger of God's justice balancing the human scale of inequalities by the perfect timing of the Eternal's Natural Laws to give history a helping hand that it once again realign itself to follow the Master Plan. Joshua fully realized without this victory his leadership would rest in a cloud of doubt. Without this victory the *aidah* multitudes who make up his camp could once again be lost in that *mass* called humanity. Therefore his victory is also their victory. It is also a victory for the indigenous people of Canaan. For millennia they have striven to rise above the demands of tyrants. Somewhere in the genetic process they feel the demand, the urge, yet cannot make it on their own because of a sea of superstition and idolatrous forces overpower their lives. Here, Israel's cause has found a harmonious pitch for a new inspiratiom in the hearts of a righteous minority who want peace, to live contentedly. Has his victory won the sovereign recognition of the people of Canaan? Joshua's exultation because of the flow of events animates his soul to offer a song of thanksgiving, that he was the Eternal's instrument *malach* to implement His action in harmony with natures ongoing process. *Yom valailah lo yishbetu,* The miracle is ever subject to the timing of our needs with natural law, to ignore God's law is to fail. Rising to the heights of his inspiration and courageous leadership, he ordered the sun to stand still in Gibeon and the moon to pause in its orbit in order to give Israel's forces the opportunity to pursue the enemy to the valley of Aijalon. The speed with which Israel's forces functioned as they reached their appointed goal, gave Joshua the feeling that his prayer was answered as the sun and the moon literally delayed their normal circuit. The complete text of Joshua's Ode was recorded in *Sefer Hayashar* (a book which circulated in king David's time). *Velo ats lavo keyom tamim,* the sun did not hasten to set (as it is sometimes blocked out from view by clouds) it was a perfect sunset with its long lasting after glow over the horizon (II Sam.1:17.18,

JOSHUA CHAPTER 10

Deut. 4:7, 33:11). V.14, Joshua felt the exultation of this day as he realized the accomplishment of all the goals so vital for the fulfillment of his life's task. He reflected upon his ineptitude (Joshua 9:14.15) that his blunder too, was the Eternal's direction (Ps.19:3) for He neither slumbers nor sleeps, nor will He permit mankind any rest until His will, progress shall be pursued in accord with His Master Plan. Joshua's exultation is inspired as he reached back in his memory (Ex. 34:10.11, 14:14) to recognize that all these epic moments have come to pass in the span of one full day under his leadership *lishmoa Adonai bekol ish.* V.15, Joshua has indeed felt the response of the Eternal, as he transmitted God's inspiration to his army, to complete the task before the sun sets. On this note of fulfillment Joshua and his men returned to Israel's camp in Gilgal. This verse belongs at the end of this chapter.

Vs. 16.21 Joshua now returned to the details of the war itself. In the heat of battle it was reported that the five kings escaped from their armies and hid in a cave in Makedah. He therefore issued an order to barricade the entrance with huge stones and place sentries in charge to make sure they do not escape. Joshua pressed his advantage, when he recognized the loss of their leadership. He ordered extra pressures upon the remnant of their armies, that they do not filter back to their communities. This spontaneous decision by Joshua was the turning point of the campaign. Joshua did not call a halt to the war until every last enemy had disappeared from the battlefield. Literally a battle to the finish. It was to serve notice to any other combination of alliances what Israel's answer will be. Joshua reported that those who managed to escape the battlefield did filter back to their fortified cities. Joshua's army reassembled at Makedah. The effectiveness of Joshua's strategy was expressed in the deadly silence which was confirmation enough, that they had it coming to them for a long time. *Lo charatz livne Yisrael leish et leshono* not one dared to raise its voice in opposition to Israel.

Vs. 22.43 Joshua ordered the cave to be opened and to bring forth the king of Jerusalem, the king of Hebron, the king of Jarmut, the king of Lachish and the king of Eglon. Joshua ordered his officers to perform an ancient ceremony of subjugation. (obviously not recorded in the Torah (Ps. 106:35) habits Israel picked up from its environment). The intent of this ceremony was to convey the message to all the leaders in Canaan, Israel will not tolerate any opposition. In keeping with past practices they were hung on a gibbet and then buried at sunset in the cave where they hid. The cave was then sealed to become a monumental lesson for the future (Deut. 21:22.23). Vs. 27.33, In these verses Joshua records the sequence of his battles with the Amorite kings. When he came to the assistance of the Gibeonites, he fought these kings in the open, frontally before the powerful walls of Gibeon. After he routed them he attacked each and every one of them individually to destroy their ability to regroup in their cities. The following cities he destroyed in this order: Makedah, Libnah, Horam king of Gezer came to the assistance of Lachish, yet he

JOSHUA CHAPTER 10

succeeded to destroy it. Vs. 34.39, Joshua continued his campaign and destroyed Eglonah, Hebron and Debir. Vs. 40.42, these verses sum up Israel's great victory as they conquered the Judean hills, the southern Negev area *haashedot* the low lying area bordering the Dead Sea. This area is swampy as it receives the run off from the hill country (Num. 21:15). This victory included the territory from Kadesh Barnea to Azah in the northeast, to Goshen in the mountains of Judah, to Gibeon in the northwest. The intent of this information is to establish the historic fact that Joshua succeeded to engage the Canaanite forces as far west as the River of Egypt. Bordering the Mediterranean at this time, the whole sea coast was occupied by the Philistines who were recent conquerors of this territory. They were called the Seapeoples, they came from the Greek Islands. Joshua, did not take Kiryat Arba in this campaign. It was conquered by Othniel the son of Kenaz, recorded in (Joshua 15:16.19). It is placed here to credit Joshua for the initial action. Gezer, was not conquered until Solomon's time (Jud. 1:29, I Kings 9:15.17). V. 43, v. 15 belongs here because Joshua did not return to Gilgal from the day he left Gilgal with his army to defend Gibeon, until the action described in vs. 16.42, was completed. He now returned with his army to Gilgal confident that his southern campaign was over.

JOSHUA CHAPTER 11

Vs. 1.5   Jabin king of Hazor initiated a call to arms to the following kings and leaders of the northern territory: Jobab king of Madon, Shimron king of Achschaph, all the kings who occupied territory north of the Lebanon Mountains, the plains below it toward the Chinnereth, the territories south of the Chinnereth, and Nafoth Dor on the Mediterranean Sea in the west. When the text does not give the name of the king, the territory was ruled by Jabin of Hazor. The text now describes the ethnic origin of these peoples and the areas occupied by them. The Canaanites occupied all the territory from the Mediterranean Sea to the eastern side of the Lebanon Mountains (Num. 13:29). This included the territory from the Mediterranean Sea to the western side of the Jordan River. The Amorites, Hittites, Perizzites, and Jebusites, occupied the mountainous areas, the Hivites occupied the territory south of the Hermon Mountain, called Mitzpah. All the above named kings mobilized their forces in great numbers armed with the latest in cavalry and chariots. They assembled in the vicinity of Merom-in the plain of Dothan. From here they planned to launch their attack against Israel.

Vs. 6.15   In every action recorded, Joshua took the initiative from the start. His surprise attack unhinged the effort of this tremendous force. Joshua forced them to retreat to Greater Zidon to Misrefot-maim, to the valley of Mitzpah in the east. Another flank was driven from the heights of the Lebanon Mountains into the Mediterranean Sea. The extent of the chaos can be ascertained by the force of the rout as they broke up into sections to escape the force of Joshua's pressure. Another branch

JOSHUA CHAPTER 11

retreated to the eastern side of the Lebanon hills. Looking at a topographical map, it was Jabin's intention to bring the battle to the Israelites from all the high ground which he occupied. Joshua's surprise strategy becomes clearer as the retreat unfolded. One of Israel's tactics was to maim the enemies horses, so they can never again be used in a cavalry action of war. Having destroyed their horses, they then burned their chariots. Vs. 10.12, Joshua having succeeded in disbanding Jabin's army, he then directed his attention to the source, the city of Hazor (its history goes back to 2700 BCE.) from where all the tyrannical leadership originated. Joshua destroyed it completely, the proof was discovered by Garstang in 1926. Vs. 13.15, Joshua spared the communities which had natural security built into their geographic-fortress-like positions, as he planned to occupy them at once. In order to settle in them he had to follow the guidelines, to destroy every vestige of its decadence as described in (Num. 21:35, 33:52, Deut. 20:16.18).

Vs. 16.19   The text describes in detail the territories conquered by this tremendous action. From the smooth hills below Mount Seir (so called because no vegetation grew upon them) to the plains of Lebanon from which rises Mount Hermon, all this territory was acquired in this single action. V. 18, informs us that the mopping up, the cleaning up of some recalcitrant pockets of this territory occupied Joshua for many years. V. 19, Joshua reminds history that Israel was morally bound to offer every community the opportunity to make peace with Israel in accord with Torah law (Deut. 20:10). Yet few communities were free to make peace with Israel on its terms; to live in peace with Israel by accepting the Seven Laws of Noah, as a basis from which to rise to the greater demands of Torah law. 3300 years have elapsed into modern times, every ethnic group has a nationality, a place in the sun. Beginning with the families of Shem, this has been Semitic territory. It is a challenge to Israel to become worthy to possess it. It is also a challenge to the rest of mankind to recognize Israel's legal title. The Amorites, the Hittites, Perizzites, the Jebusites, who now occupy the Holyland, are Indo-Aryans, Indo-Europeans or Hamitics, who terrorized the Semitic inhabitants. The original Semites either assimilated or were destroyed by these barbarians.

History has come full circle in the 20th century. Modern day Joshuas in Israel paraphrase our ancient leader Joshua, "None will make peace with Israel only Egypt."

V. 20   *Ki meet Adonai hauta* beginning with (Gen. 15:16.21) for centuries the Eternal's *tehina* mercy, has demanded a response (Gen. 6:3). Yet, these usurpers of the Holyland have ignored their genetic potential for human development. Israel's war of liberation began with the Exodus. From that moment it offered freedom to every human being that desired it (Ex. 12:38). Egypt had a desire to exploit Israel for its nation. What was the motive behind the following historic incidents: (Ex. 17:8.13.16, Num.

JOSHUA CHAPTER 11

20:14.21, 21:1.3,35, 22:, 23:, 24:, 25:1.9, 31:1.12)? It is this barbaric cruelty which the Eternal has recorded in the book of time. He has patiently waited for a sign from these barbarians that they desire to repent and therefore seek God's *tehinah* mercy, to help them rise upon a new plateau. The time has come for the Eternal to balance His account. When the Eternal observed the obstinacy of the Canaanite heart in refusing Israel's terms: 1. Those that desire to leave the Promised Land peacefully, may do so. 2. Those desiring to accept the challenge of living by the Seven Laws of Noah, in order to harmonize with Israel's moral statutes. 3. Those desiring war have the choice of being destroyed completely. (Jerusalem Talmud Sheviit 5:1, 16:2).

(Gen. 3:24) For degenerate man who strives to perpetuate the strife of the sword and war, the Eternal has established the *cherev hamithapechet*, the self-destructive force of their burning egos. Man holds the key for the recombinant choice of *tehina or ego* one leads to the development of the *Zelem Elohim-humanity* the other to self destruction, in order to secure for the righteous of all humanity the path of continuity, peace and contentment. Gibeon the only organized community in the Holyland desirous to live in peace on Israel's terms not only survived but won its protective custody throughout Jewish history.

Vs. 21.23   For seven years Joshua continued his relentless battle to clean out the pockets of resistance. With particular emphasis upon the *anakim* the mainstream of Israel's opposition in the hills of Judah (Num. 13:22, Deut. 9:2). These forces hid in their caves. Periodically they came out in guerrilla force to create havoc upon Israel. Joshua removed these pockets of resistance and we can feel his confidence come through to us as he begins to call them *harei Yisrael* the mountains of Israel. Excluded from the area designated to become the Holyland in accord with (Num. 34:) are Gazah, Gath, Ashdod, these are but representative cities of the territory bordering the Mediterranean coast, now occupied by the Seapeoples-Greeks, who arrived in the 13th century and succeeded the dynasty of Gerar, whose treaty with Israel was made by Abraham (Gen. 21:22.34, Ex. 13:17). Moses was honor bound at the time of the Exodus to bypass Gerar because this treaty was still in force. *Ki karov hu* (Deut. 2:1.27, Gen. 22:24, Deut. 3:14) see Eternal Torah, for details about these territories. From these incidents we must conclude the importance of Israel's moral position when it came to honor its treaties over centuries under changing historical conditions. With the exception of minor pockets of resistance, Joshua now feels secure that he has conformed with his charge as transmitted to him by his master Moses, whose original directives came directly from the inspiration of the Eternal. Joshua now turned to the task of dividing the Holyland. He begins to concentrate from the necessities of war to the high priorities of peace. While Joshua gave no quarter to those desirous of prolonging the war, he was most anxious to recognize those willing to accept the values which Israel is desirous to introduce into the Holyland.

JOSHUA CHAPTER 12

Vs. 1.6 — Though the Canaanite leaders-kings, were prepared for a war of extermination to their last inhabitant, entire regions of the Holyland had accepted as a *fait acompli* Israel's new plateau of civilization. For millenia the evolution of these values was in the process of development. The residents in the Fertile Crescent have felt the impact of these developments as they began to improve their humanity under these traditions and laws. Then came the invasions of the barbarians from the north and the west who turned the clock back. This coming of the Israelites was a new breath of freedom to renew the hope of those descendants of the Semitic residents who had become inured to the savage idolatrous oppression. It offered new hope for other indigenous groupings. They now began to recognize the incorrigibility of their leaders. Only they stood to lose from the new standards and values. The general populace of the Holyland was anxious for a new start. The restrictions under the new constitution was to govern the lives of Israel as well as the indigenous population who have agreed to live in peace with Israel under the guidelines inscribed in the Torah. Under its umbrella all of its inhabitants are guaranteed their human rights. 23 times the Torah repeats for emphasis, "To love the stranger." There can be no aliens in Israel. Moses' instructions not to dispossess the inhabitants willing to live in peace with Israel, recognized their tremendous know-how in the field of agriculture and animal husbandry. The Torah recognized their importance to the national economy of Israel. Two generations of Israel had been isolated from these skills. Aside from the moral aspect which has the highest priority in Jewish civilization, the good will of the indigenous population of Canaan is a vital ingredient for the success of Israel. (Ex. 23:20.33, 34:12.18, Deut. 7:1.5) see commentary in The Eternal Torah. This chapter simply reports that Israel succeeded in destroying the tyranny, the arbitrary and unjust despotism of the barbarian governments. It enumerates the 31 kinglets that ruled by clans in the Trans-Jordanian area. It is this land and its inhabitants, that will now be governed by Torah law. Heading the list of tyrants are Sihon and Og, the other 29 subordinates who were subject to their arbitrary whims are not mentioned here. This Trans-Jordanian territory was taken under the leadership of Moses. It was he and the Elders of his time that granted this territory to the tribes of Reuben, Gad and Manasseh (Num. 32:) These tribes are now in the fighting ranks of Israel, honoring their vow to Moses and the Elders. V.5, Indicates the boundary lines of Og *ad gevul Hageshuri, vehaamaachati* see Eternal Torah in (Deut. 2:, 3:1.22) these were descendants of Abraham's family. Every descendant of Abraham to infinity is honor bound by (Gen. 18:19) *laasot tzedakah umishpat* to observe righteousness in their everyday lives and to live ethically in their relations with other human beings. Israel's relationship ceased when the Geshurites and the Maacatites took up arms against Israel in David's time (II Sam. 10:6, 15:8, I Chronicles 19:6.15).

Vs. 7.24 — Enumerated in these verses are the names of kings defeated by Joshua and a listing of the territories over which they ruled west of the Jordan River. Israel honored Esau's territorial

JOSHUA CHAPTER 12

rights as a descendant of Jacob, though now listed as Seir-Edom. V.14, see commentary on (Num. 21:1.3, Judges 1:17) for the historic background on this verse. Some of the territories listed here were part of the southern campaign, while some had to be retaken and reported in (Judges 1:22.26). For an up to-date detailed understanding of the geographic positions of these communities, see commentary on the book of Joshua, published by Mosad Harav Kook, Jerusalem.

JOSHUA CHAPTER 13

V. 1 The Eternal inspired Joshua to recognize the facts of life. For 40 years Joshua led Israel's armies to safe conduct in its desert experiences. It was he that warded off the attacks of Amalek. It was he that helped Moses overcome the rebellions in the ranks of Israel. It was he that won the battles of Sihon and Og. It was he that planned the strategy for the invasion of Canaan. He has won the battles for the possession of the major part of the Holyland. He is now challenged to face the realities still facing Israel. Part of this equation is the unalterable fact that he is now 89 years old. The Eternal strives to inspire him to recognize the truth that his effectiveness as a military leader has been diminished by his inability to lead Israel's army in the field. From the above summation of his accomplishments, we must conclude that his natural ability lay in leading the army and to develop military strategy. The Eternal strives to stimulate his perception to recognize the other side of the equation. Who shall become Israel's leader to carry on the tremendous task that lays ahead of Israel? Unlike Moses, whose leadership did not come to the fore until he was 80 years of age, yet, he had the vision to choose Joshua during his lifetime. He created the organization for a smooth running nation by appointing Elders and Judges, a Sanhedrin to govern Israel during his lifetime (Ex. 18:14.27, Num. 11:14.17). *Atah zakantah ba bayamim* You are now at the height of your experience, your advanced age demands an accounting for every day remaining of your active lifetime. Joshua must recognize the reality of Israel's condition. He has defeated the major forces of those occupying the Holyland, there are many pockets of resistance which need organization to assume the responsibility of governing in order to establish law and order. There are still large areas to be conquered to accord with (Num. 34:).

Vs. 2.7 See (Joshua 11:21.23) why the Mediterranean coastal area was left unconquered at this time. See Eternal Torah, why Geshur was not conquered until (II Sam. 10:6, 15:8). V.3, Joshua outlined the territory now held by the Philistines and the nature of their government. They were divided into 5 states, each headed by a Seren, a governor over Ekron, Azzah, Ashdod, Ashkelon, Gath. Vs. 4.5, The text is indicating the territory bordering the Mediterranean Sea, beginning in the west at Shihor-Nile River, all the area bordering the Mediterranean going north into the Hermon and the Lebanon Mountains north to Hamath. The Eternal now inspired Joshua, to take into consideration his personal physical limitations in leading Israel in the

JOSHUA CHAPTER 13

field and therefore to concentrate on creating the organization and government to administer the territories already in the hands of Israel. Vs. 6.7, "Follow My inspiration to divide all the allotted territory described in (Num. 34) to the nine and one half tribes still waiting for their inheritance. You have My assurance that in the course of time and history, the above areas now held by the Philistines will be conquered by the very tribes who are destined to possess them."

Vs. 8.13   Joshua is completing the historical record begun in (Num. 32: Joshua 1:12.18) described in these verses are the territories conquered from Sihon and Og which make up the land mass known as Trans-Jordania and were officially designated to the tribes of Reuben, Gad and three families of Manasseh. V.13, is but another example of the effect of Abraham's genetic inheritance which he passed on to his posterity (Gen. 18:19) the moral demand of ethical conduct in all of Israel's human relations. Abraham gave his word in (Gen. 21:22.34, 22:24, 19:37.38, 36:1.8) to honor their legacies and treaties. Moses recorded this moral tradition in (Deut. 2:4.8, 9.12, 17.19,) for all time to honor their treaties and legacies. Joshua made a treaty with Gibeon in (Joshua 9:15) he fought five allied governments in (Joshua 10:6.7) in order to honor Israel's treaty with Gibeon. In (II Sam. 21:1.6) King David continued to honor this treaty 300 years later. Israel honored and reminds history in the record to honor the Geshurite and Maacatites territories. This was kept until (II Sam. 10:6, 15:8).

V. 14   In (Num. 35:1.8) the Torah established the overall pattern of territories to be allocated to the Kohanim and Leviim. Joshua reiterated this arrangement that the tribe of Levi were not to receive title to any land. In (Joshua 21:) he will designate 48 cities scattered in the Holyland among the tribes where they shall function as teachers to the families of Israel. The title of these cities will be held by the respective tribes. These cities were not assigned until the Mishkan was established in Shiloh. See The Eternal Torah p. 422 for the table showing the division of these cities.

Vs. 15.23   Joshua now reports for the record of history that this territory which he now is assigning to the families of the tribe of Reuben, were promised orally by Moses during his lifetime. Now that the tribe of Reuben have earned their legal title to this land by having fulfilled their promise to Moses (Num. 32:29.33), Joshua is now issuing to them the full title to the following territories to have and to hold in perpetuity: Beginning in the north on the shores of the Arnon River, the whole plain which includes the city of Medba, Heshbon and the cities of Dibon, Bamoth-baal and Beth-baal-meon, Jahaza, Kedemoth, Mephaath, Kirjathaim, Sibmah, Zereth-hashahar, all in the plain and in the rising mount from the valley. Beth-peor, Ashdoth-pisgah, Beth-jeshimoth. Included in Reuben's territory are all the cities of the plain which were part of the Kingdom of Sihon, king of the Amorites, whose capital was Heshbon. Included in these territories are Evi, Rekem and Zur, Hur, Reba, which were dukedoms of Sihon. (Some of these territories originally

JOSHUA CHAPTER 13

belonged to Moab and Midian (Num. 21:25.31, Gen. 25:1.6). In peace as in war Israel was to honor its legacies and treaties. Israel took this territory from Sihon, who had taken it from Moab. Israel took some of these land areas from Midian, when it became involved with Sihon and Og and thereby showed its animosity to Israel (Num. 25:1.9, 14.15) though descendants of Abraham and Keturah, they developed their animosity to Israel and thereby breached their rights as brothers. V.22, Israel now squared another old score with Balaam (Num. 22:, 23:, 24:, 25:) a man who started out as a prophet, he then let his ego overpower him for personal gain as he switched to become an advisor of foreign affairs to Midian. It is here in Midian that he met his waterloo because he could not resist their golden opportunities, if he would only do as a soothsayer what no genuine prophet could do. Curse Israel (Gen. 12:1.3). V.23, the western border of Reuben's territory was bounded by the eastern banks of the Jordan River. All of the above became the inheritance of the tribe of Reuben and all of their respective families.

Vs. 24.28 The following territorial boundaries include all the land areas promised by Moses to the tribe of Gad and their families on condition that they join Israel in the conquest of Canaan. They have now fulfilled their promise and Joshua hereby passes title to them for the following land rights, to have and to hold in perpetuity: Beginning with Jazer and all cities in Gilead and half of the land of Ammon to Aroer up to Rabbah. Beginning with Heshbon to Ramath-mizpeh and Betonim, including Mahanaim to the border of Debir, the valley of Beth-haram, Bet-mirmah, Succoth and Zaphon, included are the territories not assigned to Reuben from the kingdom of Sihon king of Heshbon. Gad's land rights include all the area from the eastern border of the Jordan to the edge of the Sea of Chinnereth. All the above represent the inheritance of the tribe of Gad and their respective families.

Vs. 29.33 (Num. 32:29.32) Moses gave permission to the families of Machir, Jair, and Novach, who chose to occupy the vast territories to the north of Trans-Jordania. That it can be granted this land mass as an inheritance on two conditions, that it conquer it from the Amorite kings now possessing it and that they obligate themselves to send a representative number of soldiers to join the rest of the tribes of Israel in the conquest of all the territory west of the Jordan River known as Canaan. Joshua now recognized their rights to receive title to their territory as they have met both conditions. Included in this title are the following land areas: The boundaries of Manasseh, in Trans-Jordan began at Mahanaim and included all the territory which was conquered from Og king of Bashan, all the villages of Jair in Bashan which include about 60 communities or cities. Half of Gilead, Ashtaroth, and Edrei which originally belonged to Og in Bashan were inherited by half of the families of Machir, the oldest son of Manasseh. The rest of this vast territory was divided between the other half of the families of Machir, the families of Jair and the families of Novach. Since these families met all the conditions outlined in (Num. 32:) Joshua is now passing legal title to them. This

JOSHUA CHAPTER 13

concludes the official division of all the territories to the tribes of Reuben, Gad and the three families of Manasseh, who chose to receive their inheritance of the Holyland in Trans-Jordania. V.33, in v.14, we have explained the meaning of this verse. Inferred from the repetition of the context of this verse are these facts. The portions which these tribes will have to set aside for the Leviim have been designated as quoted above. However, should this territory ever expand, these tribes will become morally obligated to set aside a proportionate amount of additional land.

JOSHUA CHAPTER 14

Vs. 1.5   All of Trans-Jordania was officially divided by Moses (Num. 32:). All Joshua and Eleazar did was to confirm and give testimony that Reuben, Gad and the three families of Manasseh honored their pledge and were honorably discharged from their pledge made to Moses. Joshua is about to distribute the allotted portions on the west side of the Jordan River to the nine and one half tribes. He therefore is reminding Israel in accord with the record, who has the authority to distribute the land in the Holyland (Num. 34:16.29, 33:53.54). In v.4, Joshua reconfirms for the record Jacob's error in the ancient common practice of primogeniture (Gen. 48:22). Moses witnessed the effect of this unfair practice and wrote a new law in (Deut. 21:15.17) to discourage this practice. (see Eternal Torah on Gen. 32:, 3?: tracing its effect in the history of Israel). V.5, Joshua reminded his generation that he is bound by the instructions given to Moses by the Eternal God of history. Neither Moses nor Joshua can wipe clean the record of Jacob's condemnation of Levi, in (Gen. 34:30, 49:5.7) Joshua's *ki im* is very instructive. Though I am honor bound to carry out Jacob's instructions, we will give the tribe of Levi its allotted portion in accord with the instructions given in (Num. 35:1.8) and we will strive to be generous in the land we set aside for its agriculture and animal husbandry, that the tribe of Levi can supplement their livelihood. (In Yebamoth 89b, Rabbi Eleazar, strives to uphold Joshua's legal right to correct any inequalities which came to their attention. He is taking Joshua, the Elders and Eleazar the high priest to task for not exercising their authority. This should have applied not only to Levi but to Ephraim, Manasseh and Simeon).

Vs. 6.15   Caleb was one of the scouts to represent the tribe of Judah when Moses sent them forth to reconnoiter, to survey the Holyland, for the purpose of establishing georgraphic and military information for the conquest of the Holyland. Caleb was 40 years of age at that time. This experience took place in the beginning of the second year after the Exodus. The details are recorded in (Num. 13:6.30, 14:6.10,30.38, 32:12). Caleb is reminding Joshua who is the only surviving witness of a promise given to him by Moses and confirmed in (Num. 14:24, Deut. 1:34.36) in recognition for his dedication. Caleb is establishing his age as 85, (it is at the end of the seven years of conquest, the place is at Gilgal). As Joshua is about to divide the land, Caleb requests permission to organize a military force in the tribe of Judah, for

JOSHUA CHAPTER 14

the purpose of acquiring the mountains of Hebron. Vs. 11:12, Caleb assures Joshua that his physical condition and his faith in his ability today are as fresh as that day 45 years ago when he returned to give his minority report as a scout. "My faith in the Eternal's promise grants me the ability and the will to defeat those mighty giants that occupy our allotted territory at this moment. We promise to defeat the Mittrani forces that occupy the hills of Hebron, if you will permit us to annex it to our official inheritance (Num. 13:28)." Vs. 13.14, Joshua recognized Caleb's reasonable request. He granted Caleb permission to establish a legal title to the tribe of Judah. Caleb's initiative corroborates the importance of distributing the land now in accord with the Eternal's inspiration in (Joshua 13:1). The responsibility and initiative for actual possession and governing each tribe's allotted territory will pass to the heads of each tribe. In (Jud. 1:20) we have the proof that Caleb succeeded in removing the *mighty giants.* V. 15, informs us that Hebron was called Kiriat-Arba because of these four mighty families. Caleb's great faith and dedication to his God and to his people once again come to the fore in his lifetime as he inspired the other tribes to assume the initiative in cleaning out the pockets of resistance. As each tribe recognized the importance of winning a war is demonstrated only by their ability to establish law and order and to govern in accord with Torah law. This was a great moment in Jewish history for those who initiated the challenge to establish law and order, in order to begin a new era in the Holyland. The land now rested from the war. Caleb's recognition in his generation, is the consistent reward of Judah in Israel's history which began to surface with the father of the tribe of Judah in (Gen. 37:26, 43:8.14, 44:18.34).

JOSHUA CHAPTER 15

Vs. 1.19 Consistent with the reverence of the tribe of Judah in Israel's history, tradition tells us that the division of the land actually began with Judah. The tribe of Judah was allotted all the *negev* southern territory which was bounded by the western border of Edom in the east and the Mediterranean Sea in the west and the Red Sea in the south. All the land area west of the Jordan to Ekron were its northern boundary. Vs. 13.15, define the actual territory allotted to Caleb and his immediate families. Vs. 16.17, Caleb offers a reward to him who shall succeed in conquering Devir-Kiriat Sefer. This challenge was assumed by Othniel a nephew of Caleb. His valiant offer was to be rewarded in becoming the husband of Caleb's daughter Achsah. Caleb's father was Jephuneh. When he died his mother married her brother-in-law Kenaz. (In later history he became known as the Kenizite) Othniel was born from this marriage. Caleb and Othniel were genealogically full brothers. It was Othniel who became the leader of Israel upon the demise of Joshua. When Othniel succeeded in conquering Devir, he also succeeded to become the husband of Achsah, Caleb's daughter. Vs. 18.19, Achsah is unhappy with the arid land allotted to her husband in the Negev, she pleads with her father Caleb, for his blessing, that he grant her the ability to cultivate this land for sustenance. For

JOSHUA CHAPTER 15

this I would need an area with springs of water. Caleb therefore granted her wish and gave her legal title to an area which received the surface run off from the hills of Hebron and the potential for underground springs from the water table.

Vs. 20.62   The following cities, towns and villages are included in the territory allotted to the families of Judah:

29 cities in the Negev	Jerusalem
14 cities in the North-shephela	Judean Hills
16 cities in the South-shephela	11 cities, south
9 cities in the East-shephela	9 cities Hebron, central
Ekron — Mediterranian	10 cities Hebron, east
Ashdod — Mediterranian	6 cities Hebron, north
Azzah — Mediterranian	2 cities Hebron, desert
	6 cities Hebron, forest

The total number of cities accounted for in these verses are 112 cities, scattered over 14 regions. In v. 32, 38 cities were enumerated because 9 of these cities were allotted to the tribe of Simeon, in order to conform with Jacob's wish in (Gen. 49:5.7). In v.36, 15 cities are enumerated, actually there should be only 14 because Enam, refers to the spring of Tapuach. Vs. 45.47, these cities and surrounding areas were not conquered until (Jud. 1:18.19) after the demise of Joshua. Some of the territory occupied by the Philistines was not possessed until David's time. V. 63, when the book of Joshua was brought up to date by the prophet Samuel, Jerusalem was still occupied by the Jebusites. This too did not pass unto Israel until David's time. Though many of the areas included in Joshua's division of the land are still held by the various Canaanite peoples, Joshua is instructing the present and future generations to strive to possess all the territory included as Israel's inheritance, that it accord with the Eternal's promise. It is up to Israel to create the reality of its inheritance.

JOSHUA CHAPTER 16

Vs. 1.4   The text establishes the general boundary lines which encompassed the territory which will be divided between Ephraim and Manasseh the sons of Joseph. Their territory was confined within the line which began at a point in Jericho fronting on the Jordan River, it then runs in a westerly direction over the hilly area to Beth-el, then to Luz (Luz was the ancient town, Beth-el was established in the time of Jacob) continuing to the border of Haarchi, then on to Ataroth. It then went westward to the border of Japhleti, on the border of lower Bet-horon and Gezer westward to the Mediterranean Sea.

Vs. 5.10   The text now defines the territory assigned to Ephraim and their respective families. Beginning at a point in Atroth-addar in the east to upper Beth-horon, continuing toward the Mediterranean Sea in the west, turning north to Michmethath, then east to

JOSHUA CHAPTER 16

Taanath-Shiloh, continuing on to Janoah. From here it descended to Ataroth and Naarath touching the border of Jericho, continuing east to the Jordan River. The westward boundary began at Tappuach to the Wadi Kanah then on to the Sea. In addition to the territory confined within the boundary lines defined above, the families of Ephraim were to receive specific cities and villages within the territory which shall be assigned to Manasseh. V.10, the people of Gezer voluntarily conformed with the conditions outlined in (Deut. 20:10.11) and remained in Gezer as day laborers. (Jud. 1:28) confirms that the same situation existed in its time. In (I Kings 9:16.17) we learn that king Solomon's father-in-law, Pseusennes II, the king of Egypt destroyed the city of Gezer and took its inhabitants as captive slaves to serve in his daughter's services.

JOSHUA CHAPTER 17

Vs. 1.2   Looking at a map of the Holyland, we must fix in our minds the territory of the tribe of Manasseh was cut in half by the Jordan River. East of the Jordan River, in the Gilead area, the families of Machir the eldest son of Manasseh and his brothers Jair and Novach had already received their inheritance as defined in (Joshua 13:29.32). This conformed with the promise made during Moses' lifetime in (Num. 32:39.42). Joshua is now to assign the territory contiguous to the Gilead land on the western side of the Jordan River, to the remaining families of Manasseh: Abiezer, Helek, Asriel, Shechem, Hepher, and Shemida.

Vs. 3.6   The appeal now being made to Eleazar, Joshua and the Nesum, who are responsible for the division of the Holyland, is but a reminder of the original appeal made by the five daughters of Zelaphchad: Machlah, Noah, Chaglah, Milkah and Tirtzah, in (Num. 26:33, 27:1.11). Moses confirmed in these verses the justness of their appeal and so established the law in the Torah, that when a father has no sons only daughters, it is they that shall inherit as if they were sons. Joshua remembered well their appeal and therefore set aside ten districts west of the Jordan River. These daughters will now receive collectively the portion their father would have received had he lived. (All the descendants of those present at the time of the Exodus and recorded in the census were entitled to participate in the division of the land). There was but one condition laid upon the daughters of Zelaphchad and included with Moses' adjudication of their appeal and recorded in (Num. 36:1.13) in order to keep the title to the land in the tribe of Manasseh, that they marry men of their choice from the families of Manasseh.

Vs. 7.13   The boundary line for the six sons of Manasseh that will receive their inheritance on the western side of the Jordan River is as follows: Beginning at the southern boundary of Asher, going south to Michmethath (near Shechem) continuing east to En-Tapuach, continuing south to the Wadi Kanah, then turning west to the Mediterranean Sea. This territory was contiguous to Asher in the north and

JOSHUA CHAPTER 17

Issachar in the east. Tappuah on the border of Manasseh belonged to Ephraim. The towns south of Wadi Kanah also belonged to Ephraim. Bet-shean and its dependencies, Ibleam and its dependencies, Dor and its dependencies, En-dor and its dependencies, Megiddo and its dependencies, were considered as three regions and are included in Manasseh's inheritance. Vs. 12.13, Manasseh failed to conquer many of the above communities, nor would the natives agree to the conditions offered them, to observe the Seven Laws of Noah, in order to live in their communities peacefully. In (Jud. 1:27.28) the situation in these regions had not changed.

Vs. 14.18 The tribe of Manasseh as the representatives of the sons of Joseph appeared before Joshua in Gilgal for the purpose of enlarging their allotted territory to meet their ever expanding needs. They came prepared with statistics to prove their position. In the census taken in (Num. 1:34.35) their number was 32,000. In the census taken 39 years later (Num. 26:34) their number had increased to 52,700. By quoting the record they proved that other tribes decreased in the same period. Yet, they received their inheritance by the same formula. Joshua recognized their just claim. However, he utilized their statistics to point up their added numbers gave them the capability to expand their territory upon the hills of Ephraim by clearing the forest land. You now have the ability and the manpower to clear out any pockets of resistance, to cultivate the land to produce your food with your increased needs. What Manasseh was seeking was a national effort to remove the Perizzites and the remnants of the Rephaim, who are armed with iron chariots limiting their ability to conquer the plain which was impenetrable at this time. Joshua countered their demand by suggesting that the tribe of Ephraim whose territory is contiguous with theirs, that they join forces for their mutual benefit to destroy these powerful forces which will continue to harrass them. When you succeed in overcoming this handicap, the plain will offer you the needed extra territory for expansion.

JOSHUA CHAPTER 18

Vs. 1.3 The time frame of this chapter is 14 years after they entered Canaan. The Mishkan has been transferred from Gilgal to Shiloh. Joshua assembled the representatives of the whole people of Israel, in order to prod the tribes of Benjamin, Simeon, Zebulun, Issachar, Asher, Naphtali and Dan, to cease squatting as transients between Gilgal and Shiloh. They were subsisting upon the booty they acquired as their share in the wars that were fought. Joshua challenged their inertia. "How long will you procrastinate from taking possession of your inheritance. Your wandering years are over. You must cease living in an atmosphere rooted in miracles. The Eternal God of Israel awaits your initiative to take advantage of the conditions He created for you to succeed in inheriting the land." (See Addendum in T.E.T. p. 553).

JOSHUA CHAPTER 18

Vs. 4.7 — Joshua proposed that each of the seven tribes listed in vs. 1.3, appoint three men from each tribe who shall represent them for the purpose of surveying the territories allotted to them. "You are to reach an agreement between yourselves how to apportion the natural resources of the territory in accord with the respective needs and skills of each tribe. Your survey is not to infringe upon the territory of Judah in the south nor on the tribes of Ephraim and Manasseh in the north, who have already received title to their land. You are to record your collective agreement and your plan for your division of this territory into seven portions and submit it to me (Joshua) here in Shiloh. I shall then substantiate your conclusions are in conformity with the instruction given and recorded in the Torah for the division of the land (Num. 26:54). The Elders, Eleazar and Joshua will then confirm your legal title to your inheritance before the Eternal our God." V.7, Joshua summed up his address to the representatives of all the people assembled. Joshua reminded these seven tribes, that when they take title to their land, Levi's portion becomes the responsibility of each tribe in recognition for the Leviim's dedication to the whole community of Israel. Joshua summed up for the record that the tribes of Reuben, Gad and the families of Machir, Jair and Novach, of the tribe of Manasseh have received title to their inheritance and are already settled in Trans-Jordan.

Vs. 8.10 — The importance of leadership and initiative are emphasized by Joshua in these verses. Looking back on the historical record of these past two generations, we observe how human beings become inured, they are willing to tolerate a primitive development at a time when opportunity demands action. *Vayetzav Yohoshua* Joshua warned, encouraged and admonished the chosen leaders, chosen to make the survey, that their inertia could endanger the whole cause of Israel's development. Every gain we have made in the seven years of intensive campaigning for the possession of the Holyland can be lost as the enemy recognizes indolence in the ranks of Israel. Survey this territory and come to a positive solution, to take possession of your inheritance, to develop its natural resources, that these cities, towns and villages become viable communities to accord with the instructions given in (Num. 33:54.56). V.10, it should be obvious to the serious student that the mission described in vs.4.7, took a considerable amount of time. We must therefore consider that Joshua's prodding took place before the establishment of the Mishkan in Shiloh. It is placed here at the end of the 14th year to conclude the record for the division of the Holyland to conform with the conclusion of Joshua's life's work as inspired by the Eternal in (Joshua 13:1.7). Joshua, Eleazar and the Nesiim gave official approval to the plan submitted by the seven tribes listed in vs. 1.3.

Vs. 11.28 — In accord with the drawing of lots, Benjamin was to receive the territory included within the following boundaries: Consistent with the historic past history of the tribe of Benjamin, their inheritance lay between Judah and Joseph. (For detailed record of

JOSHUA CHAPTER 18

Benjamin's past history see The Eternal Torah on (Gen. 49:27). Benjamin's northern boundary began at the Jordan River, it then ascended to the northern flank of Jericho, it rose westward to the hill country and continued on to Beth-aven, it then turned southward to the flank of Luz-Bethel. From this point it descended to Atroth-addar, to the hill which is south of Lower Beth-horon, it then turned southward from the hill on the south side of Beth-horon and ended at Kiriat-baala, a town in Judah, they call it Kiriat-jearim. The above details represent the western rim of Benjamin's boundary. The southern rim began at a point on the outskirts of Kiriat-jearim continued westward to the waters of Naphtoah. It then descended to the bottom of the Valley of Ben-hinnom at the northern end of the valley of Rephaim. From this point it continued down the valley of Hinnom, to the southern flank of the Jebusites to En-rogel. From here it curved northward to En-shemesh and continued to Geliloth, facing Adummim. It continued to descend to the Stone of Bohan a son of Reuben. It then veered northward to the edge of the Arabah. From this point it began to descend into the Arabah. The line then continued to the northern side of Beth-hoglah and ended at the northern edge of the Dead Sea, which is the southern end of the Jordan River, to form the southern boundary of the tribe of Benjamin. Their eastern boundary line ran parallel with the Jordan River. In vs.21.28, are recorded the names of the 26 cities included in this territory of Benjamin and was considered as two separate regions of the Holyland.

JOSHUA CHAPTER 19

Vs. 1.9   Simeon drew the second lot. Its inheritance will conform with its historic record as expressed in the will of Jacob (Gen. 49:5.7,8.12, Jud. 1:1.4). The tribes of Benjamin and Simeon became the wards of Judah, who directed their progressive historic development. (See The Eternal Torah on the above verses for details of their historic record). Simeon's territory outlined in these verses conform with Jacob's request. Their communities are not contiguous with each other. They follow the pattern of their social relationships with various families in the tribe of Judah formed over the past centuries. The tribe of Judah voluntarily surrendered 17 cities in two separate regions to the tribe of Simeon. Judah's goodwill and magnanimity are recorded in (Deut. 33:7, I Chronicles 4:24.43). The name of these cities are: Beer-sheba-Sheba, Moladah, Hazar-shual, Balah, Ezem, Eltolad, Bethul, Hormah, Ziklag, Beth-marcaboth, Hazar-susah, Beth-lebaoth, Sharuhen, Ain, Rimmon, Ether, Ashan, Ramath-negeb. Included were the villages which became the inheritance of the tribe of Simeon.

Vs. 10.16   The third lot came to Zebulun, whose natural abilities were established during the 17 years before the demise of Jacob in Egypt and recorded in (Gen. 49:13,47:28, Ex. 1:7) see Eternal Torah for details of their involvement with the Phoenicians in maritime adventures while in Egypt and beyond. They received their inheritance to

JOSHUA CHAPTER 19

conform with their abilities on the shores of the Mediterranean Sea. Starting at a point in Sarid and ascending westward to Maralah, touching at a point in Dabbesheth and the wadi near Jokneam, then on to the eastern side of Sarid, continuing on through Chisloth-tabor, to Daberath, then rising to Japhia. It then veered eastward to Gath-hepher, to Eth-kazin and Rimmon, turning to Neah its northern boundary, continuing to Hannathon. Its extreme northern limits were the valley of Iphtah-el, Kattah, Nahalal, Shimron, Idalah and Bethlehem. Making a total of 12 cities with their villages. The above boundary lines defined the inheritance of the tribe of Zebulun.

Vs. 17.23 The fourth lot was drawn by Issachar. Their expertise lay in the field of agriculture, yet they were also involved in the maritime adventures of Zebulun, Asher, Dan and Naphtali. See The Eternal Torah for details on (Gen. 49:14.15, Deut. 33:18.19). In v.21, Ein-ganim, symbolizes their expertise in agriculture. In v.22, Shachatzimah is one of the border towns of Issachar, in Sanhedrin 88a, the sages confirm that one of its boundary lines was the Jordan River. It translates this word as a lion because this town was a habitat of lions, to prove its point it quotes (Jer. 49:19, 50:44).

Issachar received 16 cities and their villages in one region. Included were the following cities: Jezreel, Chesulloth, Shunem, Hapharaim, Shion, Anaharoth, Rabbith, Kishion, Ebez, Remeth, En-gannim, En-haddah and Beth-pazzez. Their boundary touched the Tabor Mountain at Shachatzimah and Bet-shemesh and the Jordan River. Tabor, Shachatzimah and Beth-shemesh are border communities included in the inheritance of the tribe of Issachar.

Vs. 24.31 The fifth lot went to Asher, whose personality and initiative have a long history of development and were recognized in (Gen. 49:20, Deut. 33:24.25) see The Eternal Torah for details of Asher's historic record. Asher inherited 22 cities and villages contained in one region. The following communities formed the perimeter of its boundary lines: Helkath, Hali, Beten, Achsaph, Allammelech, Amad, Mishal and it touched the shore of the area west of Carmel (not Mount Carmel). It bordered on Shihor-libnath and continued east to Beth-dagon. It then touched the boundary of Zebulun and the Valley of Iphtah-el and Beth-emek and Neiel in the north. It continued north to Cabul, Ebron, Rehob, Hammon, and Kanah to great Sidon. The boundary then turned to Ramah and north to the fortified city of Tyre. It then veered to Hosah and then westward to Mehebel, Achzib, Ummah, Aphek and Rehob. Though scholars find it difficult to reestablish many of these communities, to pinpoint their geographic position, what comes through from our research is the tremendous good will which emanated from the tribe of Asher toward the families of all Israel throughout Jewish history.

Vs. 32.39 Naphtali was the sixth tribe to receive its official territorial designation. Jacob's evaluation of Naphtali in (Gen. 49.21) and Moses' confirmation two centuries later in (Deut. 33:23), Naphtali's sound thinking impressed itself upon his posterity, to establish his

JOSHUA CHAPTER 19

immortality in Israel's history. Naphtali received 19 cities and their villages in one region. Their boundary ran from Heleph, to Elon-bezaanannim, Adami-nekeb, Jabneel to Lakkum and ended at the Jordan River. Their boundary then turned westward to Aznoth-tabor, on to Hukok. It touched the territory of Zebulun in the south and Asher's territory in the west and it touched Judah's territory at the Jordan River in the east. The following cities or towns were fortified cities: Zidim, Zer, Hammath, Rakkath, Chinnereth, Adamah, Ramah, Hazor, Kedesh, Edrei, En-hazor, Iron, Migdal-el, Horem, Beth-anath, Beth-shemesh. All the above were the inheritance of the tribe of Naphtali. Considering that the boundaries of Naphtali touched Phoenicia, Asher, Zebulun, Issachar, Manasseh, Dan and the Sea of Galilee, all these factors enhanced it's international outlook. Its geographic position became the laboratory to assimilate ideas from abroad and to exercise it's native linguistic talents. All these natural talents utilized in an environment of goodwill and contentment became the envy of all Israel.

Vs. 40.48   The tribe of Dan was the seventh and last of the tribes to receive their official allotment of land. Their territory officially included the following cities-towns: Zorah, Eshtaol, Irshemesh, Shaalabbin, Aijalon, Ithla, Elon, Timnah, Ekron, Eltekeh, Gibbethon, Baalath, Jehud, Bene-berak, Gath-rimmon, Mejarkon, Rakkon at the border of Joppa. The text now tells us *vayetzeh gevul b'nai Dan mehem* that their territory slipped from their grasp. They were unable to take possession of it. So the Danites migrated to the north and took the city of Leshem, near Mount Hermon, east of the Litani River and the city of Tyre on the Mediterranean Sea. They renamed Leshem and called it Dan. Though all the above cities and villages were ascribed to Dan, they never fully took possession of it. Because, 1. The Philistines occupied most of this territory including the southern part of Lebanon. 2. They took Leshem-Dan to be close to the Phoenicians, to complement the efforts of their brethren involved in the maritime traffic with the Phoenicians. For the student interested in the sources which substantiate these facts we offer the following: See commentary in The Eternal Torah on the following verses (Gen. 49:16.17, Deut. 33:22, and the addenda pages 261, 553). To enlarge upon the involvement of the tribe of Dan in future Israel history, we offer the following sources: *(Judges 13:2.25, 18:12, 1:34.35, I Kings 4:9, 15:27, II Sam. 23:32, I Chronicles 6:54, 8:13, 11:33). Leshem was not conquered until the time of (Judges 18:) in the time of Deborah. But another proof that Samuel completed the book of Joshua. Dan was the main source of king Solomon's maritime *know-how*. Their families are found living in Ephraim, Benjamin, Manasseh and Judah.
*The references refer to Dan's activities in the above named cities or towns.

Vs. 49.51   Joshua has concluded in establishing the boundary lines for all the tribes that were eligible to inherit land west of the Jordan River. The details of this task are recorded in chapters 14 through 19. Joshua requested and received the area of Timnat-serach in Ephraim which is his tribe. This territory was already in possession of the tribe of

JOSHUA CHAPTER 19

Ephraim. Here he built a city, fortified it and spent the rest of his life there. (Jud. 2:9) records that he was laid to rest there. V.51, The High Priest Eleazar, Joshua and the Nesiim, have now officially completed their historic task at Shiloh, a task that took seven years. The emphasis now is upon Israel's individual dedication, to begin to govern by establishing law and order in their respective allotted territories. Israel has a constitution, the Torah, which shall govern their individual lives, the lives of all the human beings who are now living in their midst. The success of Israel can never be measured by Gross National Product. It is ever tied to our ability to extend the human rights guaranteed by the Eternal God, to every human being who makes up the composite *edah* community of Israel.

JOSHUA CHAPTER 20

Vs. 1.6 About 700 years in the evolutionary process which began with Shem after the period of the flood, have now become history. (Gen. 15:13.21, 18:19, Ex. 21:12.17, Num. 35:9.34, Deut. 4:41.44). All of these verses record stepping stones for a human being who is part of a community and a nation, to begin to rise to the maximum of his genetic human potential, by implementing his *Zelem Elohim* his godly image to become civilized and build a new WORLD ORDER. These six verses which are a repetition of the legal procedures dealing with manslaughter tie the book of Joshua to the Five Books of Moses. See The Eternal Torah, on the explanation of the above texts dealing with the Cities of Refuge, which Joshua is now obliged to implement. Uppermost in Joshua's mind is the experiential effect of the wars of conquest fought by the Israelites. Shall this experience inure the people of Israel, to the practice of taking a life? Will they differentiate between defense and outright murder? Joshua is therefore inspired by the Eternal to implement the Cities of Refuge, to which one who kills another person by accident, unintentionally, may flee from the avenger. There at the city gates, he shall plead his case to the recognized Elders and court of law. There he shall remain safely in their protective custody until his case is adjudicated that he in fact had no intention to kill. It was an accident. He shall remain in this City of Refuge until the death of the current high priest. There he is to live a normal life while being rehabilitated from this traumatic experience and only after the new high priest is appointed may he return to his original home. Joshua reminds Israel for emphasis, that blood revenge in this new environment is the common coin of everyday living. The enforcement of Torah law to protect every human being regardless if he or she be native born, proselyte or alien must become mandatory before this land becomes universally known as the Holyland.

Vs. 7.9 Joshua records the names of the Cities of Refuge and their geographic position in every community in the Holyland: Kedesh, in the hill country of Galil, in Naphtali. Shechem, in the mountains of Ephraim. Kiriath-arba-Hebron, in the mountains of Judah.

JOSHUA CHAPTER 20

Betzer-Trans Jordan, in the wilderness of the Tableland-plain of the tribe of Reuben. Ramoth in Gilead, in the territory of Gad. Golan, in Bashan, in the territory of Manasseh. Every human being regardless if he lived locally or was a traveler came under the protective custody of Torah law. The above named cities must be publicized, roads going to and from these cities must be kept open at all times. No one may take the law into his own hands to avenge a homicide. The court, the prosecutor under the law of the Torah becomes the avenger. Only the court can make the determination of guilty or innocent.

JOSHUA CHAPTER 21

Vs. 1.5 Now that all the territories of the Holyland have been established, the leaders of the tribe of Levi reminded Eleazar, Joshua and the Nesiim of the Eternal's promise recorded in (Num. 35:1.8) that land be set aside for their families and pasture land for their livestock. Israel recognized the dedication of the Leviim and the justice of their request. The first to be assigned were the immediate descendants of Aaron. They received 13 towns in the territories of Judah, Simeon and Benjamin. The remaining families of Kehath, received 10 towns in the territory of Ephraim, Dan, Manasseh (west of the Jordan). *Hanotarim* refers to Amram, Yitzhar and Uzziel.

Vs. 6.8 The families of Gershon received 13 towns in Issachar, Asher, Naphtali and from Manasseh in the Bashan northeast of the Jordan River. The families of Merari received 12 towns in the territories of Reuben, Gad, in Trans-Jordan and Zebulun west of the Jordan. These 48 communities included pasture land or a greenbelt, in accord with the stipulation in (Num. 35:1.8). The dimensions for these areas are given in these verses in the Torah. V.8, *bagoral* a human being's lot is established by one's conduct, effort, and lifestyle. Therefore *goral* cannot mean *fate* rather it is societies assessment of our development. Each of these families of Levi, were chosen for their natural abilities to play an important part in the development of the Mishkan-Tabernacle. From this institution was to arise the inspiration and leadership for Israel's development.

Vs. 9.19 The text in these verses specifies the names of the towns given to the immediate descendants of the Kohathites who received the first assignment. They received Hebron, as a city of refuge together with its greenbelt from the tribe of Judah. (the outlying fields of Kiriath-arba remained the territory of Caleb). The tribe of Judah also contributed Libnah, Jattir, Eshtemoa, Holon, Debir, Ain, Juttah and Beth-shemesh for a total of 9 towns and their respective greenbelts attached. The tribe of Benjamin contributed the towns of Gibeon, Geba, Anathoth and Almon for a total of 4 towns with its greenbelts. Making a total of 13 towns with their pastures.

Vs. 20.26 The other families of Kohath refer to the descendants of Amram, Yitzhar, Hebron and Uzziel. They receieved 4 towns

JOSHUA CHAPTER 21

in the hill country of Ephraim. Shechem, became a city of refuge, Gezer, Kibzaim and Beth-horon together with their greenbelts. The tribe of Dan contributed 4 towns: Elteke, Gibbethon, Aijalon, and Gath-rimmon. The tribe of Manasseh contributed 2 towns with their greenbelts: Taanach, Gath-rimmon, for a total of 10 towns with their greenbelts.

Vs. 27.33   The Gershonites received 2 towns from Manasseh, in Golan in Bashan (Trans-Jordan) which became a city of refuge and Beeshterah, together with their greenbelts. The tribe of Issachar contributed 4 towns with their greenbelts: Kishion, Dobrath, Jarmuth and En-gannim. The tribe of Asher contributed 4 towns and their greenbelts: Mishal, Abdon, Helkath, and Rehob. The tribe of Naphtali contributed 3 towns and their greenbelts: Kedesh in Galilee, became a city of refuge, Hammoth-dor, and Kartan. The Gershonites received a total of 13 towns and their greenbelts.

Vs. 34.42   The families of the Merarites received 4 towns and their greenbelts for pasture from the tribe of Zebulun: Jokneam, Kartah, Dimnah, and Nahalal. The tribe of Gad contributed 4 towns and their greenbelts: Ramoth in Gilead, became a city of refuge, Mahanaim, Heshbon, and Jazer. (There are 4 towns missing in this text). They are given in (I Chronicles 6:63.64). The Merarites received 4 more towns in the territory of Reuben in Trans-Jordan: Bezer, Jahzah, Kedemoth, and Mepaath and their greenbelt for pasture. The Merarites received 12 towns and their greenbelts. Making a total of 48 towns and their greenbelts. Each of the Levitic towns-cities were limited to approximately 10 acres of land.

Vs. 43.45   Everything the Eternal God had promised the forefather's of Israel in the following texts (Gen. 12:2.3, 22:17.18, Ex. 23:29.30, Num. 10:29, Deut. 1:8, 7:22.24,11:31.32, 12:9.10) has now come to pass. In these verses Joshua confirms to the present generation the completeness of the Eternal's promise over the centuries. They are now the recipients, the witnesses that have taken possession of the land and are settling in it. Every former opposing force has been silenced and restrained from taking up arms against Israel. Every ingredient for success is now present in the Holyland. It is now up to the present generation to integrate the inhabitants desiring to live peacefully and to participate in a higher development of civilization which guarantees every human being his ability to develop to the maximum of their natural ability. To those pockets of resistance, who fail to observe the realities of progress, Israel must establish a united nation dedicated to govern justly under the constitution established in the Torah. Malbim confirms in the following excerpts from the texts, that the Eternal God implemented the conditions which fulfilled His promise to Israel's forefathers: *Vayiten* The Eternal God fulfilled His promise in presenting the Holyland to Israel. *Vayirashuhah* The Eternal transmitted to Israel their inheritance in accord with His oath. *Vayeshvu bah* Each tribe of Israel received its inheritance when the land was divided and are dwelling in the Holyland as their rightful and legal possession. *Vayanach Adonai*

JOSHUA CHAPTER 21

The Eternal implemented and created the conditions for a peaceful continuity in the Holyland. *Velo amad* The Eternal God created the psychological fear of defeat during the conquest of the Holyland, as Israel's enemies felt the effect of the Eternal's inspiration in the battles that were fought. *Lo nafal davar* Every promise for Israel's ascendance and triumph over their enemies made by the Eternal God over the centuries have all come to pass.

JOSHUA CHAPTER 22

Vs. 1.6 These six verses establish Israel's secure position in the Holyland after seven years of conquest and seven years spent in establishing responsibility in each of the tribes that inherited a portion of the land on the condition that they become responsible for governing by law and order in their own communities, with special emphasis upon the indigenous peoples living in their midst. *Az* expresses Joshua's elation, that this moment gives him the feeling of security, that he may discharge the *halutzim* soldiers drafted by the tribes of Reuben, Gad and the families of Machir, Jair and Novach of the tribe of Manasseh, who stood by the other tribes of Israel in the conquest of the Holyland. Joshua expressed his gratitude on behalf of all Israel, for having honored their oath given to Moses (Num. 32:). He acknowledged their loyalty to his leadership during these past 14 years. "You have dilligently observed the commandments of the Eternal God. It was your dedicated sacrifices and co-operation that won for your brethren tranquility and a measure of contentment. I hereby discharge you from your original oath (Num. 32:28.33, Deut. 3:20)." V.5, *rak* Joshua has but one reservation as he discharges Reuben, Gad, and Manasseh, he pleads with them that they rededicate themselves and their posterity to the *cause* which goes back to Shem. Rededicate yourselves to the principles of genetic progression. It was this principle that brought forth the personality of Abraham, who in turn received the recognition of the Eternal (Gen. 18:19). Abraham's dedication to a new world order was inherited by Isaac as a condition for the Eternal's promise (Gen. 26:3.5). 700 years of evolution from Shem to this moment in history. You have inherited the Holyland as a *morashah* an inheritance to infinity on but one condition (Deut. 11:1, 13.25) that you love the Eternal your God by perpetuating the principle of genetic progression as set down in the Torah (Lev. 12:1.5). (See addenda in The Eternal Torah). You may now return to your families in Trans-Jordan, secure in your conscience that you have earned the Eternal God's blessings in the name of all Israel (Deut. 10:12.22).

Vs. 7.8 Joshua repeats his gratitude to the families of Machir, Jair and Novach of Manasseh, who joined Reuben and Gad, though they were not under oath to join Israel. V.8, Joshua reminds Israel of their moral obligation to share their booty with those that remained at home in Trans-Jordan during these 14 years to protect their families and to carry on the construction which started before they embarked upon the conquest of the

JOSHUA CHAPTER 22

Holyland. In (Num. 26:) when the last census was taken, these two and one half tribes of Reuben, Gad, Manasseh, totaled 110,580 men between the ages of 20 and older. From this number they drafted 40,000 men for the conquest of Canaan (Joshua 4:12.13). Joshua's reminder to divide the spoils with those who kept the home fires burning in their absence is very appropriate.

Vs. 9.20   The tribes of Reuben, Gad and Manasseh took leave of Joshua in Shiloh. When they reached *gelilot hayarden-the kikar* the shores of the Jordan River, they built a huge altar to express their gratitude to God for their safe return. They had no intention of offering sacrifices upon it. When this came to the attention of the nine and one half tribes settled west of the Jordan River, they assembled at Shiloh to express their indignation. They came prepared to enforce this law as described in (Deut. 12:). Phinehas the son of Eleazar the high priest recommended they first reveal their indignation and demand an explanation. The Nesiim of these tribes joined Phinehas and challenged the tribes of Reuben, Gad and Manasseh at *gelilot hayarden*. "Shall we consider your building an altar a sign of rebellion against the law of the Torah? Have we learned nothing from the experience at Peor (Num. 25:1.9)? We should still feel the effect of our guilt for that action. Are we to interpret your action as a desire to separate yourselves from the concept of a Central Sanctuary for all Israel? You must realize the effect of your action can parallel the experience recorded in (Num. 16:22). Are you saying that Trans-Jordan is not a part of the Holyland? There must ever be one altar in Israel as an expression of a united Israel. Do not reject our plea. We remind you of the sin of Achan, recorded in (Joshua 7:). Though only one man transgressed God's law, the whole community felt the effect of the transgression. Consider the consequences, the potential disaster for all of Israel, should you segregate yourselves from the rest of the community."

Vs. 21.23   The leaders of the tribes of Reuben, Gad and Manasseh were overwhelmed by the accusation. Their spontaneous reply is an effort to prove their loyalty and dedication to the whole house of Israel. "*El*, the one God that is the Creator of the Universe. *Elohim*, the God, Whose Oneness created everything about us to harmonize with justice for all, *Adonai*, it is this Eternal god, who is the Director of history. (I Sam. 2:3, 16:7, Jer. 17:9.10). It is this God, who fathoms the purpose of our conduct. It is He, that will testify to our motive. Should He find us guilty, may He negate our deliverance from the evil forces that surround us." The basic concept of Reuben, Gad and Manasseh's oath as expressed in V.22, are rooted in (Gen. 1:1, Ex. 20:5). "How can we assure you that our motivation to build this altar was an inspiration to express our gratitude to God for all that has come to pass? (Deut. 29:28). May the Eternal God, who knows our innermost motivation, may He punish us if it was our intent to offer sacrifices upon this altar in contradistinction to the Central Sanctuary at Shiloh."

Vs. 24.29   "We built this altar in the same spirit that our forefathers

JOSHUA CHAPTER 22

built their altars, not for the purpose of offering sacrifices (Gen. 12:7, 13:4, 26:25, 35:1, Ex. 17:15). We built this altar as a testimonial to our posterity, that we shall ever remain loyal to our God wherever the Central Sanctuary may exist in future history. *Mideaga midavar* We built this altar to express our unity with all the tribes west of the Jordan. Lest sometime in the future it be said that *ugevul natan Adonai* that the Eternal established the Jordan River as a natural boundary line to exclude us from the Holyland. We built this altar to remind our posterity of our concern with the national unity of all Israel, that we demand they honor the Central Sanctuary by their sacrifices. This altar is an everlasting reminder to history that Trans-Jordan is an integral part of the Holyland. V.29, we are hopeful that you recognize our sincerest convictions, that "rebellion" will not harmonize with our dedication to our Eternal God and His Central Sanctuary wherever it may be established."

Vs. 30.34   Phinehas the son of Eleazar addressed the leaders of Reuben, Gad and Manasseh. Your reply reflects the teachings of our master Moses (Deut. 33:10). Your exemplary conduct confirms your sincerity to live by the Eternal's law and to inspire all of us to remain a united people under the unity of God. We are grateful for your dedication. It has stayed our hands from taking action for which the Eternal God would have held us responsible. The priest Phinehas, and the Elders of Israel returned to Shiloh and gave their report to the high priest Eleazar and the representatives of all the tribes living west of the Jordan River. They were gratified by the reply of Reuben, Gad and Manasseh. They recognized it as an omen of God's blessings which can be present only when our inner thoughts are in harmony with our actions. V.22.

JOSHUA CHAPTER 23

Vs. 1.3   Joshua mounted the conquest of Canaan in his 82nd year. He was still active when the Tabernacle was established at Shiloh. This was in his 96th year. The incident reported here was sometime between his 96th and the 110th year when he passed away. Joshua assembled all of Israel's representatives, their Elders, the heads of the tribes, their judges and all the officers of the army. "You are living witnesses to the miraculous intervention of the Eternal our God. It was His inspiration to all of us, that harmonized our actions with His natural law which created the miracles that enabled us to vanquish all of Israel's enemies and to take possession of the Holyland. We in this generation have been privileged to feel the effect of the Eternal's intervention in the affairs of mankind in order to set history on the course outlined at the beginning of time (Psalms 105:)."

Vs. 4.6   Joshua referred back to chapters 13 through 21 in which he divided the Holyland among the tribes of Israel. He now reminds them that he is well aware of the many areas which

JOSHUA CHAPTER 23

are still in control of their enemies, although they are part of your inheritance. "I have succeeded to destroy the military forces in the areas west of the Jordan River. I have displaced their governing bodies. Yet, there are many pockets of resistance because you have failed to take the initiative to begin governing your individual territory and to organize a central authority to whom you are responsible for your progress. During my period of leadership I strove to inspire you with the courage vital to fulfill the instructions given to you by Moses our master in (Deut. 11:23.25). *Hu yehdafem* the Eternal has created the momentum in history for you to activate the conditions that will challenge the conscience of the opposing forces to make a choice, to live among you in peace in accord with the Eternal's blueprint for civilization (Ex. 23:29.33, Deut. 6:16.19, 20:10.18) or suffer the consequences for resisting a new plateau for civilization. For this task individual and collective resolution are vital ingredients. This is the moment for action. Should your enemies recognize your waxing and waning from your goal, you shall never succeed in taking full possession of your inheritance."

Vs. 7.8 "You are not to assimilate with the natives by accepting their lifestyle. You are not to take an oath in the name of their deities. Do not utter the names of their deities in your daily speech (Ex. 23:13). Nor may those who remain in your communities take an oath in the name of their deities (Deut. 6:13.15). In reciprocity for their accepting your standards of morality and ethics, they are to be extended the protection of the Eternal's law (Deut. 10.19). You are obligated under the law to encourage human relations in your daily activities for the advancement of a peaceful community. Do not misinterpret equanimity with any form of homage which may lead innocently to genuflection." In (Joshua 22:5.6) we are given a first-hand expression of Joshua's satisfaction with this generation whom he has known from childhood. He recognized their consistent effort to live by Torah disciplines. "Hold fast to the disciplines of the Lord your God" is a most encouraging historic note for us to consider when we evaluate this period in Jewish history (Deut. 13:5, Joshua 24:31, Jud. 2:7). "Hold fast to the Eternal your God even as you have done to this day."

Vs. 9.11 "In recognition for your dedication to the Eternal your God, He inspired you to overpower forces of mighty clans and kings. The fear created at the Exodus (14:14) has demoralized the ranks of your foes (Deut. 4:38, 9:1.4, 11:23.25, Joshua 21:41.43). V.10, your loyalty to the teachings of our great law giver Moses, (Deut. 32:30) granted each and everyone of you the courage to pursue a thousand. Your dedication to the disciplines and the mitzvoth of the Torah, will earn for you the Eternal's protective custody and the deference of all mankind as you march on through history. Your awe of the Eternal will create the consternation and panic of your enemies as they begin to perceive *ki shem Hashem nikrah alecha* (Deut. 28:10) for the Eternal God recognizes you as his own."

JOSHUA CHAPTER 23

Vs. 12.13 "Should you become remiss in your disciplines and take the line of least resistance after I am gone and assimilate with those that remain in your midst, to permit yourselves to intermarry with them and they intermarry with you (Deut. 7:3, Ex. 34:16). Be therefore forewarned, should you permit this to occur, you shall not succeed in dispossessing those that remain to pollute your environment with their idolatrous debauchery and their murderous practices. You shall become ensnared by economic advantages which shall entrap you *lepach ulemokesh* to afflict your conscience *leshotet*. Like thorns *litzeninim beenechem* they shall scourge your body *betzidechem* to sap your national vigor, so painstakingly developed over centuries of genetic progression. You shall then disappear from the Holyland which the Eternal your God gave you as a *morashah* an inheritance conditioned upon your following the disciplines outlined in the Torah." (See The Eternal Torah on (Num. 33:55.56, Deut. 11:17).

Vs. 14.16 "Behold the time has come for me to depart this life, in accord with the Eternal's natural law for all humanity. You are living witnesses that you have received your reward for your dedication to the disciplines of the Eternal your God." Joshua paraphrases the text given by Moses in (Deut. 28:63.68). "Should you transgress the Covenant made by the Eternal with Abraham, which is binding upon every generation to infinity, you shall incur the Eternal's wrath. As the Judge of your conduct, He will remove His *hashgachah* the biological and psychological anti-bodies, which normally protect every living creature. *Ad hashmido* (Deut. 4:26) your conduct shall implement and set into motion a series of events visualized by Moses our teacher in (Lev. 26:14.46, Deut. 28:15.69) miseries which humanity brings upon itself by idolatrous and depraved lifestyles. I too am concerned with human indolence, lethargy and depravity. Should you ignore the struggle from Shem to this very day. Should you forsake your God (Gen. 4.26) when man began to climb ever so slowly until he reached the plateau of Abraham." Many generations of genetic progression or a span of 2377 years elapsed from Adam to the birth of Moses, who struggled with his conscience to grasp the full meaning of the Eternal God, documented in (Ex. 6:2.3, 3:13.15).

"Should you permit yourselves to become assimilated, in this environment, the Eternal your God will erase your presence from this good land, which remains your *morashah* inheritance from the beginning of time to infinity. You shall be driven into exile to purge your genes from the excesses of your environment. To return one day to begin again."

JOSHUA CHAPTER 24

V. 1 Joshua is motivated by his conscience to deliver a major address to the whole community of Israel. He has been in retirement for some time in Timnath-serach, in the mountains of Ephraim. He had a premonition that this shall be his farewell address to Israel.

JOSHUA CHAPTER 24

He issued an order to the representative personalities of each tribe, their Elders-Nesiim, their judges and all officials involved in governing their respective communities. *Vayityatzvu* indicates they honored Joshua's order and made their appearance at Shechem. It was here (Gen. 12:6.7, 33:18.20) that Israel's history had its beginning. It was here that Jacob purchased his first piece of the Holyland.

Vs. 2.4   V.2, indicates that all the people were invited on a voluntary basis. Joshua therefore addressed *kal haam* all the people which included every future generation (Deut. 29:9.14, 32:7). Joshua's review of history follows the format of Moses. In accord with the direction of the Eternal God of history and recorded in the Torah are the records of the prediluvian generations (Gen. 6:1.8). "Observe closely and meditate over their lives. Research and study the history of your forefathers recorded in the genealogical table given in (Gen. 11:10.32). Ask your parents to enlighten you about your roots, the original modest beginnings of your forefathers. Look into the Torah and study the historic development of all humanity. Observe the orderly division of their territories, the establishment of their boundaries in (Gen. 10:1.32,13:15.16, 15:18.21). Perceive for yourselves from the record in the book of Genesis, that even at this early moment in human history, the odds were overwhelmingly stacked against the descendants of Shem. Comprehend the direction of the Eternal in the evolution of history, as He designated Israel's future territory. Observe the inhumanities of man to man and the destructiveness of man to the ecology as recorded in (Gen. 4:8.10, 10:8.10, 11:3.4)." From (Gen. 11:26.32) we learn that Ur and the area of the Euphrates River was the Semitic homeland of our forefathers from the beginning of human history. From (Gen. 10:11.12) we learn how another ancester of Terach (Gen. 10:22) Ashur expanded their Semitic territory and built the cities of Nineveh, Resen, and Calah on the Tigris River. Joshua reminded his generation that Terach was the father of Abraham and the father of Nahor, that they were idolators. From (Gen. 11:31.32) we learn that Terach's home was in Haran, this whole area of the Fertile Crescent was the ancient home of the Semitic families going back to the beginning of human history. V.3, when Abraham left Ur on the Euphrates River in accord with the Eternal's inspiration, the Eternal God directed him to establish himself in all of Canaan because this too had been Semitic territory from the beginning of human history (Gen. 12:1.9). Abraham expanded his presence in Beer Sheba, Hebron and Gerar. *Varbeh et zaro* (Gen. 17:4, 25:1.18, 21:5) Ishmael became the father of the Arab peoples who established their territory south of the Fertile Crescent in the Arabian Desert. V.4, Isaac became the father of Esau and Jacob, Esau's genealogy is in (Gen. 36:). Esau took possession of Seir-Edom and Jacob followed his historic destiny (Gen. 15:13.14) as he and his families and the multitudes of proselytes went down to Egypt. It was here in Egypt in the crucible of time and history that Israel became inured as they became ensnared by the fleshpots of Egypt."

JOSHUA CHAPTER 24

Vs. 5.7 Joshua is a living witness to the experiences he is reviewing with Israel, the epic experience recorded in (Ex. 3: with particular emphasis on v.7). "It was the Eternal God that reached out in search of a *malach* a human being with the competence and dedication to create the potential great people of Israel out of a horde of inured human beings. The Eternal found Moses brooding over the fate of his people as a fugitive of Egyptian political intrigue. The Eternal is sensitive to Moses' humility as described in (Ex. 4:10.16). This became the beginning of Moses' and Aaron's mission for the redemption of Israel from the *kur habarzel* crucible which destroyed the soul of multitudes of human beings that Egypt conscripted in its system of servitude and bondage. Study your Torah in (Ex. 5: 6: 7: 8: 9: 10: 11: 13:17.22,14:15:) for the sequence of plagues which brought Egypt to recognize the greatness of the Eternal God as He invoked and implemented the forces of His Natural Law to destroy Egyptian arrogance at the Reed Sea." The terror of this experience destroyed the tyranny of the Egyptian forces as the terrifying *tsunamis* which originated in the Aegean Sea destroyed the Island of Thiera. This created the *maafel* the pillar of fire and cloud which kept the Egyptian might from the forces of Israel. It was this tidal wave that devoured the Egyptian forces as Israel stood on the eastern shores of the Reed Sea "Most of you within the sound of my voice were born in the desert in which Israel was molded into a people during these past 40 years." (See addendum to Book of Joshua pp. 70.77).

Vs. 8.10 "You are living witnesses to the wars with Sihon and Og in Trans-Jordan, who refused to grant us peaceful passage through their territory (Num. 21:1.3, 21.35, Deut. 2:31.37, 3:1.8). Remember, our victory was the result of the phenomena created by the Eternal your God. We defeated Sihon and Og and took possession of their land in Trans-Jordan. V.9, when Balak the king of Moab observed our victory over Sihon and Og, he mobilized for war against Israel (Num. 22:2.13). He sent for Balaam the son of Beor, to destroy the inner security of Israel. V.10, look back into the historic record, how the Eternal your God inspired Balaam to recognize the historic truth that he may not curse Israel (Gen. 12:2.3,22:17.18, Deut. 23:6, Num. 24:9). Balaam recognized that Israel's genetic progress conformed with the Eternal's Master Plan for civilization."

Vs. 11.13 "We then crossed the Jordan River westward to Jericho. We offered them peace in accord with Torah disciplines (Deut. 20:10.11). Yet, they girded for war (Joshua 6:1). Had Jericho accepted Israel's terms to live in peace by accepting the Seven Laws of Noah as a beginning for a new development, none of the other tyrants, the usurpers of Semitic Canaan would have gone to war with Israel. It was at this critical juncture that the Eternal your God delivered Jericho into your hands as their barbaric egos overwhelmed their good judgment. V.12, Long before your entry into Canaan the Eternal your God sent the *hornets* of history to invade Canaan." (Hornets ... symbolize the Egyptian invaders who weakened the Hittites and the Amorites, Ex. 23:28, Deut. 7:20). "*Lo becharbecha, velo bekashtecha* it was these

JOSHUA CHAPTER 24

hornets that made it unnecessary for you to repeat the battle of Shechem (Gen. 48:22) which was fought by your ancester Jacob. When Israel penetrated the city of Shechem, their fortresses were deserted (Is. 17:9, Deut. 8:17.18)." Vs. 2.13, were a review given by Joshua in the name of Israel's Eternal God. Joshua paraphrased (Deut. 6:10.11). "I, the Eternal your God have given you land for which you did not labor to clear its forests. You took possession of cities, towns and villages which you did not build. You enjoy vineyards and olive groves that you did not plant or cultivate."

Vs. 14.15   Vs. 14 through 28, are Joshua's last wishes. As a father, whose life spans the epic experiences of Israel, from the Exodus to the conquest of the Holyland. "Now that I have reviewed with you the history of man and the Manifest Destiny of Israel, as it advances upon the ladder of evolution to become *or bagoyim* (Is. 42:6) an inspiration to all of mankind, I implore you to revere the Eternal your God. Serve Him with undivided loyalty in sincerity and with perfect devotion to truth and justice (Ps. 34:12.23, Gen. 17:2, Deut. 18:13.18, Prov. 2:21, I Sam. 12:24.25). Remove from your hearts the idolatrous concept of the Eternal God as worshipped in the religious rites of your progenitors in the Fertile Crescent, from Ur in the Chaldees to Mari on the Mediterranean Sea. Reject the idolatrous practices and concepts you experienced in Egypt. I hereby demand that you destroy the idolatrous figurines and other fetishisms, you have retained as booty from the wars we fought. Ever remember the Decalogue is the foundation for the evolution of man, a stepping stone to the perfection of human character. (Ex. 20:1.5) the Decalogue reaches into the secrets which we inscribe in our hearts. It strives to destroy the satans, the images of despair, which we create in our self-created exile from the light of God. V.15, you as human beings have the freedom to choose, the measure of your dedication, your awe and your love for the Eternal your God, the Creator of the laws of the Universe. All of humanity's choices are rooted to the measure of our dedication to observe these laws. Therefore, make your choice today. Shall you serve the primitive concepts of your forefathers, the idolatrous, barbaric procedures of the Amorites, in whose environment you are now living? Should this be your choice, you must calculate the consequences based upon human experience as recorded in human history. I, hereby serve notice to all of you within the hearing of my voice and plead that you record it for future history, that my household and I, shall ever remain loyal and dedicated to the Eternal God of the Torah."

Vs. 16.18   All those present at this convocation gave their reply to Joshua, as they paraphrased their dedication with the sensitivity expressed in (Joshua 22:22.29). "Far be it from us to forsake the Eternal our God, to serve other deities. It was He that delivered us from Egypt's house of bondage. It was the Eternal, the God of history, Who activated the powerful forces of nature to speed us on to victory. It is He, that challenges every native born Israelite or proselyte to ever remain witnesses to the

JOSHUA CHAPTER 24

greatness of the Eternal God of all humanity, Who strives to inspire every human being to rise upon the ladder of evolution, to assist in the creation of a better world order. V.17, as witnesses we must ever keep the record alive in the hearts of every human being interested in the advancement of truth. The miracle of crossing the Reed Sea and the protective canopy of the Eternal, as He sheltered us from the hazards of the desert. In gratitude we remember (Ex. 19:4, Deut. 1:31) His protective custody, as He created consternation and panic in the ranks of Israel's adversaries in whose midst we traveled. V.18, in everlasting gratitude we acknowledge the Eternal's inspiration which animated us and gave us the capability to conquer the Amorite usurpers of the Holyland. We join with you and your posterity as a united community, in recognition for all that the Eternal did for the whole house of Israel. He is our God, to Whom we shall remain loyal to infinity (Ex. 19:8)."

Vs. 19.20 Joshua is desirous to define and to punctuate Israel's dedication at this moment in their history when they are the actual recipients of the Eternal's promise which originated in the very beginning of human history. *Lo tuchlu laavod Adonai* "Remember! You cannot worship the Eternal your God with reservations in your heart. You may not wax or wane in your dedication to His statutes and judgments. He shall hold you responsible in the future, if you fail to honor your oath, which is binding upon your posterity (Deut. 29:14, Ezekiel 20:33.37). *Ki Elohim kedoshim Hu* for He is consistent in His demand, that humanity become involved in the management of the Universe. *El kano Hu* He is the consistent *Force* in the genetic process that has granted man the freedom to choose his lifestyle." A civilized human being is one who fully realizes that every living moment is an encounter with God. *El kano* is the *Force* that demands mankind's dedication to reach out for its *Zelem Elohim* maximum intelligent development. Idolatry, sexual excesses and debauchery are parental deviates from the Eternal's direction and Masterplan for humanity. *Elkano* is the *Force* that charges mankind to become the masters of their destiny. "Therefore, should you desecrate your contractual dedication to the Covenant, *lo yisah*, He will not tolerate your treasonous transgression, nor will He give you the benefit of the doubt as He weighs in the balance *chatotechem* your innocent, inadvertent transgressions (Gen. 6:3) and your iniquitous sins. V.20, should you disregard your oath and forsake your Eternal God in the future, to serve alien values, He will reverse your blessings, to punish you commensurate with your iniquity." (Deut. 32:47) Like Moses, the spokesman for God's concept of justice, Joshua is now the father figure of all Israel, who came up from the ranks of Israel. He pleads *lo davar rek hu mikem* "There are no empty promises of utopia in the Torah. Only your dedication will secure your continuity in the Promised Land."

Vs. 21.22 Joshua accepted the people of Israel's reply, that they will serve only the Eternal God, (Deut. 26:17.19). "Your testimony this day ties the past to the future as you strive to become the

JOSHUA CHAPTER 24

Eternal's *am segulah* the Eternal's model for civilization (Deut. 28:10, 7:6, Ex. 19:5)." For the record, Joshua testified that Israel's reply was their spontaneous and free choice. This testimony made in the 12th century became binding upon every generation to infinity.

Vs. 23.28   Joshua reminded all those present that their first step is to redirect their goals to complete devotion to the Eternal, by removing all tangible idolatrous objects from among their possessions. Only then can your thoughts begin to become pure and dedicated to the Eternal, the God of Israel. Once again the assembly assured Joshua, they will heed his plea and remove these abstractions, in order to worship the Eternal God totally dedicated to His Masterplan for humanity. V.25, on that very day Joshua inscribed this covenant in the Book of Joshua and annexed it to the Book of Deuteronomy, together they became *Sefer Torath Elohim* the book of Divine Instruction. Just as the Covenant made at Sinai was the initiation of the *Sefer Torath Elohim* made with the generation of the Exodus, this covenant made at Shechem was the renewal of the original Covenant with the generation who became the recipients of the Divine promise, the Holyland. This precedent by Joshua was followed on many occasions in Israel's history (II Kings 11:17, 23:3). V.26, Joshua then followed a precedent initiated by Moses in (Ex. 24:4). Joshua placed this memorial with the renewal of the Covenant at Shechem under the historic oak tree noted in (Gen. 35:4, 12:6, Deut. 11:30, Jud. 9:6). V.27, Joshua unveiled a large stone as a symbol and as a second witness that it was present and heard the testimony of Israel's acceptance of God's message in (Joshua 24:2.13). "Should you fail to keep the covenant, this permanent reminder engraved in the granite of timelessness shall prod your conscience to renew your dedication to the meaningfulness of the Eternal's Masterplan for civilization." Having completed his last message, Joshua administered the Eternal's oath with Israel, Joshua then dismissed the assembly and permitted them to return to their newly inherited territories in the Holyland.

Vs. 29.31   The rest of this chapter was recorded after the demise of Joshua, the son of Nun, the servant of the Eternal God, who died at the age of 110, the same age that his progenitor Joseph, the father of the tribes of Ephraim and Manasseh. He was laid to rest in the area of his inheritance, in the city he built Timnath-serach, which is in the mountains of Ephraim, north of Mount Goash. Joshua's life and dedication are equated with Moses. His influence upon his generation was effective, for Israel lived by the law of the Torah throughout Joshua's lifetime and the lifetime of the Elders that survived him, who were appointed in (Num. 11:16.17). It was these Elders that handed down the traditions recorded in the name of the Eternal and became part of Israel's history.

JOSHUA CHAPTER 24

Vs. 32.33 — Consistent with the continuity and dedication of Israel to their oaths, the promise made by Israel to Joseph in Egypt and recorded in (Gen. 50:24.25 was consistently carried forth by Moses as recorded in Ex. 13:19). Joseph's remains traveled with Israel throughout the 40 years of wandering. He was put to rest by Joshua in the field purchased from Shechem the son of Chamor and recorded in (Gen. 33:19). This territory was now the inheritance of Ephraim. Recorded here is the demise of the High Priest Eleazar, the son of Aaron. He was laid to rest in Gibeat Phinehas, in the allotted territory of his son Phinehas in the hills of Ephraim.

ADDENDUM

In I Kings 3:1, the text cryptically informs history that king Solomon negotiated to marry the daughter of Pseusennes-Pasebkhanu II, the last king on the king list of the 21st Dynasty. Egyptian history is not quite sure how long he reigned, 14 years, 35 years, 41 years or 46 years. From this example we may conclude that Egyptian history is not concerned with time or chronological order. Three hundred and forty one years have elapsed from the Exodus in 1304 BCE. and 963 BCE. The Egyptian king is desirous of renewing his ties with Israel. Examining the historic records included in the Books of Joshua, Judges and I and II Samuel, there is no record of contact between Egypt and Israel either in war or peace. What created these ghost centuries? There is also no existing record of the 210 years when the Patriach Jacob came to Egypt at the invitation of the Hyksos Dynasty that was in control of Egypt at this point in time. Ex.1:7, is a cryptic report of the 71 years which lapsed between the arrival of Jacob and his family in Egypt and the passing of Joseph. Israel multiplied in numbers and became a political force. They were involved in commerce domestically and in international trade. There is no evidence that Israel was in Egypt and that it made any contribution during these 210 years. Not only is there no record of Israel's presence in Egypt but no indication what happened to them.

For centuries historians, Egyptologists, Archaeologists and sundry researchers have based their information upon shards battered by the vicissitudes of time and displaced from their original resting places to make them worthless as authentic records of the past. There is no record of Israel's presence in Egypt because Egyptian monarchs destroyed the evidence. They also erased the records of the kings whom they succeeded in order to blot out their memories. These are the authentic sources upon which Biblical critics nurtured generations to create the concept that the Exodus of Israel from Egypt was a myth.

Like many other scholars I have spent years in reading the annals of Egyptian history in order to harmonize the Biblical record with the secular historic record. I shall present briefly a condensation of all my researches, that you the reader may grasp the confusion from which it is utterly impossible to establish an orderly chronological sequence for Egyptian history. From the record it is assumed that the Old Kingdom consisted from the first to the sixth Dynasty. For five centuries the Old Kingdom rulers permitted the Syrian Khurri tribesmen, the Khatti tribesmen, Hittite tribesmen and some Semitic elements to migrate and become established in the Nile Delta Valley. In accord with history their power grew as the palatial intrigues created confusion and in some moment of national catastrophe, not recorded, they became known as the Shepherd Kings. In accord with some reconstructed records they ruled Egypt from 1725-1575 BCE. Hittite records claim the Hyksos came to power in 1685 BCE.

In accord with modern historians who created the Middle Kingdom, based upon an erroneous interpretation of the Manetho Dynasties, the 18th Dynasty came into being as the Pharaoh Ahmose expelled the Hyksos after he overthrew their government which ruled from their capital city of Avaris. He spent some years in

ADDENDUM

the process of pursuing them into the southern part of Palestine. When Amenhopis I, Thutmosis I, II, Hatshepsut-Thutmosis III, succeeded each other to the throne, they continued the persecution of the Hyksos in order to exterminate them. These were the kings that initiated the oppression as they feared Israel's powerful influence under the Hyksos kings. These were the kings that fought the wars in the Holyland for the purpose of looting the prosperous communities there, and to bring back captives to augment the already enslaved Israelites. Lacking the capital for their ambitious construction projects, this became the means to accomplish their ends to build a powerful Empire.

Since the goal of this paper is to confirm the authenticity of the Exodus, I shall not encumber it with the numerous kings that reigned between Thutmosis the III and Rameses II, the Pharaoh of the Exodus, nor will I multiply the confusion by quoting the various names by which each king was recorded nor will I create complications by showing the variations by which the various Dynasties are recorded by different historians. The Merneptah Stele written by Merneptah who succeeded Rameses II, informs history that the conquest of the Holyland (by Joshua) was still in progress in 1220 BCE. This bit of information exposes the tragic decline of the Egyptian Empire. For it confirms Egypt's inability to defend its Empire against its horde of slaves completing its conquest in the Holyland. While we do not have the details for the natural disaster that enabled the Hyksos to take over the reigns of the Egyptian government for 150 years, we do have the proof for the disaster which blacked out Egyptian glory for almost four centuries. The natural disaster that hit Egypt in 1304 BCE, made possible the Exodus of two million slaves because there was no home in Egypt in 1304 BCE. where death did not strike Ex.12:29.38.

Before I present the evidence, I would like to present a chronological calendar of Israel's history going back to the Biblical Adam. There are two sources for this historic record. One establishes the birth of Moses in 2377 J.C. or 1383 BCE., the other is given in the Babylonian Tractate Aboda Zara page 9a. This record covers 2448 years; there is a variation of nine years between them. The chronology of Jewish history is as clear as daylight. It is the history of a people chosen to dedicate its place in the sun and to the Brotherhood of man and the unity of God.

Gen. 15:13.16, establishes the time table for the Exodus. 400 years from the birth of Isaac.

Jewish Calendar	BCE.	
2048	1712	Birth of Isaac.
2216	1544	Joseph came to Egypt at age 17
2231	1530	The famine in Egypt took place 217 years before the Exodus.
2238	1523	Jacob came to Egypt with his family at age 130.

ADDENDUM

2255	1506	Jacob died 17 years later at age 147.
2309	1452	Joseph died at age 110.
2368 or 2377	1374 or 1383	Moses was born
2457 or 2448	1304 or 1313	Moses was 80 years old at the time of the Exodus Ex.7:7.

All the technical data I will quote in the following for the natural disaster which made possible the Exodus are quoted from a paper compiled by Leon Pomerance and sponsored by the New York Society Archaeological Institute of America, in 1970. In it are his conclusions after devoting 10 years in archaeological research on the Island of Crete and Thiera-Santorini. His thesis is, that the collapse of Santorini could not have happened in the 15th century because there is no historical proof of disaster in that century for the destruction of the primitive economies in the Aegean and eastern Mediterannean shores. On page 19 of Pomerance's report he strongly supports the theory that all the evidence described in Ex. 13:17.22,14:1.31,15:1.19, leads him to the conclusion that the Exodus of Israel from Egypt described in these texts are the testimony of eye witnesses to the effect of the explosion and collapse of the Island of Thiera upon the powerful Empire of Egypt. Rameses II was the tyrant with whom Moses and Aaron negotiated for about a year. The details are reported in Exodus 5:, 6:, 7:, 8:, 9:, 10:, 11:. The data I have presented on the dating of the Exodus confirms Mr. Pomerance's thesis. It literally pinpoints the timing of the disaster for the people of the Aegean and Mediterannean shoreline and the beginning of new hope for civilization. The subsequent record of those who did not die by drowning, asphyxiation, plague or cremation and escaped on foot to devastate every community on the Mediterranean littoral are recorded in the Book of Judges and the Book of I Samuel. These were the 'shosim' from the Aegean that penetrated into Egypt. They destroyed the Mittani. They fought the Hittites. These were the refugees that augmented the Sea Peoples living in Gerar for centuries which eventually created the Philistines, from whom was derived the name Palestine.

History is indeed indebted to the only surviving record written by an Egyptian eye witness who survived this terrible holocaust. This record was found in the neighborhood of the pyramids in Saqqara. At last report this eye witness testimony called the Ipuwer Papyrus is at the Museum in Leiden, Netherlands (catalogue Leiden 344). The writer describes the great catastrophe. In it he laments for the horror and ruin which struck Egypt. The translation of the Ipuwer Papyrus is by A.H. Gardiner:

2:8   Forsooth, the land turns round as does the potters wheel.

2:11 The towns are destroyed. Upper Egypt has become a dry waste.

ADDENDUM

3:13	All is in ruin.
7:4	The residence (of the king) is overturned in a minute.
4:2	Years of noise. There is no end to noise. Subterranean rumbling upheaval.
6:1	Oh, that the earth would cease from noise and tumult and be no more.
2:5.6	Plague is throughout the land. Blood is everywhere.
2:10	The River is blood. Men shrink from tasting. Human beings thirst after water.
3:10.13	That is our water! That is our happiness! What shall we do in respect thereof? All is ruin.
4:14	Trees are destroyed.
6:1	No fruit or herbs are found.
2:10	Forsooth, gates, columns and walls are consumed by fire (clouds of fire).
10:3.6	Lower Egypt weeps. The entire palace is without revenue. To it belongs (the natural resources) wheat and barley, geese and fish.
6:3	Forsooth, grain has perished on every side.
5:12	Forsooth, that has perished which yesterday was seen. The land is left over to weariness like the cutting of flax (Locusts).
6:1	No fruit nor herbs are found ... hunger.
5:5	All animals, their hearts weep. Cattle moan.
9:2.3	Behold cattle are left to stray, and there is none to gather them together. Each man fetches for himself those that are branded with his name.
9:11	The land is not light (darkness). A thick cloud. The light of the sun was dimmed by dark clouds and created "the shadow of death."
4:3, 5:6	Forsooth, the children of princes are dashed against the wall.
6:12	Forsooth, the children of princes are cast in the streets.
6:3	The prison is ruined (storehouse), is common property.
2:13	He who places his brother in the ground is everywhere.
4:4, 6:14	Forsooth, those who were in the place of embalmment are laid on the high ground.

From the above we can conclude a sequence of earthquakes, the effect of the burning island is spreading clouds of darkness mixed with draughts of acid and ash.

ADDENDUM

4:2   Forsooth, great and small say, 'I wish I might die.'

5:14 Would that there might be an end of men, no conception, no birth! Oh, that the earth would cease from noise, and tumult be no more!

7:1   Behold, the fire has mounted up on high. Its burning goes forth against the enemies of the land.

6:7   Forsooth, public offices are opened and their census lists are taken away.

6:9   Forsooth, the laws of judgment-hall are cast forth. Men walk upon them in public places.

7:1.2 Weep ... the earth is ... on every side ... weep.

12:11 The realm is depopulated. The residence of Pharaoh is a heap of ruins.

3:1   Forsooth, the desert is throughout the land. The nomes are laid waste. A foreign tribe had come to Egypt.

15:1 What has happened? They seek to know the condition of the land.

14:11 They have come to an end for themselves. There is none found to stand and protect themselves (from the catastrophe).

12:6 To-day fear ... more than a million people. Not seen ... enemies enter into the temples ... weep.

The tragedy described in the Ipuwer Papyrus, is the result of the collapse of the Island of Thiera-Santorini in the Aegean Sea. This was the end of the 13th century and not the 15th. The Minoan kingdom on the Island of Crete was destroyed simultaneously with the so called Middle Kingdom in Egypt. Every coastline in the Mediterranean littoral bore the brunt of this enormous explosion, which spread from Sardinia in the west to the Anatolion Mountains in the east. Pomerance describes the speed of the *tsunamis* in the Mediterannean Sea, that it could reach wind speeds of 200 miles per hour which in turn could create sea waves in excess of 200 feet high in a series of two or more waves. Pomerance reaches back to the seismic disaster of Kraketu, in the Sundra Strait, in 1883, to point up the fact that it only involved an explosive area of 23 square kilometers. By comparison Santorini involved 83 square kilometers and an explosive force which could reach ten times the force of Kraketu. Pomerance calls our attention to the geographic position of the Mediterannean which is a three dimensional landmass; containing a substantial portion of humanity in so limited a physical area. It was this cul-de-sac effect of the Aegean and the Mediterannean that accounted for the apocalyptic disaster of the time of the Exodus. The explosive force of this *tsunamis* in the Mediterannean could reach the equivalent of 400 to one thousand nuclear bombs. The rumblings could reach around the world and its destructive affect could reach thousands of miles away. To believe that

ADDENDUM

Mycenae, Crete, Egypt and Syreo-Palestine cities and smaller communities could escape from the enormity of this disaster is indeed simplistic.

It is estimated that prior to the Exodus of Israel, there were about eight million inhabitants in greater Egypt. Assuming two million left Egypt (Ex.12:37.38). This included native born Israelites, their wives and children. Included in this figure must be the multitudes that took advantage of the opportunity to leave and become emancipated. All these families did so with the encouragement and blessings of Moses and were integrated at Mount Sinai three months later prior to the presentation of the Decalogue. The picture of survival becomes very dim. For it could have included more than a million that died by drowning, fire and asphyxiation. It is literally impossible to calculate the losses by starvation, pestilence and multiple exposure to the vicissitudes of nature over a long period of time after the original disaster calmed down. The destruction of farmland by the tremendous forces of the *tsunamis* as it denuded and salinated the soil. The middle class whose homes were destroyed bore the brunt of the tidal wave. They must have been completely wiped out. Egyptian and Aegean records testify to the loss of skills vital for survival. It left a void for centuries, causing hundreds of communities to collapse, because of the destruction of thousands of herds of sheep, goats, and cattle. The destruction of crops and graneries transmits a vision to twentieth century man of a vast graveyard strewn with corpses as pictured in the World War II Holocaust. In one half hour thousands of miles were terrorized with a lasting terror by death, pestilence, poverty and starvation. Whole communities were denuded of humans, plants, trees and animals. Culture, art, literature were traded for survival.

It seems ironical that over a period of 3300 years the only surviving record written by an Egyptian eye witness is the Ipuwer Papyrus. But another example of Egyptian intransigence, its refusal to face the moral demand for truth. While the masses struggled with illiteracy and survival, the middle and upper classes who were literate and survived this disaster busied themselves to erase every indicator that there ever was a people called Israel, who lived in Egypt and contributed their natural talents for the welfare of the nation. This idiosyncrasy of destroying the past must be coupled with Egyptian dating, which has no chronological support. Some dates are ingenious, most are incredible and inconsistent with the known facts. The Middle Kingdom is a fabrication of modern historians. It is completely erroneous. Rameses II, could not possibly have fought the battle of Kadesh in 1288 BCE. Egypt was finished as a military force. There is no mention of Egypt in the Holyland until I Kings 3:1.

Throughout the period of the Judges, Asia Minor felt the affect of the *shosim* looters, who were the refugees, also called the Sea Peoples, who escaped the seismic area-wide disaster which originated in the island of Thiera-Santorini. They drove thousands of settlers from their homes all along the Aegean and Mediterannean coastline, they murdered and looted for survival as mindless wanderers seeking a place to rest their heads in order to create a new life for

ADDENDUM

themselves. They very nearly became the "Hyksos" in Egypt after the Exodus. They became the mercenaries in the Egyptian army and rose to the top over the centuries. To place the disaster of Santorini in the 15 or 14th century, is to ignore these so called normal centuries devoted to military exploits, conquering and enslaving humanity in order to build an Empire. This conclusion not only vexes but denies any claim to scholarship.

Pseusennes II's desire to secure his needs from Israel's granary in 963 BCE. is but the necessary proof that Egypt has not yet recovered from the disaster of the Exodus at the end of the thirteenth century.

The governments of Thutmosis I, through the reign of Rameses II, included the 15th and 14th centuries. These were the centuries of military invasions of Palestine and Libya. Every campaign brought back thousands of humans to augment Egypt's slave oriented society in order to satiate the megalomaniac building appetites of the Pharaohs. There is no shred of evidence of any natural disaster in these centuries.

When the tsunamis struck at the close of the 13th century, Rameses II became an eye witness as millions of slaves ignored their masters and headed for the main military highway, the direct route to the Holyland. They welcomed the assist of the Pillar of Fire by night, for it confirmed to Israel's leaders that the great geological drama of Santorini had started and would soon develop its tremendous force. At this point Israel's leaders ordered a change in their course (Ex.13:17.18, 21.22) as they headed eastward in an attempt to cross the Reed Sea.

No modern observer of the *tsunamis* on the coast of Japan or South America has succeeded to put into words a more vivid picture of natural forces actively engaged in emancipating human beings from the terrors of slavery than Moses. For a man without maritime expertise, he described the force of the *tsunamis* as it destroyed the Egyptian forces in the Reed Sea (Exodus 15:1.19):

V.1   I will sing unto the Lord, for He has triumphed gloriously; The horse and driver He has hurled into the sea.

V.4   Pharaoh's chariots and his army, He has cast into the sea; The choicest of his officers are drowned in the Reed Sea.

V.5   The mountain of waters created the depths that covered them; They sank as a stone.

V.8   The blast of Your nostrils caused the waters to pile up, The floods stood straight as a wall as Your will froze in the heart of the sea.

V.10   You made the wind blow, the sea covered them; Like lead they sank in Your majestic waters.

V.11   Who is like You, O Lord, among the celestials; Who can compare with

ADDENDUM

your Majesty in perfection, Awesome in splendor, working wonders, to pursue Your goals!

V.12 Your right hand gave the command; The earth swallowed them.

V.13 With benevolent mercy, You have redeemed this people from the crucible of Egypt; Thy supreme power shall guide them and inspire them to become worthy to develop the Holyland.

V.14 Fear has overtaken the inhabitants of Philistia.

V.15 Terror has overtaken the chiefs of Edom. Fear and trembling has overtaken the leaders of Moab. Depression and despair has overtaken the inhabitants of Canaan.

V.16 Terror and dread has descended upon them, as they observe the mighty arm of the Eternal calling them to justice. Their arrogance and swagger has been silenced with the stillness of stone. For they fear the day when the Eternal will unfold the history of this people whom You have acquired as Your birthright.

V.18.19 Only the Eternal, Who's reign is to infinity, can avenge Israel's alienation in Egypt by tossing Pharaoh's chariots and horsemen into the sea, as Israel marched forth on dry ground in the midst of the Reed Sea.

THE ETERNAL TORAH

JUDGES
SHOFETIM

THE TABLE OF CONTENTS FOR THE BOOK OF JUDGES, has been written with the intent that it can be used as a synopsis to summarize the whole Book of Judges.

INTRODUCTION   Pages 89.90

CHAPTER 1   After the death of Joshua, the Elders recognized the erosion of
Pages 91.95 Israel's goals in the Holyland. The tribes of Benjamin, Manasseh, Ephraim, Zebulun, Asher, Naphtali and Dan, lived as aliens in the Holyland. Instead of introducing a new world order, they have assimilated with the natives. Observing Israel's failure in governing the Holyland and removing the pockets of resistance it became the signal for organized resistance.

The Elders succeeded in inspiring the tribes of Judah, Simeon and Manasseh to turn the situation around. Under the leadership of Othniel, Judah and Simeon succeed in Jerusalem, Hebron, Debir, Gaza, Ashkelon and Ekron. Manasseh fails to win the loyalty of the natives in their territory; instead it impoverishes them as peons, contrary to Torah law.

CHAPTER 2   Phinehas the kohen calls an assembly of all Israel, to remind
Pages 95.100 them that the Eternal God, shall never release them from their genetic commitment to His Covenant. The text documents Israel's failures to teach their children by creating an environment for their moral and ethical development. He reminded Israel, that the cause of their miseries are the result of failing to set an example for the newly joined proselytes.

Vs.11.13: Phinehas highlights the historic past, with its unusual opportunities to succeed. He details the conditions of anarchy created by ignoring and rejecting the Eternal God's Presence in the Holyland.

Phinehas succeeded in reawakening the Eternal's genetic demand for progressive development. Out of this convocation came charismatic leaders, who became inspired to stimulate Israel's ranks with new hope. This chapter summarizes the effect of these Shoftim-leaders during this period of the Judges, which lasted for about 225 years.

V.23: Phinehas concludes his convocation by analyzing the intent of (Ex.23:29.30), the Eternal's instructions given in the Torah. The obligation ever remains Israel's challenge to integrate its native population to live in peace as a viable thriving community under the banner of the Eternal God of Israel.

CHAPTER 3   Reviews the cause and effect of Israel's rebelliousness during
Pages 101.105

TABLE OF CONTENTS: JUDGES

the century after they had entered the Holyland. War clouds began to appear because Israel permitted itself to become assimilated and the vassals of the new conquerors of the Holyland. The Philistines in the west and Cushan Rishathaim in the north became the Eternal God's punishing rod to discipline Israel and awaken it from its lethargy.

Othniel rose to Israel's need to win 32 years of peace. Vs.12.30: Describes the disobedience of the tribes of Reuben, Gad, Ephraim and Benjamin. Ammon and Moab hired Amalekites and became the Eternal's punishing rod in Trans-Jordan. Ehud became the second of the Judges, to defeat these perpetual enemies of Israel and to win 62 years of peace.

V.31: Describes the efforts of the third of these Judges. Shamgar the son of Anath, rose to combat the infiltration of the *'Shosim'* Aegean marauders called the Seapeoples.

CHAPTER 4
Pages 105.109

Vs.1.16: Describes a new coalition of Canaanite forces formed by Jabin and Sisera, decades after the lifetime of Ehud. They plan to start their action in the north central territories occupied by Naphtali, Ephraim and Issachar. Deborah inspires Barak to issue a call to arms. Barak agrees on the condition she join him in the direction of the battle. The war ends by the destruction of Sisera's army.

Vs.17.24: Describes Sisera's escape to the tent of Jael, the wife of Heber the Kenite, her heroic action destroyed the last vestige of Jabin's political and military control of Canaan. This victory also won for Israel deliverance from years of oppression.

CHAPTER 5
Pages 109.115

Devoted to Deborah's powerful Ode. It expresses Israel's gratitude for 20 peaceful years after the destruction of Jabin's coalition of forces under the leadership of Sisera.

CHAPTER 6
Pages 116.121

Vs.1.10: Describes the chaos in the territory of the tribes of Reuben, Gad and the families of Jair and Nobach of the tribe of Manasseh. These are the very families and tribes that failed to respond to Deborah and Barak's call to arms. Their self interest became the signal to Midian, Ammon and Moab, that this was the moment to accomplish in Trans-Jordan what Jabin and his coalition desired to accomplish west of the Jordan River. The Trans-Jordanian tribes begin to see clearly the formation and threat of the clouds of war. This becomes their moment of truth as they turn inward to examine their past conduct. They now once again return to the only Source from whence cometh humanity's salvation. The messenger of the Eternal strives to inspire them in their moments of

TABLE OF CONTENTS: JUDGES

repentance to rise courageously to cope with their problems, in order to overcome their ongoing fear of the Amorites.

Vs.11.24: The Eternal's messenger implements his inspiration by seeking out Gideon and to inspire him to use his natural talents to come to the aid of his people.

Vs.25.40: Gideon's modesty challenged his manifest destiny, that he rise from his cloud of doubt to implement his resolution to become the man of the hour who shall fulfill the demand of the Eternal's messenger.

CHAPTER 7
Pages 121.124

Gideon issued a call to arms and mobilized his army at the foot of Mount Gilboa. Gideon established criteria for those who shall become his army. He offered exemption to those that desire it and is desirous of excusing those who have succumbed to Canaanite idolatrous practices. Gideon is determined that his select group of men be dedicated to his strategy of fighting the battles of the Eternal God of Israel.

CHAPTER 8
Pages 124.127

Vs.1.17: Reflect the existing disunity in the ranks of the tribal families. Their self interest prevailed to divide them from their national cause and their universal goals.

Vs.18.21: Gideon's successful war against Ammon, Moab, Midian and the Amalek mercenaries ends with the execution of their leaders Zeeb and Zalmunna.

Vs.22.23: The tribes of Asher, Zebulun, Naphtali and Manasseh and Ephraim issue a draft that Gideon become their king in perpetuity. Gideon's unique rejection of their unanimous offer.

Vs.24.28: Gideon set up an Ephod as a memorial to his victory in Ophrah-Manasseh, his home town. This was his sincere effort to express his gratitude for the peace he has gained for his people after seven oppressive years. Gideon's blunder reflects the mentality of the period. Though Gideon is dedicated to live by Torah disciplines, yet, neither he nor his generation fully grasp the symbolic meaning of Choshen-Mishpat. (Ex.28:4.30). Vs.29.35: Mirror Gideon's personal lifestyle and his family's dedication to his people's welfare. Soon after Gideon's death the tribal and familial unities fell apart as they deviated from Torah guidelines and once again opted for idolatrous worship and assimilation.

CHAPTER 9
Pages 127.133

Vs.1.6: Abimelech, the son of Gideon plans a conspiracy to execute his brothers in order to become king of Shechem-Manasseh.

Vs.7.21: Jotham, the only son to escape the massacre delivers his message to the citizens of Shechem.

TABLE OF CONTENTS: JUDGES

Vs.22.25: Records the gloom and fear that overtakes the tribes as they grasped the enormity of Abimelech's crime.
Vs.26.29: Gal ben Ebed plans a rebellion against Abimelech.
Vs.30.41: Zebul, the governor of Shechem advises Abimelech to initiate a counter revolution.
Vs.42.49: Abimelech plans to destroy Shechem's genetic treasonous hatred.
Vs.50.57: Abimelech strove to destroy all the communities allied with Shechem in this rebellion. While in Thebaz he was killed in action.

CHAPTER 10
Pages 133.136

Vs.1.2: The brevity of Tolah's written record for his 23 years of leadership cannot conceal his accomplishments of peace and enterprise.
Vs.3.5: Jair ruled his territory known as Havoth-Jair for 22 years. Hebrew literature fleshes out his accomplishments during his leadership, despite the cryptic report given here.
Vs.6.8: An historic review of Israel in the Holyland to the death of Jair, that brings to a close a period of prosperity intermingled with retrogression and new found hope via the ever receptive hope of repentance.
Vs.9.10: Israel's prosperous and peaceful years are dissipated as they assimilate with their new found gods and cults. This brings on 18 years of envy, hate and oppression by the Ammonites in the east and the new giant military force in the west. In their moments of misery Israel must recognize the facts of life, their new found gods and cults cannot intercede with the Source of human dignity and inspiration. Idolatry is a detour which leads to a dead end.
Vs.11.16: The Eternal inspired Phinehas, a descendant of Aaron, to raise his prophetic voice to turn this oppressive situation around. He traveled the length and breath of the land, to censure, to rebuke and to cajole the tribes of Israel, to recognize the truth. Only the Source, the Eternal God of Israel, can inspire new hope and courage to those dedicated to His guidelines. Phinehas speaks for the record of history, when he reports, "Israel destroyed their idolatrous symbols. They resolved to remove their new found abominations from their homes. As Israel became receptive to the Eternal's Presence, the Eternal God became sympathetic to Israel's affliction."
Vs.17.18: Israel's resolution filtered into Ammonite ranks to win the time necessary to organize their new found hope.

CHAPTER 11
Pages 136.140

Vs.1.8: Jephtah is recognized as a man of valor. He is offered

TABLE OF CONTENTS: JUDGES

the position of commander in chief of Reuben, Gad and Manasseh's army in Trans-Jordan.

Vs.9.11: Jephtah accepts on the condition that if he succeeds he shall be recognized as the head of their government.

Vs.12.29: Jephtah strives to settle this dispute with Ammon peacefully. Though Jephtah established the facts of his righteous cause, Ammon is determined to go to war.

Vs.30.33: Before Jephtah leads his army to war, Jephtah makes an irrational vow. Jephtah's confidence in his cause inspired his loyal army to rout the Ammonites from Aroer to Minnith.

Vs.34.60: Jephtah's one and only daughter comes forth to greet her father upon his victory. Enthusiastically she expresses her love and devotion only to learn that she has become the victim of her father's irrational vow.

CHAPTER 12
Pages 141.143

Vs.1.6: The leaders of the tribe of Ephraim took Jephtah to task for having ignored them in his call to arms. The roots of Ephraim's animosity goes back in history to the lifetime of Joseph. Their challenge fanned the fanatical intransigence of Jephtah to spark a fratricidal war with the tribe of Ephraim.

V.7: Jephtah led Israel for six years. It is through the experiences of its leaders that the period of Judges emerges.

V.8.10: Contrasting the personality of Jephtah, emerges the personality of Ibzan, who led Israel from Bethlehem. His democratic universal outlook bypassed all narrow tribal inbreeding. Ibzan's outlook encompassed the whole nation. His seven years of leadership served as a model for his posterity.

Vs.11.12: Elon a native of Zebulun succeeded Ibzan and led the nation for ten years.

Vs.13.15: Abdon the son of Hillel, a Benjaminite led Israel from his home territory in Ephraim for eight years. It was Jephtah's intransigence that won 25 tranquil years for Israel during the lifetime of the three leaders that followed him.

CHAPTER 13
Pages 143.147

Prefixing this chapter is a summary of how the Philistines arrived in the Holyland to become a powerful entity. This chapter is devoted to recapitulating the background of Samson who was born and raised under extraordinary circumstances by parents who had given up all hope of having a son who shall fulfill their dream of becoming a leader in Israel. The text describes his birth beginning with conception, his prenatal and postnatal environment that will develop a personality born to become a great human being. Through the eyes of the *'Malach*

TABLE OF CONTENTS: JUDGES

Adonai' we see how Manoach and his wife, two humble human beings are taught to play a part in the evolutionary process. The chapter concludes by some historical facts that created the demand for great leadership. Samson's father is a Danite. They never succeeded to inherit their territory because of Philistine occupation.

CHAPTER 14
Pages 147.150

Describes a scene that repeats itself throughout Israel's history. The basic demand of Torah discipline is rooted in genetic progression (Lev.12:1.5). Natural selection is the graveyard of civilization. Samson's choice of a Philistine woman brings forth the outcry of his parents, "Is there no woman in Israel that determines your decision to marry a Philistine woman?"
Vs.5.9: Reflects Samson's Nazirite background and how he permitted its dilution by the Philistine environment.
Vs.10.18: Illustrate Philistine permissiveness, mores and vulgarity. Samson's training as a Nazir awakens his conscience. V.18, evaluates the crudeness of Philistine mores. Vs.19.20, Samson begins to evaluate his romance, "Was it a fantasy or a mirage?" Samson's lusting with his eyes was the first cause. This made violence possible. Killing on impulse becomes an animal instinct for self preservation. A complete detachment from the *Zelem-Elohim*-the conscience; the ingredient that makes man or woman human. Samson's home environment reawakens and kindles a tiny spark to reactivate his conscience. He now concluded that the Eternal God must be ever present in our daily lives. On this noble thought he returned to Zarah, his parents' home.

CHAPTER 15
Pages 150.153

Vs.1.3: Illustrates Samson's step by step degradation. It is he (Gen.4:6.7) that opened the door to permit tragedy to enter his life.
Vs.4.17, Samson's freelance confrontation with individual Philistines that led to provoking their government. Through Samson's escapades we observe the counter measures of injustice and violence. Samson's resolution in v.14, never led to a united effort to help the tribe of Dan acquire a foothold in their allotted territory. V.17, exposes Samson's saner moments when he asked the pertinent question, "How have I departed from the dedication of a Nazir, to become a killer?"
Vs.18.20: While Samson is involved with his own self, his conscience thirsts for truth. *Vayikra Elohim* the Eternal strives to reveal to Samson the wellspring of living that creates the

TABLE OF CONTENTS: JUDGES

	"link" between God and man that demands personal involvement to help build peace into the human equation.
CHAPTER 16 Pages 153.157	Exposes the tremendous losses to private property, sparked by Samson's egotistic drive and implemented by his superhuman strength. V.17, exposes Samson's lack of fear, while his dissipation has robbed him of his reason and his natural instinct for survival. Vs.18.27: Sum up his step by step dissipation, the defiling of his natural gifts which led him in the opposite direction of *'kedushah'* perfection. His imprisonment and the mutilation of his perfectly created body are but the effect of his chosen lifestyle. Vs.28.31, Samson's life symbolizes Israel's tremendous potential, how it squanders its cumulative development. Samson's prayer has come too late. He also fails to recognize the Eternal's demand is for construction and not destruction.
CHAPTER 17 Pages 157.159	Vs.1.6: In these closing decades of the period of the Judges all of Israel's travail has become chargeable to the fact, "There is no central authority in Israel." This chapter focuses upon a woman of means and her son Michayahu. Their lives open a window for history to observe the prosperity of the period, also the lack of ethics, the permissive apostacy under the guise of Torah law. The disguise becomes apparent as the son steals from his mother, the mother crudely utters a curse and then reneges and revokes her vow. Vs.7.8: (Num.18:2.6, Deut.12:12,19 14:29,18:6.8 16:14, 26:11.13 10:8.9) The Torah had designated the tribe of Levi to become the recognized teachers and leaders in Israel. In turn they were to be supported by the community. Through the report in these verses we can observe the denigration of their status and their deviation from Torah disciplines. Jonathan a descendant of Gershon the son of Moses conveys our object example of the times.
CHAPTER 18 Pages 159.162	The tribe of Dan is determined to relocate; after recognizing their inability to take possession of their allotted territory. They dispatched scouts to investigate the Laish area. They stopped at the home of Micah in the hill country of Ephraim. There they meet Jonathan serving as a priest in Micah's shrine. Vs.8.14: When they returned home, they reported their conclusions which were accepted and the families of Dan set out to take possession of their new territory. On their way north they are determined to steal Micah's shrine.

TABLE OF CONTENTS: JUDGES

Vs.15.21: Describes the details of the theft. They also convinced Jonathan to join them as their priest.

Vs.22.26: Micah pursued the Danites and soon was convinced that in pagan law, possession is recognized as title. He returned to his home reconciled that he was not harmed.

Vs.27.31: Samuel the author of the Book of Judges speaks for the record of history as he describes the injustice perpetrated upon the settlers in Laish. The Danites rebuilt the city and renamed it Dan. They activated Micah's shrine and installed Jonathan as their priest. This whole incident has come down to us known as the *'Pesel Micah'*, the Shrine of Micah.

CHAPTER 19
Pages 162.165

Though the experience recorded in this chapter is accepted as an everyday occurrence in the news media of the world, it could not be accepted by Israelites in the eleventh century BCE., because it murdered the peace in every Jewish heart. This crime recorded by the Prophet Samuel charges every human conscience to eradicate the predatory beast from the heart of man. On the record Israel is a people refined by centuries of laws and disciplines that led to the conclusions inscribed in the Decalogue and then amplified in the Torah. These laws encompass the disciplines that must govern human behavior every moment of their existence. This crime condemns humanity until it is eradicated.

CHAPTER 20
Pages 165.169

Vs.1.7: The united tribes assembled at Mitzpah and decided upon a united action until this problem is solved. They set up a court of inquiry and accepted testimony from the Levite.

Vs.8.16: They reached a concensus to mount an action at once. They presented the charges to the tribe of Benjamin. Their reply came by issuing a call to arms.

Vs.17.25: They sought and received the concurrence of Phinehas the priest. For two days they suffered casualties as they regretted this unnecessary war.

V.26: They called an assembly for prayer at Shiloh to redefine their cause.

Vs.27.28: To bolster the courage of the men, Phinehas brought the Ark to Bethel.

Vs.29.38: Describes the war in detail. As the war drew to a close, the tragedy of this fratricidal war created the deepseated pain which can never be erased from Israel's memory.

Vs.39.48: Describes the tragic losses in the tribe of Benjamin.

CHAPTER 21
Pages 169.172

Vs.1.4: Returning to Bethel in a mood of contrition the united tribes face Phinehas the High Priest with a plea, "Why are we incapable of uniting to face our common enemies instead of destroying a complete tribe in a fratricidal war?" They pleaded with Phinehas to forgive their irrational vow taken before the war at Mitzpah.

Vs.5.12: They also regretted their decision to punish the tribe of Manasseh for failing to join in the war. It was at this point that they dispatched a messenger to intercept the force sent in v.10, and changed their instructions as recorded in v.12.

Vs.13.15: In this mood of contrition and reconciliation they invited the 600 Benjaminites that survived at the Rock of Rimon, to report to Shiloh for a plan of rehabilitation.

Vs.16.18: The High Priest Phinehas nullified their irrational vow. The reconciliation was now completed as the Elders agreed to grant the remnants of the tribe of Benjamin every opportunity for rebuilding their numerical strength.

Vs.19.25: Out of this convocation they returned home resolved to labor cooperatively and fully agreed to strive for a central leadership.

INTRODUCTION TO THE BOOK OF JUDGES

The book of Judges is the historic record which begins with the demise of Joshua, and the Elders who functioned with him during his lifetime to govern Israel. The period of the Judges ends with the fall of Shiloh in about 1050 BCE. Joshua died at the age of 110 in about 1234 BCE. Before Joshua died he divided the Holyland and decreed that each tribe assume the responsibility for governing in their individual territory. Included in Joshua's decree was the challenge to each individual tribe to integrate the natives now living in their inherited land mass.

Each of the respective tribal territories are to be governed by Torah law. In accord with (Ex.23:29.30) Israel was to recognize the natural abilities of the native population and the accumulated agricultural *"know-how"* which has taken centuries to evolve. The Torah established minimum conditions inscribed in The Seven Laws of Noah for the natives. Basic to these minimum conditions is the abolition of idolatry and all its ancient ramifications. In turn for the loyalty of the natives Israel was to guarantee their human rights, equal protection under Israel's law which demands the abolition of slavery.

Going back to the Exodus, multitudes of proselytes were integrated into Israel's ranks by Moses. When Joshua conquered the Holyland, the native population was receptive to Israel's code of law and its goals for human rights. For centuries they lived under tyrants. It was these tyrants which comprised the organized force to oppose Israel's entry into the Holyland. Therefore, the challenge to Israel's tribal society was to teach by example to observe Torah law.

History records that Joshua succeeded during his period of leadership which began with the demise of Moses, to continue the standards laid down by Moses. The period of the Judges became progressively worse because when Joshua died he failed to designate a central authority to strive for the national goal. Every tribe concentrated on their own self interest. They failed to integrate the native population. Instead they succumbed to local mores and assimilated with the natives. They accepted, condoned and became inured to idolatrous practices. The retrogression of this period of the Judges, when everyone did as they pleased was attributed to the fact that there was no king in Israel (Jud.17:6, 18:1, 21:25).

Periodically charismatic leaders arose to enforce Torah law, to encourage courts of justice, to sit as justices, and encouraged military leaders to defend their respective communities against the tyrants that arose to assimilate Israel or to expel them from the Holyland. The periods given for the effectiveness of these rulers are given in round numbers. They did not succeed in a single united effort which involved each and every tribe at one given time. Therefore, these periods overlapped each other, for a total of about 225 years.

Studying the details and the background of this important book, we derive a kaleidoscopic picture of the centuries it will yet take before Israel shall measure up to its historic destiny, to become *"a light unto the nations of the World."*

INTRODUCTION: JUDGES

Israel's score card rises or falls in just measure to its dedication to the principles of Torah law and the daily observance of its disciplines.

Included in the text of the commentary are references gathered from every source in human history which has surfaced over almost three millenia to confirm, to assist the scholar and student to clarify the full meaning of every verse in this book covering the period of the Judges.

David Lieberman

JUDGES CHAPTER 1

Vs. 1.3 The time frame of this chapter is some time after the demise of Joshua. The Elders are concerned with the chaotic conditions which are beginning to surface in the ranks of Israel. Each tribe is beginning to make peace with themselves. They are satisfied to permit the pockets of resistance to continue without enforcing the conditions decreed in the Torah. The Seven Laws of Noah, were to become the basis from which to create a new plateau to integrate the indigenous population of Canaan and to offer them citizenship. They in return are to contribute their loyalty and their natural abilities to enhance the economy of Israel. The Seven Laws of Noah are: 1. Courts of justice, 2. Prohibition of blasphemy, 3. Abolition of idolatry, 4. Prohibition of incest, 5. Prohibition of murder, 6. Prohibition of robbery, 7. Cutting flesh from a living animal. They did not at this point sign a peace treaty with the Canaanites in their respective territories. They did permit however passively, the corrupt and debauched practices of the past to exist in their environment. Each tribe became involved with their own self interest and their own survival. Israel ceased to be a united nation under the disciplines of its Constitution, the Torah. Concerned with this state of affairs the Elders started a dialogue with all the tribes of Israel, in the name of the Eternal God of Israel. They recognized the erosion of the ideals for which Israel made such heroic sacrifices. The Elders called Israel's attention to the reawakening Canaanite leadership striving to recapture the governing leadership of the Holyland. The Elders are seeking a spontaneous united response to bring all pockets of resistance under the governing tribes in their respective territories. Which of the tribes will set an example by initiating a military campaign in their respective territory to establish law and order and to clean out the pockets of resistance?

V. 2 Judah responded to the call of the Elders in the name of the Eternal God of Israel. Judah has already identified itself in past history for its leadership ability. Let us therefore look at this genetic progressive record: (See commentary in The Eternal Torah on Gen.49:8.12, Deut.33:7).

V. 3 Is another indicator of Judah's leadership ability as they requested Simeon's cooperation in this venture. The tribe of Simeon occupied nine cities in Judah's territory (see commentary on Joshua 15:20.62, 19:1.9). In return for Simeon's participation, Judah will assist Simeon to clear out all pockets of resistance in their territory.

Vs. 4.7 Judah and Simeon set out upon their campaign against the Canaanite and Perizzite population in their territory. Inspired by the cause of the Eternal, they defeated an army of about 10,000 men in Bezek (see T.E.T. Deut.32:30.31) for the meaning of this victory.

V. 5 Adoni-bezek led his forces in the city of Bezek, Judah and Simeon fought him to a standstill and completely overpowered the Canaanite and Perizzite opposition.

V. 6 Adoni-bezek fled the city and was pursued until he was caught. In keeping with the ancient military practices they incapacitated the thumbs of his hands and

JUDGES CHAPTER 1

the large toes of his feet; to handicap his ability to run and his efficiency in wielding a sword.

V. 7 The campaign continued to the outskirts of Jerusalem, where Judah established their camp. (The city of Jerusalem and its citadel was not taken until David's time). Here Adoni-bezek was brought. He recognized his punishment as just retribution for the 70 kings to whom he had administered the same punishment. Here Adoni-bezek boasted, that he continued to embarrass his enemies by forcing them to survive on the crumbs falling from his festive tables. Bezek, is in the area which is now known as Abu-dis, northeast of Judah's territory. From this record of history we can observe the ongoing wars, the changing waves of invaders, who created dictatorships, they originated from the north and had no historic roots in the Holyland. Here in captivity Adoni-bezek passed away into history as a symbol for all those that will resist Israel's legitimate position to create a new plateau for civilization.

Vs. 8.9 The tribes of Judah and Simeon proceeded from Bezek to the corridor leading to the lower city of Jerusalem. They took possession of the villages surrounding it. However, its inhabitants escaped into the citadel which became known in David's time as Mount Zion. This area was technically in Benjamin's territory and since they were in no position to govern it, Judah set it on fire in the hope that Benjamin will make an effort to rebuild it and settle there. In v.21, we are informed that the tribe of Benjamin failed to take advantage of this opportunity to rebuild it. The Jebusites grasped the opportunity to fill the void. They rebuilt it, while the tribe of Benjamin lived there as aliens. This condition remained the same until David conquered the citadel (II Sam.5:7.10).

V. 9 Judah and Simeon proceeded to the hill country surrounding the lower city of Jerusalem, the southern areas and the lowlands along the Mediterranean coast stretching from Jaffa to Gaza. The contrasting elevation can be observed from Hebron, which is close to 3000 feet above sea level. From the height of Hebron the land continues to drop to the negev steppe leading to the desert area.

Vs. 10.15 The action described in these verses goes back to (Num.14:30.33, Joshua 14:6.15, 15:13.19). Though Joshua recorded the conquest of Hebron in (10:36.41) they did not occupy it at that time. Caleb assumed command at this time and marched on to the city of Hebron-Kiriat-Arba and destroyed the myth of the three mighty giants referred to in (Gen.14:5) as Rephaim.

Vs. 11.12 Caleb continued to Devir which was known in the past as Kiriat-sefer. This is the moment when Othniel the son of Kenaz is picking up Caleb's challenge made in (Joshua 15:16.17).

V. 13 Othniel conquered Devir and won his bride Achsah.

Vs. 14.15 Caleb's daughter Achsah repeated her request for a supply of water in the territory allotted to her and Othniel. See (Joshua 15:1.20) for Othniel's genealogy and an explanation of v.15. It was this action that won for Othniel

JUDGES CHAPTER 1

the title shofet-leader. Considering the advanced age of Caleb (Joshua 14:10) he was 85 years old when Joshua began to subdivide the Holyland, it was Othniel's heroic efforts and his reputation as a scholar which qualified him as a leader in Judah. The springs in v.15, have been identified as Sell-ed-Dilbeh, between Hebron and Dahariyeh.

V. 16   The historic background of the Kenites goes back to the ancient people before Abraham (Gen.15:19). For its continuity into the 19th century ACE. see T.E.T. (Num. 10:29.32). From this historic record of the Kenites, we can understand their desire to become identified with the tribe of Judah, with particular attraction to Othniel-Jabetz (I Chronicles 4:9.10). When Joshua divided the land, the Kenites were allotted the area on the outskirts of Jericho, in the vicinity of the ancient palm trees (Deut. 34:3). Since they were basically shepherds and lived only in tents this was acceptable to them. When Judah succeeded in taking control of their territory, they requested and received their allotment in Arad, which is about 16 miles south of Hebron. Heber the Kenite was the husband of Jael (Jud. 4:11, 5:26, I Sam. 27:10, 30:29). These references establish firmly their dedication to Israel's goals and their ability to evaluate the future of the tribe of Judah.

The important role of the Kenites in early Israelite worship is confirmed by the discovery of an Israelite Sanctuary at Arad. They settled in Arad as soon as Judah and Simeon established its rule because they were anxious to conform with Torah disciplines given in (Deut. 11:31.32).

Vs. 17.21   Judah now joined Simeon to clear out the pockets of resistance in the territory allotted to Simeon. They made it clear to the Canaanites that were living in Zephath, (a negev-south community. It is identified as modern Sebaita or es-Sufah), they would have to accept the terms inscribed in the Torah (Deut. 20:10.18) and become integrated into the welfare of the country. When they rejected these terms, Judah and Simeon destroyed the city and renamed it Hormah.

Vs. 18.19   Judah proceeded to conquer the three cities of Gaza, Ashkelon, Ekron and their surrounding territory. These cities are in the hill country north of Gaza. Judah did not challenge the cities of Gath and Ashdod because they recognized Philistine superiority there. It was in these cities of the Emek valley that they maintained their superior forces of iron re-enforced chariots.

Vs. 20.21   These verses confirm the action described in vs. 10.15, and the action described in vs. 8.9. The Benjaminites lived as a minority among the Jebusites because they lacked the initiative to unite their kindred tribes of Ephraim and Manasseh, for a united action in the manner of Judah and Simeon. When this information was recorded by the prophet Samuel, the above described conditions in Benjamin's territory had not changed.

Vs. 22.26   Some time elapsed when the tribes of Ephraim and Manasseh, the tribal descendants of their father Joseph, followed the example set by Judah and Simeon. They fully realized that

JUDGES CHAPTER 1

with every passing year, the inhabitants living in their territories were beginning to organize a military force in order to by-pass the conditions under which they agreed to live as citizen's of Israel. Their united action created the blessings of *vaAdonai imam* the Eternal God of Israel.

Vs. 23.24 Ephraim and Manasseh sent scouts to survey their chances of entering the walled city of Bethel. It was known as Luz in antiquity. This is the same city mentioned in (Joshua 8:17) when the battle of Ai was fought. This city is now called Beitin and is northeast of Ramallah. Since Israel had neither the equipment or the technical know-how to attack the fortifications, it was strategically important to find the secret passageway by which their people left the city upon their daily affairs. The scouts bided their time and finally observed a man emerging from the secret passage. They confronted the man with an offer to deal kindly with him, if he would disclose the method of exit and entree.

Vs. 25.26 Confirms the fulfilment of their vow to this man and his family when they conquered the city of Bethel. They escorted him and his family to safety away from the dangers of combat. The text validates the extent of their kindness. They enabled him to relocate and build a city north of Syria in the land of the Hittites. In commemoration of his past, he called it by the ancient name of Bethel-Luz.

Vs. 27.29 More than a century has elapsed since the last census was taken and recorded in (Num. 26:28.37). In this census these three tribes numbered 130,800 men between the ages of 20 and older. Despite their numerical strength there was no unity of purpose. Israel's situation was becoming more untenable with every passing year. The indigenous population was beginning to rearm in order to prove that Israel was not invincible. Manasseh lacked the initiative to govern in Beth-shean, Taanach, Ibleam, Megiddo, Dor and their surrounding territories. Periodically when the tribes did rise above their self interest, they only succeeded to impress the inhabitants to work for the public good under duress. Even this insincere and half hearted effort did not come about until the defeat of Jabin (Jud. 4:23) of Canaan. Ephraim too, failed to govern its territory at Gezer, while Benjamin failed at Jebuz.

Vs. 30.36 The author of the book of Judges continues to describe the conditions of the Holyland toward the end of Joshua's life and into the period of the Judges. V. 30, informs history that Zebulun failed to govern in its allotted territory. This included the cities of Kitron and Nahalol. They did periodically draft the natives for forced labor but not as free citizens.

Vs. 31.32 The tribe of Asher, whose territory was located in the highlands of the Holyland, failed to govern in Acco, Ahlab, Achzib, Helbah, Aphik and Rehob. The Asherites assimilated with the indigenous settlers.

V. 33 The tribe of Naphtali, whose territory lay east of the Upper Galill, north of Zebulun and Issachar and east of Asher, did not take possession of their

JUDGES CHAPTER 1

territory. They were considered alien settlers among the Canaanite inhabitants of Beth-shemesh, and Beth-anath, the center for the worship of the goddess Anath. They strayed completely from the intent and purpose of the Exodus and the conquest of the Holyland.

V. 34 The tribe of Dan failed completely to defeat the Amorites in their allotted territory. They were confined to the area of Zorah and Eshtaol. It was at this time that Dan sought, found and established the majority of its families at Laish and renamed it Dan. The full details of this action are reported in (Jud. 18:1.31).

V. 35 The Amorites remained in the original allotted territory of the tribe of Dan, which included Har-heres, Aijalon and Shaalbim. Some years later the tribe of Ephraim succeeded in displacing the Amorites. Even then, they failed to introduce the conditions outlined in the Torah for the conquest of the Holyland. This record of inertia and assimilation on the part of the tribes of: Manasseh, Ephraim, Zebulun, Asher, Naphtali and Dan, exposes their lack of initiative, to follow through upon their commitment to become a governing force in accord with the ideals and purpose of the Torah, to build a new plateau of civilization in the Holyland. As time went by the indigenous population fully concluded, they need not take their conquerors seriously. The demagogues and the would be dictators succeeded to win the loyalties of the population, while the Israelites became the underdogs.

V. 36 Describes the vast area being governed by the Amorites at this moment in Israel's history. They held all the territory from Scorpions Pass in the Wilderness of Zin to Selah in the south, near the kingdom of Edom. Scattered throughout this Amorite territory were Israelites living as aliens instead of a nation in its own Holyland.

JUDGES CHAPTER 2

V. 1 At this juncture in Israel's history, came Phinehas, the prophetic *malach Adonai* messenger of the Eternal God of Israel. He came from Gilgal to Bochim, in the vicinity of Bethel. Here he summoned all the leaders of Israel for a major address. He reminded his audience of the Eternal's intention and purpose for the Exodus of Israel from Egypt. Phinehas quoted from the record, the promise made to our forefather and recorded in (Gen. 15:18, Ex. 34:10.13, Deut. 7:1.6). "You are ever to remember, your lives must ever remain dedicated to the Covenant made with your forefathers. *Lo afer beriti leolam* The Eternal God shall never permit you to withdraw from this oath and His Covenant with Israel (Ex. 19:18, Deut. 9:14)."

V. 2 The binding force of the Eternal's Covenant made with Abraham, binds every generation of Israel to eternity. When you make a peace treaty with the inhabitants of the Holyland, who reject the conditions laid down in the Torah, you invalidate the oath taken by your parents (Ex. 23:32.33,34:12.18, Deut. 7:2.4). "It is not the intention of the Eternal God of Israel, that you subjugate the indigenous people of Canaan.

JUDGES CHAPTER 2

Your obligation is to destroy their idolatrous practices which imprison their bodies and minds. Your task is to elevate them to the standards set down in your Torah. Their opposition to this challenge denies them the right to become beneficiaries of the values of human development. Your coming to terms with the inhabitants of Canaan on their level of development challenges your presence in the Holyland, as they drag you down to their standards. Rethink yourselves, examine your conscience. When you negate your oath to uphold the Covenant, you not only retard your growth and development but fail to enrich the lives of those who agree to live by the standards of your Torah disciplined environment."

V. 3   Phinehas reminded his audience of Moses' admonition given in (Num. 33:55.56) in the name of the Eternal God of Israel. Joshua too reiterated this warning to Israel in (Joshua 23:12.13). "Be you therefore forewarned, should you fail to remove every negative force from your environment, this diversionary force shall rise to ensnare you from your goal in history to become a light unto the Nations. Should you succumb to their idolatrous and debauched standards of living, you shall become entrapped into that bottomless pit of despair."

Vs. 4.5   When Phinehas completed his admonition, the leaders of Israel's tribes broke into tears as they recognized their failing judgment and lack of leadership. To commemorate this important moment in Israel's history, they named or renamed this area Bochim-weeping. This turning point in the history of Israel at this very place, where Jacob, who was in the midst of making critical decisions in his life (Gen. 35:8) was confronted with the demise of his mother Rebecca and her nurse Devorah, probably influenced the renaming of Bochim. Phinehas recognized their weeping as confession for their lack of leadership. This act of recognizing past failure and resolution to inspire their respective tribes, legitimized their ability to offer a sin offering. This offering was made upon the original altar built by Joshua in Gilgal, which has remained intact for centuries as the Central Sanctuary before Shiloh. It also confirms that Bethel and Gilgal are in the same contiguous area where Jacob recorded his most marvelous experience (Gen. 28:10.22).

Vs. 6.8   Phinehas as the moral and spiritual leader of Israel was morally bound by Torah disciplines to accept the leaders contrition as sincere. This he did in the name of Moses and Joshua as recorded in (Gen. 6:3, Ex. 34:7, Joshua 24:25.28). The text follows verbatim the text recorded in Joshua.

V. 7 Phinehas confirmed for the record of history, that during his lifetime which exceeded the lives of the Elders present at this convocation, the Elders renewed their efforts to inspire their respective tribes to get on with taking possession of the areas conquered by Joshua and to enforce disciplines in their midst.

V. 8 Phinehas as the successor to Joshua, memorialized the dedicated life of Joshua by repeating for the new generation of his time, that Joshua who was the

JUDGES CHAPTER 2

successor of Moses died at the age of 110, that like his teacher Moses, Joshua was also dedicated as a servant of the Eternal God of Israel. He reminded the new generation that will one day succeed him where the burial place of Joshua is, that it would be fitting and proper to pay their respects to his memory for a lifetime of dedication to Israel's cause (Joshua 24:29.30).

We who live almost three millenia removed from this period in Jewish history must ever remember the great number of proselytes that filtered into the ranks of Israel. Their individual lives were but one generation removed from the mores of a debauched and idolatrous society.

Vs. 9.10   It was the dedication of Moses in his time, Joshua in his time, Phinehas and the Elders in their generation, who remonstrated with the native born Israelites and the newly joined proselytes, to remain loyal to their oath. The text establishes the time frame when the following experiences took place. In v.9, the text changes the name of Joshua's burial place from Timnath-serach, to Timnath-hereth, to remind history that this generation was into idolatrous sun worship. They placed a symbol of this worship on Joshua's grave to indicate their doubt with Joshua's triumph recorded in (Joshua 10:12.14). The text continues to tell us that the previous generation, who had first hand experience with the past events had died. The current generation were completely ignorant of the past events because parents failed to observe the mitzvah of *veshinantam levanech vehigadeta et bincha* (Ex. 13:8, Deut. 6:7,11:19). Parents involved with survival and making it in a new economy, in a new land failed to teach their children of the new generation the events which had won the faith of their fathers. This new generation challenged the triumphs given in past testimony. Israel's concept of the Eternal God, the disciplines recorded in the Torah and the events which molded Israel into a nation and a civilization were forgotten.

V. 11   At this juncture in Israel's history, the Book of Judges describes the anarchy which set into the ranks of Israel in the Holyland. Let us pause to examine the world scene which made possible the conquest of the Holyland. The "Finger" of the Eternal God, is ever inspiring mankind to take advantage of moments in history, when great strides can be made in the process of humanity's evolution. Moses' miracle timing of the Exodus was inspired by the *tsunami* which devastated Egypt and the Aegean Seapeoples. For 40 years Israel was welded into a nation, as it bided its time in the desert of life for the right moment to enter upon its national life in the Holyland. When Joshua entered the Holyland, the Hittite empire had been completely wiped out. The Hurrian state of Mittani was gone. The Cassite dynasty in Babylonia had sunk into a weakened condition. The new Assyria in the east, a product of Semites and Hurrians, were defending themselves against the encroaching Arameans along the Euphrates River. Had the tribes of Israel assumed full control over the Holyland at this point in time and history as a united people under their constitution the Torah, this would have rocked all the

JUDGES CHAPTER 2

imperial dictators from their thrones. It would have established a new world order. This is the true meaning of (Ex. 14:14). The Eternal God of history is the "Man of War" as He strives to encourage the righteous forces of humanity to move off dead center, to help build a better world order. This is the real world as we review it from the 20th century. This was the inspired view given by the Eternal to Moses as he received it and recorded it in (Ex: 33:18.23). See commentary in T.E.T. When mankind rejects the Eternal's direction in history, My Presence is not perceived nor acknowledged.

Vs. 12.13 This new generation provoked and incited their Eternal God by their ingratitude for their blessings. The sequence of Israel's actions are described: 1. They desecrated their humanity by their conduct in the secrecy of their own homes. Only God can monitor our private lives by challenging our individual conscience. 2. They worshipped the variety of gods created by each individual to harmonize with their own individual lifestyle. These imaginary gods became their masters. The *Bealim* were their nature gods. They were associated with immoral rites and human sacrifices. The Eternal God of history ceased to play a part in their lives. See commentary in T.E.T. on (Deut. 6:14.15, 7:14.15).

Vs. 14.15 When Israel short circuited the Eternal's normal progressive demand, this created the simile of the Eternal's anger. The *shasa* the nomadic robber-tribes of Canaan instinctively felt the chaos, which Israel itself created in their settlements. It is not God that creates the conditions of anarchy but man himself. When law and order subsides, the evil forces of society take over and chaos sets in. Israel's communities were plundered because they relied upon miracles promised by their new cults and gods. They failed to defend themselves as they were being subjugated. Instead they resigned from history. Their fears became so great that even the stirring of a leaf created terror of pursuit (Lev. 26:36, Num. 14:42). Only after the Eternal's wrath encircled them, did they begin to examine their reason for being Israel. Their defeat became a fixed certainty in their conscious stricken minds. *Vayimkerem* they voluntarily sold themselves in order to bribe their oppressors to deal kindly with them. With every turn of the screw the pressures and the oppression became unbearable. Israel's enemies concluded they have removed their "halo" (Num. 14:9). Israel is but one of them now. V. 15 (Lev. 26:14.18), when the tribes began to link the Eternal's anger with their oppressive situation, they began to link their blessings with their ability to perceive the Eternal's direction in history. Israel's problems during this period of the Judges are the result of their rebellion against the Divine demand engraved in the genes of mankind for progressive development.

V. 16 The prophet Samuel who wrote the book of Judges has described in vs. 11.15, as vividly as possible the cause and the effect of Israel's rebelliousness upon their individual lives and the collective national welfare. V.16, informs us that the Eternal's demand for

JUDGES CHAPTER 2

social justice remained alive, however dormant in the lives of a few, dedicated to the cause of Israel's position in history. From this minority of inspired and dedicated leaders arose the inspired men and women who have developed leaders who shall help Israel against these nomadic robber-tribes who plundered and oppressed the territorial settlements. From these efforts there arose periodically Shoftim-leaders who organized military units to defend themselves against these marauders. These charismatic leaders stimulated and animated the rank and file to recognize the current dangers of being decimated or absorbed into the melting pot of their barbarian environment.

V. 17   The *Shoftim* counselled the tribes in which they exercised their sphere of influence, to follow the disciplines outlined in the Torah. They met with opposition from the rank and file because of their exposure to the environmental mores of their surroundings. This chaotic period lasted for about 225 years, from about 1234 to 1009 BCE., when Saul was anointed as king of Israel. During these 225 years, the following *Shoftim*-leaders-judges, rallied their respective tribes in which they lived. Sometimes they succeeded to unite some of the other tribes but never as a completely united nation.

Judges-leaders	Recorded in Chapter	The Enemy
Othniel	Judges 3:9	Ahram-Naharayim
Ehud	Judges 3:13	Moabites
Barak-Deborah	Judges 4:2	Jabin-Sisera
Gideon	Judges 7:8:23	Midianites
Jephtah	Judges 11:12	Ammonites
Samson	Judges 13:16	Philistines

Despite the sincere efforts of the above named leaders, Israel ignored the disciplines developed from Abraham to Joshua, they ignored their leaders while each man and woman continued to remain immersed in the sensual worship of existing deities.

Vs. 18.19   When these judges-leaders came to the fore and succeeded to throw off the yoke of terror and plunder, the people in their respective tribe showed signs of contrition and repentance during the lifetime of these charismatic chieftains. This sign of remorse harmonized with the Eternal's long suffering compassion for mankind as they strive to rise upon the ladder of evolution (Ex. 34:7, Gen. 6:3).

When these leaders died, they once again retrogressed into their debauched, dissipated and corrupt lifestyle. In some instances the next generation was more depraved and demoralized than the previous generation.

Vs. 20.21   Only the Eternal God, Whose existence is to infinity has the ability to recognize genetic retrogression as it surfaces in the lives of individuals or nations. He recognizes the cause which has kindled His wrath. Israel has failed to uphold the Covenant made with their

JUDGES CHAPTER 2

forefathers. "They have ignored My Blueprint, the Torah, they have abdicated the disciplines inscribed therein for human development."

"No longer shall I inspire the momentum to create the moment which shall harmonize with My Natural Law for Israel to succeed in driving out the pockets of resistance left by Joshua when he died (Joshua 13:1.6).

V. 22 *lemaan nassot* (Ex. 23:22.31, Deut. 20:10.11) This is Israel's test, that Israel can deal justly with the indigenous population of the Holyland. Only the hard core may be destroyed. From Shem to Abraham, to Moses and through this moment in Israel's history, the period of the Judges, represents a span of about 1000 years. The laws in the Torah are disciplines refined in the human heart through genetic progression by the demand inscribed therein and the inspiration of the Eternal God, cultivated through the *Zelem-Elohim*-human capacity for intelligence. *Hashomrim hem derech Adonai* Israel must pass through the crucible of time and history to demonstrate to the Eternal and all of humanity, that they can measure up to the stature of their forefathers, when the Eternal God *chose* them (Deut. 14:2) to become a light unto the nations (Is. 42:6). Israel's test must substantiate to the Eternal God and to all of humanity, that its dedication to *Torath Adonai*, is so secure in their own hearts, that the indigenous inhabitants of the Holyland, who have resolved to live by the Seven Laws of Noah, may never again lapse into their idolatrous and depraved mores. Israel's test, is the measure of its dedication to Torah principles, in the daily give and take of the market place. The moral bankruptcy of the 20th century can be traced to this very test. Humankind cannot justify their existence when it desecrates human rights or when it destroys the ethics and standards demanded by the ecology. *Im lo* was Joshua's challenge in (Joshua 23:12.13). Israel failed in the period of the Judges, because it did not create copartners of the indigenous population. The effect of these 225 years of backsliding will be felt for centuries to come.

V. 23 *Vayanach Adonai, lemaan naasot eth Yisrael*, the real test to Israel was to transmit to the indigenous population their dedication to the disciplines of evolution inscribed in the Torah. Reciprocally, Israel was expected to integrate and accept the centuries of experience of the natives as an asset to the overall welfare of the nation. To destroy the native know-how and to destroy the ecology is to create a jungle out of ongoing thriving communities. *Derech Adonai* is to follow the details inscribed in the Master Plan-the Torah, for all of humanity. *Velo netanam beyad Yehoshua* Joshua's conquest of the Holyland conformed with the Eternal's preconceived plan (Ex. 23:29.30) that the Holyland may not become a wasteland in the manner and example of the empire builders of history. The Holyland was to remain as a viable thriving community. It was Israel's ongoing responsibility to establish the Eternal's values in the hearts of its citizens who voluntarily accepted the challenge to stay in order to build a new world order.

JUDGES CHAPTER 3

Vs. 1.2 The time frame of this chapter is three generations after the conquest of the Holyland by Joshua. When the Holyland was divided by Joshua, it was his intention that every tribe assume the responsibility to enforce law and order in their respective territory. It became their individual responsibility to enforce the conditions laid down to the indigenous population, in order for them to be granted citizenship and to enjoy the benefits of a thriving peaceful community. There were several factors which surfaced after the division of the land which handicapped this ideal goal: 1. Joshua did not anticipate the importance of central leadership in the Holyland. Joshua was anxious to transfer the responsibility of governing to the individual tribes, though they had no past experience in this area. Up to this point in time Joshua ran a tight military camp which goes back to the first encounter with Amalek (Ex. 17:8.13). Moses and Joshua's central leadership was augmented by the Nesiim and the Sanhedrin. 2. Despite the lack of experience in managing their own affairs, the individual tribes were most anxious to enjoy the freedom which was granted them. However, the responsibility overwhelmed them and the ideals they intended to plant in the Holyland began to elude them. 3. We must never forget that the majority of those who entered the Holyland were either second or first generation proselytes. During and after the first three decades thousands of new proselytes joined the ranks of Israel.

It was the second generation proselytes that swelled the numbers that became exposed to the idolatrous and licentious environment surrounding their communities. The children who made up the current generation of this chapter were almost completely ignorant of Israel's goals and ideals to build a new world order.

It was this third generation who assimilated with the natives, although they had agreed to Israel's conditions, the tribes never enforced them. While these generations were assimilating with the natives of Canaan, the clouds of war were beginning to gather as the would be dictators and kinglets planned to oppress and enslave this whole new population. Three generations have passed and the skills of war have been forgotten. V. 2 The scene changes in the Holyland from an economy of peace, to acquiring skills of warfare.

Vs. 3.6 The text proceeds to establish for the historic record the names of the new military forces waiting in the wings to challenge Israel's Manifest Destiny. Israel now has the choice of either rededicating themselves to the first cause, to observe their Torah and its commandments in order to justify their position in the Holyland or to permit itself to become enslaved by these newly formed super-powers consisting of: The five principalities of the Philistines, Gaza, Ashkelon, Ashdod, Gath and Ekron and their constantly expanding territories. These territories were expanding eastward away from the Mediterranean coastline. The Philistines were immigrants from the area of the Aegean Islands. They were uprooted by the *tsunami* which occurred at the time of the Exodus (Joshua 3:5.8). They arrived in Canaan after the Egyptians were expelled from the Holyland. North of their territory was a new

JUDGES CHAPTER 3

concentration of indigenous Canaanites. Further to the north were the Zidonim, who later in history became known as Phoenicians. In central Canaan were the Hivites, who were also Achaens. Their territory was Baal-Hermon, from Baal-gad below the Hermon to Hamath-Hasbeiya. Scattered in and about the six nations named in v.5, are Israelite settlements established at the time of the conquest. In all of the above named communities the Israelites intermarried with the natives, contrary to the instructions given in (Deut. 7:3). They also succumbed to their idolatrous practices and worshipped many gods.

V. 7 At the end of the 19th Egyptian Dynasty, Cushan-Rishathaim from Syria-Palestine, was engaged in war with the Egyptians as he strove to expel them from Palestine. In the process of his campaign he spread his oppression against Israel. When this exposed Judah in the south, Othniel came to the fore as leader and prophetic personality. He recognized this moment as correct to nip in the bud Cushan-Rishathaim's grandiose intentions. His spontaneous response harmonizes with the expulsion of the Hurrians-Cushan Rishathaim, by the Pharoah Sethnakhte, in about 1200 BCE. at the beginning of the 20th Egyptian Dynasty.

It was Israel's ingratitude and faithlessness which gave Cushan-Rishathaim the incentive to recognize this moment when in Israel's ranks they were dissipating their lives in the service of a whole panthean of Canaanite gods. This rift in Israel's society tore the fabric of unity as they lost the ability to remain united as a military force to defend themselves. Their involvement with sensuous practices ignored the historic storm warnings as Cushan-Rishathaim took advantage of this split in the ranks of Judah. To be attentive to the voice of the Eternal God of Israel is to crystalize our awareness to the realities of our daily problems. The Eternal's voice tuned into our conscience inspires us to find ways and means to cope with the truth which faces human beings daily.

V. 8 The anger of the Eternal reflects upon the desecration of human intelligence, when we fail to respond to the dangers which develop when we short circuit the truth. The sin is our challenging God's Natural Law. Recorded in these verses is the defection of the tribe of Judah. It is not the Eternal God that created the conditions which made possible the eight years of subjugation to Cushan-Rishathaim, but the series of sinful acts which challenged the Eternal's Natural Law, Moral Law, and Ethical Law.

V. 9 Israel's conscious awakening that it was their own conduct that created and implemented the social conditions which invited their enemies to take advantage of their distraction from their normal responsibilities. This was the spark that activated their ever present foes to take advantage of their dissipated lifestyle (Gen. 4:7), *Vayizaku* When humanity recognizes the limitation of their own powers, they then turn to the only Source that can help them (Gen. 6:3, Ex. 34:7). The Eternal God of human history desires but one condition in consideration for His ongoing

JUDGES CHAPTER 3

blessings, contrition, when we do something which is contrary to His Law and resolution to implement our decision. The Othniel in this verse is the same person who's spontaneous resolution implemented Caleb's challenge in (Jud. 1:12.14). Othniel now recognizes Judah's problems. He resolves to lead Israel out of its dilemma with Cushan Rishathaim.

V. 10   *Vathehi alav ruach Adonai* Othniel is inspired to leadership. *Vayishpot* He strives to teach Israel, to recognize the root of civilization is law and order. He then rallied the tribe of Judah to gird their loins against their common enemy *dissipation* and *sinfulness*. Cushan Rishathaim is but the Eternal's instrument to teach Israel, that all of its problems are of their own making. *Vataz yado* Othniel's prophetic leadership transcended his everyday responsibilities as he inspired Judah to their maximum potential. Othniel was about 53 years of age when he rose to lead Israel in war and to win 40 years of normalcy in the territory of Judah. His greater contribution was to win a generation of loyal Israelites to the disciplines of their Eternal God.

V. 11   *Vatishkot haaretz* Faced by a determined and resolute people, Cushan-Rishathaim retreated to the north. These Hurrians were an assimilation of the original Cassite invasion of Canaan. The tribe of Judah enjoyed 40 years of peace to the end of the Othniel's lifetime.

Vs. 12.14   Chronologically the disobedience and demoralization of the tribes of Reuben and Gad, whose territory was east of the Jordan River and the tribes of Benjamin and Ephraim, whose territory was west of the Jordan River, was in the process of developing during the lifetime of Othniel. What these four tribes had in common was their boundary line, the River Jordan. While Judah under the influence of Othniel's leadership was enjoying a renaissance in their communal life, this renewal and dedication to Torah principles had no effect upon the four tribes of Reuben, Gad, Benjamin and Ephraim. This fact highlights the displeasure of the Eternal, there was no national goal or unity between the tribes. The defection of these four tribes from Torah disciplines created the chaos which motivated Eglon the king of Moab, to ally himself with Ammon. Ammon and Moab then hired Amalek roving mercenaries (Ex. 17:14.16). See (Deut. 2:9.19) for Israel's relationship with Ammon and Moab which the Torah insisted that Israel shall honor. The allied forces then took possession of the Jericho valley with the intention of infiltrating the rest of the Holyland from this central position. Ammon and Moab exposed their intentions when they hired the Amalekites the symbolic enemy of civilization (Deut. 25:17.19). For 18 years these four tribes were subjugated and oppressed.

Vs. 15.16   When these four tribes reached the end of their endurance, *Vayizaku* they cried for help to the Eternal God of Israel. In

JUDGES CHAPTER 3

keeping with God's ongoing mercy (Gen. 6:3, Ex. 34:6), there arose from the ranks of Israel, Ehud the son of Gera, of the tribe of Benjamin. We are told that although Ehud was left handed, he was *iter* also ambidextrous. Ehud's strategy was to become the representative of Israel, that he will deliver the annual tribute to Eglon the king of Moab, who master minded this whole tyranny. Ehud sought the opportunity to destroy the chief of operations in order to create chaos in their ranks. Included in Ehud's strategy was a double edged sword without a hilt about 18 inches long. This he carried underneath his outer garment on the hip of his right side. A sword is normally carried on the left side and is manipulated by the right hand.

Vs. 17.19   Ehud and his men delivered the tribute and Eglon's guard received it in behalf of their king. Eglon now discharged Ehud and his men. Ehud returned with his men to the area of the *pesilim* stone quarry near Gilgal. It was from here that Ehud returned by himself under the pretense that he had a most secretive message for Eglon, which he must deliver in privacy. Whereupon the king discharged all those in his presence, and invited Ehud to retire with him to the cool upper chamber on the north side of his home.

Vs. 20.22   When Ehud entered the room, the king was already sitting there. Spontaneously Ehud announced, "I have a message from the God of Israel for you." Instinctively Eglon rose to be close to Ehud's lips. At this very split second Ehud's left hand reached for his sword-dagger and plugged it deep into Eglon's stomach. His excess fat enclosed the blade including the handle. As Eglon's tremendous girth enclosed the dagger, the *parshandona* the fecal material in the intestines oozed forth.

Vs. 23.25   Ehud exited from the *misderonah* vestibule and locked the door behind him. When the courtiers returned and observed the locked doors, they assumed that the king was attending to his personal needs and desired maximum privacy. V. 25. They waited a reasonable length of time confused by this strange condition. In their confusion they unlocked the door and discovered Eglon's dead body.

Vs. 26.30   While the courtiers lingered in their confused hours, Ehud made his safe retreat to the quarries which marked the boundary line of Moab. Ehud then proceeded to Seirah, the Ephramite highlands. V. 27. Upon Ehud's safe return, he issued a call to arms in the territory of Ephraim. From here he marched them toward Moab. "Follow me for the Eternal has created the moment for us to overthrow Moabite oppression." V. 28 Ehud then issued a command to take control of all the fords of the Jordan, in the vicinity of Gilgal. Ehud was desirous of cutting off all Moabite forces now west of the Jordan and those east of the Jordan from joining together. V. 29. At this juncture they stood their ground against the army of occupation on the western side of the Jordan and those on the east trying to enter the fray. The text

JUDGES CHAPTER 3

reports the loss of about 10,000 valiant warriors. V. 30. The heroic action by Ehud's generalship gave Israel a normal peaceful period of 62 years. The 80 year period in the text includes the 18 years of the oppression.

V. 31   Shamgar the son of Anath, his name is of foreign origin and therefore we may conclude that he was the son of one of the mixed marriages. He was recognized as a man of war and therefore he was named after the goddess of war. Anath appears many times in Mari records and from the information recorded, Shamgar was recognized by his violent method in attacking his enemies. An ox-goad was a bat-like piece of wood about 10 feet long, it was shaped like the letter *lamed*. At its sides and end it was studded with metal spikes. Its basic use was to teach oxen how to plow *malmad habaker* it is from this shaped instrument that the letter lamed is derived. Shamgar was active in a period when the Seapeoples of the Aegean Sea area were driven from their homeland in the beginning of the 12th century by a tremendous tidal wave (Joshua 3:5.8) see commentary for details and Addendum in Book of Joshua. When their homeland was devastated they roamed by foot and inundated the whole Mediterranean littoral with terror and pilfering. This wave of Seapeoples arrived in the Holyland at the end of the 12th or the beginning of the 11th century BCE. Israel was experiencing the effect of these marauding bands that made the roads most dangerous. Therefore, Shamgar's natural and abnormal defensive weapon and his heroic attack with those that joined him to make the roads safe was very effective as he lashed out at these roving bands. Shamgar's leadership was limited to the southwest along the seacoast area in the territory of Judah, Simeon and Benjamin. It is therefore assumed that he originated from one of these tribes. There was no connection with Ehud, who functioned mainly in the Jordanian area and had the cooperation of the four tribes that he represented. Shamgar's effort was a limited action by a handful of men, directed specifically against these wandering marauders interested in plunder only in order to survive. These marauders are called Philistines in the text because their kinsmen who came to Canaan by the sea from Crete and possibly Cypress began to infilter the land of Gerar from the 15th century (see Gen. 26:6.7 in T.E.T.).

JUDGES CHAPTER 4

V. 1   This chapter begins decades after the death of Ehud. The effect of his leadership to unite Reuben, Gad, Benjamin and Ephraim, was completely forgotten. The Canaanites were biding their time while observing the effectiveness of assimilation. Observing the intractability of Israel's efforts to establish their new world order inscribed in their Torah, the Canaanites began to regroup. Jabin the king of Hazor determined that this was the propitious moment to take advantage of the social chaos in Israel's community.

V. 2   150 years have passed by since Joshua destroyed the major

JUDGES CHAPTER 4

forces of the coalition of kings enumerated in (Joshua 11:).
We recognize the common practice of kings assuming the names of previous dynasties, though the government has no genetic connection with the previous dynasty. For example Pharoah in Egypt, Abimelech in Gerar-Philistia and Jabin the king of Hazor in this text. All the evidence records the complete destruction of Hazor in Joshua's time. This new force under Jabin is a new regrouping of those that survived and he therefore assumed the name of Jabin of Hazor and by his influence and ego is called king of Canaan. Jabin's present state is located in Harosheth-hagoyim, in the northern Galilee, in the territory of Naphtali and Zebulun. Jabin's economy consists of handcrafted merchandise which found its distribution in the export trade of Zebulun. For details see T.E.T. (Gen. 49:13, Deut. 33:18.19) and addenda in the Eternal Torah. The ruins of the old city of Hazor are now in the vicinity of the modern kibutz of Ayeled-hashachar, in the southwest of the modern state of Israel. The Sisera in our text traces his origin to Goyim (Gen. 14:1) Gutium in Kurdistan, north of the Persian Gulf, in the area of the Zagoros Mountains.

V. 3   For 20 years the oppressive actions of the allied forces of Jabin and Sisera, oppressed the tribes in this area. During this period they armed themselves with 900 chariots introduced by the Philistines into the Holyland. Sisera and Jabin's strategy was either to absorb Israel by assimilation or to expel them from their territories. The activities of Jabin and Sisera were concentrated in the north, specifically in the territory of Naphatali and Zebulun. It was these tribes who concentrated all their efforts in the export and import trade which was their forte beginning with the 17 years of Jacob's life in Egypt. The above information grants us the opportunity to observe the development of Israel's presence in the Holyland in many areas. They were prospering economically but were failing in their national life but most importantly in the area which gave Israel its reason for being in the Holyland. Only when Israel's position and daily life becomes untenable does Israel begin to turn to the Source, that is ever mindful of human failings above all the error of its lifestyle when it assimilates the delusion of idolatry (Gen. 6:3, Ex. 34:6.7). Israel's *vayitzaku* outcry for help from its Eternal God, is the symbol that it recognized its error.

Vs. 4.5   In anticipation for this moment of return, the Eternal is ever evaluating the evolutionary process; in search for human beings dedicated to the Eternal's disciplines. It is this dedication which makes them receptive to the Eternal's inspiration, that they create the vital correction in society. History now introduces the prophetess Deborah, the wife of Lappidoth, who devoted much of her time to the cause of justice in Ramah and Bethel, in the hill country of Ephraim. Here she presided daily under the shelter of palm trees to administer justice, to all those dedicated to the disciplines of Torah law. Historically her seat of justice conforms with (Gen. 35:7.8). Here she presided and dispensed justice with mercy. Her love and

JUDGES CHAPTER 4

dedication to the Eternal won the hearts of Israel. Her inspired leadership was spontaneous as it came to the fore in this chaotic period in Israel's history.

Vs. 6.7 Deborah summoned Barak the son of Abinoam of the tribe of Naphtali. His home town was Kedesh in Naphtali. Through her message to Barak she strove to transmit her inspiration, that now was the moment to overthrow Jabin's oppressive rule. V. 7 Deborah requests Barak to issue a call to arms to the tribes of Naphtali and Ephraim. She demands that he muster 10,000 men for the purpose of defeating Jabin and his allied forces. Barak is directed to mobilize his army at Mount Tabor, south of Ephraim. Advance your forces to the wadi-Kishon to confirm your intentions to Jabin and Sisera that you intend to make the wadi-Kishon your battle ground.

Vs. 8.9 Barak agrees to follow Deborah's instructions on the condition that she join him on the battlefield as an inspiration to their united command. Should you decide not to honor my request, I shall not issue the call to arms. It is Deborah's tremendous prestige which can inspire his men to fight against the tremendous odds of a standing military force supplied with chariots and other military equipment. Deborah agrees to Barak's conditions *haloch elech imach* that not only will she lead jointly with him but will issue the call to arms to her tribe of Ephraim. It was Deborah's intention that Barak receive full credit for this military action. However, under these circumstances Barak will have to share the credit for Siserah's defeat with a woman. Tractate Sotah 44b, elaborates upon this incident and concludes that it is a mitzvah which obligates women to join their men in war against Israel's enemies. Deborah issued her call to arms in Ephraim and joined Barak in Kedesh-Naphtali.

V. 10 Barak is now sure of Deborah's unlimited cooperation. He issued a call to arms to Naphtali and Zebulun. This call must have included Issachar for their name and credit for their loyalty is recorded in Deborah's Ode. These groups numbering 10,000 men assembled at Kedesh-Naphtali and marched south to Mount Tabor, which is northeast of Emek Israel and centrally located between Naphtali, Zebulun and Issachar. From this elevation they could observe the operations of Sisera in the valley.

Vs. 11.13 The author of the book of judges anticipates the question. How did Heber the Kenite get to Kedesh Naphtali when the Kenites were located in Arad in the South? We are therefore informed that when the Kenites settled in Arad in the Negev, Heber chose to join Naphtali and settled in Zaanannim in the district of Kedesh Naphtali.

Barak's decision to rise upon Mount Tabor exposed his intentions to Sisera, who therefore mobilized his full complement of 900 chariots and their charioteers at Harosheth-hagoyim and together with his army marched directly to the wadi-Kishon.

JUDGES CHAPTER 4

V. 14 Deborah now conveyed to Barak her divine inspiration. She recognized the sequence of the battle formation is now in place just as she had visualized it in her divine inspiration. Deborah gave the command to Barak. "This is the day and now is the moment that the Eternal has designated to deliver Sisera and his army into your hands." Barak's advantageous position, the suddenness and spontaniety of the attack, plus the weight of numbers overwhelmed Sisera's mechanical advantage and his trained military force.

Vs. 15.16 Barak's split second timing, the confidence inspired by Deborah's presence gave every man in Barak's army the assurance that their leadership harmonized with the Eternal's inspiration for victory over their enemy. The speed of Barak's action created panic in Sisera's ranks. Recognizing the reality of Barak's strategy, Sisera dismounted from his chariot and fled on foot from the battlefield. Barak pressed his advantage as he pursued the retreating army in the direction of Harosheth-hagoyim. The text reports the complete destruction of Sisera's forces.

Vs. 17.18 Sisera fled in the opposite direction in the hope that he can reach the Kenite community between Kedesh-Naphtali and Zaannanim. He was on good terms with their inhabitants. Jael the wife of Heber the Kenite observing Sisera's fear encouraged him to enter her tent for safety and encouraged him to rest from his arduous pursuit. She covered him with a garment to comfort his fears.

Vs. 19.20 Reassured by Jael's thoughtfulness, Sisera requested water to quench his thirst. She ingratiated herself further into his confidence by offering him milk. Jael then covered him with a coverlet to induce him to sleep. Sisera requested that she guard the entrance to her tent and to assure those that may be seeking him that there is no one but she in the tent.

V. 21 Sisera's exhaustion and extreme fatigue lulled him into deep slumber. Jael the wife of Heber Hakeni, a member of a dignified and moral people weighs this heroic moment and prays for Divine guidance. Jael recognized this opportunity to redirect the history of Israel by destroying this sworn enemy of Israel. While weighing the facts she spontaneously seized a tent pin in one hand and grasped a hammer in the other and made her way stealthily to her sleeping guest. Her dedication rose with her indignation, should she fail Israel's cause at this critical moment. Her action was her reply as she drove the tent pin deep into the temple of Sisera's head. She did not pause in her determination until she observed the tent pin submerge itself into the ground of this sleeping enemy of Israel. Sisera's death was instantaneous; he never awakened from his deep slumber.

V. 22 Barak pursued Sisera after the destruction of his army, lest he reorganize for another opportunity to defeat Israel. Jael

JUDGES CHAPTER 4

greeted Barak with elation and confidence as she pronounced, "Come! I will direct you to the man you are pursuing." Barak entered the tent to see for himself the miracle of this day. The defeated dead body of this boasting enemy of Israel.

Vs. 23.24 Israel recognized its indebtedness to God's concept of justice. It was His inspiration that created the moment and the motivation to defeat Jabin, Sisera and their allies. V. 24 The high-point of this great moment in Israel's deliverance from years of oppressive environment under Jabin's yoke, created the incentive and stimulation, that Israel rededicate itself to the mitzvah of *horashtem* to assume full responsibility to govern its territory. Israel's victory wiped out Jabin's political and military control of Canaan.

JUDGES CHAPTER 5

V. 1 The song of Deborah stands as a literary masterpiece. It is considered on a par with the Song of Moses, written at the greatest moment in Israel's history, the Exodus from Egyptian oppression. It was the Exodus that launched Israel upon its historic destiny. A destiny which shall continue to refine its development through the disciplines of its Constitution-the Torah, until it emerges in the process of evolution to become an inspiration, "A light unto the nations of the world." The Exodus marked the birth of a nation. This victory became a turning point in Israel's history, as it rose to a new plateau. The forcefulness of its text, the sparkling diction of its nuances, its brilliant imagery conveys the anomaly of Israel's behavior as it departed from its historic destiny in the period of the Judges. Deborah describes Israel's irregularities. She envisions that Israel's rebellion is reflected and influences the movement of the planets. It is Barak that created the action while Deborah developed the animation. Together they announced their gratitude to the Eternal God of Israel for their victory over their enemies on the very day when it became a reality. Deborah and Barak equate their victory with that of Joshua.

V. 2 Scholars place the action in this chapter in the period of 1200-1125 BCE. It is also assumed to have been the last major battle against the indigenous Canaanite forces. *Bipheroa peraot* When Israel contritely acknowledged, that its disciplinary breaches were the cause which created the period (the 20 years of Jabin's oppression) the period of unfaithfulness *Sotah* (Lev. 13:45, Num. 5:18) when Israel was subjected to drink the cup of bitterness, which could have ended by banishing Israel from the Holyland. It was precisely at this critical junction that Deborah and Barak took the lead *behithnadeb am* to stimulate and to breathe new life and hope into the heartbeat of Israel. It was at this crucial juncture that the tribes of Naphtali, Zebulun, Issachar and Ephraim arose from their inertia to join hands in order to throw off the yoke of Jabin the son of Hazor. For this rededication to the

JUDGES CHAPTER 5

Eternal's cause *barchu Adonai* we are obliged to utter gratitude to the Eternal God of history.

V. 3 "Hear O you tyrants, that call yourselves kings. Be attentive to my message, you who proclaim yourselves as princes among men. *Shimu melachim* hearken to my voice you pompous kings. *Haazinu roznim* Be attentive to my message, you, who aspire to become kings. While you accredit your heroic deeds to your egos, I, *anochi LaAdonai* shall confirm my reliance upon the Eternal (Ex. 14:14). *Anochi ashirah* I shall express my gratitude to Him. *Azamer Ladonai Elohei Yisrael* I shall dedicate my Ode to the Eternal God of History. It is He that is Israel's God."

V. 4 *Adonai, betzetcha miSeir* Deborah reviews the present in light of the past. "Eternal God of History, I shall recapitualate Israel's history as it stood at the doors of Seir-Edom, to plead for peaceful passage through his territory (Deut. 2:1.8). Their negative reply challenged the Eternal's direction in history. At this critical juncture, the Eternal spread His protective canopy over His wandering horde. He inspired Israel to rededicate itself to its historic destiny. He marched them directly to Obot and on to the river Arnon." (see T.E.T. Num. 21:1.5 for details of this experience Deut. 2:4.10). Deborah recalls this critical period, "*Eretz raashah* the Earth quaked as Israel marched from the borders of Edom, determined to sweep away every obstacle in its path. *Gam shamayim natafu* The very heavens cooperated to supply Israel with manna. *Gam avim natafu mayim* The clouds sympathised with Israel's manifest destiny as it supplied it with abundant rain-water."

V. 5 Deborah describes the supernatural setting at Mount Sinai. "The normally immovable mountains quaked as the Eternal God of Israel proclaimed to mankind His Divine truth, to awaken and activate the Divine spark (the Zelem Elohim) embedded in the human soul. *Harim nazlu* Deborah is contrasting the enormity of the Divine force-His natural law, which hollows out the mountains to create pools for water. The same law polishes the pebbles to create a fountain. Yet, man having witnessed the Eternal's epic revelations, fails to reach out for its potential greatness as a human being to become a co-partner with the Eternal. *Zeh Sinai* This was the intent and purpose of My revelation at Mount Sinai. *Mipnei* This was the genesis the causality of My demand of human history. *Adonai* The Eternal God of Israel shall ever pursue His demand of Israel, that it fulfil its manifest destiny to become an inspiration to mankind, to lead the way toward the evolution of men and women who resolve to live and develop in accord with My Blueprint revealed at Mount Sinai."

Vs. 6 Having reviewed the highest moment in Israel's history, the pronouncement of the Decalogue, Deborah turns to the immediate past. It is her intention to highlight the retrogression of Israel over a period of less than two centuries. Deborah begins

JUDGES CHAPTER 5

with the record of Shamgar ben Anath (Jud. 3:3.31), to the lifetime of Jael, a period of many decades. She describes how the highways were infested by bands of marauders and thieves. The normal life of commerce ceased. Travelers were forced to take detours. They were coerced into devious paths in order to survive.

V. 7 — "*Chadlu perazon beyisrael* Unfortified communities ceased to exist in Israel, as they could not defend themselves against these marauders and pilfering bands of robbers. *Chadelu* All life in the Holyland was coming to a standstill." It was these conditions which created the demand for leadership. Deborah's leadership and fame as a judge was known locally. The critical conditions of the times demanded the dedication of a mother. Therefore her consent to become Israel's national leader had the effect of motherhood, as every Israelite became her responsibility, her children. Her dedication as a mother involved her in every detail of Israel's life.

V. 8 — *Yivchar Elohim chadashim* Israel created new spectors, apparitions and ghosts from local practices. These abominations became stumbling blocks in Israel's progress, as Israel adopted Canaanite idolatrous practices. Israel's anarchy introduced Jabin's oppressive conditions. Rebellion broke out in the cities which led to Jabin's disarming every individual Israelite. Not a spear or a shield could be found among 40,000 Israelites.

V. 9 — In Vs. 1.8, Deborah described the existing conditions when she assumed command with Barak. Deborah now describes the heroic efforts of all those who participated to stem the tide and turned Israel's hopeless condition to victory. "*Libi lechokeke Yisrael* As a mother in Israel, my heart beats in gratitude to Israel's Nesiim-governors. It was their courageous efforts that harnessed the opposition against law and order. *Hamithnadvim baam* To all those that volunteered to enlist in the army of Israel, *baruch Adonai* we offer our gratitude to them for their dedication. Their spontaneous inspiration set an example for others to follow, it merits the blessings of the Eternal God of Israel."

V. 10 — Deborah addressed her remarks to merchants, travelers and those dependent upon law and order, "You, who exult your position in society by riding upon tawny white asses, and you who expose your station in society by *yoshevei al midin* sitting in judgment upon others by your lifestyle. *Holchei al derech* You who travel about to sell your wares, *sichu* it is you, so dependent upon peace in the land, more than any group in society that owe a debt of gratitude to the Eternal God of Israel for this victory. Raise your voices in the market place in behalf of all those that endangered their lives and answered our call to arms."

V. 11 — "Raise your voices *mikol mechazezim ben mashabim* louder than the trumpeters at the central watering places. *Sham yetanu zidkot Adonai* There in the public square in the

JUDGES CHAPTER 5

presence of the multitudes chant your gratitude to the gracious acts of the Eternal God of Israel. It is He that made possible *pirzono beyisrael* the restoration of open cities in Israel. *Az yardu lashearim am Adonai* It is the Eternal's victory that made possible the rehabilitation of our cities."

V. 12 "Awaken! Awaken yourself Deborah, measure up to the demand, to the need of the hour. Inspire the whole house of Israel. Animate the leaders of Israel to utter a song of gratitude, to all those that participated in the war. Arise Barak and *usheveh shevyecha* justify your reason for taking captives, you son of Abinoam. Alert them to Israel's standards of rehabilitation. Breathe new hope into their lives. Animate them to join the family of civilization by accepting the Seven Laws of Noah. Retrain them to enter the portals of Israel. Inspire them to refine their lives under the guidance of Torah laws."

V. 13 "*Az-then* refers to (Jud. 4:14.16) This was the moment that the Eternal God of Israel delivered the mighty Sisera *leadirim am* and his mighty allies to the nobility of mankind. The Eternal's Prophetic inspiration *Adonai yerad li bagiborim* gave me the privilege to become one of the heroes."

V. 14 Deborah expresses her gratitude to those who answered the call to arms, "From Ephraim *sharasham* whose territory originally was occupied by Amalek, came the volunteers who answered the call of Deborah. From Benjamin came the hosts of dedicated *amecha* soldiers. Machir the son of Manasseh came down from the north of Trans-Jordan (Num. 32:39.41, Deut. 3.15) led by their Nesiim leaders to set an example to their dedicated soldiers. The tribes of Zebulun directed the call to arms. With their soldiers came their leaders to prove to Sisera and Jabin, the pen is mightier than the sword."

V. 15 "Standing side by side with Barak and Deborah were the Nesiim-leaders of Issachar as they led their soldiers into the heat of battle in the valley of the Emek. Contrasting Isaachar's tenacity and spontaneous response to Barak's command, the tribe of Reuben was divided in many factions. *Biflagoth Reuben* Their response was missing because they lacked the determination and dedication. They were involved in determining their self interest." For a composite historical record of the tribe of Reuben see (T.E.T. Deut. 33:6).

V. 16 Deborah now expressed her contempt to the tribes that failed to respond to Israel's call to arms. "Reuben ... Why did you remain among the sheepfolds? Was the bleating of your sheep of greater consequence than the distressful cry of your brethren? *Liphlagoth Reuben* Reuben's factions and inner conflict must have been involved *im chikre lev* with the problem of searching your soul for an answer to Israel's question, where is Reuben?"

JUDGES CHAPTER 5

V. 17 — Gilead in this verse refers to the tribe of Gad and the families of Jair and Nobach of Manasseh, that did not reply to Barak and Deborah's call to arms. "Gilead, you, who are our immediate neighbors and dwell east of the Jordan River, you have failed Israel in its greatest moment of distress. Deborah challenged the tribe of Dan, whose territory northwest of the Argob, is Laish-Dan. What is your excuse? *Yagur aniyot* What motivated your decision to remain with your ships? Were you fearful of rocking the commercial boat with the Phoenicians and the Philistines? Was your loyalty to them greater than aiding your brethren at this critical moment in their history?" See Addenda in T.E.T. on pages 261, 553 for Dan's involvement in international marine commerce.

Asher's territory bordered the Mediterranean. They were involved with Dan, Asher and Zebulun in the maritime affairs of the Middle East. They held a co-prosperity treaty with the Phoenicians and the Philistines. Deborah pours forth her cryptic ironic and sarcastic question to Asher. "What is your excuse for not heeding the call of Israel? Her irony spurts forth the answer *veal mifretzav yishkon*. Were you more concerned with the bays of Gebol, Acco, Sidon and Beirut, than Jabin's threat to expel Israel from the Holyland?" (Asher was the caretaker of these ports for Dan, Asher and Zebulun).

V. 18 — Deborah contrasts Zebulun as *am cheref nafsho* though vitally involved in the above maritime projects, Zebulun jeopardized their lives unto death. There were no conditions or limits to their involvement and dedication to come to the aid of their brethren to defeat their common enemy. Deborah equates the dedication of Naphtali, who answered Barak's call to arms with the dedication of Zebulun. "With fearless courage they scaled *al meromeh sadeh* Mount Tabor at the direction of their leader Barak. Fearlessly they imperilled their lives as they rose to the rigorous demand of the battlefield which culminated in the wadi-Kishon."

V. 19 — Deborah describes the action of the war in detail. When the Canaanite forces mobilized to destroy Israel's forces at Taanach, they made their stand at the waters of Megiddo-Nahr-el Lejjun, which flows into the Kishon-Nahr-el Muqatta. Taanach's history goes back to 2700 BCE. Taanach was destroyed many times during the next 1400 years. It was rebuilt again in 1300 BCE. Archaeological researches fix the dates of the war led by Barak and Deborah against Jabin and Sisera between 1125-1100 BCE. Jabin and his allies fought with the intention of dividing the north of the Holyland from the South and then create two separate actions. One shall destroy every northern community and the other will destroy every community southward until every Israelite is banished from the Holyland. Sisera, the commander in chief of the allied forces deployed his army along the Kishon, from Megiddo to Taanach. Barak deployed his forces on Mount Tabor. He chose this position because it gave him total command over the whole Jezreel Valley. Deborah now gives us an overview of Jabin who spoke for all the opposing

JUDGES CHAPTER 5

forces of the Canaanites and tells us what their intentions were. "*Betzah kesef* They intended to plunder but were forced to retreat quite emptyhanded, *lo lakachu* they took nothing from Israel. Even those that survived Israel's onslaught were fortunate to escape alive."

V. 20   Deborah vividly portrays her visual and prophetic concept of the battlefield from the heights of Mount Tabor. "It was the Eternal God of Israel, Who mobilized His forces in the heavens above (Ex. 14:14). The stars in their orbit harmonized with Israel's need. From the heavens came a freshet which inundated the whole plain of the Kishon, to mire Sisera's chariots into a sea of mud. The Eternal's heavenly bodies offset the odds created by Sisera's allies and their superior military armaments."

V. 21   "*Nahal Kishon gerafam* The normally modest Kishon swelled with pride as it swept Israel's enemies off their feet. *Nahal kedumim* This ancient humble and modest stream fought Israel's battle with pride as it performed to the demand of *hakochavim mimsilotham* the heavenly bodies which rule the seasons from their orbit. *Tidrechi nafshi oz* My soul was girded with strength as I urged Israel's army to pursue the enemy with determination."

V. 22   "*Az halmu ikve sus* This was the epic moment, when the heavens and the Kishon performed in harmony to mire the hooves of their horses into the muddy plain. *Midharoth daharoth abirav* The egotistical arrogance of the charioteers stimulated the massive confusion, as the fleeing horses responded by prancing and pounding their hooves ever deeper into the mud of the plain."

V. 23   Deborah is the *malach Adonai* it is she that is performing in accord with His inspiration. Deborah proclaims a curse upon the inhabitants of Meroz-al Ruz (near al-Lajjun). They failed to answer the call to arms nor did they make an effort to capture Sisera when he fled. The inhabitants of Meroz failed to identify themselves with Barak and Deborah. The inhabitants of Meroz had become enslaved by Jabin. This was their opportunity to become emancipated; yet they failed themselves and the people of Israel. Deborah's curse is vocal. Its enduring effect is to bore deep into their conscience to awaken their potential as human beings.

Vs. 24.25   Deborah contrasts the heroic act of Jael, the wife of Heber the Kenite. "Most blessed of women is Jael in the household of Israel. May the Eternal God's blessings in (Deut. 28:1.8) come to pass in her lifetime to reward her faith and trust in the Eternal God of Israel. Jael's faith is the psychological secret weapon which destroyed Sisera and turned Jabin's tyranny into a rout." V. 25, graphically illustrates the scene at Jael's tent. "Though Sisera asked for water, she offered him milk. She recognized his position in his society and served him elegantly with curd."

JUDGES CHAPTER 5

Vs. 26.27   Despite her good manners, Jael was sensitive to Sisera's despotic and brutal conduct. Determined to avenge his cruelty upon her people, Jael firmly held a tent pin in her left hand; resolved to avenge all of Sisera's brutal and despotic persecution. She grasped a workman's hammer and pounded the tent pin into Sisera's head (Jud. 4:21). *Umachatzah vechalfah rakato* With dispatch and devotion to her people Jael punctured and pierced through Sisera's temple. "At her feet he lay outstretched as he sank into everlasting sleep. The slumber of death *Shadud* plundered his lifelong arrogance."

V. 28   Deborah describes a scene which took place in many Israelite homes during the 20 years of Jabin's despotic oppression as mothers anxiously awaited their children who never again returned. The subject now is Sisera's mother. "Sisera's mother looked through the window, with anxiety she strained her vision as she peered through the lattice. *Madua echaru* Why is his chariot late in coming home? What has muted *paame markevotab* the rythm of the prancing charioteers?"

Vs. 29.30   "Her ladies in waiting perceive her anxiety and strive to console her, while she strives to reconcile her unjustified concern. Blustering with pride of past experiences, she jests; they must be having difficulty to divide the booty or perhaps their dilemma of choosing a *rechem-a womb* a consort or two for each soldier. (A practice forbidden in (Deut. 21:10.14). Sisera's mother humors her fears. Perhaps the soldiers are delayed while choosing a dyed garment befitting his rank or perhaps they are delayed trying to find embroidered neckpieces."

V. 31   Deborah concludes her Ode with a prayerful wish; "May Sisera's doom become an example for every future tyrant who strives to surpress human dignity. May he be punished by Divine judgment. *Veohavav* May those who recognize the Eternal's Blueprint for living the good and contented life perceive the effectiveness of the Eternal God's directives. *Ketzet hashemesh bigevuratho* May every human being who chooses to live by His Divine disciplines inscribed in the Torah, become the force to be endowed with the dedication to contain every wicked endeavor. May their effectiveness become as powerful as the sun when it reaches its zenith in the firmament of the universe as Israel reaches its manifest destiny, to become a light unto mankind." Deborah prays for the day when all of mankind will join hands to keep the wicked forces from infecting the moral and ethical fibre of the genetic progress of all humanity.

(Jud. 4:3) From the low point recorded in this verse, the prophet Samuel records 20 peaceful years after the destruction of Jabin and Sisera. The territories of Naphtali, Zebulun, Issachar and Manasseh in Trans-Jordan experienced the effectiveness of normal living. The tranquility of these latter years wiped out the misery of the past. Therefore the text reports 40 years of quietude and peace.

JUDGES CHAPTER 6

Vs. 1.3 Examining the record established in the previous chapter, we find the families of Jair and Novach of Manasseh, the tribe of Gad and the tribe of Reuben completely missing from Deborah and Barak's united effort. Deborah has cryptically pronounced her displeasure with these tribes in Trans-Jordan for their unfaithfulness to Israel's national cause in the Holyland. It is this disloyalty that gave Midian the audacity to do in Trans-Jordan what Jabin hoped to accomplish west of the Jordan, to banish Israel from the Holyland. The period we are about to deal with in this chapter is about 1100 BCE. Looking back upon these symptoms which were offensive in the eyes of the Eternal God of history, we see the nucleus of problems which will surface generations later.

The Eternal God has inspired mankind through his Zelem-Elohim embedded in his soul, the capacity to expand his intelligence to learn His Natural Law. When the Eternal God inspired Moses to write down these laws which had been evolving in the human experience over millenia, they became the guidelines by which every human being can live and prosper. To desecrate these laws is to begin to die. When man or woman bypasses these disciplines, they sow the seeds of infection into the environment which find their way into the genetic process of evolution. Every human being has the responsibility to pass on the progress they have inherited to the the next generation. Now let us examine the record of history. Midian is a direct descendant of Abraham (Gen. 25:2). Midian's territory is northern Hejaz, east of Akabah. Periodically it extended itself eastward toward Moab. Moab too, is related to Abrahm (Gen. 19:30.38). This is also the genealogy of Ammon. The effectiveness of Midian's expansion was implemented in this period by the chaos existing in Trans-Jordan. The Midianites as descendants of Abraham recognized Israel's rights in the Holyland. Therefore it made no effort to conquer territory. It simply exercised its ancient way of life of marauding wherever and whenever it observed weakness in a community (Num. 25:16.19, 20:14.21). For seven years Midian plundered and pillaged the tribes in Trans-Jordan. The Israelites were forced to establish *minharot* dens or lookout posts in the mountains from which they can observe the enemy. They hid their possessions in *mearot* caves and created *metzadoth* fortresses from which to attack those who came to plunder them. Midian is joined by the Amalekites and the Semitic children in the east (Gen. 29:1). We may assume this refers to the same allies described in (Jud. 3:13) meaning Ammon and Moab.

Vs. 4.5 The text now describes their method of pilfering and plundering. When the Israelites finished plowing and seeding their fields, the Midianites and their allies would raid the tribal territories, destroy the new growth and any perennial standing crops. Their plundering spread across the Jordan in the direction of Azza-Gaza. They deprived the settlements of their food supplies, they devastated the condition of the soil which made it extremely difficult to reseed a new crop and above all they did not leave a sheep or an ox or an ass, depriving the Israelites of their use for food or replowing and reseeding the land. These Bedouin nomadic hordes would

JUDGES CHAPTER 6

swoop down upon Israel's communities with their countless camels, cattle, sheep and goats, like locusts they destroyed everything in sight. Midian's intent was to force the Israelites to abandon the land.

V. 6 Israel's weakened and impoverished condition turned their thoughts inward as every indicator of their depression pointed to their failures to live by guidelines inscribed in the Torah. They now confess to their conscious awakening that they failed their Manifest Destiny in the Holyland. Recognizing their hopeless condition, they turn to the historical Source of human hope. In distress they cried out to the Eternal God of Israel, to come to their aid before they disappear as individuals and as a people.

V. 7 It has taken Israel centuries mired in oppression and depression to fully grasp their place in history. Their dependence and security were vouchsafed by the Eternal, subject to their dedication to live by the disciplines inscribed in the Eternal God's Torah. *Vayehi ki zaaku* Israel must recognize these everlasting truths, that when man falters, it is because he lacks the ability to rise by himself. The Eternal God is ever consistently patient (Gen. 6:3, Ex. 34:6.7) and hopeful that mankind will mend its ways of living to conform with guidelines inscribed in his genes for progressive evolution. The Eternal waits for the bud of man's humanity to inspire his daily living.

Vs. 8.9 Israel's repentance brings forth the Eternal's response. *Vayishlach Adonai ish Navi* The Eternal chose from the ranks of the ever loyal remnant, one who recognizes the Finger of the Eternal God in human history. A prophet is no star gazer. He is no visionary with a chimera for delusion. A prophet is one that analyzes the facts of cause and effect in order to introduce meaning into daily living. The prophet in this text is a descendant of Phinehas. He admonishes Israel with the same theme used in (Jud. 2:1.5). He enlarges upon this format by quotations from (Lev. 11:45, Ex. 20:2, Deut. 6:1.15, 32:1.29). This is the consistent format followed by every prophet in Israel.

V. 10 The prophet who speaks in the name of the Eternal, strives to stimulate and to encourage this generation not to fear the Amorites, referring to any group that may challenge Israel's rights in the Holyland. Your fears are the psychological effect of your inattentiveness to the voice of the Eternal God of history. It is the result of your guilt complex for deviating from your manifest destiny in history.

Vs. 11.12 The prophet in vs. 8.10, has succeeded in activating the consciences of his audience, however, there was no effort on their part to resolve their problem by implementing a plan for their salvation from the oppression in their communities. It is the prophet that now becomes *Malach Adonai* the one who shall initiate the Eternal's consistent mercy. It is the Eternal that recognizes human shortcomings (Gen. 6:3). It is His

JUDGES CHAPTER 6

long suffering patience (Ex. 34:6.7) that grants mankind the opportunity to rise upon the evolutionary ladder until he recognizes the Eternal's goals for humankind. The *malach Adonai* is striving to implement his inspiration for a solution of Israel's dilemma. His destination is Ophrah, there he sat down under a terebinth tree on the property of Joash, a descendant of the family of Abiezer, of the tribe of Manasseh, in Trans-Jordan (Num. 26:29.30, Joshua 17:2). The Eternal's messenger has already concluded that Gideon the son of Joash is the long sought leader who can become the man of the hour. He therefore sat under the tree to admire the skill and deftness of Gideon as he was threshing wheat in the winepress, where he threshes a small quantity at a time. He then stores it safely in one of the caves, to keep it from the marauding Midianites. From this verse we learn the extent of Israel's poverty. He threshes wheat in a winepress because he does not own an ox.

V. 12 The *malach* presents himself before Gideon. I have been observing your efficient and intelligent method of working. I conclude from your successful procedure that you are a man of valor and courage. Your faith in the Eternal God grants you the self-reliance to overcome the oppressive conditions of the times.

V. 13 Gideon is provoked by the *malach*-messenger's conclusion in v. 12, *Adonai imcha*. "If the Eternal God of Israel is with us as you imply, why has all this misfortune befallen us? Where are the miracles about which our parents and grandparents have been assuring us (Ex. 13:14, Deut. 6:4.8)? What was the intent of delivering us from the Egyptians *veatah netashtanu Adonai* only to abandon us now to every mercenary and marauding oppressor, such as Midian and Amalek?" Gideon's sincere query can be equated with Moses' indignation and plea in (Ex. 32:11.13).

V. 14 The *malach* now identifies himself to Gideon. "I speak with the authority of the Eternal God of history (Ex. 3:10). I, the Eternal's messenger recognize your sensitivity and sincere concern with Israel's problems. I therefore charge you in His name *lech bechochacha Zeh* go forth and dedicate your zealous sensitivity and indignation which you have demonstrated to me for the purpose of helping the plight of your people. Your conscious awareness confirms your capability to help Israel in the name of the Eternal."

Vs. 15.16 Gideon recognizes the reality of the situation. He now addresses the *malach* on a man to man basis. "What are my qualifications to help Israel? My family is the poorest in the tribe of Manasseh. I am the youngest in my immediate family." V. 16 Gideon's modesty parallels and is analagous with that of Moses in (Ex.4:10.17). The *malach* gives Gideon the same assurance received by Moses *ki eheyeh imach* (Ex. 3:14). This is the ineffable name of the Eternal God engraved in the genes of man from creation when He created the nucleus of all living matter. "Examine and search your conscience to discover your potential strength which only awaits

JUDGES CHAPTER 6

your implementation. You shall then defeat the multitudes of Israel's enemies as if they were but one man."

Vs. 17.18   "I am grateful for your confidence in choosing me. Although I recognize your authority as the messenger of the Eternal, and in keeping with the dedication of my forefathers (Gen. 15:8, Ex. 3:12), I request a sign that shall confirm your authority, that you indeed speak with the authority of the Eternal God of Israel."

V. 18   Gideon is desirous of expressing his gratitude to God by a gift offering. He requests that the messenger remain until he can prepare his gift offering.

Vs. 19.21   Gideon went into his house, he baked unleavened bread and prepared a kid. He then placed the meat in a basket and poured the broth into a pot and presented it to the messenger waiting under the terebinth tree. *Malach Adonai*, is the Eternal God's messenger. The dialogue in vs. 15.18, gave Gideon the inspiration to recognize the plea of the messenger, in the name of *Elohim*, the Justice of Israel's cause. He therefore prepared a gift offering in gratitude for having been singled out to assume Israel's leadership. Gideon anticipated that the messenger would refresh himself by eating his cooked food. Gideon was instructed by the messenger to pour out the broth upon the rock. This made it clear that he is still *malach Adonai* and therefore, it must be offered only to *Adonai*. Gideon placed the meat and the unleavened bread upon the rock. The *malach* touched the meat and the unleavened bread with the tip of his staff, the flame rose and consumed the meat and the bread upon the rock. While Gideon concentrated on the meaning of the offering and his encounter with *malach Adonai* that he is now fully committed to initiate a plan of action in order to defeat Israel's enemies, when he looked up the *malach* was gone.

V.22   Gideon's involvement came in three stages. In vs. 11.13, Gideon assumed he was the host of a distinguished guest. In vs. 14.19 Gideon concluded that his guest was a prophet. In vs. 20.23, Gideon fully realized that he was indeed confronted and challenged by *Malach Adonai* one who was inspiring him to create and implement a plan to throw off the yoke of oppression of his brethren in the name of the Eternal God of Israel.

V. 23   In keeping with mankind's common and popular conception of the text in (Ex. 33:20) that none can see the face of God and live, the Eternal God penetrated into Gideon's conscience, to assure him that he will not die. It is his task to become a copartner with the Eternal God of history in the management of the universe. "Peace be with you Gideon, try not to see God but perceive His Presence on an I-Thou basis. Only humans who cannot perceive God in their lives cease to be and live like human beings."

JUDGES CHAPTER 6

V. 24 — Gideon built an altar as a memorial to remind him and all future generations of his encounter with the Eternal God and his struggle with his *Zelem Elohim-intelligence*, to comprehend the Eternal's guidelines for ruling the universe. Gideon called his altar *Adonai Shalom* the Eternal's objective for all humankind that they strive to live in peace. The prophet Samuel reports in this verse that during his lifetime when he recorded the book of Judges, Gideon's altar stood intact in his hometown in Ephrath in the territory of his family Haezri-Abiezer.

V. 25 — That very night after his encounter with the Eternal God, recorded in vs. 11-24, he resolved to implement two positive commandments (Ex. 34:13, Deut. 16:21). By destroying idolatry in his own home, Gideon set an example for others to follow. Gideon destroyed his father's altar designated for the worship of Baal and the *Asherah-tree* planted next to the altar. It was customary to breed animals specifically for this purpose. Gideon took the sire of the young bull which was reserved for Baal worship and slaughtered it upon the altar before he destroyed it. (The bull was kept for seven years to insure continuity).

Vs. 26.27 — Gideon then built an altar *al rosh hamaoz* upon the flat side of the rock, where he had offered his gift offering *bamaarachah*.

He then took the young bull which was intended for Baal worship and sacrificed it upon his altar and built a fire to burn it with the *Asherah* which he had cut down. V. 27 gives the reason why Gideon offered sacrifices at night when it was not permitted. He anticipated reprisals for his action and therefore took ten men to defend his desecration of their idolatrous worship and did it at a time when none were about. The intent of this whole procedure was to establish Gideon's own dedication. By carrying out these instructions he endangered his own life as he faced reprisals from the whole community.

Vs. 28.32 — The next morning the townspeople discovered the extent of the destruction of their altar and the two bulls. V. 29. They instituted an inquiry and concluded that it was Gideon the son of Joash that was the culprit. V. 30. They confronted Joash with the facts and charged Joash to produce his son Gideon to punish him for his desecration of their god.

V. 31 Joash challenged their presumptuousness, "If Baal is a god, let him fight his own battles. Let Baal vindicate himself by destroying him that is guilty of this offensive act."

V. 32 The townspeople reconciled Joash's logic and openly stated *yirev habaal-Jerubaal* let the Baal fight his own battle to justify his position against Gideon. From this verbal picture we can grasp the extent of Israel's retrogression from Torah disciplines.

V. 33 — Midian, Amalek and the bnei kedem-Arameans organized

JUDGES CHAPTER 6

their forces to begin their seasonal marauding and pilfering as described in v.3. They crossed the Jordan River westward and camped in the valley of Jezreel, cradled between Mount Carmel and Mount Tabor, where it branches off at Beth Shean. From here it is overpowered by Mount Hermon and Mount Gilboa.

Vs. 34.36 Gideon evaluated the situation and he issued a call to his own immediate family. When they responded he felt encouraged, he then sent messengers to Zebulun and Naphtali to mobilize. (Gideon is unaware what happened to these messengers. (See Jud. 8:18, for details). There are many incidents in history where genuine leaders challenge their manifest destiny (Gen. 15:1.8, Ex. 3:11.12). Gideon is challenging his own ability to lead a military action. Gideon is seeking a symbol that his encounter with the *malach Adonai* was authentic. He denigrates his ability to become an instrument of the Eternal. He challenged his right to cause others to jeopardize their lives in an action that could fail.

Vs. 37.40 Gideon chooses the fleece of sheep as his symbol. He is knowledgeable of its natural law under which it functions. He decides to place the newly shorn fleece of sheep upon the threshing floor that under normal conditions would create dampness upon the floor. Gideon conditions his symbol, that the fleece absorb the atmospheric dew, while the ground beneath the fleece remains dry.

V. 38 Gideon rose early the next morning before sunrise. He pressed the fleece to test it. He then wrung a bowlful of water from the fleece while the floor remained dry.

V. 39 Gideon's selfdoubt seeks reassurance for his conclusion. He requests that the fleece remain dry while the area underneath the fleece become moist.

V. 40 That very evening Gideon examined the fleece and was satisfied that it alone was dry, while the area underneath was damp from the dew. Gideon's self doubt has been resolved. The effect of his experiment has bolstered his courage. He is now ready to set out upon a predestined mission.

JUDGES CHAPTER 7

Vs. 1.3 Gideon-Jerubaal arose the very next morning to assume the leadership of the men who answered his call to arms. They marched to the well of Harod-Ain-jalud, at the foot of Mount Gilboa, in the valley of Jezreel. Here they set up their camp. The Midianites were camped north of Gibeon, in the valley of Gibeath-moreh.

V. 2. Gideon is overwhelmed by the response to his call. The weight of numbers in his ranks challenged the strategy of his military action to totally defeat the Midianites.

V. 3. Gideon reached back into Torah law (Deut. 20:8) to create an army of excellence. He bid all those desirous to become exempt from this action to return to their homes. *Veyitzpor* take the shortest route (make a beeline home like a

JUDGES CHAPTER 7

bird). Early the next morning 22,000 men who claimed exemption left the mountain of Gilead-Ein-charod. 10,000 men remained with Gideon secure in their resolution to stay the action to defeat the Midianites.

Vs. 4.5 Gideon's strategy calls for fewer numbers. The remnant that fits his needs must prove their dedication to qualify for his army. He therefore devised another test that shall prove their past conduct to Israel's disciplines. He marched his men to the spring of Harod, to observe how they drink water from the stream. *Vehayah asher omar elecha* Gideon is inspired to conclude, that only those who have resisted the idolatrous assimilation with the indigenous settlers have the courage to resist environmental temptation, and remain dedicated to Torah principles. Gideon's test was to single out those who genuflected-bowed before the idol Baal and those who were ever conscious of the inference conveyed by this posture.

V. 6. Only 300 men out of his army of 10,000, met his criteria by lapping water with their hands, while the rest knelt because their subconscious reflex became fixed in their habits. 9,700 men were rejected because Gideon used the Eternal's inspiration *bochen kelayot valev* to test their inner strength. *Lo yelech imach* is Gideon's inspired resolution. "These 9,700 men shall not go with you for they have not met the test. They could jeopardize My plan for your success."

Vs. 7.8 The subtle test conveyed its message to the majority that were disqualified. Gideon's selectivity conveyed its full meaning to those that were disqualified. There will be no submission to idolatry nor to Midian's tyranny. Those excused from serving in this action transferred their food supplies to the 300 men selected for military service. The group commanders also transferred their trumpets. Gideon's selectivity *hechesik* reinforced the resolution of Gideon's hand picked army as they left Ein-charod at the foot of Mount Gilboa. From here they marched in the secrecy of the night to Gibeat Hamoreh. From this elevated position they kept their enemy under surveillance in the valley of the Emek. Midian was aware of Israel's mobilization of a large army. They therefore paid no attention to a small band marching in the distance.

Vs. 9.14 Gideon is inspired to recognize the timing of his action. V.10. His conservative and humble attitude seeks additional confirmation for his conclusion. Gideon therefore took his armor bearer Purah to reconnoiter the Midianite camp. V. 11. Approaching closer, he listened attentively to discern any tension in the Midianite camp. V. 12. Getting closer he made a mental note of the vast number of men and camels encamped in the valley.

V. 13 Reaching the edge of the vanguard, Gideon overheard a soldier narrating a dream to his neighbor. "I dreamed that a loaf of barley bread is whirling in the Midianite camp. It then struck a tent which flopped about as it collapsed."

JUDGES CHAPTER 7

V. 14 The listener replied, "These symbols would indicate that Gideon the son of Joash, is running rampant among our camp with sword in hand. It indicates Gideon's confidence, that the God of Israel has surrendered the Midianites into his hands."

Vs. 15.18 Gideon analyzed the effect of the dream upon the dreamer *veshivro* and the breakdown of the constituent parts of its symbolism. Gideon expressed his gratitude to the Eternal for having endowed him with the sensitivity to remain attentive and alert to His directives. He returned to camp to reinforce the courage of his men. He strove to instill confidence and resolution into their hearts. "We shall succeed in overcoming their numbers for the Eternal has confounded our enemy (Ex. 23:27)."

V. 16 Gideon divided his 300 men into three separate groups. Each man was equipped with a ram's horn and a torch concealed in an earthen jar.

V. 17 Gideon instructed his men to follow his directions throughout the attack. He explained the importance of split-second timing in exposing their covered torches, not only to confound the enemy but to convey the message that their only avenue of escape is eastward toward the Jordan River.

V. 18 Wait for my signal to blow your ram's horn from your position in the north, the south and the west, that the sound surround and confuse the Midianites. This is the moment to announce our pledge, our dedication to the Eternal God of Israel and to the leadership of Gideon.

Vs. 19.22 The night is divided into three parts for guard duty. The first began at 6 P.M. the second at 10 P.M. Gideon arrived at the outer edge of the Midianite camp at the beginning of the middle watch at 2 A.M. just as the sleepy guards assumed their positions; while the slumbering multitude were in their deepest sleep. At this exact moment the three groups harmonized the blasts of their horns, they shattered their earthen jars to expose their burning torches.

V. 20 They secured their torches into their left hands and the ram's horn in their right hand and initiated their battle cry. "We raise the sword in the cause of the Eternal God of Israel and we pledge our loyalty to Gideon our leader."

V. 21 Gideon's three legions surrounded the Midianite camp and observed the pandemonium in the ranks of the enemy as they fled toward the east, the only avenue open for retreat.

V. 22 Gideon issued the order for the blast of the horns and the beginning of their charge in pursuit of the fleeing masses. They fled in the direction of the only uninhabited area between Bet-shitah and Zererah, close to the border-line of Abel-mecholah near Tabbath.

Vs. 23.25 In (Jud. 6:35, 8:18) Gideon had sent messengers to alert Zebulun and Naphtali. They were cut off. From this verse we learn that Gideon sent another set of messengers to Naphtali, Asher and throughout Manasseh, with instructions to cut the Midianites off, to

JUDGES CHAPTER 7

keep them from recrossing the Jordan River at Beth-barah or any of the other fords near by.

V. 24 confirms that this time the messengers got through to Ephraim and it was they that manned all the crossable fords.

V. 25 Ephraim pursued the Midianites and captured two of their generals, Oreb and Zeeb. They killed Oreb at the Rock of Oreb and Zeeb at the winepress of Zeeb. They then brought the heads of Oreb and Zeeb to Gideon in Trans-Jordan. He had crossed into Midianite territory in pursuit of Zebach and Zalmunna, who were responsible for the death of Gideon's brothers described in chapter 8.

JUDGES CHAPTER 8

Vs. 1.3 — Gideon is of the tribe of Manasseh. Manasseh and Ephraim are the sons of Joseph (Gen. 48:5). The tribe of Ephraim took Gideon to task for having bypassed them in his first call to arms in his battle against Midian. "How could you have ignored us, when the battlefield was close to our territory?"

V. 2 Gideon's reply is brief to the point and indicated his diplomatic leadership. "How can you compare my efforts with your results?" Your gleanings *oleloth* the capture of Oreb and Zeeb, are far greater than the *"mibtzir"* the vintage of Abiezer-Gideon's father."

V. 3 Gideon's reply passified their resentment as he built up their ego. "It is true I organized the operation. I made the plans and led the dedicated soldiers. However, it is your good fortune to have made the greater contribution to the defeat of Midian."

Vs. 4.6 — Gideon and his men are in pursuit of Zebach and Zalmunna. They arrived in Succoth in the territory of the tribe of Gad (Joshua 13:27). Gideon requested some bread to succor his famished soldiers, so that he can continue his pursuit of the kings of Midian, Zebach and Zalmunna. V. 6. The tribe of Gad were loyal to the Midianites and therefore they refused to help Gideon, in fear of reprisals against them. "You talk as if Zebah and Zalmunna have already surrendered to you." They continued to challenge his ability to overcome the formidable odds. This incident reflects the tremendous schism in the ranks of the Israelites in Trans-Jordan.

Vs. 7.9 — Gideon replied to the leaders of Succoth, "I take an oath that when I succeed in accomplishing my goal, I shall return to punish you for this act of treason. I shall thrash your bodies with wild briers and thorns."

V. 8 Gideon continued eastward in pursuit of the kings of Midian. When he arrived at Penuel, near the Jabbok River (in the territory of Gad) Gideon made the same request and was refused. They too doubted Gideon's ability to accomplish his goal.

V. 9 Astonished at their betrayal and inhuman act, Gideon spoke his mind. "When I return in peace from my mission, I shall establish the source of our

JUDGES CHAPTER 8

faith which gives us the courage to pursue our just cause. Contrast our faith in the Eternal God of Israel with your faith and trust in this fortress which sits on the hill. You are dependent upon it to protect you from the enemies that surround you. Your faithlessness and treasonous conduct challenges our relationship. I vow to destroy this fortress into which you have placed your trust, when I return in peace from my mission."

Vs. 10.12   Zebach and Zalmunna escaped with but a remnant of their large force, to Karkar, east of the Dead Sea. V. 11. Gideon pursued his goal and continued through Bedouin territory east of Nobach and Jogbehah. The Midianites retreated here and assumed they were safe and out of Gideon's reach. V.12. Gideon routed the whole camp in his search for Zebach and Zalmunna. He was intent upon destroying the root and branch of Midianite leadership. He therefore terrorized the Midianites as they fled, Gideon captured his long sought after prey, Zebach and Zalmunnah. (Jagbehah borders Midian on the eastern side of Gad's territory. Karkar is an area of springs in a valley cradled by mountains).

Vs. 13.17   Gideon is now on his way back from his battle with Midian at the ascent of Heres. V. 14. By chance he encountered a young man who lived in Succoth, Gad. He requested and received from him the names of the 77 elders responsible for their refusal to supply him with food for his men on his way eastward (Jud.8:5.7).
V. 15 "Here are Zebach and Zalmunna, *heraftem othi* for which you taunted me when I requested food for my men who fought your battles."
V. 16. Gideon gathered the elders of Succoth and charged them for their refusal to succor his men. He then took clusters of thorns and briers from the wilderness to teach them the meaning and the consequences of their cruel conduct.
V. 17. Gideon continued on to Penuel (Jud. 8:8.9) to make good his threat, to punish them for refusing to supply him with food for his men. When he started to destroy their fortress in accord with his warning, the men of the city defended their position. *Vayaharog* indicates that in the course of their resistance some paid with their lives.

Vs. 18.19   In (Jud. 6:35) Gideon sent messengers to alert Manasseh, Zebulun and Naphtali, to mobilize for war. These messengers were intercepted and killed by Zebach and Zalmunna. He now requests from his captives that they produce the bodies of his brothers that were killed at Mount Tabor, that he may identify them. Zebach and Zalmunna assure Gideon that they looked like him. "They looked like the sons of a king. Their stature and facial appearance resembled you. We therefore assumed they were your sons."
V. 19 Gideon replied. "These were my brothers, the children of my mother. Had you delivered them to me alive, I would have spared your lives. I now have no alternative but to avenge them."

JUDGES CHAPTER 8

Vs. 20.21 Gideon called upon his first-born son Jether to draw his sword. Because of his youth he demurred from the task. Zebach and Zalmunna, demanded that Gideon a man of vigor and resolution make the ordeal of defeat brief. Their heroic minds would feel shattered should a mere boy destroy their egos. Gideon complied with their request and delivered the coup de grace. He then removed their leadership insignia-crescents from their camel.

Vs. 22.23 The body of men that fought with Gideon initiated a petition and it was confirmed by the popular consensus, that Gideon become the first king in Israel, with the proviso that his sons and their posterity shall succeed him. Gideon replied, "I will not rule over you, nor shall my posterity rule over you. Only the Eternal God of Israel shall be your ruler."

V. 24 Gideon is desirous to establish a memorial in Ophrah-Manasseh to parallel the one in Shiloh-Ephraim, to commemorate their victory over Midian. The singular purpose of the Ephod in the Torah is to remind the kohen of his dedication to the unity of all the individual tribes of Israel. From Gideon's conduct on the record, we cannot conclude that he had any other intention. For this purpose Gideon requested a united contribution from all the tribes that fought the battle with Midian-Amalek-bnei-kedem, for the glory of the Eternal God of Israel. Gideon made no request in his own behalf, he had already refused the highest honor that Israel could offer him. He now requested that each man surrender one of the golden nose-rings which they had taken as booty from the Ishmaelim and the Midianim. These two names have become interchangeable by tradition. Their genealogy goes back to Abraham and Keturah-Hagar (Gen. 25:1.2, 16:15).

Vs. 25.26 By unanimous agreement they spread a coverlet and each man made his contribution to the general collection.

V. 26 These nose rings totalled 1700 shekels (a shekel is equal to 13 grams of gold. 13 x 1700=22,100 grams of gold). They also contributed *saharonim* golden crescents, *netiphoth* pearl eardrops and luxurious purple garments worn by the kings of Midian. They also contributed the golden chains worn ornamentally about the necks of the camels.

Vs. 27.28 Gideon melted down all this gold and had it reconstructed into an *Ephod-Choshen mishpat* (see comm. in T.E.T. on Ex. 28:4.30). Gideon is inspired by (Num. 31:50.54) after a war with Midian in Moses's lifetime. Gideon's well intentioned memorial to their victory was set up in Ophrah Manasseh. In principle it desecrated the basic warning given in (Ex. 20:1.5) for it became an oracle by which the people of Israel sought answers to their destiny, fate and fortune. From the records of this experience we derive a graphic picture of Israel's retrogression. Gideon's *memorial* in Ophrah-Manasseh was conceived and conformed with the primitive

JUDGES CHAPTER 8

mentality of its environment. The Tabernacle in Shiloh and its *Choshen Mishpat*, is a concept which even the popular mentality of 20th century man has difficulty in grasping in order to implement its teachings as a guide for living.

V. 28 Offsetting Gideon's blunder is the historic record of Gideon's accomplishments. After seven years of oppression by Midian and their allies, Israel enjoyed 33 years of tranquility in the lifetime of Gideon.

Vs. 29.32 Gideon-Jerubaal the son of Joash, retired to his home in Ophrah. He concentrated upon his personal domestic affairs.

In keeping with the times and his popularity as a national hero, he had many wives and is reputed to have had 70 sons. In addition to his many wives, he also had a concubine who remained living with her family in Shechem. When she gave birth to a son, Gideon named him Abimelech, may his aspirations train him for leadership. After some years in retirement Gideon the son of Joash died and was laid to rest in the family burial plot in Ophrah.

Vs. 33.35 Gideon's dedicated leadership was effective during his lifetime as he strove to unite the tribes of Asher, Zebulun, Naphtali, Manasseh and Ephraim. Gideon's character sought inspiration to confirm his leadership and dedication. From the record we observe a prudent human being dedicated to his cause, his people and ever mindful of his place in history. When Gideon died the above named tribes became disunited in their national purpose as they introduced Canaanite forms of worship. They adopted and opted for the god Baal-berith.

V. 34 Their old enemies observing their retrogression from national goals once again took advantage of their disunity as a sign of weakness.

V. 35 Gideon's followers soon forgot the principles for which Gideon had united them. This gap destroyed their unity as their loyalties toyed with the dominant popular demand for assimilation with ideas that made no demands for principles in daily life nor a responsibility to follow the goals and guidelines established in the Torah for the advancement of civilization.

JUDGES CHAPTER 9

V. 1 The city of Shechem dates back to the second millenium. The people of Shechem are always called *baale Shechem* in the name of their ancient god. When Joshua conquered the Holyland the Shechemites agreed to adopt the Seven Laws of Noah, to be permitted to remain in their territory and promised to become dedicated to the national goals of Israel. The original founders of Shechem were Hivites (Gen. 34:2, Joshua 9:7). Abimelech, whose mother is a Hivite is sensitive to the fact that his genealogy (Jud. 8:31) does not conform with the law in (Deut. 17:15). Though his brothers have no aspirations for kingship in the spirit of their father Gideon, Abimelech has no qualms about desecrating his father's principles. Nor does he have any moral reservations to destroy the potential obstacles to his kingship-his brothers.

JUDGES CHAPTER 9

V. 2 — Abimelech was in Ophrah, where collectively with his brothers they were engaged in the affairs of the tribes of Asher, Zebulun, Naphtali, Manasseh and Ephraim. From this tranquil scene, he went to Shechem for the specific purpose to organize and plan a conspiracy against his half brothers. He sought and received the cooperation of his maternal grandfather and his immediate family (Hivites). They are to initiate a demand for him to become their king. He challenged their choice of being governed by the 70 sons of Gideon or by one (him) who's mother is a Hivite.

Vs. 3.4 — Confirms the intrigue set into motion by the relatives of his mother, who have already won the consent of the *baale Shechem* to activate Abimelech's murderous intrigue.

V. 4. The men of Shechem withdrew 70 shekels of silver from the treasury of their house of worship *Baal-berith*, to pay for the worthless and reckless men who shall implement Abimelech's treacherous plan of intrigue.

Vs. 5.6 — Abimelech led them to Ophrah. There they succeeded to round up 69 of Jerubaal's sons and beheaded each and every one of them. Only Jotham, the youngest son escaped the massacre when he succeeded to hide from the killers.

V. 6. Abimelech, the men of Shechem and Beth-milo (a nearby fortified town) assembled at the terenbinth of Schechem (Gen. 35:4, Joshua 24:26) and proclaimed Abimelech as their king.

V. 7 — When Jotham was informed of Abimelech's murderous act, he rose upon the natural platform which juts out at Mount Gerizim. It is from this platform, the curses inscribed in (Deut. 11:29, 27:11.26) were pronounced and projected to those standing on Mount Ebal. Jotham standing on this platform addressed the citizens of Shechem. "Be attentive to my message if you desire to be judged by Him Who administers justice to all of humankind."

Vs. 8.9 — "One day the trees of the forest convened to anoint a king. They requested that the olive tree become their king. Whereupon the olive tree replied. Have I ceased yielding my rich oil, for which I was created and by which kings are anointed, lamps are lit in both Temples and homes? Shall I resign from such worthwhile service, in order to exult my superiority over the other trees?"

Vs. 10.11 — "The trees then turned to the fig tree. Come reign over us. The fig tree replied. Have I paused yielding my sweet delicious fruit, that I should elevate myself as a ruler over all the other trees?"

Vs. 12.13 — "They then turned to the grape-vine. Come reign over us! The grape-vine replied. Have I failed to yield my wine which gladdens the heart of man? It is with my fruit that man praises

JUDGES CHAPTER 9

God, shall I resign from this glory to elevate myself to rule over all the other trees?"

Vs. 14.15 "The trees then turned to the thornbush. Come reign over us! The thornbush replied. If it be your intention to honor me as your king, come and prove your loyalty by taking shelter in my shade. Should you refuse my conditions, I shall become the source from which forest fires start in the hot summer, to spread and consume every tree in the forest including the mighty cedar."

V. 16 Jotham challenged the men of Shechem. "What motivated you when you chose Abimelech as your king? Was it your desire to honor the memory of Jerubaal and his household? Or, was it your desire to show your gratitude for all he had done for you during his lifetime?"

Vs. 17.18 "Considering that my father laid his life on the line of fire for your well being and saved you from the oppressive Midianite forces, was this that motivated you to kill his sons, to diminish his standards of greatness, to choose Abimelech only because he is the son of Jerubaal's concubine, a daughter of one of your kinsmen?"

V. 19 "Was it indeed an action motivated by truth and sincerity that you selected Abimelech as your king because you were desirous to glorify the memory of my father and his household? If this be truly your intent and purpose, then enjoy your choice and may Abimelech rejoice in becoming your king."

V. 20 Jotham's sarcasm turns to a curse. "However, if all I have said in truth is but a sham in your hearts, may a conflagration detonate Abimelech's government to destroy the citizens of Shechem and Beth-milo, in just retribution for his horrendous act of treason."

V. 21 Jotham having completed his exposition and critique, put distance between himself and the people of Shechem and his brother Abimelech. Jotham fled to Beerah, in the vicinity of the Brook of Zorek, in the territory of Judah.

Vs. 22.23 Abimelech's rule was limited and confined to the tribe of Manasseh. The other tribes rejected his claim to kingship. His rule lasted but three years. V. 23. Abimelech's treachery was complemented in kind by the people of Shechem. They were overcome by the guilt of so much innocent blood having been shed. They recognized their culpability in Abimelech's treachery and their faithlessness and desecration of the memory of Jerubaal.

V. 24 *Lovo chamas* A pall of gloom and fear descended upon Abimelech and the people of Shechem and Beth-milo (Gen. 9:6, Deut. 28:66.67). The scene of Jerubaal's dead sons faced

JUDGES CHAPTER 9

them daily as they could not remove the sight from their conscience. Daily they anticipated their call to the bar of justice, in just retribution for their treachery.

V. 25   Abimelech responded to the social friction and intrigue which surfaced in Shechem and removed his seat of government to Tarmah (v. 31). This enabled them to set up an ambush upon the hills of Shechem. They once again retrogressed to their ancient mores of robbing every traveler instead of the normal tax collections which granted peaceful passage through their territory. This was reported to Abimelech in Tarmah.

Vs. 26.27   The above verses report a growing rebellion against Abimelech by the lords of Shechem. Taking advantage of the developments, a shrewd demagogue, by the name of Gal ben Eved came to live in Shechem. It was he that ignited the rebellion against Abimelech. It was Gal ben Eved that brought the rebellion to fruition. Though the Shechemites had agreed to become loyal citizens of Israel, they ever remained a doubtful enclave. It ever remained a hotbed for dissension. Another factor which encouraged rebellion was the reality of assimilation. The Israelites living there merged their loyalties and sympathies with the lords of Shechem. They ceased to be an independent voice loyal to Israel's cause. Gal ben Eved reintroduced ancient pagan practices in the process of harvesting their vineyards and the trodding of the grapes, they introduced pagan festivals in their house of worship. These social changes became political rallying points as they ate and drank together they began to initiate open rebellion. Under the influence of Gal ben Ebed and his followers, these celebrations climaxed by openly cursing Abimelech.

Vs. 28.29   At the high-point of one of these gatherings, when their emotions were relaxed by wine. Gal ben Ebed rose to detonate the passive rebellion into action. "Who is Abimelech that we should serve under him? We reject his authority and our loyalty to the memory of Jerubaal. We reject the authority of his lieutenant Zebul. We denounce alien rule, let us once again reestablish our loyalties to the ancient founders of Shechem. V. 29. Were I, in command of the city of Shechem, I would reject outright this alien government. I would challenge Abimelech to open warfare to prove his weakness in governing by defeating him in battle."

Vs. 30.31   Zebul, Abimelech's acting governor in Shechem, incensed by the public response to the demagogue Gal ben Ebed, set into motion a series of actions secretly to put down the rebellion. V. 31 He also dispatched a secret message to Abimelech in Tarmah, informing him of the developments.

Vs. 32.33   Zebul advised Abimelech for a military action against the city, to mobilize his forces at night and to lie in waiting upon a nearby field until sunrise of the next morning. Establish your

JUDGES CHAPTER 9

forces, surround the city on the ready for Gal ben Ebed's attack. Take advantage of your preparedness to meet Gal ben Ebed in open combat. Engage him in battle with your effort and intention to fully destroy him, with everything in your military experience.

Vs. 34.37 Abimelech mobilized his forces and followed Zebul's advice. He waited for Gal ben Ebed to leave the city. Abimelech divided his force into four separate troops, to insure the capture of Gal ben Ebed. When Gal and his army reached the exit of the city of Shechem, only one troop was released to attack him from the west. When Gal saw movement in the distance, he addressed Zebul, "I see a group of people coming from the hills." Zebul chided him. "You are imagining things, you must be observing a mirage of trees and thinking they are people." V. 37. Gal persisted in his conclusive observation. "I see people emerging from the central hill district. I also see another group rising from the plain of Meonenim."

Vs. 38.40 Zebul observing his plan in place, is encouraged by the scene. He addressed Gal ben Ebed. "Where is your boasting mouth, that denigrated Abimelech's ability to rule? This is obviously the Israelite force, the people you despise. This is your opportunity to translate your venom into action. Go out there and defend your arrogance and hostility." Vs. 39.40. Gal ben Ebed led the dissenters of the lords of Shechem in battle against Abimelech. Abimelech's strategy was to draw the enemy outside the city. He is well aware of the treasonous elements inside the city, he therefore avoided being boxed into that environment. Gal's boasts proved greater than his courage to stand and fight. He fled from the scene as Abimelech pursued him, many of his followers were slain as they tried to find their way back into the city.

V. 41 Abimelech decided to remain close by in Arumah, the modern el-Ormah, southeast of Shechem, and await the development of events before he finalizes his own strategy. He was hopeful that Zebul may succeed in turning things around in that treacherous city. Zebul succeeded in dispossessing the followers of Gal ben Ebed. Some time after they were forced out of the city of Shechem, Abimelech calculated the risk of living in the midst of a time bomb. He evaluated the deep seated hatred fanned by the sands of time, he concluded that only its complete destruction would deny a replay of past intrigues. It would also discourage other communities in the Holyland who had agreed to remain in their settlements on Joshua's conditions from following the example of Shechem.

V. 42 *Vayehi mimacharat* After the lapse of a reasonable period of time, the Shechemites were satisfied that they have succeeded in appeasing Abimelech. They gradually returned to their normal habits and routines. They came and went at will. They are now satisfied that Abimelech had forgiven their past rebelliousness. *Vayagidu laAbimelech* It

JUDGES CHAPTER 9

was reported that the lords of Shechem had once again reactivated the robber bands, v. 25.

Vs. 43.44   Abimelech is motivated to destroy both root and branch of Shechem's treasonous hatred. Its perfidy if allowed to exist in the Holyland will plague Israel for centuries. It must become a symbol for history. Abimelech organized his military force into three companies. They encamped outside the city and waited for the robber bands to leave the city. They attacked and struck them down.

V. 44. Abimelech led his company to man the gates of the city. The other two companies were at the ready to strike all those passing to and from the city of Shechem.

V. 45   Abimelech and his company fought inside the city from door to door to destroy every potential effort for defense. He was intent upon rooting out the people who kept the virus of hate alive in the Holyland during these past two centuries. Once again Abimelech's heroic act is contrary to Torah law, Abimelech razed the city of Shechem and sowed its territory with salt, to insure its desolation. Abimelech the symbol of fratricide becomes the instrument of history to root out Canaanite hatred.

Vs. 46.48   Observing the destruction of their city, the lords of Shechem went into hiding in the excavated secret tunnel beneath the citadel, that housed the temple of *El-brith*. V. 47. Abimelech was informed that the lords of Shechem were in the secret tunnel of their citadel. V. 48. Abimelech marched his troops up to Mount Zalmon, one of the plateaus on Mount Gerizim, northeast of Shechem. He instructed his men to follow his instructions. "Take an axe, cut off a tree limb and place it upon your shoulder."

V. 49   Abimelech's troops followed his example, they cut a limb from a tree and carried it upon their shoulders and placed it at the entrance of the *hatzeriach* secret tunnel. They then set the tree limbs on fire to destroy those inside. From the number reported (1000) who hid in the citadel, we can conclude the approximate size of the shrine.

Vs. 50.53   Abimelech resolved to destroy every village or community allied with Shechem, in their rebellion against his rule. He encamped against Thebaz and occupied it. Vs. 51.53. Many of its inhabitants escaped into the tower which stood as a fortress in the center of the city. They locked themselves in and went up to the roof. Abimelech had planned to destroy it by fire. However, this was not to be. A woman threw the upper part of a millstone from a corn grinder mill and crushed his skull.

Vs. 54.55   Abimelech is embarrassed that he met his fate at the hands of a woman. Abimelech in keeping with the times charged his armsbearer to deliver the coup de grace, that history may not claim that he met his end at the hands of a woman. V. 55. When Abimelech's

JUDGES CHAPTER 9

soldiers became aware of his death, they withdrew from Thebaz. It is identified with the modern Tubaz, 13 miles north of Shechem.

Vs. 56.57 Abimelech's death is considered just retribution for the death of his brothers. However, for us in the 20th century, we begin to have a concept of the long haul demanded for man to cease from the inhumanities of man to man. Even in our time man is not yet civilized. From the record we must recognize the Eternal God's long suffering patience (Gen. 6:3, Ex. 34:6.8) as He waits through the centuries for the bud of human kindness to evolve in the hearts of men and women dedicated to His goals. History testifies to the fulfillment of Jotham's prophetic curse for Abimelech's barbaric act recorded in (Jud. 9:5). It is ironic that Abimelech is the instrument which administered justice upon the people of Shechem. Its very name has become a symbol of barbarism.

JUDGES CHAPTER 10

Vs. 1.2 Tolah the son of Puah, son of Dodo, of the tribe of Issachar, who lived at Shamir in the hill country of Ephraim, was one of Israel's leaders during this period of the Judges. However, the text is not establishing the fact that he succeeded Abimelech chronologically. V. 2. Though he is reputed to have led Issachar for 23 years, we have no information to flesh out the record of his leadership. He lived, he led his tribe and died in Shamir. We can not pinpoint its location on a map, though it was in the territory of Issachar, south of the Sea of Chinerreth, north of Ephraim. It is not the Shamir of Judah. It is ironical that the prophet Samuel devoted 57 verses of chapter 9, to give us a blow by blow description of Abimelech's barbaric activities, which were concentrated in the three years of his rule. Here the record is limited to two sentences though Tolah's leadership lasted for 23 years. Let us therefore look into the records available to us to surface what we do know. See commentary in T.E.T. on the following texts (Gen. 49:15, Deut. 33:18.19, Num. 26:23, Num. 1:28.29, IChron.7:1.5). At the census of Mount Sinai, Issachar numbered 54,400 men. Forty years later in Trans-Jordan they numbered 64,300 men. Six generations later in David's time the family of Tolah alone mustered 22,600 men for service in the army. Tolah's brother Uzi mustered 36,000 men for service in David's army. While the whole tribe of Issachar was able to record 87,000 men (all above figures are age 20 and older). From the record we do know the tribe of Issachar developed a high priority for education-knowledge-philosophy. Their influence had engraved itself upon the genes of every human being who by birth or by voluntarily accepting Torah disciplines have brought civilization to the whole world through their international involvement with humanity. Abimelech's evil was interred with his bones, the good created by the goodwill of the tribe of Issachar lived on to influence 23 years of continuous peace and enterprise.

Vs. 3.5 Jair the Gileadite led Israel (in Trans-Jordan) for 22 years. See

JUDGES CHAPTER 10

comm. T.E.T. on (Num. 32:41, Deut. 3:14.15) for historic details of this important territory. The families of Jair-Manasseh played an important role even before the conquest of the Holyland. V. 4. Jair had 30 sons who were all involved in administering various territories belonging to Jair. They were distinguished personalities and identified by their regalia as they traveled on 30 male donkeys while administering the affairs of their family in 30 different townships. Their territory was identified as Havoth-Jair, Jair conquered it during the lifetime of Moses. Jair ruled in the teritory of Havoth-Jair for 22 years. When he passed away he was laid to rest in Kamon modern Kumen, east of the Jordan River.

V. 6 When Israel arrived in the Holyland, they were influenced by the idolatrous practices of their local environment. Their exposure to these idolatrous practices slowly filtered into their lives and while they remained loyal to their sacrificial disciplines at the Mishkan-Tabernacle, they permitted themselves in various degrees to toy with the local cults and oracles, fortune telling, magicians, they deified trees, animals and humans. As Israel's roots struck deeper into the environment of the Holyland, they shed their responsibilities to Torah disciplines and adopted not only the local deities but imported others from peoples with whom they were engaged in commerce. All the above developments confirm the material successes of the various tribes. Periodically when their successes became the envy of the indigenous population, with whom they assimilated and intermarried, this envy became the source of political unrest which brought into the open the hostility of local communities and neighboring nations. Israel's prosperity ever enlarged their identity with their neighbors deities. They now worshipped Baal-gad, Baal-hazor, Baal-meon, Baal-perazim, Baal-tamar, Chemosh-Moab, Molech-Ammon, Dagon-Philistia, Baal-zebub. Israel forgot the reason for their emancipation, their place in history, their reason for being Israel. Had Israel remained loyal to their Torah disciplines, their neighbors envy would have stimulated their desire to follow Israel's disciplines, which would have created the blessings of tranquility and contentment, which is the universal goal of the Eternal God's objective for all humanity.

V. 7 When the Eternal God of history observed Israel's retrogression, when their prosperity balanced with their loyalty to their neighbors cults, their envy created the atmosphere, "Leave us because you have become too powerful." This became the cause which ignited the Philistines in the west and the Ammonites in the east. When the pressures of historic events detonated Israel's conscience, the clouds of war and oppression loomed on the horizon. Israel suddenly and gradually felt the effect of their retrogression as the Philistines and the Ammonites decided to call a halt to Israel's prosperity.

V. 8 Beginning with the period immediately after the death of Jair, these two belligerant forces created a pincers movement to

JUDGES CHAPTER 10

oppress, enslave and batter Israel wherever they were settled in the Holyland. For 18 years the tribes in Trans-Jordan bore the brunt of this crushing effort of the Philistines, the Ammonites and the Amorites. Israel's continuity is conditioned upon the following conditions, when they fail to observe the conditions written into their contract, the tables of history are turned around (Ex. 15:2.19, Lev. 26:2.26, Num. 21:21.35, Deut. 28:25.29,29:11.19).

V. 9 Israel's guilt-ridden conscience is aware that it has strayed from the Blueprint which has guided its existence. This glimpse into reality destroyed their morale and hope for a future. This became the signal for Israel's enemies to increase their pressures and to seek a quick resolution to their efforts. They attacked Judah in the south, Benjamin and Ephraim in the north.

V. 10 Faced with the realities of truth, Israel cried for help to its only ally, the Source of its salvation. Israel's confession to their Eternal God-their conscience-their Zelem Elohim, stirred their sense of justice. In their moments of distress Israel must admit however reluctantly that these newly found gods and their cults cannot save themselves nor help others. Elohim, God becomes apparent to men and women when they obey the Eternal God's natural law. To know God, we must live by His law every moment of our lives. He must be present in our thought processes, our conduct, our perception, our methods of doing business and in the private moments of our lives in the privacy of our homes. Human progress is the result of living perceptively by the disciplines of the Eternal God of history.

Vs. 11.12 If we examine the history of Israel's past into modern times, we discover that every generation produced prophets who spoke in the name of the Eternal God of history. The prophet in these verse is Phinehas, a lineal descendant of Aaron. He remonstrated with Israel for their ingratitude for all the Eternal God of Israel has done for them through the centuries. "Yet, you have forsaken His disciplines, you have strayed from His truth, to worship the deities of the nations surrounding you. You have done this despite your collective experience that in your moments of distress, it was not the god of the Egyptians, the Amorites, the Ammonites, the Philistines, the Sidonians, Amalek or the Maonites (Meunim in the territory of Judah), that enabled you to overcome the terror of our enemies." Phinehas reminded his listeners that whenever in the past Israel repented their past conduct and resolved to try again, to live by Torah disciplines, this sparked new hope as the Eternal activated His mercy (Ex. 34:6.7) see comm. in T.E.T. From the Eternal's mercy came forth inspired leaders to create new hope and succeeded to throw off the yoke of despair.

Vs. 13.16 "You cannot expect deliverance when your repentance is insincere and superficial. Until you resolve your doubts, turn to the gods you have chosen to worship." (Deut. 4:24.40,

JUDGES CHAPTER 10

32:36.38)." V. 15. Spontaneously, those within the hearing of his voice implore Phinehas to intercede in their behalf. "We stand guilty as charged. We are resolved to recognize our disobedience. Punish us for our transgressions but save us from our immediate enemies who seek to remove us from the Holyland."

V. 16 Phinehas testified for the record, that Israel's repentance began by their sincere effort to remove every symbol of idolatrous worship from their homes and communities. Phinehas speaks in the name of the Eternal as He recognized Israel's distress. He is sympathetic with Israel's grievous affliction.

V. 17 The Ammonites mobilized their forces and encamped at Gilead. Israel countered by mobilizing its forces and mounted a defensive action at Mizpah. The Ammonites recognized Israel's resolution to stand their ground. The Ammonites respected Israel's challenge and withdrew without any action taking place.

V. 18 The tribal leaders in Trans-Jordan took advantage of this lull before the storm and decided unanimously to organize a campaign against the Ammonites which shall free them from Ammon's ongoing tyranny. They agreed to search for a military leader who shall unite their efforts for a successful campaign. They further agreed to recognize his ongoing leadership with a voluntary standing force for all of Trans-Jordan.

JUDGES CHAPTER 11

Chapters (11: to 12:1.7), are devoted to settling an old historic dispute between Ammon and the Trans-Jordanian tribes of Reuben, Gad and the families of Machir, Jair and Nobach of the tribe of Manasseh. The historic details are recorded in (Num. 21:21.35, Deut. 2:1.19). Moses and Joshua were to recognize Ammon's historic territorial rights. However, when Sihon and Og dispossessed Ammon and Moab from portions of their historic land, Israel took possession of this land from Sihon and Og, for it no longer belonged to Ammon or Moab. (Jud. 10:17.18) introduces a new problem. For 18 years Ammon disregarded their kinship with Israel. During these 18 years it exercised every oppressive action against its Israelite kinsmen in Trans-Jordan. Taking advantage of the social and moral chaos recorded in (Jud. 10:6.18), they are ready to mount a military action to dispossess Israel from land it has occupied for 300 years.

Vs. 1.3 Jephtah is introduced as a mighty man of valor. His father's name was Gilead, his mother was a native woman married to Gilead as a concubine and consummated outside the framework of Israel's law. The text therefore calls her a harlot. Jephtah was born from this marriage. Gilead had another wife to whom he was married in accord with Israel's laws. From this marriage Gilead had sons. V. 2. Describes the stigma and the animosity by which his brothers pursued Jephtah. Since they considered him an outsider, they strove to deny him his legal rights as a member of the family. Gilead traces his genealogy to (Num. 27:1). V. 3 Jephtah being forced to

JUDGES CHAPTER 11

leave home settled in the area of Tob, northeast of Gilead near Syria. Tradition teaches that Jephtah left home after his father died. Though he was a legal heir to his father's estate, he refused to enter into controversy with his brothers. Jephtah became a freebooter and attracted other personalities with similar familial circumstances. Essentially they were men without property *rekim*.

Vs. 4.5   In accord with the decision made in (Jud. 10:17.18) it was decided to seek Jephtah's services in organizing a military force for the purpose of carrying the war to Ammon. There is a lapse of about four years between the time Jephtah left home and the time when he is being offered the leadership by the tribes of Israel in Trans-Jordan. It was in this interim period that he earned the reputation as a man of valor.

Vs. 6.8   When the official offer was made to Jephtah to become the Trans-Jordanian commander of Israel's forces there, Jephtah challenged their inconsistency. "How do you reconcile your actions against me in the past, when you forced me to leave my father's home? Now, that you are in distress you suggest that I sacrifice my life in your behalf, to prove my pardon of your contemptible conduct." V. 8. The Elders of Trans-Jordan replied to Jephtah's charge of inconsistency. "We are here to beg forgiveness for our transgression. Come with us to lead our wars against Ammon, we shall prove our profound remorse for having offended you. We desire to appoint you as our permanent leader of Gilead-Trans-Jordan."

Vs. 9.11   Jephtah restates his conditions of their agreement. "I shall return with you as your military commander to lead the war against the Ammonites. As a dedicated Israelite, I have the faith that the Eternal God of Israel shall create the conditions for me to defeat the Ammonites in battle. When I succeed with my part of the agreement, you shall be obliged to recognize me as your head of government." V. 10. The Elders replied to Jephtah. "May the Eternal God be our witness that we shall recognize you as the head of our government in Trans-Jordan." V. 11. Jephtah accepted and went with the Elders to Gilead. There he started by becoming *kazin* their commander in chief of their military forces. When Jephtah arrived in Mitzpah, he repeated his understanding with their leaders before an assemblage of the tribes of Reuben, Gad and Manasseh.

Vs. 12.15   Jephtah sent messengers to Ammon. He requested that Ammon define its reasons for declaring war on Israel. V. 13. "When Israel arrived in Trans-Jordania, they took possession of the territory which is bound by the Arnon River in the south, the Jabbok in the north and the Jordan in the west. We request that you restore this land to us peacefully." Vs. 14.15. Jephtah categorically denies Ammon's claim. He reminded them that when Israel took possession of this territory it was in the possession of the Amorites (Num. 21:21.35) who had originally conquered it from Moab. Jephtah challenged Ammon from claiming land which never belonged to them.

JUDGES CHAPTER 11

Ammon and Moab are now one state. Ammon is therefore basing its claim upon this point.

Vs. 16.20   Jephtah's messengers review the details of Israel's historic wanderings in the Sinaitic Peninsula, from the time they left Egypt until they arrived in the vicinity of Kadesh. V. 17. Arriving close to the borders of Edom, they requested peaceful passage through their territory (Num. 20:14.21) and were refused despite the recorded admonition to Israel in the Torah (Deut. 2:4.19) to respect Edom, Moab and Ammon's territorial rights because of their historic kinship (Gen. 19:30.38, 25:19.34). V. 18. Israel honored Edom, Moab and Ammon's traditional territorial rights, at great peril to itself as recorded in (Num. 21:4.5). V. 19. Arriving closer to the border line of Sihon, we sent a message to the king of the Amorites, requesting peaceful passage through their territory in order to continue on our journey to the Holyland. V. 20. Sihon the king of the Amorites (who then possessed this very territory you are now claiming) doubted our sincerity. His reply was given by mobilizing his army at Jahaz to stop us from continuing upon our journey to the Holyland. When we pursued our goal, they attacked us (Num. 21:21.35).

Vs. 21.24   Jephtah's messengers point out that Sihon's threat left Israel no choice, "We either defended our rights or perished. There was no room for manouver. With faith in the Source of our strength we fought Sihon, his army, his people to a stand still. We won this land from the Amorites, we have possessed it for the past 300 years." V. 22 "We the descendants of those who fought Sihon, received it as an inheritance (Num. 32:33, Deut. 3:12, Joshua 13:15.32)." V. 23. "For centuries you have known these facts, that we took this land from the Amorites, you now have the temerity to demand that we return it to you." V. 24. "We feel justified in retaining this land because of our moral right, confirmed by the counsel of the Eternal God of Israel. Even as you justify the possession of your territory because your god Chemosh granted you the capability to conquer it."

Vs. 25.26   "Though this land which you now claim belonged to Moab before he lost it to Sihon, yet, Balak the son of Zippor, respected our rights (Num. 22:). He did not go to war with Israel. What law grants you preeminence over a piece of land which you never owned?" V. 26. "When Israel settled down in Heshbon and its adjoining towns and Aroer and its adjoining towns bordering the Arnon River, did you make an effort then to repossess this territory?"

Vs. 27.28   Jephtah's representatives pleaded with Ammon as with a brother, in their effort to avoid war and bloodshed. "Where are your prior territorial rights to this land? Over the centuries Israel has respected its kinship. It has proven its goodwill with its neighbors to act justly. May the Eternal God of Israel, Who is devoted to the establishment of justice in human relations, may He give His verdict in recognizing the

JUDGES CHAPTER 11

impropriety of Ammon's claim." V. 28. Ammon's king was determined to go to war with Israel, he ignored the rational and truthful position of Jephtah.

V. 29   Jephtah's indignation rose with Ammon's rejection of the justice of Israel's cause. Jephtah's diplomatic effort to establish justice in human relations has a parallel in (Gen. 18:17.19). Jephtah transcended his finite ability as he grasped *the Finger of the Eternal* to inspire him and to guide his every step in his preparations for this defensive war against Ammon. Jephtah mobilized his forces and marched through Trans-Jordan, passing north to Mitzpeh-gilead. He penetrated into Ammonite territory, resolved to counter Ammon's arrogance by attacking every town that lay in his path.

Vs. 30.31   In the highest moment of Jephtah's dedication, he made an irrational vow. Should he be successful in defeating the Ammonites and return safely from the war to his home, whatsoever (animal or human) that shall come forth to greet him, he shall offer it to the Eternal as a burnt offering. Jephtah's senseless vow, a fanatical *high* is made in the fever pitch of his delirium. The Torah denigrates and discourages all vows. (see T.E.T. on Num. 27:). Jephtah's vow cannot be compared to Jacob's vow in (Gen. 28:20) nor with Hannah's vow in (1 Sam. 1:11). Almost 1000 years have elapsed from the Akedat Yizchok (T.E.T. on Gen. 22) yet, it shall take centuries to eradicate this barbaric practice from Israel's conscience.

Vs. 32.33   *Vayitnem Adonai beyado* Jephtah's emotional ecstacy inspired his leadership as he felt the full power of justice on his side. (Deut. 20:1.4, 10.13). He is no longer bound by the admonition given in (Deut. 2:9.19, 23:4.6). Ammon and Moab's antagonism became the historic basis for denying them the shelter of their kinship, which survived the centuries because of Israel's dedication to the principle of justice. V. 33. Jephtah routed Ammon's forces from Aroer, east of Rabbath-Ammon to Minnith, east of the Jordan River and pressed on to Abel-cheramim-Kurm Dhiban. In this stretch of territory Israel conquered 20 cities.

V. 34   Tradition teaches that Jephtah had but one child that he fathered, though he had adopted many other children. It is this one and only daughter that greeted him with timbrel and dance, to celebrate his victory over Ammon.

V. 35   When Jephtah recognized his only daughter, that it is she that shall become the subject of his vow, *hachreah hichratani* he rent his garments to express the impact of his irrational vow. "You have brought me to my knees in distress. You have turned my victory to ashes, for I dared to utter a vow to the Eternal, which I may not retract." Jephtah exposed his ignorance of the law. An irrational vow is null and void when it is made. In accord with Torah law, the kohen was legally bound to nullify it. That Jephtah would be permitted to contemplate the fulfillment of his vow, confirms

JUDGES CHAPTER 11

for the record of history the adoption of human sacrifices was an accepted norm. It will yet take centuries to eradicate it from Israel's midst.

V. 36 — The love and spiritual affinity of Jephtah's daughter for her father are the underlining commentary of this verse. She is quite content to yield her life in order that her father fulfill his vow in gratitude for his victory over Ammon.

V. 37 — The pathos of Isaac for his father (Gen. 22:1.8) are paralleled in the words of Jephtah's daugher. Her lamentation is heroic as she resigns herself to the fate that awaits her. In her one and only request she encapsulates her dreams, her hopes, her immortality in the process of genetic progression. "Permit me a two month delay, that I may join with my friends in our common cause, to lament the future which could have been mine."

V. 38 — Jephtah granted his daughter's request. Her friends joined her to roam upon the hills of the Holyland, to evaluate her heroism and the full meaning of her sacrifice. As a potential mother in Israel, she evaluates woman's position in society as the *matrix* of humanity. Penetrating her consciousness during these two months, we who live in the 20th century must try to perceive the depth of her thoughts. Though the Eternal God shows us the way to nobler living, it is we by ourselves that create the evil and the pain we endure until we cease to stumble and bumble into misery. Man fails to establish the Eternal God's ideals as the solution for his human problems. Man emerges from the womb of time as the child of the Eternal God, to perfect his freedom. He is inspired to perceive justice and to master his choices which become our heritage. We join Jephtah's daughter in evaluating the needless human sacrifices when we deviate from the Eternal's Torah.

V. 39 — Jephtah's daughter returned home to her father. He never relented from his resolution to carry forth his vow. Nor was there a public demand to cease and desist from this barbaric practice. *Vatehi chok* Subconsciously the multitude felt guilty in not having raised their voices to stop this tragedy from coming to pass. It became tradition to lament this savage act. There was no need to make it illegal. It has been an abomination since the time of Abraham.

V. 40 — A *chok* is a statute written into the Torah, for mankind to observe, though they have not yet reached a plateau in their evolution to rationalize it. By public acclaim they established an annual fast day which introduced a four day memorial period each year to mourn the fate which befell Jephtah's daughter (and countless others who were so needlessly and mercilessly sacrificed).

JUDGES CHAPTER 12

V. 1   Once before in (Jud. 8:1.3) the tribe of Ephraim reproached Gideon with the same complaint they are now making against Jephtah. "Why didn't you call upon us to join with you in the war against Ammon?" There is but one difference, in the previous incident their murmurings *vayomru* were made in a peaceful format. Gideon being of a different disposition pacified their insolence. In this verse they amplified their arrogance and contempt. *Vayitzaek* (Jud. 10:17). Their intention was to confront Jephtah in Mitzpeh-gilead but were intercepted at Zaphon-amatha, in the territory of Gad (Joshua 13:27) by Jephtah's representatives. Their complaint and threat was made to these representatives.

V. 2   Jephtah's reply confirms our understanding of v. 1, they obviously were put in their place by Jephtah's representatives.

Ish riv hayiti ani Reflects Jephtah's controlled anger as he addressed the Ephramites. "You were certainly aware of Ammon's belligerence. Over a period of 18 years the Trans-Jordanian tribes were beleaguered and involved in constant strife with the Ammonites (Jud. 10:8). Every time we endeavored to mount an action you were notified and your assistance was requested. Yet, you ignored your moral obligation."

V. 3   "Taking into consideration your disloyalty to the cause of Israel and your belligerence to the tribes of Gilead, I concluded we will have to go it alone despite the reality that the Ammonite forces outnumbered us and were better equipped for war than we were. I therefore took the initiative (Jud. 11:29) at great risk to my life, I mounted an offensive to carry the war into Ammon's own territory. The outcome is now history; for the Eternal God of Israel, inspired me to create the conditions for the defeat of the Ammonites. What is the point in your coming here to mount a civil war against me? Your quarrel is with your own conscience. Your treasonous convictions have condemned you."

V. 4   After the defeat of the Ammonites, Jephtah disbanded his volunteer army. He now recalled them to settle his score with Ephraim. Ephraim called the Gileadites-Trans-Jordanian tribes, refugees from the Holyland. They taunted the tribes of Reuben, Gad, and the families of Machir, Jair, and Nobach of Manasseh, for having separated themselves (Num. 32:) from the main body of the Holyland. (Joshua 22:) is another incident which fanned their animosity that reaches all the way back to (Gen. 37:). Arbitrarily, they argued that Trans-Jordan was contiguous with the main territory of Ephraim and Manasseh and therefore had no right to choose a leader by themselves. Ephraim now completed the evolution of their animosity by slandering the root of Jephtah's army and his origin (Jud. 11:1.3).

Vs. 5.6   The Gileadites controlled the fords of the Jordan. When the Ephraimites tried to cross over to their territory in the west, the Gileadites challenged them to identify themselves. The

JUDGES CHAPTER 12

men of Ephraim were asked to pronounce the word *shibboleth*, despite the fact that it was known nationally that they had a speech difficulty and could not pronounce the *sh* instead they pronounced the word *sibboleth*. This became Jephtah's court of justice as he arbitrarily avenged himself against any Ephraimite that could not meet his criteria. Jephtah's capability as a military leader was offset by his fanatical intransigence. Just as he could not mitigate his imprudent vow, to show mercy to his own daughter, neither could he forgive his deepseated animosity toward Ephraim.

V. 7 Jephtah led the Trans-Jordanian tribes for six years. When he died he was laid to rest in Mitzpeh-Gilead, his birthplace.

Many legends have been woven around Jephtah and his personality. We are only interested in the known facts in order to draw a composite picture of this chaotic period. The Torah stands as the psychoanalytic Force, which contains the doctrine, that establishes criteria for human development as man evolves from his primitive origin to become a civilized human being. The Torah has warned Israel against assimilation and intermarriage. Israel's doors must be ever receptive to accept those who desire to reach for a higher level of human development. This has put the onus, the burden and responsibility upon native born Israelites and its proselytes to become exemplary individuals for the rest of society. Israel's failure to uphold these standards created the chaos, the disunity and even the civil war depicted in these three centuries after Joshua.

V. 8 Some time after Jephtah, Ibzan, became a leader and judge. He established his seat of government in Bethlehem, in the territory of Zebulun (Joshua 19:15), located in the northwest of the lower Galil, north of Nahalal. Tractate Baba Bathra 91a identifies Ibzan, with Boaz. He was called Ab-zon, because he led his people as a shepherd. He exercised his authority like a father. Rabbinic tradition traces his genealogy to Bethlehem in the tribe of Judah.

Vs. 9.10 Boaz deviated from marrying his children to their own immediate tribal families. History reports that he had 30 sons and 30 daughters. He sought mates from outstanding families in Israel. Boaz was dedicated to the national welfare of Israel. He therefore crossed tribal boundary lines to inspire national unity. Boaz married Ruth, from their marriage came Obed, Yishai, the father of king David. He led his people for seven years and the brevity of his leadership record, reflects a period of tranquility. The background and setting for the events recorded in the book of Ruth, are set in this period and in this territory. V. 10. When Boaz died he was laid to rest in Bethlehem in the territory of Judah.

Vs. 11.12 Elon succeeded Boaz in the leadership of the tribe of Zebulun. He was a native of the tribe of Zebulun. For 10 years he led this important tribe from the city of Ayalon in Zebulun. From

JUDGES CHAPTER 12

the brevity of the record, we can conclude the effectiveness of his leadership. To flesh out the record see commentary in T.E.T. on (Deut. 33:18.19). To confirm this conclusion see what Deborah has to say about Zebulun in (Jud.5:18). When Elon died he was laid to rest in Ayalon, in Zebulun.

Vs. 13.15 — Elon was succeeded by Abdon the son of Hillel, the Pirathonite. This town was southwest of Schechem, in the hill country of Mount Gerizim, in the territory of Ephraim. In accord with (I Chron. 8:23.30) he was listed as a Benjaminite. The text records the effectiveness of his leadership, by telling us that he had 40 sons and 30 grandchildren, who were all involved in striving to establish the state as they rode about the country on government business on 70 colts and wore regalia to dignify their position in the government. Upon Abdon's demise he was laid to rest in Pirathon, Ephraim, after a successful leadership of eight years. Examining the record of Tola, Puah, Jair of Gilead, Ibzan, Elon and Abdon, we observe the search for leadership among the tribes. We also must conclude the breakdown of clans as they crossed lines to develop a central government.

JUDGES CHAPTER 13

The book of Judges is a most valuable document. It establishes a kaleidoscopic picture of generations on the move in their search for their Zelem Elohim, their potential human capacity. In the center of this struggle is a small minority called Israel, in the process of being refined in the crucible of 2000 years of evolution. As the children of Shem who have survived the melting pot of assimilation, in an environment of barbarity, idolatry and a debauched society, they are striving to establish a new world order in the Holyland, a piece of land that has been Semitic from the time of Noah.

Refined in the crucible of Egyptian slavery, Israel emerges from the Exodus with a written Constitution, inspired and written by the *Finger of the Eternal God of Israel.* A Universal document which guarantees every human being his and her rights of life, liberty and the pursuit of contentment. Israel's initiative of overthrowing the powerful Egyptian government inspired hundreds of thousands of human beings to join Israel's initiative to become free men and women. At Mount Sinai, they were inducted officially into the household of Israel and extended every right and privilege, even as every native son of Israel. The Decalogue-Israel's Constitution welcomes every new proselyte by repeating the admonition to every member of Israel, "Love the stranger. Ever remember the abominable treatment you yourselves received in Egypt." 23 times the Torah, the enlargement of the Decalogue, repeats this admonition.

The forty year struggle in the desert of life was spent to integrate the new body of Israel into a new way of life. Emerging from this period of trial and error, faced by a powerful opposition of kin-Ammon, Moab-Edom, they mounted a united conquest of the Holyland. Once again Israel is challenged to absorb, and

JUDGES CHAPTER 13

integrate thousands of new proselytes. The native Israelites have now become the minority, who must uphold the standards established by the Torah for a new world order. To enter the world as *Cain* and to emerge in the image of the Godly man Moses. It is he that inspired humankind to dream dreams of freedom, to obey the disciplines of Torah law, in order to create *messianic* human beings, who shall activate the *messianic age* and destroy the principle and concept of the survival of the fittest.

V. 1 The history of the Philistines, the Exodus from Egypt, the crossing of the Reed Sea, the abrogation and annulment of Abraham's treaty with Abimelech the king of Gerar, are all part of the rise and fall of nations. Nations rise and fall like stars. They are created and come into being to serve a purpose and then disintegrate. Let us therefore look into the record and observe when the Philistines were a nebulous aggregate. See commentary in T.E.T. on the following texts (Gen. 21:22.34, 26:6.8, Deut. 2:17.23, Joshua 3:5.8, Jud. 3:31). Had Israel emerged in the Holyland on target instead of losing 38 years in the crucible of the desert, there never would have been a Philistine rod to oppress Israel for 40 years (Ex. 13:17:).

Chronologically (Jud. 3:31) belongs to a period before the main wave of Seapeoples invaded Gerar. Shamgar's war was fought with the forerunners of the people who became known as the Philistines. The present Philistines emerged from the *tsunami* in the Aegean Sea to invade Egypt, Anatolia, and Syria. It was this wave that destroyed the Hittite Empire. All of this happened during the reign of Rameses III. He succeeded to impress many of the professional warriors into the Egyptian army. Only a small number of this last wave made it to the Holyland. It was this well organized force that is now fully established on the Mediterranean coast. The 40 years of oppression started long before Samson appeared on the scene and lasted into the time of Eli the High Priest. It is this organized Philistine government that forced the tribe of Dan to go north to Laish. The time frame is the end of the 12th or the beginning of the 11th century BCE.

Vs. 2.3 Manoach lived in Zorah-Surach between the allotted territory of Dan and Judah. His genealogy is traced to Dan. His wife Hatzlalponie, was from the tribe of Judah (I Chron. 4:3). Her name is a contraction of *pnei-zel*. She acknowledged the inspiration of an angel, who assured her that she would conceive a child, despite her pessimistic point of view that she shall remain barren.

V. 3 The effect of the angel's inspiration challenged her inferiority complex, to think positively and she will indeed conceive and give birth to a child.

V. 4 The angel's inspiration strove to turn her thoughts around from negative degradation of a guilt complex, to positive optimistic hope that she will be able to conceive if she follows the disciplines outlined in (Num. 6:3) for a *nazir*, one that is dedicated to reach for the highest moral standards by dedicating his or her lifestyle to the disciplines of a *nazir*. Part of the discipline is to avoid wine or liquor, any beverage or food

JUDGES CHAPTER 13

which intoxicates. They may not expose themselves to a dead body, which can introduce morbid thoughts to depress the mind or even become exposed to potential infection, *tame laneflesh*.

V. 5   She is admonished to follow these disciplines of positive thinking, that she may conceive. She is instructed to transmit these disciplines of a *nazirite* to her child when he is born and to dedicate his whole life to become a leader of men who shall help Israel from its dilemma and oppression by the Philistines.

Vs. 6.7   Hatzlalponie reports her experience to her husband Manoach. "I was so overwhelmed by his appearance and inspiration, I failed to ask him to identify himself to me." She exuberantly reports the good news, that she will indeed conceive and give birth to a son. Hatzlalponie tells Manoach, how the angel instructed her in the details how to raise her son. Yet, she avoided telling Manoach of the angel's psychoanalytic conclusions for her being barren. She also failed to report that her potential son was to abstain from cutting his hair. She exaggerated when she enlarged upon the angel's instructions that her potential son would be obliged to be a *nazirite* from birth to the day of his demise. In every inspiration reported by man or woman in a dream, an inspiration or a vision, they mostly always fail to repeat the message as they receive it. Human beings fail to comprehend that God's metaphoric message is clear, factual, and exact. We may not enlarge upon its details nor are we at liberty to modify it. See commentary in T.E.T. on (Gen. 41:1.38).

V. 8   Manoach is piously receptive to his wife's inspiring vision. He therefore pleads in his prayers, that the Eternal God (Gen. 25:21) send His messenger-malach once again to enlighten them with further instructions. "Teach us how we may implement Your *Malach's* inspiration by our *melachah-efforts*, to create the environment vital to train our potential son after his birth.

Vs. 9.12   Manoach's sincere plea was acknowledged as the *messenger* reappeared as Hatzlalponie was sitting by herself in the field. *Vs. 10.12*. She hastened to report her experience to Manoach. Arriving at the appointed place, Manoach expressed his desire for further instructions. "Are you the one that inspired my wife that we shall be blessed with a son? May your inspiring words be perceived, that my wife shall indeed conceive. Instruct us we pray, how we may implement and complement your wonderful prediction by our efforts in prenatal and postnatal care"

Vs. 13.14   "Your wife is to implement the instructions I have already given her. She may not eat or drink any product that originates from the grapevine nor may she eat or drink any intoxicant food or beverage. She may not eat any food that is condemned by our dietary laws, or permitted foods which have been declared unclean. Obviously, it

JUDGES CHAPTER 13

shall be clear to you that my prediction and inspiration is totally contingent upon her compliance with the details of my instructions."

Vs. 15.17   Manoach pleads with the Eternal's messenger. "Grant us the privilege of becoming your host. Stay in our midst while we prepare a kid in gratitude for your message of hope." V. 16. The messenger-*malach* replied to Manoach's invitation. "Should you detain me, I cannot partake of your food. However, if it be your desire, to express your gratitude, you may offer a burnt offering to the Eternal God. I am but His humble messenger."

V. 17 Manoach pursued his interrogation of the *malach*. "What is your name that we may acknowledge our gratitude for your wonderful message of hope when your prediction comes to fruition?"

V. 18   The *"malach Adonai"* is perturbed by Manoach's perplexity and reservations. "What purpose would it serve you to know my name? Is it not gratifying that I have inspired you and your wife to resolve your ongoing problem, that I have breathed new hope into your lives, for the fulfillment of the most desired goal in your lives?" *Vehu peli* "I further recognize your human reservations are rooted in your human limitations. Should it not have been sufficient for you to recognize the Eternal's intervention in the affairs of mankind? Yet, you are requesting additional proof of the authenticity of my credentials. It is now up to you both to create the pysychological environment; the determination to dedicate your lives to the implementation of my message of hope. Your faith in the Eternal God's natural law, will resolve your doubts and reservations as it indeed will come to pass." For a fuller understanding of this difficult verse and the subject of *nazir*, see commentary in T.E.T. on the following texts (Gen. 18:17.19, Ex. 33:16.23, Num. 6:1.2, 11:23).

V. 19   Manoach took the kid, the flour and oil, which he had planned to prepare for his guest-the malach-messenger. *Vayaal al hatzur* and he offered it as a burnt offering upon the rock. A deviation from Torah law. This incident exposes the common practice of offering sacrifices during this period of the Judges on private altars. Manoach and his wife stood transfixed as *umafli laasot* the *malach Adonai* transcendented their finite concentration upon the flames that rose from their offering upon the rock. They assumed the *malach* rose heavenward in the flames of the sacrifice. See (Jud. 6:17.25) for Gideon's paralell experience.

Vs. 20.21   When Manoach and his wife concluded that the *malach Adonai* rose heavenward in the flames of their sacrifice, they had the same reaction as the experience recorded in (Lev. 9:24, see comm. in T.E.T.). They both fell upon their faces to avoid the challenging effect of this miraculous experience.

V. 21 When the *malach Adonai* did not reappear, both Manoach and his wife

JUDGES CHAPTER 13

were reconciled and elated over the effect of this most marvelous experience.

Vs. 22.24 Manoach said to his wife, "Now that we have come face to face with God's angel, we shall surely die." Manoach's wife tried to rationalize their experience, "Were it the Eternal's intention to kill us, He would not have accepted our gift offering. Neither would we have been given, the privilege of observing this marvelous scene. Neither would we have been granted the ability to comprehend the angel's message (Gen. 33:10)." V. 24. Manoach and his wife reviewed in their moments of privacy, the full meaning of the instructions given to them, for their responsibility to create the home atmosphere of tranquility for the prenatal conception of a child that shall become endowed with the perfection of body and mind. Hatzlalponie succeeded to conceive and gave birth to a son. She named him Samson. *Vayevarachehu Adonai* The Eternal God blessed Samson in the name of his parents who succeeded in fulfilling the disciplines of His natural law, to procreate a human being worthy to receive God's blessing (Ps. 84:12, 19:6).

V. 25 Samson's physical and mental development were forged in an atmosphere of *kedushah* of tranquility. His parents succeeded in imbuing him with *yirat Adonai* the awe of the Eternal God. This in turn inspired him with *ruach Adonai* the desire to dedicate his life to serve his people. Samson's consecration echoed his desire to *lepaamo* develop courage to spring into action. Samson became aware and sensitive to the plight of his people in the tribe of Dan. Their inability to take possession of the territory allotted to them described in (Joshua 19:40.48, 15:33), forced the majority of the tribe of Dan to conquer Leshem in the north. Samson belonged to the minority of Dan that lived in Zarah and Eshtaol in the territory of Judah. He is growing up in a time when the Philistines are mounting an effort to move eastward in the Holyland.

JUDGES CHAPTER 14

Vs. 1.2 Samson is now an adult, he goes to Timnah-Tibneh, a Danite city. While there, he is attracted to a Philistine woman. V. 2 He returned home to Zarah and told his father that he has become infatuated with a Philistine woman. In accord with ancient custom he is requesting his father to arrange for her marriage to him.

V. 3 In light of Samson's parents dedication described in v. 25, they challenge his choice. Both of his parents in unison disputed his decision, "Is there no woman among our kinsmen or among the other tribes of Israel, that you are determined to marry a Philistine woman, who is the daughter of an uncircumcized Philistine?" Samson's reply was emphatic. "It is this specific woman that has attracted and enamored my affection for her. *kach li* Take her for me as a proselyte, she shall then disassociate herself from her people. It is she I intend to marry and not her parents or her family". A

JUDGES CHAPTER 14

statement which has its echo expanded into the 20th century. Samson's parents whose objections were quite clear, are at a loss how to avoid their dilemma.

V. 4 — They looked back upon their dedication to raise Samson in accord with the instructions given them by the *malach Adonai*, where have they failed? They analyze the meaning of being a *nazarite* dedicated to the cause of Israel and concerned with the hostility of the Philistines. This controversy is bound to strain their relationship with their son. How can they reconcile their resentment with their hope for their one and only son? (Gen. 27:46) How does the Eternal God of Israel intend to resolve their dilemma?

V. 5 — With perfect faith in the Eternal's guidance of their destiny, Manoach, Hatzlalponie and Samson went down to Timnah. When they arrived at the nearby vineyards of Timnah, Samson remained there, while his parents went ahead to meet the bride's parents and to discuss the details of Samson's forthcoming marriage. While roaming through the vineyard a young lion roared toward him. Unlike English, in Hebrew every stage of a lion's growth is described by a different word, gur, kephir, aryeh, labi, layish. The symbolism in the narrative is indicative of Samson's detour from the guidelines for his life. As a *nazarite* he tempted himself by being present in a vineyard. Having ignored the first barrier, he is being challenged by his second misstep, the lust for a Philistine woman.

V. 6 — *Vatizlach* Samson instinctively was endowed with the vitality and determination to meet his challenger. He tore the young lion apart with his bare hands as one would rend a kid asunder. Samson did not tell his parents about this experience, for fear that they would confirm his instinctive suspicion that these symbols were challenging the new path he is taking in his life. Samson is also deeply impressed by his supernatural strength which gave him the capability to dispatch a ferocious beast.

V. 7 — Samson joined his parents. He now met his bride and her family. He spoke to her for the first time and confirmed for himself that in addition to being attractive, she was also intelligent. When he was informed that she consented to convert to meet his standards as a *nazarite, vatishar beene Shimshon* his evaluation of his bride elated him.

Vs. 8.9 — Samson returned the following year with his parents to make the necessary preparations for his wedding. Enroute he detoured to the area where he had encountered the young lion. He found the carcass and observed a swarm of bees in the skeleton and an accumulation of honey. V. 9. He scooped up some of the honey into the palms of his hands and ate the honey as he rejoined his parents. He offered them some of the honey and they ate it. He did not disclose the source of the honey, that it came from the carcass of the dead lion. The symbolism of this experience was to

JUDGES CHAPTER 14

caution Samson, that the beauty of his affianced bride, like the sweetness of the bees honey could return to its natural instincts and sting him.

Vs. 10.11　　Manoach met with the bride's parents to finalize the details for the bride's conversion in accord with his previous agreement. Samson gave a bachelor party in accord with Philistine custom for thirty friends of the bride. V. 11. These 30 groomsmen were designated to impress Samson with their position in society and were to entertain him before the wedding.

Vs. 12.14　　Samson proposed a riddle and gave them seven days until the end of the wedding reception. Should they guess the riddle, he would reward each of them with linen under garments and outer garments. V. 13. Should you fail to solve my riddle, you shall be obliged to give me 30 sets of linen under garments and 30 sets of outer garments. V. 14. Samson stated the riddle. "Out of the eater came something to eat. Out of the powerful came sweetness." For three days they pondered the riddle. Though they would have been justified to receive some modification had they asked, their arrogant attitude toward Samson considered it beneath them to ask questions.

V. 15　　Rashi suggests that the riddle was proposed on a Wednesday. *Yom Hashevii* was the fourth day after they resolved that the solution was beyond them. *Pati et ishech* "Entice your husband to give us the answer to his riddle. If you do not comply with our request, we could put you and your father's household to the torch." (Obviously a common practice of revenge which even the tribe of Ephraim acquired from the indigenous environment (Jud. 12:1, 15:6). "Have you invited us here in order to impoverish us? If this was your intention, rest assured we shall implement our threat."

V. 16　　Samson's wife exposed her tormented fears as she badgered him with tears and disputed his love, for in fact he hated her. "Your intent and purpose of challenging my countrymen with your riddle was to embarrass them. If you loved me you would have confided me with the answer." Samson replied, "Since I did not divulge the answer to my parents shall I reveal the answer to you?"

V. 17　　For the full period of seven days of the wedding feast Samson's wife harassed him with tears. On the seventh and last day of the wedding festivities, Samson could no longer resist her distress, he gave her the answer to his riddle. Because of the fear of her countrymen she divulged the answer to them of Samson's riddle.

V. 18.　　The following Wednesday, the wedding festivities are about to end as the sun set, Samson's groomsmen addressed him. "What is sweeter than honey, and what is stronger than a lion?" Samson recognized and acknowledged the source of their intelligent reply.

JUDGES CHAPTER 14

"Had you not plowed with my heifer, you would not have guessed my riddle." Samson expressed his annoyance. *Charashtem beeglathi* Your unethical and immoral method of involving my wife to find the answer to my riddle forces me to expose your vulgar and lewd way of living. As my guests you were obliged to receive me graciously. This you did not do. You persisted in your hostility, it came between me and my wife. By threatening my wife you created the enmity between us which initiated mistrust and deception. You reduced my wife's character to that of a dumb animal, that can be led astray from her master to plow with her. It was my intention to cherish her and shelter her in accord with the mores and standards established by my people of Israel, where the Jewish woman is the queen of the household. You have destroyed this potential by persecuting her conscience with your coarse and obscene intervention into our lives.

V. 19 *Vatizlach alav ruach Adonai* Samson's distress motivated him and his resolution, he was determined to avenge his distress against the Philistines, who symbolized the mores and injustice of their people. For two days he traveled in the direction of Ashkelon. His anger and his hostility rose as he walked deep into Philistine territory. Samson evaluates his romance, was it a fantasy or a mirage? He had pinned great hope and anticipated much happiness in his marriage. He now sees quite clearly through the antagonistic environment during the wedding reception, and the intimate relationship between his wife and his best man. Samson climaxes his infuriated rage by killing 30 Philistines. Samson took their clothing and paid his debt to his groomsmen. *Vayichar apo* He obviously put into words the thoughts that prevailed in his mind during his trip to Ashkelon and back. Samson's wrath turned to remorse that he rejected his parent's advice in v. 3, repentantly and with an inflamed conscience, Samson asks, how did he permit himself to justify his heroic act of killing 30 Philistines in order to pacify his anguish? How did all this violence begin? Samson cannot bypass his guilt, for lusting with his eyes. Repentantly he left Timnah, to return to his father's home where the Eternal God of Israel, is ever present in the daily lives of his parents.

V. 20 To confirm Samson's repentant conclusions, this verse reports that Samson's father-in-law, in keeping with Philistine mores gave his daughter in marriage to his best man. It was he that was his rival before his wedding. This information was not available to Samson at this time.

JUDGES CHAPTER 15

Vs. 1.3 Some time later during the beauty and bounty of the wheat harvest, amidst the splendor and radiance of nature in bloom, Samson in keeping with Israel's mores, resolved to revisit his wife. In keeping with the oriental agricultural mores, he took with him a kid as a

JUDGES CHAPTER 15

token of his reconciliation. Arriving at her father's home, Samson desired to enter his wife's room. However, her father would not permit him to enter.

V. 2. Samson's father-in-law, tried to justify his conduct reported in v. 20. "I concluded that you no longer desired my daughter because of her past conduct, I therefore gave her in marriage to your wedding companion." To appease Samson's feeling, his father-in-law offered him his younger daughter, "who is even more beautiful than your former wife."

V. 3. Samson's indignation magnified his resolution as he declared openly to all those present. "Be it known that from now on any harm I can inflict upon the Philistine people, shall be in just retribution for the grief and distress you have caused me."

Vs. 4.5   Beginning with these verses Samson initiated a personal *war* against all Philistines. There is no national or local effort to throw off Philistine oppression against Israel in the Holyland. His personal escapades are carried on in an environment of daily commercial enterprise between Israel and the other indigenous communities of the Holyland. We must not overlook the effectiveness of international trade despite the unorganized and chaotic conditions in the Holyland. The Philistines have the organized military force to expand its commerical operations. Their presence is vital for the development of daily commerce. It must be recognized that at no time in the period of Judges has Israel made an organized counter reply to Philistine progressive effort to limit Israel's ability to govern the Holyland. Samson's freelance effort described in these verses eventually stirred the conscience of Israel to build an awareness against Philistine inroads. Samson's pin-pricks of the Philistines were the compulsive awareness of one man which kept the Philistine question alive for the next century, when Saul and David will organize a national effort to deal with it positively.

V. 4. Samson trapped 300 foxes, he tied a wooden torch to the tails of every two foxes, for a total of 150 torches soaked in flammable material.

V. 5. He lit the torches and turned the foxes loose among the standing fields of grain in the vicinity of Timnah. The flames spread from the sheaves of grain already harvested to the standing crops not yet harvested. It spread from here to vineyards and unto the olive trees.

Vs. 6.8   Upon investigation, it was established that this was the work of Samson, that he did this to avenge himself against his father-in-law. The people whose crops were destroyed now turned to avenge themselves by putting Samson's father-in-law, his daughter and his home to the torch, in accord with Philistine mores.

V. 7. Samson challenged their moral concept of equating the loss of their crops with the deaths of his wife and his father-in-law. "I shall not cease until I avenge your injustice."

V. 8. Samson gathered a group to join him. He waylaid those responsible for putting to death his wife and her father. They rampantly maimed those riding on

JUDGES CHAPTER 15

donkeys on their thighs and those walking on their legs. At this point he went into hiding in the cave of the Rock of Etam. (South of Bethlehem, in the wilderness of Judah).

Vs. 9.10   From a local affair, the Philistine authority sent an expedition, they ascended to Lehi and pitched their camp there. V. 10 The men of Judah challenged their right to encamp in their territory. "We are in search of Samson in order to imprison him." (Jud. 14:4)

V. 11   Philistine strategy confirms their tyrannical rule. They have the knowledge that Samson is in hiding here. They also know that he is a Danite. Yet, they demand the Judean's to organize a unit to capture him and turn him over to the Philistines as a prisoner. Both sides have calculated that Samson has organized a force of his own (something he never achieved). The Judean's recognized the Philistine official command and organized a force of 3000 men to arrest Samson. They entered the cave and demanded a reason for Samson jeopardizing their relations with the Philistines. "Why do you do this to us?" Samson replied, "I have simply repaid them for the pain and grief they have caused me."

V. 12   The Judean's informed Samson they have come to arrest him and turn him over to the Philistines in accord with their military order. Samson agreed to permit them to bind him on condition they swear not to contend with him. "For if you do, I shall defend myself. I am loath of causing bloodshed among my fellow Israelites."

V. 13   The Judeans assured Samson they will just bind him but will not contend with him or even harm him. They certainly will not kill him. Samson permitted them to bind him with two new ropes and they brought him up from the cave.

V. 14   Samson proceeded with them to the Philistine camp at Lehi. When they faced each other, the camp roared with joy. *Vatizlach ruach Adonai* Samson became endowed with resolution, the Philistines shall not win this round. Determined to give a good account of himself, he garnered his strength and broke loose from his bonds. The ropes dissolved like flax touching a flame.

Vs. 15.16   In the moments which divided Samson from his captives, he sought and found a fresh jawbone of an ass (a common experience in the mid-east, where carcasses of dead animals are permitted to dehydrate in the hot sun). Like a hunter he routed his attackers, who feared his approach. V. 16 Samson's courage rose and in retrospect he said, "With the jawbone of an ass I slew many jackals."

V. 17   Analyzing the meaning of his victory, he discarded the jawbone in digust as he mumbled to himself, "One day history will remember my heroic accomplishment and call it

JUDGES CHAPTER 15

Ramath-Lechi. How have I, descended from the goals and dedication of a *nazir* to become a killer of men?"

Vs. 18.20 Samson reviewed his experiences beginning with (Jud. 14:3, 19,15:1.8, 14.15) his thoughts wearied him, his conscience challenged his judgment *vayitzmah meod* his thirst for the ability to perceive the truth by far outreached his physical thirst for water. Samson called upon the Eternal for guidance out of his dilemma. "It was You O Eternal God, that gave me the courage, the determination to turn my capture and defeat into a victory. Shall I wander about in Philistine territory searching for water to quench my thirst? Should I succumb to my physical need I most certainly would be made to pay with my life for my courageous self defense? Should I make no effort to save my life, I most certainly would die of thirst? I cannot believe or even perceive by the remotest concept, that You saved me from death by the Philistines only to permit me to die of thirst." V. 19 *Vayivka Elohim* In justice to Samson's sincerity, his dedicated desire to perceive the *link* how every living creature draws its existence from the Source of all life, Samson was granted the inspiration to search for water in the *machtesh-hollow* the natural hollow which is a potential for springs of water. Samson's experience has a parallel in history (Gen. 21:15.19). Hagar had encouraged Ishmael to become a *mezachek* one who denigrated the meaning of Isaac's birth in the life of Sarah. Samson too denigrated the meaning of intermarriage and assimilation as conceived by his parents. The Eternal God of his father Manoach, is challenging Samson's ego. It was he that followed the desire of his senses to Timnah, now faced with the threat of dying of dehydration, he lacks the common sense, the practical understanding of God's natural law, that in the cleft of the rock was the ongoing potential for a spring of water. It was God's natural law that forced the water from the hollow of the rock to make it visible to the embattled Samson. While he satisfied his need for water and began to regain his strength, he recognized his past errors which almost cost him his life. Samson named this spring, "The spring that made itself visible when Samson prayed for water." *En-hakkore.*"

V. 20. Samson's effectiveness as a force against the Philistines was a spontaneous periodic leadership, which only held the Philistines at bay. He never mounted an organized endeavor to expel the enemy from Israel's territory. His distractions and his detours from his potential destiny limited his efforts to hit and run tactics during the 20 years of his active lifetime.

JUDGES CHAPTER 16

Vs. 1.3 Samson's recklessness is indicated by another escapade. He is aware of Philistine resolution to square matters with him for his past performances. Yet, he challenged his fate by checking in at the home of a libertine woman, who lived in Gaza, about 30 miles from Zorah. V. 2 Samson's presence in this specific home was reported to the local

JUDGES CHAPTER 16

authorities. They created an ambush and marked time all night to capture him as he attempts to leave in the morning and kill him on sight. V. 3 Anticipating trouble, Samson rose at midnight, when he attempted to leave the city the gates were locked. He lifted the doors and the doorposts in one piece, including the bars that secured them to the enclosure, upon his shoulders and carried them to a nearby hill overlooking the city of Hebron in the distance.

Vs. 4.5   From these verses we observe a man endowed with superhuman strength and physical powers, he dissipates and squanders his ability. What drives Samson is his ego, to establish his lack of fear, yet fails to utilize his superior gifts to help his people overcome their enemies waiting in the wings to destroy them. Consistent with his lifestyle, he now falls in love with Delilah, from the area of the Wadi-Sorek. This is part of the allotted territory of Dan and is now occupied by the Philistines. V. 5. The governors of the five Philistine provinces went up to Wadi-Sorek and offered Delilah 1100 x 5 = 5500 pieces of silver (in Jacob's time in the 15th century the shekel weighed 275 grains) or a total of 1,512,500 grains of silver. In consideration for this fabulous sum, Delilah is to entice Samson to reveal to her the source of his superhuman power. This information gives us a slight concept of the success and wealth of the times. It also enlarges upon the tremendous losses Samson created by his individual escapades. It also magnifies the extent of the chaos in Israel's ranks. Samson a member of the tribe of Dan fails to help his kin from taking possession of their allotted territory. The small area in which they live is occupied by the Philistines.

Vs. 6.7   Delilah prodded Samson to reveal the source of his power. She periodically suggested jestingly that he permit her to tie him with heavy cords in order to demonstrate the limits of his strength. V. 7. Samson's self confidence permitted Delilah to test his brute force. He suggests, "that she bind him with seven-ply fresh tendons, their combined tensile strength would prove beyond his capability to free himself."

Vs. 8.9   Delilah procured seven-ply fresh tendons. In a nearby room she created an ambush of Philistine men, to take Samson prisoner when she will succeed to tie him up securely. All things in readiness for her test, Delilah cried out "Samson! the Philistines are coming to imprison you." Samson tore the seven-ply tendons apart as if they were strands of hemp or flax exposed to a flame.

Vs. 10.12   Delilah charged Samson with lying to her. His ego permitted him to amuse her diversion and contest. V. 11 "If you tie me up with triple stranded ropes used for carrying loads, I doubt I could free myself even as any other man."

V. 12. Delilah procured the specific ropes, she bound him securely and once again ordered the ambush to wait for the moment to seize Samson as a prisoner. "Samson! the Philistines have come to arrest you." Samson mustered his supernatural strength and tore the ropes from his arms as if they were but thread.

JUDGES CHAPTER 16

Vs. 13.14 Delilah charged Samson with deliberate lies, that his intention is to make her look like a fool. Over a period of time as these experiments of Delilah took place, Samson is unable to resist her persistent effort to destroy him. There is no effort on his part to recognize the trap she is setting to challenge his endurance. Samson succumbs to yet another test, despite the fact that as a *nazir* he may not tear or cut his hair. In his moments of fatuity, he entices Delilah with an invitation. Should she succeed in his sleeping moments to weave his seven locks of hair into the warp of the cloth on her loom, he could not possibly tear himself loose (for fear of tearing his hair). Delilah waited until Samson was fast asleep, she plaited his hair into the warp of the cloth on her loom. She secured the cloth with the roller and entwined it to keep his hair firmly in place. (Was Samson asleep during all this preoccupation with his hair? Or is it the intensity of his dissipation that failed to alarm him, how far he has strayed from his original goal?) Having spent hours in her preparation, Delilah is now ready to reap her reward. "Delilah cried out, Samson! the Philistines have come to imprison you!" Samson stirred from his deep sleep, he pulled out the peg, the roller on the loom including the warp and woof of cloth secured to it.

Vs. 15.16 Delilah confronted Samson. "Your love for me is a deception, even as the confidences you have pretended to share with me." V. 16. Delilah nagged Samson over a period of time. Her persistence was reinforced by her curiosity and the great reward that awaited her success in imprisoning Samson. She utilized every womanly wile to entice him to divulge the secret of his superhuman power. She wearied him unto death as she fumed and agitated him to share his secret.

V. 17 To appease Delilah, and to satisfy his sexual demand, he bore his soul to her. "No razor has ever touched my head. I have been a *nazir* from the time I was conceived in my mother's womb. Should I cut my hair my strength would leave me. I would be reduced to the strength and vigor endowed to all makind." Samson lacked the moral force to determine the difference of right from wrong. His tremendous confidence in his superstrength challenged every physical force about him. Like a child he lacked the fear and sensitivity that would warn him against betrayal.

V. 18 Delilah is satisfied that Samson has divulged his whole personality to her. She has drained every detail of his personal life. She is confident that she can deliver him to the Philistines and receive her reward. This time she demands that the governors come personally and bring her reward with them. In effect she is telling them she will not surrender him to any one else unless they uphold their part of the agreement to pay in kind as promised.

V. 19 Delilah felt at the height of her conceit as she lulled Samson to sleep in her lap. She satisfied his every whim and wish, her

JUDGES CHAPTER 16

guile and deceit had no bounds as she ordered his seven locks to be shorn from his head. Delilah molded Samson's helpless body as his strength slipped from his grasp she bound him with ropes in preparation for his new masters.

Vs. 20.21 Delilah tested her strategy as she cried out. "Samson!! The Philistines are upon you." Samson awoke from his trance, he made an effort to free himself from his fetters as he had done on previous occasions. Samson's hypnotic seance had bypassed his *Zelem Elohim*-intelligence. He has defiled his natural gifts. Excellence can only function in an atmosphere of *Kedushah* sanctity. Samson has dissipated his natural gifts, his superhuman potential for greatness. His sensual desires retarded his natural ability for the disciplines of survival and continuity.

V. 21. Samson was seized by the Philistines. They took him to Gaza, mutilated his eyes and shackled him in bronze fetters as a mill slave in the prison.

Vs. 22.23 Indicates a lapse of considerable time as expressed by the fact that Samson's hair began to grow back. V. 23 The governors of Philistia declared a festival to express their gratitude to their god Dagon, for the capture of Samson.

V. 24. They invited their people to come and celebrate the capture of this natural monster who had wreaked havoc on the countryside as recorded in (Jud. 14:19, 15:4.5,15, 16:3). They offered sacrifices to their god Dagon for having delivered Samson into their custody. "It is he that devastated our land and slew many of our people."

Vs. 25.27 They humiliated Samson as they demanded that he be brought from the prison to dance for them. The spectacle of seeing him stumble about in his fetters became a source of amusement. To make it possible for all to see him, they placed him on the terrace between the two main pillars of the building entrance.

V. 26. Samson appealed to the lad that was guiding him about in his state of blindness, to place his hands upon the pillars that he may rest from his exhaustion. Samson had a mental concept of the building from his past experiences.

V. 27. The text records, there were about 3000 people assembled on the roof of this vast auditorium in addition to those inside the building which included the governors of the five municipalities and their women folk. All this vast assembly gathered to amuse themselves with their great victory and to view Samson's misery in chains.

V. 28 Samson has had adequate time to define the meaning of his escapades. Though denied the ability to see with his eyes, he analyzed with his mind, and evaluated with his heart, the cause and effect of his philandering. He now fully conceived how he dissipated his strength, never fulfilled the promise placed upon his shoulders by the

JUDGES CHAPTER 16

messenger of the Eternal God of Israel (Jud. 13:5). In this moment of total distress he fully perceives that he has become the symbol of Israel's dissipated power. It is not he that is being mocked but the whole poeple of Israel. From the most inner depth of his soul he prays, "*Adonai* Master of my life, *Elohim* the God of Justice, *zachreni na*, remember the moments of my life when I walked in Your paths and observed Your disciplines. *Chazkenie*, grant me the full powers of my potential strength, *ach hapaam*, this one and final moment of my life; remove the shame I have caused the people of Israel. Grant me this one request O God of justice, that I may avenge the loss of my eyes and the humiliation I have brought upon my people Israel. For this I stand ready to offer my life."

Vs. 29.30 Samson embraced the main pillars of the temple *vayilpoth* and twisted them out of place. He then braced both of his arms as a fulcrum to push the pillars apart simultaneously with both hands.

V. 30. Samson mustered every fiber of his body to avenge the shame he has brought upon his people. "Let me die with the Philistines!" his voice rang out as the temple edifice came crashing down to crush all those on the roof and in the interior of the building. Samson's heroic death accounted for more lives lost than the total of his whole lifetime.

V. 31 The members of Samson's family were joined by others of the tribe of Dan, who came from Zorah to Gaza and retrieved the body of Samson. They carried his body to Manoach's family tomb between Zorah and Eshtaol and laid it to rest in the tomb. The 20 years recorded here included the period of imprisonment by the Philistines. Just as this verse records the physical death of Samson, (Jud. 16:20) records the declining fortunes of Samson and his spiritual death.

JUDGES CHAPTER 17

V. 1 It is generally conceded that the incident reported in this chapter belongs to the period of Samson. Because of Philistine superior organization and military superiority, the tribe of Dan could not take possession of its allotted territory. In the time of Deborah the Danites were already settled in Laish-Dan. The prophet Samuel describes the following incident to give future history a window from which it can view the past. Though the people of Israel were drifting from their national and spiritual goals, there were pockets of prosperity and well being.

In the hill country of Ephraim, there lived a man by the name of Michayahu. His mother obviously a wealthy woman had 1100 pieces of silver in her possession until it was taken from her. When she discovered its loss she uttered a curse upon the one who took it.

V. 2 Michayahu's conscience was stirred with remorse because he was present when his mother uttered the curse. Yet, he failed

JUDGES CHAPTER 17

to come forward to confess that he had taken it (Lev. 5:1). Though no one saw him take it and no one accused him of taking it, he was innocent legally but morally he was guilty.

Vs. 3.5   Michayahu came forward to his mother and confessed to her that he had taken the 1100 shekels of silver and is ready to return it to her. His mother too, is perturbed because she had uttered a curse. She is now remorsefully trying to neutralize her curse, she therefore tells her son that she had consecrated this money to the Sanctuary of the Eternal, in the name of her son, that he receive His blessing for his honorable conduct. I now transfer title to it officially to create a graven and molten image. When he transferred the 1100 shekels of silver to his mother she took 200 pieces of silver from the 1100 and gave it to the foundry and they made a graven and molten image, which was set up in the home of Michayahu. V. 5 Though his given name was Michayahu, the author feels he is no longer worthy to bear the name of the Eternal, he now calls him Micah. For it is Micah that established a house of worship for all his images in accord with Canaanite common practice. Micah made *teraphim*-human figure, he clothed it with an *ephod*-a replica of the priestly garment used for the purpose of fortune telling. He now consecrated one of his sons to become the priest in his house of worship.

V. 6   Verses 1.5, describes the effect of no central authority in Israel. Each person went his own way. They ignored the values, and disciplines inscribed in the Torah. A son steals from his mother is but a symbol of the general conditions that prevailed at this time because of the lack of a central authority. The symbol of the 1100 shekels of silver describes the affluence of the times which paralleled the prosperity that existed in Philistia (Jud. 16:5). The fiction described, is the sanctification of money to bypass the mother's curse and change it loosely to a blessing. Micah's mother unmasks her apostasy as she reneges on her vow. She finally contributes but 200 shekels for her idolatrous worship. All of these machinations can only be called moral and ethical in the framework and fiction of idolatry which can take on as many forms as the human mind can fashion. This breakdown is impossible when a human being, a family, a community or a nation recognizes *Adonai Melech* God, the Eternal King of all humanity and His disciplines inscribed in His Torah. It was a free for all, everyone did as he pleased. This is the formula of retrogression which has engraved itself in the conscience of every historic period of mankind.

Vs. 7.8   The young man referred to in this verse was a direct descendant of Gershon the son of Moses (Jud. 18:30). He came from Bethlehem in Judah, north of Jerusalem. He was related by marriage to one of the families in Judah. Leviim generally were designated to live among all the tribes in Israel. This conforms with (Gen. 49:7, Deut. 12:18). The young man referred to in our text was Jonathan, the grandson of Gershon the son of Moses. He was traveling in search of a community where

JUDGES CHAPTER 17

he can serve as a Levite in order to earn his livelihood. In the course of his travels he came to the home of Micah, in the hill country of Ephraim.

Vs. 9.13   Micah his host inquired, "Where is your home?" I am a Levite, my home is in Bethlehem in Judah. I am in search of employment wherever I may find a need for my services. V. 10 "Stay with me," Micah said to him, "and be a father and a teacher to me. I will compensate you 10 shekels a year, an allowance for your clothing and an allowance for your food."

Vs. 11.12.   Jonathan the Levite agreed to Micah's offer and consented to serve him as a teacher, priest and father. Micah accepted Jonathan as a member of his household.

V. 13.   Micah is gratified by his good fortune, "that the Eternal God will bless the labor of my hands. He will enable me to prosper in all that I do, now that I have an authentic Levite as a priest to guide me, to teach me and to perform my sacrifices." Jonathan the Levite is sometimes called an *ish* a man and sometimes he is designated as *naar* an adolescent. The text is pointing up his adventurous mood as a youth and at other times his seriousness as a grown and experienced man.

JUDGES CHAPTER 18

V. 1   This verse dates the period of Pesel Micah, described in chapter 17. We are told that the tribe of Dan was unable to take possession of its allotted territory which stretched from Jaffa in the north, down to Eshtaol in the south (Jud. 1:34, 2:11.23). It was soon after Joshua died that the tribe of Dan resolved to seek another territory. It fully realized and recognized Philistine superiority in organization and military strength. They had chariots while Israel only had primitive armaments. The escapades of their kinsman Samson was no organized serious force of a united Israel. This development was still a century away. It did not happen until David and Solomon's time. Israel had the opportunity in Joshua's time when the Philistines were beginning to migrate in great numbers and invaded Gerar (see comm. in T.E.T. Gen. 26:). It was called Philistia even in Moses' time because the Seapeople were already becoming a majority. Had Israel mounted an organized united action at the end of Joshua's lifetime or even soon after his demise, they could have become the major force. In the 12th century the Philistines had dispossessed the Gerarites, where their kinsmen from the Aegean were well established.

V. 2   In (Gen. 46:23) the son of Dan is Chushim. A branch of this family never traveled in the desert with Moses. For a reconstruction of this conclusion (see addenda in T.E.T. pp261, 553). In the final census recorded in (Num. 26:42.43) those that did travel in the desert and participated in the conquest are listed in the name of Shuham. There is ample historical and archaeological evidence that the first branch of the

JUDGES CHAPTER 18

family of Dan, were living in Laish, to be near the Phoenicians long before the conquest of the Holyland. This new survey is being made by the families of Shuham. It is these families that were part of the Exodus that were counted in the second census and were allotted the coastal territory which is now being occupied by the Philistines. Therefore this survey recorded here is to reinstate the Danite settlement in Laish. While traveling north from Zorah and Eshtoel, they went to the home of Micah, in the hill country of Ephraim, with the intention of spending the night there.

Vs. 3.5   While in the home of Micah, they identified the voice which they overheard praying as that of a Levite they had met in Bethlehem, Judah. They immediately began to pry him with questions. "What brings you here? What are you doing here?" Jonathan replied, "I came here in search of a livelihood and Micah hired me to officiate as his priest." V. 5. As a kohen-priest, "Would you inquire for us from your Ephod, if our trip to the area of Laish will be successful?"

V. 6   Jonathan replied, "Go in peace, God recognizes favorably your intentions. Your mission shall succeed." (see comm. in T.E.T. on Ex. 28:13.30). The Ephod was a garment worn by all priests when actively officiating in the Mishkan. Only the High Priest had access to the Hoshen Mishpat. It was not used as an oracle.

V. 7   The five Danites arrived in Laish-Leshem. they surveyed the area and were impressed with the atmosphere of confidence and security, in the manner of Sidonians-Phoenicians. They occupied this area after the Egyptians defeated the Philistines. The main body of the Sidonians-Phoenicians are now established on the Mediterranean coastline, north of Israel. The settlers here now are squatters with no political commitments to clans or governments.

Vs. 8.9   The five Danites returned to Zorah and Eshtaol and gave their report. "We recognize excellent possibilities in this territory. Why are you silent, where is your response to our report? V. 9 We recommend that you make your plans to take possession of this excellent opportunity. Do not procrastinate."

Vs. 10.12   "Every factor in our investigation indicates that God in His graciousness has placed before us an opportunity which we must not miss. The territory has ample room for expansion. The present settlers are a tranquil group of people, they are industrious and will prove co-operative. It has natural resources in abundance and every possibility for development and its potential for good living is promising. Their lack of political ties to the surrounding communities is in our favor. We can possess it. Every ingredient for success indicates we must act at once." V. 11. The Danites mobilized 600 fighting men, they took with them their families and personal possessions. These were families that could not find opportunities in Zorah and

JUDGES CHAPTER 18

Eshtaol and were dedicated to the success of their mission.

V. 12. Enroute to their destination, they encamped at Kiriath-jearim, the area which is now called Abu-gash. It is four miles east of Beth-shemesh. This area at one time was part of Gibeon (Joshua 9:17). The surrounding communities respected Dan's courageous action and named it the Camp of Dan.

Vs. 13.14 From Kiriath-jearim they headed straight for the hill country of Ephraim and to the vicinity of Micah's home. When it was suggested that they pause there, the five original scouts reported their previous experience. "In one of these homes there is an ephod and teraphim, a sculptured image and a molten image."

Vs. 15.18 The five scouts went directly to Jonathan's house and greeted him peacefully. They engaged him in conversation while the 600 armed men approached the entrance of the house and subtly made it clear what their intentions were should he resist their demand. The five scouts took the ephod, the teraphim and the molten images. Jonathan is overwhelmed that the sons of Dan would stoop to steal, he challenged their right to take property that did not belong to them.

Vs. 19.20 The scouts replied, "We advise you to be silent. You would be well advised to come with us and become our father and priest. Would you rather become a priest to a tribe than be a priest to one man and his family?" Jonathan became receptive to their offer. He took the ephod, the household gods and the sculptured images and joined the tribe of Dan.

V. 21 The families of Dan rearranged their line of march. They placed their children in front, following the children were their families and their cattle and their movable property. Then followed the 600 armed men who formed the rear guard. They anticipated that Micah would pursue them with his townspeople.

Vs. 22.26 Some time had elapsed before Micah and his group overtook the Danites. Micah challenged them to stop. The Danites continued their march *vayasebu penehem* but turned their faces to inquire, "What is the purpose of your call?" Micah replied, "You have taken my gods and my priest and walked off with my possessions. How do you justify your innocence by asking me what is the matter?"

V. 25 The Danites replied. "You would be well advised not to shout and become abusive. We have some desperate men that would take exception to your accusation. You could provoke them to attack you and your family."

V. 26 Micah recognized the fate accompli, the odds were too great, he gathered his group and returned to his home.

V. 27 The author of the book of Judges speaks with irony for the record. Out of the voices of the silenced dead speak the

JUDGES CHAPTER 18

instructions of (Deut. 16:20, 20:10, Gen. 18:19). "When you approach a city with the intentions to conquer it, and take possession of it, you are obliged to offer them peace on the condition that they accept the observance of the Seven Laws of Noah." Where is Israel's concern with Justice shall you pursue?" The prophet Samuel therefore records the facts, that future Israel may recognize the injustice of the tribe of Dan. They stole the property of Micah, upon which he had expended his treasure and effort. They then threatened his life because he made an attempt to recover his property. They forced Jonathan to join them as their priest. Their whole procedure denigrated the concept and intent of the conquest of the Holyland. Sardonically, the prophet Samuel writes, *vayavou* they pounced upon a quiet peaceful people without warning. They attacked them and put them to the sword. When they attempted to defend themselves, they destroyed the city completely by fire. Dan cannot defend its action by charging, that Laish-Leshem was defiled by idolatry (Ex. 20:23). The scouts too bore their share of the guilt. They reported that this tranquil people would not defend themselves.

Vs. 28.29 The intent of these settlers was to build a community away from the intrigue and political strife of the Sidonians now settled on the Mediterranean coast. Laish was located in the valley of Beth-rechob, northwest of the Hulah valley, in the area of the modern Banias. Samuel effectively describes the people of Laish, they were desirous of living quietly by themselves. The Danites rebuilt the city. In accord with Daath Sofrim, this territory was out of bounds from the Holyland.

V. 29 We may conclude that with the exception of the families of Dan, that were roaming the high seas and the families of Dan, that had settled in various Judean communities and those living in Zorah and Eshtaol, the rest of the tribe of Dan settled in Laish and renamed it Dan.

Vs. 30.31 The Danites set up their own shrine with the sculptured images stolen from Micah. They installed Jonathan the grandson of Gershon and great grandson of Moses (Ex.2:22) as their priest. The prophet Samuel wrote the name Mosheh, with a *nun*, to illustrate Israel's embarrassment that a descendant of the godly man Moses had become the symbol to describe the retrogression of Israel in the period of the Judges. Here in Dan, Jonathan and his son administered to the spiritual needs of the tribe of Dan. V. 31. I am inclined to side with Ralbag, that the shrine of Dan existed simultaneously while the Mishkan was the official shrine attended by the other tribes. The destruction of Shiloh reported in (I Sam. 4:10.22) happened close to the 10th century. V. 31, therefore refers to the period reported in (Jud. 4:2).

JUDGES CHAPTER 19

V. 1 Beginning with chapters 17,18,19,20,21, the prophet Samuel describes several embarrassing and tragic incidents by which is

JUDGES CHAPTER 19

illustrated the effect of *ein melech beYisrael* the result of ignoring the laws of the Eternal God in the daily lives of Israel. In this chaotic period, a Levite whose residence was in Bethlehem in the hills of Ephraim married a second wife legally. However, by the mores of the times she was called a concubine.

Vs. 2.9 At a point in their marriage, she decided to desert him and return to her father's home in Bethlehem, in Judah. There she stayed for a year and four months. V. 3. At this point in time he overcame his pride and set out with an attendant and two donkeys, to convince her to return with him. His wife received him very cordially and when her father saw him, he too was pleased by his presence. He had resolved to persuade his daughter to return to her husband.

V. 4. Having succeeded in his effort of reconciliation, he insisted that his son-in-law celebrate the occasion and stay with him for the next three days.

V. 5. Early on the fourth day the Levite was prepared to leave but his father-in-law insisted that he first have breakfast.

V. 6. They broke bread together, feasted and had something to drink. Once again the Levite was convinced that he stay another night.

V. 7. When he arose and tried to leave, his father-in-law induced him to stay another day and night.

Vs. 8.9. On the fifth day the Levite rose at dawn to leave, once again his father-in-law advocated he have breakfast first and as the morning moved on to noon, the father's intuitive fear of his leaving grew with the day. He therefore expressed his fear of their traveling in the dark and once again he pleaded that they stay another night.

Vs. 10.14 The Levite insisted on leaving at once as he was anxious to go back home. He set out with his attendant, they loaded the donkeys, he took his concubine and arrived on the outskirts of Jebus-Jerusalem. V. 11. His attendant suggested that they stay here as the day was beginning to wane.

Vs. 12.13. The Levite was reluctant to stay in Jebus, because it was inhabited at this time by aliens. He therefore continued on to Gibeah, in the territory of Benjamin.

V. 14. Observing the sudden setting of the sun they decided to stop at the outskirts of Gibeah.

Vs. 15.16 They proceeded to the main square in Gibeah, to expose their presence, in the hope that someone will offer them their hospitality to stay the night. But none was forthcoming. V. 16 As the evening became night, an old man whose home was in the hill country of Ephraim but owned fields in Gibeah, he therefore resided in Gibeah. He was now returning from his labors in the fields.

Vs. 17.18 Observing the wayfarers, he inquired as to their destination

JUDGES CHAPTER 19

and where is their home? The Levite replied. "We are traveling from Bethlehem in Judah and our home is in Bethlehem, in the hill country of Ephraim. I am planning to go to Shiloh-the House of God. I stopped here anticipating that I could stay the night in one of the Benjaminite homes. However, no one invited us in."

Vs. 19.21   The Levite was quick to explain. "We have adequate supplies both for our animals and our own needs. All we had hoped for was shelter." The old man replied, "I bid thee peace, permit me to be your host. I will also provide your needs. You shall not spend the night outdoors." Arriving at the old man's home he provided food for the animals first, then offered them washing facilities, he then served them with food and drink.

V. 22   While they were enjoying the old man's hospitality a depraved group of Gibeanites, pounded on the door and demanded that the old man turn his guests over to them, that they may get to know them *"homosexually"* in accord with Canaanite practices.

V. 23   The old man went outside and pleaded with them. "Do not commit this abominable act. These people are my guests." The author uses the same language recorded in (Gen. 19:1.10) to illustrate the fact, 800 years separate these two eras, the practice is still prevalent in Canaan and its abominable practice has infiltrated the tribe of Benjamin.

Vs. 24.25   In keeping with the above described mores of ancient Sodom, the old man pleads, "Here is my virgin daughter and my guest's concubine. Have your pleasure with them, but do not abuse my guest." They refused his offer and continued to challenge him whereupon the Levite exposed his concubine to them outside the door. They raped her and abused her all that night. At the dawn they released her.

Vs. 26.28   Toward morning the Levite's concubine made her way back by herself after having been abused and disgraced. She collapsed at the door of the old man's house where she was to spend the night. There she lay until her husband-lord arose in the morning to continue his journey. There was his concubine *veyadehah al hasaf* her mutilation was so complete, that only her outstretched hand was able to reach the threshhold of the door. V. 28. The Levite called her to rise, "come let us continue our journey." There was no reply because she was dead. He placed her body on one of his donkey's and returned to his home.

V. 29   By the time the Levite arrived home, the impact of the terrible tragedy implicated him. He reflected upon his conduct in V. 25, he visualized his arbitrary, barbaric and self-centered conduct, as he forced his concubine out of the house to appease the mob. The enormity of his guilt grew with every step the donkey took before they arrived

JUDGES CHAPTER 19

home. How can he bypass his personal guilt? Though he fully recognized his acceptance of Canaanite mores, his conscience, having been molded by centuries of Torah disciplines, points its finger of guilt at him with an emphasis that he cannot escape. His next step is but an effort to share his transgression. He strives to implicate every tribe in Israel by his valiant and heroic act, to force them to share his blame for his barbaric conduct. He cut the dead body of his concubine into 12 parts and dispatched the symbol of his tragedy with a description of the details to each tribe in the Holyland. His misfortune he calculates, must become the rallying point to unite Israel against Canaanite debauchery which has infiltrated into Israel's daily life. The enormity of this tragedy rooted in the 11th century BCE. will continue to stir the conscience of every God-fearing human being to infinity.

V. 30   It took tragedy to spark the genetic development of the centuries. It murdered the peace of everyone that heard the details and viewed the gory symbolism distributed among the tribes by the Levite. It condemned every individual in Israel as guilty for Benjamin's dastardly crime. This united outcry of a people honed by disciplines which strove to eradicate the predatory beast from the heart of man, was instinctive and spontaneous.

JUDGES CHAPTER 20

Vs. 1.2   The enormity of this tragedy challenged Israel's right and reason for being in the Holyland, *Justice, Justice, shall you pursue*. This awareness was felt from Dan to Beer-sheba and throughout the Gilead-Trans-Jordan. Spontaneously they assembled at Mitzpah, northwest of Gibeah, in the territory of Benjamin. They were resolved to dedicate their lives to defend the honor of the Eternal God of Israel, by eradicating this blight upon the conscience of Israel. The leaders of the tribes mustered 400,000 men, who consecrated their lives to eradicate this injustice against the Levite's humble concubine. Israel has written it into the record which has survived for 3100 years to challenge every generation to infinity.

Vs. 3.5   The tribe of Benjamin to a man is aware of the assembly at Mitzpah. They too assembled to determine their course of action. A court of inquiry was set up to investigate the details of the charges. V. 4. The Levite testified, "We came to Gibeah, in the territory of Benjamin, to spend the night." V. 5. "The citizens of Gibeah surrounded the home of my host with the intention to kill me." (The Levite omits to tell them that it was he that substituted his concubine). "They ravished my concubine and abused her unto death."

Vs. 6.7   "Incensed by this depraved and outrageous act, I was motivated to challenge the conscience of Israel with this crime. I cut my concubine into 12 pieces as a symbol of my grief. My

JUDGES CHAPTER 20

intention was to rouse your sense of justice. Will you permit this degenerate and violent action to become a way of life in Israel? It is now up to you as Israelites, to prove that you are dedicated to the pursuit of justice. Take counsel and produce a plan for action and implement it at once."

Vs. 8.12 The indignation of all those present produced a consensus. They resolved to mount a united action at once. They decided no one will return to his home until this tragedy is resolved. Vs. 9.10. Their firm decision was to mobilize an army by drafting 10 out of every 100 eligible men in each tribe. Each tribe is to be responsible for its arms and its food supply for the duration of the action. Vs. 11.12. As a united action they decided unanimously, they will send representatives to the leaders of Benjamin and demand an official explanation. "How did you permit such a depraved and outrageous action to take place within your jurisdiction?"

V. 13 "We demand that you surrender those chargeable with this crime, that we may find them guilty and punish them with the death penalty. It is our intention to root out such depravity from the ranks of Israel." The Benjaminites resisted this demand. Their refusal to cooperate dishonored and disgraced their heritage as grandsons of Jacob. (Samuel omitted the word sons from the text, to record their disgraceful conduct in not shouldering their moral responsibility). See comm. in T.E.T. on (Gen. 49:27, Deut. 33:12) how Jacob and Moses evaluated Benjamin's development. Their prophetic evaluation has taken about 400 years to surface at this time in the experience recorded here and known as Pilegesh Begibeah.

Vs. 14.16 Instead of surrendering the culprits, the Benjaminites issued a call to arms. They mobilized in the town of Gibeah, which mustered 700 men. They were prepared to defend their conduct against the united action of the other tribes. The other families of Benjamin volunteered 26,000 men. Among these men there were 700 men though lefthanded were ambidextrous (Jud. 3:15) and specialists with the sling. It was reported that they could sling a stone at a hair and not miss.

Vs. 17.18 The tribes collectively mobilized 400,000 men with outstanding skills in warfare at Mitzpah. They marched to the House of God in Shiloh to take counsel with the High Priest as to the moral validity of their decision and their planned action, and under whose leadership shall they fight. Both answers are included in the last phrase. The High priest concurred in their decision and advised that they take this action under the leadership of Judah.

Vs. 19.21 The very next morning they encamped at the outskirts of Gibeah. They launched their attack against the Benjaminites, who were in the city of Gibeah. This advantage resulted in the loss of 22,000 men of the united Israel forces. The cause of this loss is challengeable to their dependence upon a miracle. War had to take into

JUDGES CHAPTER 20

consideration every angle of the potential action. Benjamin anticipated to be defeated, and therefore took advantage of the weakness in the allied strategy.

Vs. 22.23 Once again they consulted with Shiloh, and were advised that they must rededicate themselves to the justice of their cause in order to gain the upper hand in the strategy.

Vs. 24.25. On the second day they returned to Gibeah to storm the city and once again lost 18,000 men. At this point in time they fully realized they must refine their cause, their method of dealing with a brother Israelite. Their heavy losses are the effect of a deficiency in their own moral standing. Though the Benjaminites are outnumbered by the united tribes of Israel, 'Why have they failed?'

V. 26 They issued an order for an assembly at Bethel-the House of God, in Shiloh. They declared this day a fast day and followed the procedure designated for the Day of Atonement (see comm. in T.E.T. on Num. 15:22.26). They sought repentance for past transgressions in the hope they can merit a fresh start. In keeping with the fullest meaning of the Day of Atonement, that requires confession to our own inner conscience and resolution in our hearts, that we develop the ability to recognize our own deficiencies before we are given the right to correct the inequalities and the injustice of others. In this particular instance the injustice and incorrigibility of the tribe of Benjamin. Heeding the above disciplines to resolve their problem, all the men serving in the army and every other member of their households, it included men, women and children, they assembled in the House of God, in Shiloh. Collectively they fasted until the evening of that day. They offered burnt offerings and peace offerings, in order to share their wellbeing with the Priesthood and the Levites, who stood in the vanguard to discipline and remind all the children of Israel of their ongoing responsibility to live by the disciplines of Torah law.

Vs. 27.28 Phinehas, the High Priest, a descendant of Aaron, recognizing the sincerity of the soldiers in the united tribes of Israel, proceeded with the Ark of the Covenant to Bethel, in order to give his blessing to their dedicated effort and to be close at hand for all the soldiers of the army. He felt this would add another dimension to their rededication and reenforce the meaning of their cause. Bethel is midway between Shiloh and Gibeah. It is here at Bethel, that the High Priest Phinehas gave his blessings to the army, that on the morrow they shall succeed in their objective. It is here that he remained for an extra measure of faith in the justice of their cause.

Vs. 29.31 The united tribes of Israel emerged from their solemn experience with the fullest realization that the help of Israel's Eternal God, can be activated only when their faith in God is harmonized with their sincere initiative and effort to pursue the Eternal's standards for justice. Through this new light they recognized their past errors.

JUDGES CHAPTER 20

They strategically created an ambush and refined every detail to cover every contingency, they completely surrounded the city of Gibeah.

V. 30. When every detail was fully in place on their third attempt, they opened their feigned attack. V. 31. The Benjaminites countered with an offensive, while the united forces began a slow retreat as planned, in order to draw them out of the city and into the open countryside. The united forces continued their planned retreat from the hills of Gibeah and the hills leading to Bethel. This did cause them about thirty casualties.

Vs. 32.34 While the Benjaminites began to feel they were fighting the main force, the real force was the ambush waiting to swing into action at Baal-tamar. Another ambush was moving from its fixed position at Maareh-gebah. V. 34. Unaware of the surrounding action which was in the process of development, the Benjaminites were locked in battle on the highways leading from Gibeah and stretching in the direction of Bethel. At this very moment a force of 10,000 chosen men arrived south of Gibeah and unhinged the arrogant Benjaminite force.

Vs. 35.36 The original retreating force now became part of the pincers action as they turned frontally from retreat to attack. The Eternal's inspiration to the forces of Israel, created the initiative for a new beginning. Yet, their victory was tinged with remorse as they evaluated the lives lost in this civil war right at the beginning of Israel's national life.

Vs. 37.38 The ambush fighting in the city of Gibeah, deliberately opened a gap for the Benjaminites to escape, confident they will be intercepted outside the city of Gibeah. the ferociousness of the action was such that anything that moved inside the city was destroyed. V. 38. The united forces having attained their objective inside the city of Gibeah, sent up a smoke signal to inform the various armies and groups spread over a large area in Benjaminite territory, that the war was essentially over.

Vs. 39.43 These verses credit the outcome of the civil war to the strategy which began to develop as recorded in Vs. 31.32. When the Benjaminites outside of their city observed the smoke signal rise heavenward, they instinctively grasped the full meaning of their disaster. *Vs. 42.43.* The Benjaminites began to retreat from their presumptuous position as the united forces encircled them at Menuhah, where they had planned to rest. The massacre began at Menuhah and stretched toward the west side of Gibeah.

Vs. 44.48 The text sums up the dreadful casualties in the tribe of Benjamin, in a war which they brought upon themselves, 18,000 lost their lives in battle. Some fled to the Rock of Rimon, where they survived for four months. 5,000 met their fate on the highways as the united forces literally combed the area to Gidom, where another

JUDGES CHAPTER 20

2,000 paid the maximum penalty for their treasonous behavior. V. 46, sums up the total of 25,000 Benjaminites that fell that day in a war that should never have happened, were the disciplines of the Torah a part of their reason for being. V. 48. The united forces of Israel regrouped. In the process they put to the sword every Benjaminite that came within their reach. As the final touch of this dreadful war, the troops avenged themselves against every community that participated in this ferocious action, as they put these communities to the torch.

JUDGES CHAPTER 21

Vs. 1.2   When the united tribes of Israel assembled at Mitzpah, they had taken an oath that none would permit his daughter to marry any surviving Benjaminite. They now returned to Bethel, where the High Priest was encamped with the Ark for the duration of the offensive (Jud. 20:27.28). Here at Bethel in the presence of Phinehas they evaluated the tragic results of the civil war. They wept bitterly as they analyzed the salient meaning of their victory which removed a whole tribe from the ranks of Israel. What shall be its effect upon Israel's future history?

V. 3   They confronted Phinehas with their query, "O Eternal God of Israel, is this the victory you promised us in (Jud. 20:26.28)? O Eternal God, why did we have to become Your instrument to punish the tribe of Benjamin for a succession of transgressions, planted in its genetic seed centuries ago?" (See comm. in T.E.T. on Gen. 49:27, Deut. 33:12). In (Gen. 35:18) Rachel, Benjamin's mother prophetically named him Bin-oni. Was this a prediction of his evolution? What is the historic meaning of Jacob's inspiration to break camp at Bethel before the birth of Benjamin? How do we explain Israel's lament at this moment in Israel's history over the doom of Rachel's Bin-oni, at this very same geographic position in history?

V. 4   Though there has been an altar in Bethel, going back to Abraham (Gen. 12:8), they now built an altar dedicated to their self doubt and a memorial to their survival. The High Priest Phinehas offered burnt offerings and peace offerings as an expression of rededication to the Eternal God of Israel. They prayed for foregiveness for their involvement in *Pesel-Micah* and for any soldier that may have helped himself to the *herem*-booty of the war (Num. 31:50,54). At this moment of soul searching and self doubt, they strive to rationalize their involvement in the incident of the *Pilegesh Begibeah* they concluded it is rooted in the self doubt of their sainted teacher Moses. Together they must continue man's dialogue with the Eternal God of Israel (Ex. 33:13.23), "Show us Thy glory during our lifetime. Grant us the ability to comprehend Thy direction in the management of the Universe."

V. 5   When the united tribes organized a united force to deal with the problem of *Pilegesh Begibeah* they took a unanimous oath

JUDGES CHAPTER 21

to punish any tribe that would fail to answer their call, their failure would be punishable by death.

Vs. 6.7 Arriving at Beth-el, they evaluated with tremendous regret the elimination of a whole tribe from Israel's ranks. At this precise moment they fully grasped the excesses of their action in becoming the punishing rod of the Eternal, it can be traced to their indiscriminate vow. This sad page in Israel's history is rooted in Joshua's example set in establishing *herem* in (Joshua 7:10.13). Each of these excesses are contrary to the intent and purpose of Torah law, as described in our commentary on (Joshua 1:5.7). While in the atmosphere of the High-Priest at Bethel, they reviewed the past in light of the above facts. *Vayinachamu bnei Yisrael* They are most anxious to rehabilitate those that survived the massacre by escaping to the Rock of Rimmon (Jud. 20:47). These are the *notharim* in v. 1, the remnant of Benjamin, to whom they had vowed not to permit their daughters to take them as husbands.

Vs. 8.11 These four verses belong at the end of chapter 20. After the battle with Benjamin, they discovered that the community of Jabesh-gilead-Manasseh, which borders on the Jordan did not show up at Mitzpah. It was well known that the families living in Jabesh had close ties with the tribe of Benjamin. At the height of their mopping up operations described in (Jud. 20:42.43), it was in this mood and context that they dispatched 12,000 men to punish Jabesh in Gilead-Trans-Jordan. The rest of the united force went on to Bethel.

V. 12 At this moment of regret they changed the instructions to the men that have been on their way to the city of Jabesh on the east side of the Jordan and instructed them to bring back as many maidens as they could round up for the *notharim* of Benjamin. They were instructed to bring them to Shiloh. The scene described in Vs. 1.3, belongs here. There is no record written or implied that the city of Jabesh-gilead was destroyed at this time. The order given in Vs. 10.11, was rescinded and the instruction of V. 12, substituted. Resulting in *vayimzeu* the peaceful rounding up of 400 maidens which came in accord with Torah law voluntarily to become wives of the *notharim* the remnant which escaped to the Rock of Rimmon.

Returning to the reason Jabesh in Gilead did not join the rest of the tribes have deep roots. Let us examine the cause which produced the effect described in chapter 21:5.12. Joshua divided the Holyland recorded in (Joshua 13:31, 17:5.6). In (Joshua 22:) the rift began at this point with the Trans-Jordanian tribes. See our commentary on details. In (Jud. 12:4) they are called renegades by Ephraim. This animosity broke out in Jephtah's time and resulted in (Jud. 12:4.6) a civil war. See (I Sam. 11:,31:11.13, II Sam. 21:12.14) for the proof of Jabesh in Gilead's continuity. There was no military action taken. The presence of the United tribes in Jabesh was settled by bringing back to Shiloh 400 potential brides.

JUDGES CHAPTER 21

Vs. 13.14 While still at Bethel and in consultation with Phinehas, the united tribes sent messengers to the *notharim* Benjaminites at the Rock of Rimmon, they offered them peaceful asylum in their own territory, in the spirit of a new beginning. The 600 men at the Rock of Rimmon accepted the offer for rehabilitation. They agreed to close ranks with the rest of Israel. In this spirit of reconciliation the 600 men arrived in Shiloh (V. 12). They were given the choice of choosing a wife from the 400 maidens brought from Jabesh-gilead.

V. 15 The tribal Elders recognize their dilemma now that they have repented, in having made an indiscriminate vow. They are seeking a solution to have their irrational vow rescinded, that they may offer their daughters in marriage to the additional 200 Benjaminites. The Elder's *ki asah Adonai* that the Eternal's verdict can be observed retrospectively, was the result of centuries of retrogression from the major demand of Torah law, *taharath hamispachah* is the demand for genetic progression. From these seeds of moral behavior grow the progressive development of families, communities and governments which create the demand for social justice. The incident of *Pilegesh Begibeah* became the point of no return for the tribe of Benjamin. The tragedy that it represents stands as a warning for all time to Israel and every man and woman striving to rise upon the ladder of evolution. The Eternal God demands it, and stands ready to enforce it in every decadent society.

Vs. 16.18 The High Priest Phinehas is ready to nullify their irrational vow. However, he cannot cancel the curse they uttered. Only he that pronounces its potential *terror* must first eradicate it from his heart. There can be no moral fiction. Only our just and kind behavior can nullify a curse. The Elders are agreed that Benjamin must be given every opportunity to rebuild its numerical strength.

V. 19 This verse is the solution and resolution to rededicate the united goodwill of all the tribes in Israel, to once again reenforce the observance of Torah designated festivals. The Elders issued a proclamation, "That on the 15th of Ab, the annual festival will be held at Shiloh." The text gives the geographic location of the Tabernacle at Shiloh. It lies north of Bethel, east of the highway that runs from Bethel to Shechem and South of Lebonah. The details of its geographic location are attributed to the fact that the Tabernacle had lost its effectiveness during this period of the Judges. This day became a national holiday and it was designated for young people to meet and choose their mates.

Vs. 20.21 The remaining 200 Benjaminites are instructed to hide in the surrounding vineyards at the time of the festival. V. 21 "When you observe the maidens joining the festivities, come out of your hiding place and make your choice of a wife." In accord with Jewish

JUDGES CHAPTER 21

law and mores it was important that she consent voluntarily.

Vs. 22.23 "Should the father and brothers responsible for the girls complain to us as the Elders, we shall advise them to be gracious and generous. This would harmonize with our resolution to help the Benjaminites to a fresh start. As to our oath, it is not we that are giving our daughters to them in marriage. As long as our intentions are sincere, we shall have no feeling of guilt."

V. 23. The Benjamites followed the advice of the Elders, they each chose a wife and returned to their allotted territory, to rebuild their homes and their towns.

Vs. 24.25 The happy ending of this tragic period gave the united tribes of Israel the peace of mind to return to their homes and rejoin their respective tribes. They resolved to labor and cooperate with each other. The Book of Judges closes with a demand which is crystalizing in the hearts of all Israel. They are beginning to form a consensus for a central authority, a central government. They are fully resolved that all their problems are the result of, that there is no king in Israel, which created the chaos as each and everyone did as he pleased.

Baruch Hashem

Completed on the eve of the 13th day of Nisan 5741.

THE ETERNAL TORAH

SAMUEL ONE
SHMUEL ALEF

TABLE OF CONTENTS FOR THE BOOK OF I SAMUEL
A summary of the Book of I Samuel

CHAPTER 1
Pages 185.188

Vs.1.10 In a period of spiritual laxity the text describes the dedicaton of Elkanah as he celebrates the annual festivals with his family at the Central Sanctuary at Shiloh. The text sets forth the contrasting lives of Peninah and Hannah.

Vs.11.19 Records the inaudible vow of Hannah in the presence of Eli, the High Priest and Eli's blessing to Hannah.

Vs.20.23 Hannah's prayer is fulfilled when she gave birth to a son. In gratitude she named him Samuel.

Vs.24.28 Elkanah and Hannah discharge their vow by dedicating Samuel to the Service of the Eternal God of Israel.

CHAPTER 2
Pages 188.193

Vs.1.10 Hannah's Ode describes her fulfillment in Samuel's dedication to the service of God.

Vs.11.21 Elkanah observes the corrupt practices of Hofni and Phinehas, the sons of Eli at the Sanctuary. Contrasting Elkanah's disappointment is Eli's great respect for Elkanah and his dedicated son Samuel.

Vs.22.26 Describes the corrupt practices of Hofni and Phinehas in the management of the daily sacrifices in the Sanctuary.

Vs.27.36 Eli's soliloquy with the *Ish Elohim*, his conscience, as he reviews the national scene and his permissive passivity with his sons' demoralized conduct.

CHAPTER 3
Pages 193.195

Vs.1.15 Samuel's dedicated development becomes impatient with the demoralized scene. His maturity demands that he spring into action, to become involved to turn the situation around.

Vs.16.17 Eli seeks Samuel's validation as to the source and substance of his inspiration in vs.4.15.

Vs.18.21 Confirms for the record Samuel's physical and mental development, the public recognition of his dedication.

CHAPTER 4
Pages 196.198

Vs.1.3 Despite Eli's and Samuel's opposition to a war with the Philistines at this time, Israel went to war and suffered casualties in the first round.

Vs.4.18 Hofni and Phinehas brought the Ark into the vicinity of the battlefield to bolster the courage of Israel's men. The text describes the Philistine fear of its effectiveness in creating new courage in Israel's army. Described is the disintegration of Israel's army, the capture of the Ark and the death of Eli as he received the shocking news.

TABLE OF CONTENTS: I SAMUEL

                    Vs.19.22 Symbolic of new born hope the text concludes in reporting the birth of a son to the wife of Phinehas. In this tragic moment she names her son Ichabod, to commemorate the loss of the Ark of God.

CHAPTER 5
Pages 198.199

Vs.1.5 Describes the effect of the Ark upon the primitive, idolatrous Philistine mentality.

Vs.6.12 The text contrasts the imagery of idolatrous philosophy as compared with the simplicity of God's Natural Law, contained in the Ark of the Covenant. Philistine ignorance sees the Ark as an ill omen in their society. Therefore the Ark must be returned to Israel.

CHAPTER 6
Pages 199.202

Vs.1.12 The Philistine priests are consulted in the procedure they must follow when they return the Ark.

Vs.13.15 The exultation of the Leviim in Beth-shemesh upon the return of the Ark by the Philistine Governors. Their sin and their resolution described in vs.20.21.

Vs.16.18 The Governors of Ashdod, Azzah, Ashkelon, Gath and Ekron, are pleased by their conduct, the return of the Ark, and their generous indemnity.

V.19 Explains the discrepancy of the 70 men lost at Beth-shemesh and the 50,000 men lost in the Philistine war.

Vs.20.21 The Ark is transferred from Beth-shemesh to Kiriat-jearim, in light of their sin in vs.13.15.

CHAPTER 7
Pages 202.204

The Ark is placed in the home of Abinadab in Kiriat-jearim, in the vicinity of Gibeah. Samuel's effectiveness as a moral teacher. Israel's rebellion against the Philistines at Mitzpah. Samuel's effectiveness as a judge.

CHAPTER 8
Pages 204.208

Chronology of the lives of Samuel, Saul and king David, whose active lives are intertwined in the development of Israel's history.

Vs.1.3 Joel and Abijah, the sons of Samuel are appointed to act as judges in the territory of Judah, Benjamin and Ephraim.

Vs.4.9 The Elders of Israel report to Samuel in Ramah, on the misconduct of his sons and to request that he invest a king with full authority to govern Israel. Samuel's displeasure of their request is modified by the Eternal's soliloquy.

Vs.10.18 Samuel analyzes the meaning of their request for "A king in the manner of all kings."

Vs.19.22 Samuel exposes his distressed feelings to the Elders of Israel. Samuel's failure to empathize with their request challenged his authority by demanding their right to choose a king. The commentary analyzes the conduct of Moses, Joshua and Samuel in light of history as written in the Torah.

TABLE OF CONTENTS: I SAMUEL

CHAPTER 9
Pages 208.211

Vs.1.2 Saul the nameless messenger in (I Sam.4:12.17) is now mentioned as a potential candidate for Israel's kingship. Described is his genealogy, his stature and personality, from the viewpoint of Samuel.

Vs.3.14 Describes the efficient manner in which Saul searched for his father's lost asses. Disclosed here are the details leading to his first encounter with the Prophet Samuel.

Vs.15.19 Reports the details of Saul's first official meeting with Samuel.

Vs.20.23 The Prophet informs Saul that his father's asses have been found. Subtly Samuel informs Saul of the great honor that awaits him. Saul modestly reminds Samuel that he is a Benjaminite, who rose from the fratricidal civil war.

Vs.24.25 The Prophet Samuel ignored Saul's modest comments and ushered him into the festive hall where he shall be the honored guest.

Vs.25.27 Saul spent the night at the home of Samuel. In the morning the prophet explained the full meaning of his being chosen to become a candidate for the kingship of Israel.

CHAPTER 10
Pages 211.214

Vs.1.7 Saul is anointed as king of Israel by the prophet Samuel. The three incidents established by Samuel are to remove any doubt in Saul's mind that he is not only Samuel's choice, but has the confirmation of the Eternal God of history. Samuel strives to inspire Saul to immediate involvement with the welfare of Israel.

V.8 belongs to (I Sam.13:8) it is out of context here.

Vs.9.16 The incidents described in these verses tend to inspire Saul to rise to his exalted position. For the responsibility overwhelmed him.

Vs.17.24 The tribes of Israel represented by their leaders assembled at Mitzpah. They polled the tribes and chose Saul. Samuel commended the leaders upon their choice.

Vs.25.27 Samuel defined the laws for the monarchy, the responsibilities of the king to the nation and the leaders' loyalty to their king.

CHAPTER 11
Pages 214.216

Saul's spontaneous response to the call of Jabesh-gilead. He mobilized his forces as the tribes heeded his call to arms. He established his strategy against Israel's perpetual enemy in the east, the Ammonites.

V.15 Following this military action a united nation assembled at Gilgal and celebrated the inauguration of king Saul.

TABLE OF CONTENTS: I SAMUEL

CHAPTER 12
Pages 216.219

Vs.1.5 The Prophet Samuel relinquishes his position as leader to king Saul.

Vs.6.15 Samuel reviews Israel's historic record from Jacob's entry into Egypt to this point in time.

Vs.16.17 Samuel articulated his resentment. He charged them with deprecating the value of his leadership and thereby destroying the mood of this great moment in Israel's history.

Vs.18.25 The greatness of Samuel shines through as he expresses his regret for stepping down completely. He promises to continue to pray for Israel's continuity.

CHAPTER 13
Pages 219.222

Vs.1.12 Two years after Saul's inauguration, he established a standing army. Jonathan his son, initiated the war of independence against the Philistines, while Samuel handicaps Saul by exposing his arbitrary pique.

Vs.13.23 Samuel's reprimand at this point in time has despoiled his position in history. He offered no advice to Saul as he left Gilgal. The text clearly describes Saul's eroding position.

CHAPTER 14
Pages 222.226

Vs.1.15 Describes Jonathan's initiative in face of Saul's bewilderment created by the prophet Samuel.

Vs.16.23 Jonathan's heroic initiative created the tremendous victory for Israel.

Vs.24.30 Saul's interdiction ordered a fast day while in battle. The stress it created in the ranks of his soldiers.

Vs.31.35 The procedure of breaking their fast.

Vs.36.46 Saul's irrational vow stirs the Eternal's wrath and inspires Saul's soldiers to challenge his sense of justice. Unanimously they nullified Saul's irrational vow.

Vs.47.52 Saul secured his monarchy by challenging every potential enemy in the Holyland. In the process he built the finest army of his time. Included in the text is the genealogy of Saul and the names of his wife and children.

CHAPTER 15
Pages 227.232

An analysis of the Amaleks in human history.

Vs.1.9 Samuel's instructions to Saul for his war with the Amalekites. Details of the war and Saul's modifications of Samuel's instructions.

Vs.10.12 Samuel's monologue with his subconscious guilt that has been building from the day Saul was inaugurated as king of Israel. Saul's desire to establish a memorial to his successful execution of the war is the fuse that detonates Samuel's decision to replace Saul.

Vs.13.21 Samuel's showdown with Saul at Gilgal, where he planned to offer sacrifices from the Amalekite booty.

TABLE OF CONTENTS: I SAMUEL

Vs.22.24 Saul's irrational defense and Samuel's denigration of sacrifices.

Vs.25.31 Saul's plea that Samuel appear with him in public surfaces to expose his distress by tearing Samuel's garment. Saul's confession destroyed Samuel's intention to embarrass Saul before the Elders. Samuel joined Saul in prayer for the last time in public.

Vs.32.35 Samuel the man dedicated to the service of the Eternal God of all humanity executes Agog the king of Amalek. Samuel never put Saul out of his mind.

CHAPTER 16
Pages 233.237

Vs.1.3 Samuel seeks the Eternal's approval for his arbitrary decision to replace Saul. These verses represent Samuel's confession of his guilt. The Eternal insists that he solve his dilemma and implement his decision. It is the Eternal God of history, Who will judge Samuel on the merits of his conduct.

Vs.4.13 Describes Samuel's procedure when he arrived in Hebron and finally made his choice and secretly anointed David.

Vs.14.23 Records the details of Saul's psychological distress. From the details we observe its progressive stages of development. David's musical therapy becomes the vehicle by which he comes into contact with king Saul.

CHAPTER 17
Pages 237.241

A chronological review for an understanding of this difficult chapter.

Vs.1.11 Describes the battle positions of the Philistines and the battle position of Israel.

Vs.4.11 Goliath's challenge to Israel's army.

Vs.12.27 Introduces David to the scene as he carried forth his father's instructions.

Vs.28.30 Eliab's embarrassment of David as he challenged his presence on the battlefield.

Vs.31.37 David repeats his challenge to king Saul.

Vs.38.51 David proves his courageous faith as he dispatched Goliath.

Vs.52.58 Saul ordered the pursuit of the Philistine army. After the pursuit Saul requested the identity of David.

CHAPTER 18
Pages 241.245

Vs.1.5 David meets Jonathan for the first time, their spontaneous affection for each other. David was chosen to appease Saul's melancholia. He then became a permanent resident at the palace. David is successful in carrying out every mission to which he was assigned.

Vs.6.8 David's popularity created the public response, "Saul slew thousands and David slew tens of thousands."

TABLE OF CONTENTS: I SAMUEL

Vs.9.16 The step by step development of Saul's schizophrenia.
Vs.17.27 Saul's demand for a dowry before David can marry Michal.
Vs.28.30 As David's stature grew, Saul's enmity visualized him as his successor.

CHAPTER 19
Pages 245.248

Vs.1.8 Jonathan's loyalty to David stimulates Saul to take an oath, that he will not be the cause of David's death. David returns to Saul's service. He led Saul's army to a successful battle with the Philistines.
Vs.9.10 David is forced to flee to safety as Saul's spear pierced the wall behind him. David is resolved never to return.
Vs.11.20 David flees from Saul's terror. He went directly to Samuel's home in Ramah.
Vs.21.24 Saul sent soldiers to capture David in Ramah. Saul comes to Ramah. His confrontation with Samuel.

CHAPTER 20
Pages 248.252

Vs.1.17 David fled from Ramah and went to the home of Jonathan. There he confided his innermost fears. Though Samuel advised David to return to Saul's government, David enlists Jonathan's help to confirm his conclusion, that he must not return. David and Jonathan extend their covenant to include their posterity. For it is quite possible they may not survive from their involvement with Saul. Jonathan already knows of David's anointment by Samuel.
Vs.18.23 David goes into hiding while Jonathan is to return to Saul's Rosh Hodesh festival. His advice to David is to be based upon his experience with his father Saul.
Vs.24.33 Confirms the ever existing danger to David.
Vs.34.40 Jonathan advises David that he must seek safety from Saul's murderous mood.
Vs.41.42 Jonathan and David tearfully reconfirm their covenant and take leave of each other.

CHAPTER 21
Pages 252.253

Vs.1.10 After David left Jonathan, he went to Nob, to seek the help of Ahimelech the kohen. Doeg the Edomite observes Ahimelech's cooperation with David.
Vs.11.16 David calculated the risks and went to Gath in Philistia. When recognized he feigned insanity.

CHAPTER 22
Pages 254.255

Vs.1.5 David escapes to Adullam. Those that empathized with him joined his cause. This gave him a force of 400 men. David transferred his parents to Moab for their safety. The prophet Gad advised David to expand his operations, not to

TABLE OF CONTENTS: I SAMUEL

limit his movements as a fugitive from Saul's wrath. David goes to the forest of Hereth in Judah's territory.

Vs.6.23 Saul issued an order to Doeg the Edomite to destroy Nob-Gibeah, the kohanim and the Nethinim-Gibeonites that served in the House of God. Abiathar the son of Ahimelech escaped and reported to David in the forest of Hereth. David's vow to Abiathar, "I hold myself responsible for your life."

CHAPTER 23
Pages 255.257

Vs.1.15 David and his men go to the assistance of Keilah.
Vs.16.18 Jonathan comes to Horshah to rededicate himself to David's cause.
Vs.19.28 Saul is informed by the Ziphites, that David is in the wilderness of Ziph. Saul pursued David until the pursuit was called off.

CHAPTER 24
Pages 258.260

David spared the life of king Saul at En-gedi.
King Saul imposed an oath upon David in vs.20.23.
This parallels Jonathan's oath in (I Sam.20:15).
V.22 Saul fears the common practice of ancient dynasties as described in (IKings 15:29,16:11, 2Kings 10:7).

CHAPTER 25
Pages 260.265

The demise of the prophet Samuel.
David in Midbar Paran. David's brush with Nabal and David's encounter with Abigail. David's first wife was Ahinoam. Abigail became his second wife. Recorded here is Michal's marriage to Palti.

CHAPTER 26
Pages 265.266

Vs.1.5 Once again the Ziphites report on David's whereabouts in the Wilderness of Judah.
Vs.6.20 David takes Saul's spear and his jug of water. He challenged Abner with negligence of duty. David takes Saul to task for pursuing him.
Vs.21.25 David offers to return Saul's spear. Saul blesses David for his loyalty.

CHAPTER 27
Pages 266.267

David concludes a pact with Achish, the governor of Gath. He is granted permission to live in Ziklag. Here he lived for 16 months and cleared the corridor from Beersheba to Egypt from the following marauder tribesmen: Geshurites, Gezerties and Amalekites.

CHAPTER 28
Pages 268.272

Saul's encounter with the Witch of Endor.
An analysis of witchcraft and other mediums by Maimonides.

CHAPTER 29
Page 272

The Philistines mobilize for war with Israel.
David and his men are released from their commitment to Achish, the governor of Gath.

TABLE OF CONTENTS: I SAMUEL

CHAPTER 30 Pages 272.274	The pillaging of Ziklag by the Amalekites. David's counter attack and the return of their families. David distributes gifts of gratitude to all the communities listed in vs.26.31, who helped him survive the fugitive years.
CHAPTER 31 Pages 275.276	Saul's defeat by the Philistines at Gilboa, his death and the death of his sons, Jonathan, Abinadab and Malkishua. The people of Jabesh-gilead honor king Saul's memory, retrieve their bodies from Bet-shan and bury their remains. They observed seven days of mourning to express their respect for his years of loyal service.
Page 277	ADDENDUM: The historic record of Michal.

INTRODUCTION TO THE BOOK OF SAMUEL

Examining the arbitrary conclusions of world historians, we must resolve to rely upon the preeminence and the authenticity of Biblical history, in order to flesh out the essential facts of the ancient world. Every archaeological finding of the 20th century, consistently confirms the record of Biblical data. The universality of this literature records the facts. It strives to tell it as it was and as it should be. It underscores the truth and repeats its message to every generation, "Let the chips fall where they may," the intent of the record is to inspire man and woman to reach for the ideals of the Eternal God's Masterplan for all of humanity. To read the Bible with discipline as our goal, creates the demand that we examine human experiences of the past, in order to evaluate their failures and successes in light of their dedication to the Masterplan. The original guidelines set down in the Torah are as valid in the 20th century as they will be to infinity. To bypass them or to ignore their direction in our everyday lives is to promote failure.

In the first eleven chapters of Genesis, Moses the Great Law-giver, gave us the essence and results of the 'Big Bang Theory', the authentic history of the ethnic groupings of peoples in accord with their genealogy and the early formation of nations. This information existed as an oral record before his time. The Torah, the Pentateuch, the Five Books of Moses, is a written record covering 1000 years of Semitic history and the refinement of human experiences, as humanity strove to find the reason for its existence upon Earth. "Only those who observed the statutes of the Eternal God, have survived the centuries to grant our human efforts immortality. (Deut. 4:4)." Moses handed down his goals and his experiences to Joshua. For 40 years Moses strove to inspire Joshua (Num. 11:29, 27:15.23, Deut. 31:7.13), to carry on and immortalize his life's work. Joshua compiled and completed the record of his lifetime and recorded it in the Book of Joshua.

The prophet Samuel recorded the Book of Judges and the Book of Ruth, and part of the First Book of Samuel (I Sam. 10:25). Throughout the centuries both books of Samuel were one continuous manuscript. When the Bible was translated into Greek in Alexandria, in the third century BCE, it became known as the Septuagint. They at that time divided the Book of Samuel and the Book of Kings. They then became known as: I Samuel, II Samuel, I Kings, II Kings. They also organized the system of chapter and verse, in order to standardize the Bible as a Universal Document. In 1518 of our era, the printer Daniel Bomberg introduced the above described innovations in his new edition of the Hebrew Bible. Every new edition since that time has followed this format.

Both Books of Samuel cover a period of about 120 years, from the close of the life of the kohen Eli, which marked the end of the period of the Judges, to the end of the lifetime of king David. The material for the composition of these two books are credited to the prophets Samuel, Gad and Nathan and the following personalities in the courts of king David and Solomon. The kohen Abiathar of

INTRODUCTION: SAMUEL

Anathoth (IKings 2:26.27), Jehoshaphat, the recorder in king David's court and Ahimaaz, the son of the kohen Zadok. There is evidence that the prophet Jeremiah (Jer. 1:1.4) who was born in Anathoth in 645 BCE, a descendant of the kohen Abiather in king David's time, may have been among those that completed the Books of Samuel.

The Book of I Samuel begins with the genealogy of Samuel. His parents were Elkanah and Hannah. They both dedicated their lives to raise a son who shall become consecrated to the cause of the Eternal God. They created the environment prenatally and postnatally to refine his values. They molded his character to fill the void of his time, which followed the destruction of the Tabernacle at Shiloh and the loss of the Ark of the Covenant to the Philistines. The corrupt practices of Eli's sons, the death of Eli, Samuel's mentor, heightened the sensitivity of Samuel, to the reality of the spiritual and political misfortunes of Israel. Samuel recognized the root cause of Israel's problems, as they were emerging from the disarray of the period of the Judges. Samuel's goal was to create unity in the Holyland. His efforts created the demand for a central authority to lead the country. Samuel recognized the first order of business was to develop security for its inhabitants. To conform with the peoples demand for a king and his priority for secure borders, he chose and recommended Saul of the tribe of Benjamin, to fill the military needs of his time.

King Saul emerges as a humble, modest, heroic and dedicated human being. Saul succeeded in the demand of his time to constrain Israel's enemies from destroying their daily lives. However, he lacked the statesmanship to expand his authority, to breathe new hope into a divided country. The text creates a vivid record of Samuel's failure to guide and direct his anointed king. Samuel's excessive demand of this humble shepherd created and enlarged King Saul's inferiority complex that led to his schizophrenia. King Saul never rose above being the humble shepherd with a natural gift for heroic military prowess. He lacked organizational ability. The text gives very little information from which we can reconstruct his government. Yet, despite this executorial handicap, we can observe a fairly prosperous environment emerging to create individuals of wealth. Though Philistine strategy disarmed the people and controlled the development of metallurgy to the point that every plow or sickle had to be made or maintained by Philistine labor, there grew a military force well equipped and resolved to defend itself against the Philistine venture in the west and the Ammonite enemy in the east. Both of these forces independently had a tacit understanding to either assimilate Israel into its polyglot of people or to force Israel to leave the Holyland.

Like Moses in his time, Samuel's dedication to his God and to his people strove to inspire Israel to higher goals and spiritual values. Samuel's innovative ability introduced lyrical psalms into the sacrificial service at Gibeon and Nob, to elevate Israel's spiritual life upon a higher plateau. This led to the creation of the

INTRODUCTION: SAMUEL

prophetic school, from which came forth the important personalities of Gad and Nathan.

The detailed record of king Saul's pursuit of David, gives history a vivid picture of David's schooling to think on his feet while honing and refining his leadership ability. From the moment he appeared upon the scene of history in his triumphant confrontation with Goliath, to the tragic scene of his exile in the rebellion of Absalom, and the crushing blow of his death, we observe a personality born to be a king. David's greatness lies in having been blessed with the most important element vital to succeed, *Nose chen beene Elohim veadam*. The ability to transmit his charm, to captivate the loyalty of the nation and to earn the recognition of his Creator for his dedication to further His cause upon Earth. The precise mix of this formula plus king David's outstanding natural ability to lead and to organize his government created the harmony of his charmed personality. These natural gifts enabled him to rise from despair to the greatest heights.

King David's humility encompasses his spiritual devotion as he communes with his Eternal God, in order to align his decisions with the Masterplan of the Eternal God of history and justice. King David's personality is the supreme example of a human being, though endowed with a maximum of natural ability, fails in the simple personal disciplines to mar his supreme accomplishments. King David's life is a mirror for those who desire to become great and those who have attained greatness and seek the security so vital to maintain their equilibrium. King David's constitutional monarchy was based upon a *Social Contract* the Torah. Its laws and statutes demand human rights for every human being, be he or she of high or low station, be they natives, proselytes or aliens.

The material included in both Books of Samuel covers about 120 years from the end of Eli's life, through the lifetime of king David. From the biographical material which describes the lives of Eli, Samuel, king Saul and king David, we can receive a cryptic and vivid picture of Israel in the Holyland. Beginning with the anarchy recorded in the Book of Judges, we observe the evolution of the monarchy, the fulfillment of inheriting the Holyland to its maximum perimeter as outlined in (Num. 34:1.15). Examining the detailed record, we observe the self centered interest of the individual tribes and clans, their tenacious individualism is pitted against the Torah's demand for evolution. How they fail to grasp the realities of their historic position in the Eternal's Masterplan for humanity. Israel's goals are rooted in a common language, common ancestry and a common demand upon the multitudes who voluntarily joined Israel to escape the oppressive, tyrannical conditions existing in the ancient world. The integrating pressure made upon both native born and proselyte, created the complications as each group established its own interests above the central demand and purpose outlined in the Torah.

The record of king David is vivid, concise and detailed. The text literally takes us into his personal life and impartially exposes his personal weaknesses, his

INTRODUCTION: SAMUEL

physical passions, his love for and the indulgencies of his children. The retrogressive affect of his weaknesses, result in fratricide and anarchy, only to mar a perfect record of a most sensitive and dedicated human being. King David's spiritual sensitivity are imprinted in his marvelous legacy to humanity, his magnificent Psalms. Every generation into the 20th of the common era, vie with each other to expound the spiritual, musical potential rooted in the depth of meaning in the words that came forth from king David's very soul. Had he not dissipated his tremendous natural gifts, he would have handed down to his posterity a National Central Sanctuary, with an established spiritual service in the advanced spirit of Samuel, whose intent was to minimize the sacrificial service, in order to elevate the cultural and spiritual values.

David Lieberman

I SAMUEL CHAPTER 1

The book of Judges closes on a sad note. In those days going back to the period of Phinehas the son of Eleazar, the kohen, there was no king in Israel, everyone did as he pleased. The sacrificial service in the Tabernacle at Shiloh was forsaken, assimilation was rampant. The disciplines inscribed in the Torah were abandoned. Those who offered sacrifices did so upon the idolatrous highplaces of the indigenous population. Only the tribe of Levi remained loyal to the traditions and upheld the concept of the Central Sanctuary.

The book of Samuel reports that the priesthood was reactivated by Eli who was a descendant of Itamar. He not only assumed the position of kohen, but acted as a shofet-leader-judge and counselor. His effort to inspire a new beginning began before the demise of Samson, in the period reported in (Jud.10:3) when Jair governed in Trans-Jordan. Eli's effort to create a renaissance to offset the idolatrous assimilation was the spiritual force which inspired a new beginning. Eli became the recognized successor to Moses, as he repeated Moses's revelation in the words of the Eternal God of all humanity (Gen.6:3), "I must wait patiently for the day in humanities history when mankind shall reach out for My goal engraved in their genetic potential."

Eli's dedication was recognized and won the respect and loyalty of the tribes of Manasseh and Ephraim and a new beginning in the ranks of the other tribes. Eli made his headquarters in the Mishkan, he reenstated the sacrificial service in the Central Sanctuary. From here in Shiloh he dispensed counsel and adjudicated every dispute that came before him. His sincerity won the hearts of the people. Eli strove to unite the tribes for unified action against Israel's external enemies. He never aspired to become a military leader. Eli's every effort was to inspire a rebirth of the nation by every peaceful means through the daily conduct of accepted norms advanced in Israel's Torah. From this rebirth of a nation came Elkanah, a descendant of Kehath, of the tribe of Levi.

Vs.1.3   The scene described in this chapter is the symbolic result of Eli's influence over a lifetime of dedication. Elkanah was the son of Jeroham, whose grandfather was Elihu, whose genealogy goes back to Tohu the son of Zuph (1 Chronicles 6:7.12). Elkanah's home was Ramathaim Zophim, in the mountains of Ephraim, which is one of the Levitic cities assigned to them by the tribe of Ephraim. Elkanah had two wives in accord with the norm of his time. Peninah had children with Elkanah, while Hannah was childless. Elkanah in accord with the new renaissance came annually to celebrate the festivals to (Ex.13:10) accord with Torah discipline, to pray in behalf of Hannah's dilemma and to offer sacrifices. Elkanah's dedication was so complete, that when he came to Shiloh, he took a different route each time in order to inspire others by his example.

Vs. 4.5   It was Elkanah's practice that when he came to Shiloh, he would distribute funds to the members of his family, that they may offer peace offerings. Though he distributed these funds on an equal basis to all, when it came to Hannah, whom he loved dearly, he

I SAMUEL CHAPTER 1

empathized with her embarrassment. Hannah grieved over her inability to conceive a child, Elkanah therefore gave her more than he gave to the others.

Vs.6.8 Whenever Peninah observed Elkanah's solicitous conduct toward Hannah, she would taunt her in order to provoke her to tears. Peninah would ridicule Hannah for her inability to bear a child. This Peninah did upon every annual pilgrimage. Hannah's embarrassment caused her untold anguish and therefore was unable to participate in the festivities. Hannah lapsed into a crying and sorrowful mood at the slightest provocation. Elkanah made every effort to appease her. "Why do you cry and why do you deny yourself the vital necessities of sustenance? Why do you torture yourself because of Peninah's insensitivity? It should be clear to you that even if you were able to bear ten sons for me, this phenomenon could not in anyway increase my great love and devotion to you."

Vs.9.10 Hannah sat through the meal considerate of all those participating in the festivities. She did not leave the table until they had finished eating and drinking, though she did not partake of any food or beverage herself. In this mood of desperation she rose from the table and made her way to the Mishkan, to appeal to the Eternal God and to express her innermost anguish and embarrassment because of her predicament. She prayed and cried silently in the presence of Eli, who sat nearby upon his official seat in the doorway of the Mishkan. It was here that people came to seek his counsel.

V.11 This was the mood and background which inspired Hannah to take the following vow, "O Eternal God of history, *Adonai Tzvaot* You are He that directs the evolutionary process of the extraterrestrial interplanetary system that makes life possible upon Earth. It is also You, that guides and directs the body of the cell and its development. I pray that You recognize the anguish of Your maidservant. *Uzechartani* I Pray that You take into consideration my dedication to Your disciplines, inscribed in the Torah, I plead that You recognize the source of my suffering. Be attentive to my contrite soul. Grant me, I pray, the capability to conceive and to produce the vital hormone mix to create a male embryo that shall develop into a complete anatomical male, (see Addenda in T.E.T. p.338). I hereby vow to create the prenatal and postnatal environment, that he become a nazirite, dedicated Ladonai, to You the Eternal God of history." (see T.E.T. on Jud. 13:2.14)

Vs.12.17 Eli, who sat nearby took special note of Hannah's inaudible prayer that eminated from the depth of her heart and conscience, only her lips indicated motion. Eli therefore concluded that Hannah was drunk. Eli admonished Hannah, "How long will you make a drunken spectacle of yourself? Set aside your drinking bouts, that you may sober up." Hannah answerd Eli in her moments of embarrassment and distress. "I beg your pardon sir, I am a most unhappy woman. What you

I SAMUEL CHAPTER 1

observed is the inaudible distress that pervades my heart. It is this anguish which I have exposed before the Eternal God. I have neither participated in drinking wine nor any other intoxicating beverage. Do not belittle me as a worthless woman, for I have been venting my deeply ingrained distress." Eli recognized his insensitivity, he failed to recognize and to empathize with Hannah's problem. "Go in peace and may the God of Israel grant your *shelah*". This is the moment that Eli prophetically observed his insensitivity as he offered Hannah his blessing. "May God's justice grant the substance of your prayer, that *shelah*-your posterity in whose behalf you prayed so fervently. May he become the inspired *malach*-instrument for Israel's metaphysical destiny." (see T.E.T. in Gen.12:2).

V.18   Hannah gratefully expressed her gratitude to Eli, for having recognized and extended his empathy in her moments of distress. She thanked him for his blessings and returned to her family and participated in satisfying her physical need for food. Hannah begins to recognize that her despondency was a contributing factor to all of her distress. Hannah emerged from her encounter with Eli, resolved to remain cheerful and hopeful at all times, to project a countenance of optimism confirming her innermost faith in the Eternal God of Israel.

V. 19   Elkanah and his family rose early the next morning, they prayed reverently before the Eternal's Central Sanctuary, in gratitude for all their blessings and returned to their home in Ramah. Elkanah recognized the effect of Hannah's resolution, *Vayeda Elkanah eth Hannah ishto* their animation and love for each other inspired new hope, a new and fresh beginning.

V. 20   In the course of time Hannah's optimism created the wellbeing, the perfect physical and psychological conditions for Hannah to conceive. After a normal pregnancy she gave birth to a son. Hannah named him Shmuel-Samuel, in gratitude to the Eternal, Who responded to her plea in v. 11.

Vs. 21.22   When Elkanah and his household set forth for their annual visit to the Mishkan, Hannah did not join them. She was morally bound in accord with her vow to create the postnatal environment for Samuel's physical and mental development, that he become dedicated ideally to the welfare of his people Israel. She reminded Elkanah, "When their son shall be weaned, (at the probable age of two years Gen. 21:8). I will bring him personally to the Central Sanctuary in accord with my vow. He shall then remain there dedicated to devote his life to the cause of the Eternal God."

V. 23   Elkanah recognized Hannah's consistency and dedication, together they must strive to recreate the *Zelem Elohim* the intelligent development of the Divine Creator. The extra security Hannah will give her new born child by nursing him and creating the

I SAMUEL CHAPTER 1

environment of contentment and tranquility, will help create a human being prepared to cope with the challenges of daily life.

Vs. 24.26   Some time after Hannah had weaned Samuel, she resolved to fulfill her vow. Hannah made the vital preparations for peaceful offerings at the Mishkan, to celebrate the highest moment in her life. As the festivities began Elkanah and Hannah presented the boy Samuel to Eli. V. 26. "I am the woman who prayed in your presence to the Eternal God. *Chey nafshechah*, I now charge you with the responsibility to look after his welfare, even as you are responsible for your own life."

Vs. 27.28   "When I prayed, I vowed that if the Eternal will grant my request, he shall become dedicated to the Eternal God for the rest of his life, *Hu shaul Ladonai*. "I hereby entrust him to your care, to guide him and to instruct him, to become dedicated to the Eternal God." Hannah and Elkanah prostrated themselves before the Eternal's Sanctuary in gratitude for their ability to fulfill their vow.

I SAMUEL CHAPTER 2

The following ten verses represent Hannah's Ode, to commemorate this important moment in her life. It was obviously written during her lifetime to express her dedication to the cause of the Eternal God of Israel. It was included by Abiathar the High Priest, in the 6th century BCE. when the Book of Samuel was completed.

V. 1   In this moment of triumph my heart is jubilant, it bolsters my faith in the Eternal God. For in my moments of depression, it did not permit me to falter or despair. Triumphantly, I celebrate my victory, for the Eternal God has granted me the courage to expose the hostilities of my adversaries. I exult and rejoice in Thy salvation.

V. 2   The immutability of Thy law demands excellence, leading to sanctity and perfection. None can transcend Thy holiness. *veein tzur Kelohenu* Your endurance is to infinity. Your Holyness demands justice, ever tempering law with mercy in order to assist those who lack the ability to rise by themselves.

V. 3   (Peninah) Permit not your accomplishments to augment your arrogance by embarrassing others with insolent speech, for the Eternal recognizes the loins as the source of man and woman's deepseated animosity and hate (Jer. 11:20, Gen. 6:3). Therefore the Eternal God takes into consideration the motive of the thought (Pr. 16:2, 21:2, 24:12) as it evolves into an evil deed.

V. 4   The weapon of the arrogant is insolent speech. This is the source of their destruction (Ps. 31:11). *Venichshalim* While

I SAMUEL CHAPTER 2

those who are offended, the Eternal girds with strength to conform with His law (Deut. 32:4).

V. 5   The scales of justice are ever in balance, human beings strive to rationalize how those satiated by prosperity lose their good fortune and become hirelings, while those struggling for bread cease to be hirelings. She (Hannah) that was barren gave birth to many-seven, and (Peninah) that boasted of many children languishes and is forlorn.

V. 6   It is man and woman's arbitrary resolution to ignore the Eternal's law that shortens the normal lifespan and creates the cause which brings them down into the grave in the midst of their allotted years. While those who choose to live by His physical, moral and ethical laws, though handicapped by genetic inequalities continue to prolong their lives.

V. 7   It is the Eternal's genetic progressive law of evolution that grants human beings the cumulative intelligence and their potential initiative, to lead rich lives, to accumulate wealth, the wisdom to pass it on to their posterity as an inheritance governed by the Eternal's physical, moral and ethical law. It is this same law that grants every generation of man and woman to begin again when they falter, to rise upon the ladder of their potential development.

V. 8   Hannah who was deprived in the past to satisfy her greatest demand, to have a child and to fulfill her maternal instinct, compares herself to a *dal* the lowliest category on the social ladder. One who has no inherited desire to participate in the creative responsibility of a human being. He finds his needs upon the dunghill and is content to remain in this category. It is the Eternal's law which grants even this lowly and handicapped individual the potential to rise above his genetically inherited environment. *Evyon* is one who has resigned to live in everlasting poverty (see comm. in T.E.T. Deut. 15:4.5). In both of these categories the Torah charges society with the responsibility to rehabilitate them, in order to remove them from the poverty rolls. It is the Eternal's law that prods our conscience (Gen. 4:9), "I am my brother's keeper." As the Eternal's *malachim* every human being must be helped to reach the highest category with the noblemen of society. The genetic process of evolution are the Eternal's *pillars* upon which He has set the foundation of humanity.

V.9   The Eternal's disciplines and laws are the bedrock of civilization, they guard the paths of the faithful, while the wicked perish in the arrogance and hate which originates in the darkness of their loins (Jer. 11:20). Let no one delude himself that he is a selfmade being. "Be not like the colossal beast-behemoth whose vaunted strength is in the sinews of his powerful body (Job. 40:16)."

I SAMUEL CHAPTER 2

V. 10 They that strive with the righteous, challenge the Eternal's resolution, therefore they shall be shattered. From the heavens He will thunder His command. His justice will pursue the wicked to the ends of the earth. May He grant strength to the righteous who rule by the Eternal's law. May Israel's leaders triumph as the anointed of the Eternal God.

V. 11 Elkanah reports on existing conditions at the Mishkan after one of his regular visits to see his son Samuel at the Central Sanctuary. From the text we may conclude that Samuel is already in his teens, for he is old enough to assist Eli in his daily routines. Elkanah's report was probably augmented by Samuel's daily experiences. In (Lev. 1:2:3:4:) the Torah establishes the procedures for the sacrifices and their symbolic meaning. In these texts are recorded the ethical, moral standards of conduct for the kohanim-priests. Their portions of the sacrifices are prescribed by law. These tithes are reciprocal, in recognition for the kohen's dedication to the service of all the people of Israel. They may not demand it.

V. 12 Contrasting this orderly and dignified procedure, we are told that Hophni and Phinehas, the sons of Eli were scoundrels. They ignored the symbolic meaning of the sacrifices, they disgraced the respected position of the kohen as an intermediary between the people and his Eternal God.

Vs. 13.14 The text describes the prevailing scene in the courtyard of the Mishkan. When one brought a sacrifice the young assistants of Hophni and Phinehas came along with a large three pronged fork, they thrust the fork into the various types and sizes of pots used for cooking the meat and picked their share at random.

Vs. 15.16 Describes their demand for their arbitrary share even before the symbolic ceremonial procedures were completed. They demanded raw meat instead of cooked meat, when challenged by the bringer of the offering, they arrogantly threatened to take it by force.

V. 17 The conduct of these assistants reflected the instructions of Hophni and Phinehas. They made a mockery of the procedure as it contradicted and desecrated the sanctity of the Central Sanctuary. When Moses refined the system of sacrifices into law, he also limited them to be brought at the Central Sanctuary. The intent and purpose of these elaborate procedures was to elevate Israel to a new plateau. These laws banned and prohibited all primitive idolatrous procedures of the past. Moses was aware of the deepseated practice of sacrifices (which included human sacrifices) in the psyche of man. It became an educative process against the excesses of the ancient world. It established procedures for humane slaughtering and standards for the selectivity of what we may eat. It banned the eating of fat and blood. When we equate the fact that people in the 20th century still eat fat and blood as delicacies

I SAMUEL CHAPTER 2

despite the modern scientific prohibition, we must fully acknowledge that Moses was indeed the instrument of the Eternal God.

Vs. 18.19   The text desires to call our attention to the development of Samuel. His dedication and training are inferred as it contrasts with Eli's sons. As an attendant at the sacrificial service Samuel wore a linen *meil* apron. The official description of Ephod, which was worn by the High Priest is given in (Ex. 28:6.43). Looking back into the book of (Jud. 18:17) we observe the interchanging of the accepted meaning of *meil* as *ephod*. When Elkanah made his annual pilgrimage to the Central Sanctuary, Hannah would join him and bring Samuel a new robe by which to enhance his presence at the services.

Vs. 20.21   Eli had a deep respect for Elkanah and Hannah, he recognized their dedication in their self-denial of the love of their only son. He therfore extended his blessing to them that Hannah be blessed with additional children in place of Samuel whom she loaned to the Eternal. In the course of time Hannah conceived and bore Elkanah three additional sons and two daughters.

Vs. 22.23   The conditions described in vs. 11.17, are now enlarged by additional charges that confirm the inadequacy of Eli's sons as unworthy to succeed him. Rumors spread by innuendo that they made it a practice to detain the women who came to offer their modest offerings of a dove, prescribed by law in (Lev. 12:6) when they emerged from childbirth. Greedily they concentrated on the sacrifices where the pickings were more lucrative, rather than processing the offerings of the women with dispatch because of their tender conditions and their responsibility to their newborn infant. Since no sacrifices were permitted after sunset, the women were detained in the courtyard through the night until the next morning. This led to rumors of midsconduct.

Vs. 24.25   Though Eli is knowledgeable of Hophni and Phinehas's management recorded in vs. 11.17, he is embarrassed by the gossip of *am Adonai*. Eli recognized this common gossip as a sin (Num. 12). "When Eli called his sons to task he reminded them, *im yechta ish leish* when individuals gossip on a man to man basis, *ufilelo Elohim*, a human judge has the capability to adjudicate their grave sin. But you have implicated *am Adonai*. You are both guilty of instigating the *lashon hara*-the gossip. *Mi yithpalel lo*. Who is there among us that can plead with the Eternal in behalf of the whole nation?" Hophni and Phinehas ignored their father's reprimand. Their refusal to repent or to defend their conduct, confirmed their guilt as charged. This was the cause of their verdict pronounced in v.34, Hophni and Phinehas shall receive their punishment in one day.

V. 26   Samuel, though but a youth is being recognized for his dedication to the house of God. He indicated devotion to the

I SAMUEL CHAPTER 2

national welfare. The text very aptly in brief and concise terms states, he has found favor in the eyes of the Eternal God, and in the respect he received in his human relations.

Vs. 27.28 The *ish Elohim*, is Eli's own conscience. As an old man he is limited physically. Though his mind, his long experience is capable of administering counsel to others, he is incapable to discipline his own sons, let alone a nation. He has trained Samuel to become a trustworthy and dedicated disciple while preparing him for leadership. Therefore Eli has the time to evaluate the national situation. In this verse he is reviewing the history of the priesthood going back to Aaron and his important part in the negotiations with Egypt before the Exodus from Egypt.

V. 28. Refers to (Ex. 28:1.43) when Aaron was chosen to represent the tribe of Levi, as the father of the priesthood. In (Lev. 1: 2: 3: 4:) are described the *ishe bnei Yisrael* emoluments which the kohen shall receive for his dedication to the welfare of the people of Israel.

V. 29 "Why do you trample upon My benevolence, represented by the offerings brought into the Sanctuary in order to honor Me and to accord with My disciplines for Israel's development. Your failings (Eli) to rebuke your sons' conduct supersedes your allegiance to Me. You have permitted yourselves to become satiated and corpulent upon the gift offerings of My people Israel who come to honor Me."

V. 30 Eli reflected upon the history of the priesthood, how it passed down from Aaron to Eleazar (Num. 20:26). He recalled Phinehas' heroic act in (Num. 25:7.8), the kohen's failure to release Jephtah from his tragic vow (Jud. 11:34.40), his failure to respond to the national need in the disgraceful incident of *Pilegesh Begivah* (Jud. 19: 21:). "I therefore bypassed the kohen's continuity to you (Eli) a descendant of Itamar, in the hope that you would distinguish yourself in My Sanctuary. Under the present developments, I am limited by My law to honor only those that cooperate with My direction in history. Therefore, those that denigrate My direction shall be discredited."

V. 31 Eli pondered the effect of Hophni and Phinehas' scandalous conduct. All that he has stood for shall cease and be cut off upon his demise. His immortality shall be interred with the evil conduct of his sons. This will mark the end of the house of Eli.

V. 32 Eli is prophetically confident that the Eternal's Masterplan for Israel shall be implemented by Samuel (I Kings 8:56, 4:20, 5:5) and succeed where he has failed. *Vehibateta tzar meon* Enviously Eli recognized that no elder shall come forth from his household to continue his life's work.

V. 33 Eli consoled himself that the end of his life's work shall come only after he dies. He therefore prayed in the words of Moses

I SAMUEL CHAPTER 2

(Num. 11:15) that he may not survive to witness the degradation of his posterity who shall live out their lives as ordinary mortal men.

V. 34   Eli courageously continued his prophetic vision as he strove with his conscience. As a prophet Eli is a realist; the infamy of his sons' corrupt conduct calls for a complete new beginning. It would be fortuitous if both of them would die in one and the same day. My guilt in this whole matter is due to my passive validation of Haphni and Phinehas' conduct. This created the implacable resolution of the Eternal God to deal resolutely before a new beginning can be implemented.

V. 35   The effect of Eli's sad analysis recorded in the above eight verses unfolded itself in the course of the normal give and take in human relations in everyday living. The house of Eli continued: to Ichabod the son of Phinehas, it then passed on to his brother Ahitub, followed by his son Ahijah, followed by Ahimelech who served when the Mishkan was at Nob and the final member of the house of Eli was Abiathar the son of Ahimelech, (I Sam. 4:21, 22:11.22, 21:2). The nebulous aggregate which became the star that shone brightly in the house of Israel did not surface until about a century later when Zadok was appointed as High Priest by David and then officially installed by Solomon in the newly built temple in Jerusalem. Zadok's descendants served in an unbroken line until the time of Ezra in the fourth century BCE. (I Chronicles 5:27.41).

Eli continued his soliloquy with the *ish Elohim* in the hope that he would mitigate the Eternal's decree. Eli is therefore informed that through the process of genetic progression the Eternal will find the personality that will conform with My demand for leadership as inscribed in the Torah. Through My inspiration in the process of history, I shall stimulate the dedication of Israel's leaders to build a permanent Sanctuary *Bayit Neeman* which shall be devoted to uphold My law and My disciplines. The High Priests whom I will recognize and confirm shall guide and direct My anointed kings all the days of their lives.

V. 36   Eli is still enrapt in prophetic analysis of the future, visualizes the denigration of his posterity as they pay homage to the successor of the House of Eli, as they are beholden to him for a monetary handout of a small coin or even a piece of bread. Eli visualized them pleading for an appointment to the priestly divisions in consideration of a morsel of bread.

SAMUEL CHAPTER 3

V. 1   The young Samuel was in the service of the Eternal under the direction of Eli. The commitment to Torah disciplines was limited to few individuals. Even those that brought sacrifices in the Mishkan, failed to understand the symbolic meaning of these disciplines. The leadership as described in vs. 27.35 in Eli's soliliquy with God, were corrupt

I SAMUEL CHAPTER 3

and demorilized. Prophecy was limited to individuals such as Hannah as confirmed by her Ode in (I Sam. 2:1.10).

V. 2 One night in the advanced period of Eli's life, as his eyesight was failing, he was sleeping in his appointed sleeping quarters outside of the Mishkan. *Veenav hechelu kehoth* his thought processes were beginning to dim, he had lost all hope for turning the situation around as described in chapter two. *Lo yuchal liroth* he was limited mentally from perceiving a solution and was bound physically from implementing one.

V. 3 Describes the time frame, it was before dawn before the wicks in the *Menorah* had consumed their normal supply of oil. Samuel too was sleeping in the special quarter assigned to the Leviim outside of the Mishkan. These sleeping quarters were separate from the *Hechal Adonai* where the Ark stood in the Holy of Holies, where even the High Priest was limited from entering but once a year on the Day of Atonement.

Vs. 4.9 Samuel's conscience awakened him; he spontaneously replied, 'I am coming!' For Samuel assumed that Eli was calling him. Samuel ran to Eli's bed chamber in answer to his call, and learned that Eli did not call him. Eli suggested that Samuel return to his bed.

V. 6. Once again Samuel's conscience stirred him to awaken from his slumber. Confusedly he walked to Eli's bed chamber and reported in answer to his call. However, Eli denied that he called him. He once again suggested that he return to his bed and lie down to sleep.

V. 7. Samuel's youth and inexperience had limited his ability to grasp the source (the Eternal God) striving to inspire him, for the time had come to become involved and to take an active part in creating a renaissance in the House of God.

V. 8. When Samuel was awakened a third time and reported to Eli as he did on the previous two occasions, Eli's lifetime experience alerted him to the Source of the call.

V. 9. Once again Eli ordered Samuel back to his bed. However, he instructed him, "Should you again be called in a like manner, you should reply, speak O Eternal God for your servant is attentive and awaits your message." Samuel returned to his bed, and anxiously waited for the message which would grant him the opportunity to become involved in the cause of Israel.

Vs. 10.14 When Samuel's conscience was stirred a third time as he heard his name pronounced, he had the feeling that the *Speaker* stood close by his side. Samuel replied, "Speak O Eternal for I, your servant Samuel am receptive to your message."

V. 11. "I am about to implement an action in Israel which shall send a shudder of fear into the hearts of those that hear about it. The message shall quiver and tremble until it penetrates the conscience of its hearers and stirs them to action."

V. 12. "For on that day I shall activate and implement all that I have already revealed to Eli (I Sam. 2:27.36). I shall balance My account with the house of Eli, until it ceases to be a factor in Israel's history."

I SAMUEL CHAPTER 3

V. 13. "I hereby charge him for all the iniquitous conduct he new about but failed to take action. For the disgrace his sons brought upon themselves."

V. 14. "I have taken an oath that the wrongdoings of the house of Eli shall never be expiated by sacrifices and offerings *ki mekalelim lahem banay*. They not only brought disgrace upon themselves but upon My Sanctuary."

V. 15 Samuel lay upon his bed until it was time to rise and resume his morning chores in the Mishkan. Samuel feared a showdown with Eli. He is the recipient of Eli's finest qualities. Passively he knew Elis' shortcomings. Eli trained Samuel with the ability to implement the dedication he inherited from his prophetic mother Hannah and his sincere and devoted father. Samuel's devotion to Eli, his dedication to the Eternal God, gave Samuel the ability to recognize the prevailing conditions in the Central Sanctuary. Eli's soliloquy recorded in (I Sam. 2:27.36) is the momentum which will inspire Samuel in (I Sam. 3:4.14) to spring into action and to fulfill the purpose for which his mother Hannah had dedicated him to the cause of the Eternal God. Represented in the first three chapters of I Samuel, are Eli, who permitted himself to become corrupted. Hophni and Phinehas represent the assimilation and degradation of the surrounding environment. Elkanah, Hannah and Samuel typify the ever existing nucleus in the human conscience striving to reach for *their Zelem Elohim*, the maximum meaning of human intelligence, the dedication to the cause of the Eternal God of history and justice.

Vs. 16.18 Eli seeks verification from Samuel as to the details of His divine communication. Eli's conscience has already analyzed the Eternal's verdict. He is now seeking confirmation from Samuel, how his misconduct and mismanagement will effect his posterity.

V. 17. Eli threatened Samuel (with an idiomatic malediction) should Samuel conceal the details of his divine inspiration.

V. 18. Samuel's devotion to Eli and his prophetic authenticity obliged him to give Eli a verbatum report on his divine communication. Eli has lived with his passive leadership, he lacked the courage to reprimand his sons scandalous behavior. Eli is therefore resigned to the Eternal's judgment. *Vayomer* he therefore said to Samuel, "He is the Eternal God. He shall do with me and my posterity as He deems right and just."

Vs. 19.21 Samuel's personality grew with his physical and mental development. Samuel's counsel was recognized as sound. His dedication to the Central Sanctuary won the respect of its worshippers. His inspired dedication to his people won him the recognition as a statesman. From Dan in the north to Beersheba in the south the authenticity of his prophetic advice and counsel was attributed to his Divine inspiration. His sincerity and dedication to the Central Sanctuary at Shilo, influenced the daily lives of multitudes throughout the land.

I SAMUEL CHAPTER 4

When Israel appeared in the Holyland under Joshua, multitudes were ready to accept the new world order it was bringing. They recognized the advantages of Israel's laws for human rights. Multitudes in the land of Canaan became proselytes in the ranks of Israel. Israel would have succeeded with its original Master Plan and could have swept aside every opposition. What kept Israel from suceeding was the laxity of the second generation of Israelites whose parents became proselytes at the time of the Exodus. The anarchy which existed in the period of the Judges, has reached this moment in the fading lifetime of Eli.

The background for this war with the Philistines goes back to (Jud. 13:). See commentary in T.E.T. for historic details. For decades the Philistines who entered the Holyland on the Mediterranean Coast, and the Amonites in the east fought with Israel, to create a pincer action, to oppress and to assimilate the newly organized communities.

V. 1   The pressures of the Philistines at this point in time are becoming unbearable. They recognized the anarchy in Israel's ranks; yet, Israel is in no position to go to war. The officially recognized leaders are Eli, Hophni and Phinehas. At this critical moment when Israel is planning to go to war with the Philstines, Samuel utilized his accumulated prestige and challenged the widsom of going to war at this moment in time. To reenforce his conclusions, Samuel revealed the essence of his divine inspiration described in (I Sam. 3:11.14) to the followers of Hophni and Phinehas. Despite his opposition to the action, Israel mobilized for war at Eben Haezer, a name which came to pass in (I Sam. 7:12) when Samuel reversed the defeat reported here. The Philistines mobilized at Aphek, in the open fields where their iron chariots could manouver to their advantage.

Vs. 2.3   The Philistines carried the war into Israel's ranks, the battle became enlarged and resulted in the loss of 4000 men. The Israelites took their defeat badly as they retired to their camp. The Elders are at a loss to evaluate the meaning of Israel's defeat. By popular demand they ordered the bringing of the Ark from the Sanctuary at Shiloh, to bolster the fighting courage of the soldiers in the volunteer army. May the presence of the Ark of the Covenant help them against the enemy.

Vs. 4.7   Hophni and Phinehas responded to the request and it was they that brought forth the Ark to the battlefield. When the troops saw the Ark, they shouted for joy in unison. The Philistines took into account the effect of the Ark of the Covenant upon the outcome of the battle. The primitive fear of the Philistines was matched by Israel's primitive, elementary concept of the Eternal God of Israel.

Vs. 8.9   The Philistines matched Israel's joy at seeing the Ark of the Covenant by wailing. "Woe be to us, who shall save us from this Mighty God? This is the same deity that slew the Egyptians with a variety of disasters in the wilderness."

V. 9.   "Gird yourselves with courage and prove your Philistine manhood.

I SAMUEL CHAPTER 4

Should you lose this battle, you shall become enslaved by the Hebrews even as they have served us these past decades. Measure up as heroic men and fight our battle for survival with courage."

Vs. 10.11   The Philistines fought valiantly and routed the Israelites. As the battle formation disappeared it became a rout as the Israelites retreated to their homes. The decisiveness of this battle at Aphek cost the Israelites 30,000 foot soldiers.

V. 11. In the Ark of the Covenant were kept God's basic laws of justice and the formula how it must apply to all of humanity. It was captured by the Philistines. The sons of Eli were slain in the process of defending its safety.

Vs. 12.14   From the battlefield a Benjaminite fled to bring the news to Eli in Shiloh. His garments were torn and earth covered his head, he was a symbol of mourning the terrible tragedy that befell Israel. (There is a tradition that this man was Saul, who later became the first king of Israel). It was the messenger's intention to go directly to Eli, who was sitting anxiously in his official seat at the entrance of the Mishkan. With a trembling heart he waited for news from the front. Yet, it was the multitude in the city who heard the news first. It was their spontaneous wailing that Eli heard in the distance. When Eli inquired as to the meaning of the tremendous outcry, the crowd made way for the messenger to give Eli the sad news first hand.

Vs. 15.17   Eli was 98 years old, his eyes were fixed in a blind stare as he anxiously awaited confirmation of his prophetic fears (I Sam. 2:34). The messenger came forward to give his report to Eli. "I have escaped from the battlefield as we broke ranks and retreated." Eli interjected as he asked for the details. The messenger continued, "Israel's soldiers fled as they suffered heavy losses. Your sons Hophni and Phinehas were slain and the Ark of the Covenant was captured."

V. 18   The first part of the report confirmed the wisdom of Eli's reservations on the decision of going to war at this time. Eli was knowledgeable of Samuel's public statement and admonition in v.1. The demise of Hophni and Phinehas conformed with Eli's prophetic warning given in (I Sam. 2:34). The capture of the Ark was the catastrophic blow which unhinged Eli's mental balance. The impact of this tragic news confirmed the implementation of Eli's prophetic warning recorded in (I Sam. 2:31.36). This represented the fulfillment of the Eternal's punishment for his passive leadership in the management of the House of God. When Eli fell from his seat, he broke his collarbone, the cervical vertabrae. He died instantly as the result of his fall, his age, his heavy weight. Eli's blindness gave him the capability to see through his failures retrospectively of the 40 years that he functioned as counsel, judge and High Priest. He was the wrong man for this period. He lacked the courage to deal decisively with principles which may not be compromised.

I SAMUEL CHAPTER 4

Vs. 19.20 Eli's daughter-in-law, the wife of Phinehas was pregnant and was nearing her term to give birth. The tragic news of the national disaster, the death of her father-in-law and her husband caused her to weep convulsively. This brought on her severe labor pains and the abnormality and complications of early birth. Those attending her delivery consoled her with the same words expressed in (Gen. 35:17.19) "Be consoled and fear not for you have given birth to a son." She ignored their consolation as she remembered Rachel's effort before she died to name her son.

Vs. 21.22 She named her son Ichabod, to commemorate the loss of the Ark, the capture of the Ark of the Covenant, the death of her father-in-law and the death of her husband. She drew her last breath while mourning the loss of the Ark of God, the glory of Israel.

I SAMUEL CHAPTER 5

V. 1 When the Philistines captured the Ark at Eben-ezer, they brought it to Ashdod and set it up in the temple of Dagon next to their adopted god Dagon. The lower part of this idol represented a fish and the upper part was the figure of a man. Hammurapi in the 19th century BCE. called Dagon -Banija-my god. Ugaritic documents of the 15th and 14th centuries BCE. establish Dagon as a west Semitic god. Mari records identify Dagon in their culture. It is mentioned in the Tel-el-Marna Letters. The Philistines when they came to Canaan, came as mercenaries of Rameses III. They took advantage of Egyptian political upheaval and threw off the Egyptian yoke and established the five principalities which became known in history as Philistia. It was at this point that they adopted the local god Dagon. In (Joshua 19:27) Beth-Dagon was an established community. Philo of Byblos in the first century ACE. identifies Dagon with Chronos, the father of the Greek gods.

Vs. 2.5 The Philistines placed the Ark in their temple and awarded it a place of great honor alongside their god Dagon.

V. 3. Symbolically expresses Dagon's respect for the Ark of God. When Dagon bowed low, he was unable to rise by himself. The text describes Dagon as an inanimate object.

V. 4. Is a repeat performance of the previous day with a new experience, Dagon's enthusiasam to show his respect for the Ark, caused it to fall. The text demonstrates that even idolatrous gods are subject to the Eternal's law of gravity. When it fell it shattered its hands and smashed its head on the threshold of the temple at Ashdod.

V. 5. Jestingly the text informs history that the priests of Dagon declared the threshold as hallowed ground. Anyone entering the temple was obliged to jump over the threshold not to desecrate the hallowed ground where the god Dagon fell.

Vs. 6.7 At this point in time the Philistines became subject to an outbreak of a bubonic disease. When the Philistines summed

I SAMUEL CHAPTER 5

up the havoc caused by this outbreak they concluded that this was their punishment for having detained the Ark of God. Their primitive idolatrous mentality ignored the fact that Ashdod's potential for a rodent and vermin environment ever exists. It is held back by observing the Eternal's laws of hygiene and sanitation. See T.E.T. on (Deut. 7:14.15, 28:27.29) in order to fully grasp the implications of this verse.

V. 7.   The government of Ashdod summed up their conclusions and decided that the Ark of the Covenant must leave Ashdod.

Vs. 8.9   They then assembled the other four governors of the other principalities to confirm their decision. It was resolved that the Ark be removed from Ashdod to Gath. When the Ark was brought to Gath, the psychological fear already existed. Every symptom of the terrifying disease was anticipated, the rumor spread even faster than the infection. The people of Gath insisted that the Ark must be removed at once. They decided to take it to Ekron.

Vs. 10.11   Fear and terror overtook the people of Ekron even though they had not observed any symptoms of the dread disease. They charged the governors with the deliberate intention to destroy the community.

V. 11.   The governors of Philistia were called into session once again and it was decided unanimously to return the Ark to Israel. For the panic of death pervaded throughout their territory.

V. 12   Even those not exposed to infection became victims of *baafolim* their idolatrous ignorance, which initiated their outcry to heaven as a last resort because their god Dagon could not help them in this crisis. Bubonic plague is caused by the genus Pasteurella and is transmitted to man by fleas who become the carriers from infected rodents. The text in this chapter describes the backwardness and ignorance which invades the human mind. The same basic ignorance, creates the images which they reenforce by superstition and black magic to help them out of every dilemma. In contrast to all this stands the Ark of the Covenant. Its power is contained in its laws which harmonize with the laws of nature. The disciplines inscribed in the Covenant-the Torah, are vital exercises in daily living to avoid the disasters which can overtake all forms of living organisms, including human beings, when the laws contained in the Ark of the Eternal God are ignored. See commentary in T.E.T. on (Num. 21:6.9) for a parallel human experience.

I SAMUEL CHAPTER 6

Vs. 1.2   The Ark of the Covenant was in Philistine territory for seven months. During this period of time they experienced the misfortune described in chapter five. At this point the Governors of Philistia decided to return the Ark to Israel.

V. 2.   To ease their conscience they turned to their priests and diviners for

I SAMUEL CHAPTER 6

advice. "What shall be the correct procedure in our effort to return the Ark of God to Israel?"

Vs. 3.4 The priests and diviners replied. "Firstly you must do it as repentants. As repentants you are obliged to offer a guilt offering to the Ark of God, that He may pardon your wrongdoing. You can then justify your position and hope for forgiveness, which in turn may result in curing all your problems, as you begin to feel the effectiveness of His pardon. Do not send the Ark of God back without a guilt offering." V. 4. The Governors now sought the advice of their priests and diviners, as to the nature of their guilt offering-indemnity. The priests and the diviners replied. "Since each of you as Governors of a territory felt the impact of the plague, each of you have become obliged in order to make peace with the Ark of God, to share in the guilt offering."

V. 5 "Symbolically your indemnity shall represent the natural phenomena which the Eternal God of Israel has implemented in order to punish you for your misdeed. We advise you to make exact images of hemorrhoids and rodents, to represent the medium by which His Eternal law, *yakel yado alechem* activated His punishment against you, your gods and your territory."

V. 6 "We urgently caution you against a replay of the Egyptian experience (Ex. 10:2). Do not challenge His authority by your obstinacy, lest you become ensnared and lose your freedom of action. Should you not heed our advice, He shall make a mockery of you by implementing His natural forces as He did to the Egyptians."

V. 7 In keeping with their advice to honor the God of Israel, the priests and diviners suggested the following: "Build a new wagon, choose two milch cows, that have never borne a yoke (for labor). Hitch the cows to the wagon. Detain their calves at home that they do not follow the mother cows."

Vs. 8.9 "Place the Ark of The Eternal God upon the wagon. Next to it place the chest containing the gold images which represent your indemnity, to the Eternal God of Israel. Send the wagon away and let it travel at its own momentum."
V. 9 "Observe from a distance if the cows will travel in a direct route to Bethshemesh, the nearest Israeli settlement to the Philistine border. This will be our indication and proof that the God of Israel, is He that wrought the plague upon us. It is He that is directing these cows to return His Ark to Israel. Should the cows go astray, this will be our evidence, that all our problems were the result of chance, a coincidence."

Vs. 10.12 The Governors accepted the advice of their priests and diviners, they implemented every detail in accord with their specific instructions given in vs. 2.9. They followed the wagon

I SAMUEL CHAPTER 6

at a distance until it was nearing Beth-shemesh. They then took note of its reception. When they returned they reported, "That the cows lowed, indicating they longed for their calves. However, they did not veer to the right or left but traveled in a direct line to Beth-shemesh."

Vs. 13.14 The text informs us that it was at the time of the wheat harvest, therefore the people were in the fields en masse, when the Ark came into their view. Collectively they rejoiced as the wagon came to a halt in the field of Joshua the native Beth-shemeshite. Spontaneously they decided to offer a burnt offering on the *large rock* which is an historic landmark. (The sack of the Mishkan in Shiloh took place during these seven months). They took the wood from the wagon, split it and built a fire on the large rock and then slaughtered the cows and offered them as a burnt offering in gratitude for the return of the Ark of God.

V. 15 Beth-shemesh was a Levitic city (Joshua 21:16). The Leviim then took the Ark and the chest which they had removed from the wagon and set them both on the large rock. They offered peace offerings in gratitude for this event. The sin of the Leviim at Beth-shemesh that caused them to lose 70 men in v. 19 was not because they viewed the Ark in desecration of the law stated in (Num. 4:20). Their natural exposure to its presence when it arrived obliged them to receive it. This was not the reason for their punishment. They were punished because *rau baaron* they opened the Ark to examine its contents. Their desecration stood in juxtaposition to the respect the Philistines attached to the Ark of God. For a fuller understanding of the law which these Levites desecrated, see T.E.T. on (Num. 4:20 and follow the references quoted there on the fuller meaning of *kevala et Hakodesh vametu).* This incident highlights the ineffectiveness of the House of Levi, in the period of the Judges.

Vs. 16.18 The five Governors of the Philistine territories observing the joy of the Beth-shemeshites are satisfied that they followed the advice of thier priests and diviners. They returned to Ekron that very same day. All the symptoms they observed convinced them that their indemnity was acceptable to the God of Israel that they shall be forgiven for their transgression. V. 17. The five golden hemerrhoids represented the indemnity for each of the principalities which made up the Philistine territories: Ashdod, Azzah, Ashkelon, Gath and Ekron.

V. 18 Though in v. 4, the Governors were advised to contribute one golden rodent for each principality, we now learn that every fortified city and every open village voluntarily contributed one golden rodent as their indemnity in the hope that the Ark of God will forgive their transgression and free them from the ravaging plague.

V. 19 It is impossible to understand this verse as it stands. The phrase 50,000 men is completely out of context here. It

I SAMUEL CHAPTER 6

belongs in (I Sam. 4:10). The 30,000 men lost at the battle of Aphek was but the result of the second encounter which ended in a rout. There is no account of the sacking of Shiloh and the destruction of the Mishkan. This bold strike was made possible after the Philistines succeeded in cutting the defenses of the Holyland in two. The whole central range of territory then collapsed and fell into Philistine hands. Considering the fact that the Philistines controlled the coastal roads, the plain of Esdraelon became the center of the war. When Beth-shean, at the eastern end of the valley of Esdraelon, near the Jordan River fell, the Philistine conquest was complete. (I Sam. 31:6.10) is the proof of this fact. Recent archeological findings confirm this conclusion. The 50,000 men reported in this verse are those killed in the above described battles. The Philistine onslaught resulted in the control of the whole territory from the Mediterranean coast to the Jordan River. Beth-shemesh was a Levitical city in Judah (Joshua 21:16). Its population was extremely small. The 30,000 men reported in (I Sam. 4:10) were those that died at the battle of Aphek. The 50,000 men reported in v. 19, are those who died in the overall campaign. Josephus Antiquities VI, i.4, reports that some ancient manuscripts did not report this loss of 50,000 men.

Vs. 20.21 The experience described in v. 15, confirms our conclusions by the contents of these verses. The Leviim considered themselves unworthy to possess the Ark in their community. They therefore sought to find a reputable community of Leviim, who were recognized by their dedication to be worthy to assume its responsibility.

V. 21 This was their purpose to send messengers to Kiriath-jearim about four miles east of Beth-shemesh in the hill-country of Judah (Joshua 15:60). "The Philistines have returned the Ark of God, it is now with us in Beth-shemesh. We would like you to assume the responsibility for its safe keeping."

I SAMUEL CHAPTER 7

V. 1 Abinadab sent representative kohanim from the priestly city of Kiriath-jearim to Beth-shemesh. They brought the Ark to the home of Abinadab, located on the hill of Gibeon (2755 ft. above sea level) in the territory of Benjamin. Abinadab designated his son Eleazar to become responsible for the safety and sanctity of the Ark. The following texts identify Kiriath-jearim and Gibeon in Israel's history: (Joshua 9:17, 18:15, 25, 21:17. I Sam. 10:5, 11:4, 13:3, 15:34, 22:6, 23:19. I Chron. 2:50, 13:17, 18:7). It must be clearly understood that although the Ark was here for 20 years until David brought it to Jerusalem as recorded in (II Sam. 6:3.4) Gibeon never replaced the Central Sanctuary in Shiloh. The Philistines ruled with an iron hand over Israel, as confirmed in the following texts: (I Sam. 9:16, 13:5, 19, 17:1, 23:27). They disarmed Israel. To permit the reestablishment of the Mishkan would have led to unification.

V. 2 During these 20 years after the destruction of Mishkan Shiloh

I SAMUEL CHAPTER 7

and the House of Eli, Samuel operated as a free agent as he traveled from Dan to Beer-sheba, to create a renaissance in the ranks of Israel. Therefore (I Sam. 3:19.21) belongs here. Samuel drove home into the hearts of Israel the cause of their alienation. The Philistine oppression was the effect and result of Israel's estrangement from Torah principles. It not only retarded Israel but it impeded and postponed the development of the Eternal's concept of civilization.

Vs. 3.4 — Samuel's formula for a renaissance in Israel, is the established configuration of the Torah, which will be followed by every Prophet in Israel from Moses to the end of time. Samuel's dedication has earned him the mantle of Moses. Every rung upon the ladder of Israel's development is the result of Samuel's initiative at this time in Israel's history. He developed courage in the hearts of his people as he invited them to come on a voluntary basis for an assembly at Mitzpah. This was done as a challenge to Philistine oppression breathing down the neck of Israel. The Philistines countered by placing administrators and soldiers at Kiriath-jearim, to discourage these efforts of reorganization. Despite these obstacles, Samuel forged ahead during these 20 oppressive years to lay the groundwork for a new beginning. "If your repentant return is sincere, you must resolve to remove your alien gods and wishful thinking and direct all your hope for a renewal to the disciplines of the Eternal God of Israel. This will grant you the courage, inspiration and hope for a deliverance from Philistine oppression."

Vs. 5.7 — Samuel's bold defiance of Philistine authority at Mitzpah was the climactic effect of his years of traveling among Israel, to breathe new hope into every individual heart. At Mitzpah they fasted, they prayed, they poured out their hearts freely, as they made confession to themselves of their past disaffection from the goals of the Torah. Symbolically, they poured water to cleanse their souls of their past idolatrous dissipation. They acknowledged their dilatory *and laggard behavior* as they hedged their faith in the Eternal God of Israel while worshipping idolatrous images as God. V. 7. Though Samuel's assembly at Mitzpah was an unarmed convocation for prayer, inspiration and hope, the Governors of Philistia mobilized their forces to challenge Israel for rebellion.

Vs. 8.11 — Samuel offered sacrifices to raise the morale of all those present and prayed that Israel's Eternal God recognize their oppressive plight. Samuel succeeded to touch their very souls as they banished all fear for Philistine power. At this high point in the process of Samuel's prayer service, the Philistines closed ranks and attempted to disband them. Spontaneously the assembly challenged their authority to break up this peaceful gathering. The courage of Israel's assembly rose to challenge the Philistine soldiers. A tremendous storm of thunder and lightning augmented the outcry of Israel's convocation in gratitude to the Eternal's symbolic challenge to the arrogant forces of the Philistines. The timing of the Eternal God's natural

I SAMUEL CHAPTER 7

phenomena intensified the challenge of the assembly to stand up for their human rights to freedom of assembly. The mob pursued the retreating soldiers in their moment of confusion and panic unto Beth-car, where they dibanded in this pastureland. V. 11. *Vayetzeu* Inspired by the panicking soldiers as the result of the supernatural phenomena, the Israelites left Mitzpah resolved to rearm and pursue the Philistines at every opportunity.

V. 12   Samuel took advantage of the inspired mob action and established a landmark between the peak-*Shen*-tooth and the area of the assembly at Mitzpah and renamed this jutting stone peak *Eben-haezer* to commemorate for history the effect of Israel's moment of repentance upon the implementation of the Eternal's natural forces, as it came to Israel's rescue.

Vs. 13.14   The Philistines relaxed their control, they made no effort to disband Israel's assemblies which became a fact of life and met at frequent intervals to fill their need of the moment. From this step the Israelites in Ekron and Gath once again resumed self government. The Amorites-the indigenous Canaanites, took advantage of Israel's challenge to Philistine authority, they too rebelled against the heavy oppressive methods of the Philistines. They lived in peace with the Israelites.

Vs. 15.16   Samuel continued his inspired leadership for the rest of his life. Every year he made a circuitous round by a convocation at Bethel, Gilgal and Mitzpah. His presence attracted ever greater numbers and inspired self discipline by administering justice, counsel and new hope.

V. 17   He then returned to Ramah, his home. From every corner of the Holyland, the people looked to him for leadership, advice and inspiration. After the destruction of the Central Sanctuary at Shiloh, it was permitted to build an altar locally and to offer sacrifices. Samuel therefore built an altar at Ramah, to encourage the practice of self discipline as a stepping stone away from the idolatrous *highplaces-Bamoth*. The effectiveness of Samuel's renaissance marked the end of the tragic period called the Judges. His sincerity, his dedication and his devotion to the cause of the Eternal God of Israel, created a new heart in the people of Israel.

I SAMUEL CHAPTER 8

The information vital for us to understand the chronology of Samuel's active lifetime are extremely tenuous. That Samuel was 52 years old when he died must be rejected because it does not harmonize with the chronology of Saul and David. They were his choices for the office of king of Israel. Saul's rule has been calculated to fall in the following period: 1031-1016 or 1025-1010 BCE. David ruled from 1016-976 or 1010-970 BCE. It is impossible to crowd Saul's active life into less than 15 years. Encylcopedia Judaica, gives Saul's rule as 1029-1005 BCE.

I SAMUEL CHAPTER 8

and David's as 1010-970 BCE. Therefore David's rule in Judah overlapped the rule of Saul by five years.

When Samuel appointed his sons as judges for the district of Beersheba, they must have been between the ages of 40-50 in order to be eligible. To accord with Biblical marriage records Samuel would have to be between 60-70 years of age at the time of their appointment. The written record of Samuel's active life indicates that he must have been between the ages of 75 to 80 at the time of his death, which antedated Saul's tragic death on the battlefield by several months.

May the above information serve to enlighten the serious Bible student and encourage both student and scholar to search further to verify the exactness of the above conclusions.

Vs. 1.3 — Samuel appointed his two sons to become judges in Beersheba in order to extend his authority on a more permanent basis in the south, while he continued to make his circuit in the north. Samuel was at an advanced age when he did this, for he was obliged to wait for the day his sons matured to qualify as judges in Israel. Joel was the elder and Abijah his second son was the younger. He was hopeful they would follow his initiative by establishing a circuit from Beersheba to Jerusalem. This would give them a control in the tribes of Judah, Benjamin and Ephraim. However, they divided the southern territory between themselves, they made their headquarters in Beersheba and informed the litigants to come to their central courthouse. This created the impression it was beneath them to come in contact with the people in their home territory as justices and sons of the renowned Samuel. It was also rumored that they took bribes in order to advance the dates of the hearings. The effect of their conduct created rumors and innuendos, that their conduct was a perversion of justice.

V. 4 — The elders of the tribes of Israel assembled for the purpose of clarifying their conclusion that the time has come for Israel to establish a central authority, who shall unite the country as a national entity. Having agreed upon a plan of action they came to Ramah to consult with Samuel.

V. 5 — "We recognize your advanced age in years (probably 70). We have reviewed the conduct of your sons. We are concerned and perturbed that they have deviated from your standards in administering justice. We have therefore concluded that now is the time to conform with the popular demand which accords with Torah law (Deut. 17:14) *simah alenu melech*, that you as our dedicated and respected leader choose for us a king, who shall dispense justice in accord with international standards." While the first part of their request is rooted in the Torah, the second part contradicts the standards demanded by Torah law of Israel's king.

Vs. 6.7 — Samuel's displeasure at their request for a king was his spontaneous natural reaction that they were denigrating his

I SAMUEL CHAPTER 8

ability to lead. Samuel's better judgment prevailed after he resorted to prayer. (To pray is *pilel* to ask for inspiration and guidance, how we may react to a given situation). For the Eternal inspired Samuel to recognize the justness of the first part of their request, however, He rejected the second part *leshaftenu kechol hagoyim* to administer justice by the standards of other nations does not conform with the Eternal's criteria for justice. The Eternal continued to console Samuel's feelings of rejection by the elders, "Though the second part of the elders request rejects My standards for Israel's king, you are obliged to heed their every request. Even I, as the Eternal God of all the Universe, am obliged to observe My law as inscribed in the Torah (Gen. 1:27). For I have endowed humanity with the genetic potential of Zelem Elohim, the dynamic force of intelligence. Man's ability to discern his freedom of action ever remains answerable to My law of the nucleus. (Gen. 6:3) I must wait patiently for the day when Israel matures to implement Torah disciplines in order to help create a better world order."

Vs. 8.9   The Eternal continued His soliloquy. "Samuel! Review Israel's conduct from the Exodus to this day. They have forsaken Me and My disciplines by accepting the behaviorisms of their environment. Your rejection reflects Israel's inability to fully grasp the intent of your teachings and the dedication of your leadership even as they cannot comprehend the full impact of My laws for their development." V. 9, "Be attentive to the elder's request Samuel, however, define the laws ever patiently by which Israel's king shall be chosen in the framework of My laws-My Constitution-The Torah, which shall govern the king's day to day conduct in dispensing justice throughout the Holyland."

Vs. 10.11   Samuel reconvened the assembly of the elders in order to transmit the Eternal's instructions in v. 9, which is consistent with the Eternal's long suffering patience from the beginning of time (Gen. 6:3, Ex. 34:6). Contrasting the Eternal's instructions Samuel gave the elders a detailed summary of the type of king they requested who shall lead them in accord with the standards and the normal practices of the nations of the world. "This king of your choice will draft your sons to magnify his glory by appointing them as runners, charioteers and horsemen."

Vs. 12.14   "He shall commission your sons to become responsible for the multitudes of soldiers in his army. He shall feel free to rob you of your freedom, to demand that you plow his fields and reap his harvests. You shall become obliged to produce the weapons of war and the equipment for the chariots."
V. 13. "In accord with the common practice of the kings you wish to emulate, he shall feel free to draft your daughters as perfumers, cooks and bakers."
V. 14. "By the universal rule of the divine right of kings, he shall feel it within his divine right to seize your choice fields, vineyards and olive groves and then distribute them at will to his courtiers."

I SAMUEL CHAPTER 8

Vs. 15.16 "To maintain the dignity of his court he will usurp the right to tax you (ten percent) of your produce, in order to maintain his eunuchs and courtiers."

V. 16. "In accord with the *divine rights* you will bestow upon him, he shall draft your male and female hired hands (slave or free citizens). Your charge, that he conduct himself in the manner of kings, shall grant him the authority to impress your cattle and livestock in order to serve his purpose in the name of the national good."

Vs. 17.18 "The numerous tithes of your flocks will diminish your ability to earn a livelihood. As a slave you shall then be beholden to the king of your choice."

V. 18. "On the day when you fully realize the impact of your self inflicted misery by the king you have chosen, you shall cry out to the Eternal God, to come to your assistance. I warn you, He shall ignore your call. On that same day you shall fully realize your inability to extricate yourselves from your self imposed misery."

V. 19 The elders differences with Samuel are implied. It exposed their lack of appreciation for a lifetime of dedication as expressed in v. 8. Yet, it is difficult to reconcile his distress at their request for a central authority. It is Samuel that traveled among the communities to emphasize the importance of unity. All of his teachings highlighted the significance of central leadership eminating from a Central Sanctuary. Samuel failed because he created friction, when he exposed his own hurt feelings in vs. 11.18, instead of following the Eternal's instructions given in v.9, to recognize the elders demand for a king as a just request consistent with the national need and their Constitutional right (Deut. 17:14). This was his opportunity to patiently establish the foundation of Israel's national life.

This is the third time in Israel's national history that great leaders failed in their leadership at a critical moment. It ever demands tact, diplomacy and an effort to emulate the Eternal God of Israel's long suffering patience (Gen. 6:3, Ex. 34:6). Moses failed in (Num. 20:7.13), Joshua failed when he was overzealous and tried to exceed the purpose and intent of the Eternal's law. (Joshua 1:7), created the fiasco in 7:10.13, see T.E.T. on the above quotations to clarify this point of view.

V. 20 Samuel's conflict of interest was a miscarriage of the Eternal's instructions given in v. 9. He never told the elders that he concurred and granted their request. He never succeeded in explaining patiently the basic differences between world kingdoms, who function under the *divine right of kings*, the law is what they decree it is. Or, that Israel's king, must ever govern his daily conduct by the standards prescribed by the Eternal God, in His Torah. Because of Samuel's failure to convey the Eternal's guidance (Num. 20:12) in v. 9, it is the elders who have now taken the initiative by telling Samuel, what they shall expect of their king. "He shall have the

I SAMUEL CHAPTER 8

authority to mobilize an army for our wars, wars not dictated in the name of the Eternal, as wars for the advancement of justice. It shall be our king who shall enforce his concept of justice."

Vs. 21.22 Samuel's failure obliged him to reserve his answer to the elders and consult with his conscience-*The Eternal God*-the source of all human intelligence. However, the Eternal did not succeed in correcting Samuel's mental block. Israel's leaders are governed by the Eternal's law-The Torah, they may not modify nor enlarge upon its intent (Joshua 1:7). No leader can arbitrarily digress from the Eternal's Master Plan for the evolution of Israel, to become a "light unto the nations of the world." Without this goal, Israel has no position in history. Samuel did not convey the Eternal's instructions to the elders. He discharged them without a meeting of their minds. Samuel failed to grasp the Eternal's conclusion, that even He must obey His own law of human rights, the law of freedom of choice in the life of every human being (Deut. 30:19).

I SAMUEL CHAPTER 9

Vs. 1.2 In (I Sam. 4:12.17) Saul appeared on the scene of history as a nameless personality. Samuel took note of him then and was deeply impressed with his dedication as expressed by his concern for the loss of the Ark of God and its effect upon the national cause of Israel. (I Sam. 4:1) Samuel's outspoken position against going to war with the Philistines at that time was the first public position he took and was proven right by the loss of the Ark of God and the tremendous defeat recorded in (I Sam. 4:10.14, 6:19). We may conclude that Samuel and Saul's ages were 20-30. From that moment until Samuel and Saul meet officially in this chapter, Samuel watched the development of Saul. It is Samuel who recorded his conclusions about Saul in v. 2. "Saul was an excellent young man, none in Israel was handsomer than he. Saul was a head taller than any one in the ranks of Israel." V. 1, Records for the record of history for the first time Saul's genealogy. Saul was a Benjaminite, his father was Kish, the son of Abiel, the son of Tzeror, the son of Aphiah. Samuel tells us that Kish was a man of renown, a man of valor in the cause of Israel and he was a wealthy man. From (I Sam. 13:2) we can conclude the approximate age of Saul when Samuel chose him as king of Israel. Jonathan his son was old enough to lead 1000 men in a battle against the Philistines.

Vs. 3.4 The text describes an incident in the daily lives of Kish and his son Saul. Kish reports the loss of some female asses that went astray and he now requested that Saul take one of their employees and organize a plan in order to find them. Saul and his companion traveled in the hill country of Ephraim, he crossed into the district of Shalishah, then proceeded into Shaalim. He proceeded to traverse the territory of Benjamin.

I SAMUEL CHAPTER 9

The intent of this detail is to establish the capability of Saul to follow through. Yet, he did not succeed in finding them.

V. 5   When they reached Zuph, Saul suggested to his companion that they turn back, lest his father stop worrying about his asses and worry for the safety of his son and his companion. This territory was called Zuph because it belonged to Zuph, the grandfather of Elkanah, the father of Samuel. Ramah is located in this territory of Zuph.

V. 6   Saul's companion recognized and recalled that Ramah was the home of the Godly man Samuel. "He is renowned for his advice and counsel. Perhaps he can advise us what to do under the circumstances." The intent of this verse is to establish for the record, that although Samuel observed the development of Saul, Saul, who was aware of Samuel's travels in his annual circuits to advise, to counsel, to sit as a justice, to preach his message of unity wherever he went, had no occasion to meet Samuel face to face.

Vs. 7.8   Saul replied to his companion, "If we go to see him, we have nothing to give him in appreciation for his advice, our food is gone, we have nothing fitting to present to this man of God as a gift for his counsel." V. 8. Saul's companion replied, "I have a quarter shekel of silver. I will give it to the man of God and he will advise us how we may go about finding the female asses." Both were unaware that Samuel did not accept any remuneration for his services.

V 9   It was a common practice in Canaan for people to visit the *seer-a fortune teller*. Going back to the time of Abraham and Isaac, this was not the practice of Israel (Gen. 25:22). Rebecca went to seek advice *lidrosh et Adonai* from those endowed with wisdom from the Source of man's intelligence, from the Eternal God. (In Is. 30:10) "Isaiah mocks those that go to see the seers in order to tell them what to see, what they would like to hear."

Vs. 10.13   Saul agreed to his companion's suggestion, "Come let us go to the home of the man of God in Ramah. As they proceeded up the hill to Ramah, there they met some maidens on the way to the well. They paused to inquire of them, "Is the Seer at home?" It is obvious from their reply, they were aware of Samuel's travels when he made his periodic circuit.

V. 12. The maidens replied, "He has just returned from his circuitous travels for a special sacrificial festival at the shrine (I Sam. 7:15.17).

V. 13. "If you will hurry you will find him as you enter the city before he leaves for the *mizbeach-the shrine* for the festivities. There are people there awaiting his arrival that he may bless the sacrifice before they start to eat."

Vs. 14.16   As Saul and his companion entered the city, Samuel came

I SAMUEL CHAPTER 9

from his home toward them on his way to the shrine.

Vs. 15.16. The day before Saul arrived at Ramah, Samuel was inspired by the Eternal, that on the morrow about this same time, "I shall send you a man out of the tribe of Benjamin and you shall anoint him as the ruler of Israel. It is this man that shall relieve My people from the distress imposed upon them by the Philistines. I have become perceptive to their affliction (Ex. 2:23)."

Vs. 17.19 When Samuel saw Saul (this verse follows verse 14) the Eternal granted Samuel the capability to perceive, that he is the very man whom he had recognized for his outstanding qualifications and his potential as described in the commentary on vs. 1.2. V. 18. Saul approached Samuel inside the gate of the city and asked him, "Where is the *seer's*-the prophet's home?" V. 19. Samuel answered Saul, "I am the *seer* that has observed you beginning with that tragic day when the Ark of God was confiscated by the Philistines (I Sam. 4:10.17). I have been expecting you today. Go up ahead of me to the shrine, for you shall eat with me today. In the morning you shall take leave of me. However, before you leave, I shall answer the questions for which you sought my help. I shall also explain the full meaning of this festive reception for you. I shall strive to help you resolve the national problems which are so close to your heart."

V. 20 "Now as to your immediate problem of finding your father's asses, which were lost three days ago, be not concerned about them. I can set your mind at ease that they have been found. Now, even if they had not been found, put your mind at ease, for you cannot evaluate their loss with the honor which awaits you and all the members of your father's household. *Kal chemdath Yisrael*, every material advantage awaits *halo lecha* you as the *chosen* of Israel."

V. 21 Saul replied to Samuel, "I trust that you have taken into your calculations the fact that I am a Benjaminite. Have you overlooked the tragedy recorded in (Judges 20:21:) which reduced my tribe of Benjamin to become the smallest tribe numerically? How can you overlook the animosity borne by my tribe? Take into consideration that my family is insignificant when compared to the other great families in Benjamin." Saul's reply is not an indication of modesty but significant for the historic record of Benjamin. The progress made by the remnant of Benjamin as they literally rose from the ashes of civil war in the incident of *Pilegesh Begibeah*. "For you (Samuel) to recognize my family over the outstanding families of Benjamin, is to ignore the advantages they can bring to the position of a ruler in Israel."

Vs. 22.24 Samuel ignored Saul's review of the historic facts, he directed Saul and his companion to enter the chamber for the festivities. He further directed him to take a seat at the head of

I SAMUEL CHAPTER 9

the table, where about 30 guests were already seated awaiting his presence with Samuel.

Vs. 23.24.   Anticipating the coming of Saul, Samuel made the preparations for this festival. He instructed the cook to reserve the choicest portion (normally given to the kohen) for the most honored guest. As the cook served Saul, Samuel announced that this banquet was planned in anticipation of his becoming their honored guest. When Samuel observed Saul's reservations to eat the kohen's prescribed portion, Samuel urged Saul to eat what was set before him as their most honored guest.

Vs. 25.27   After the banquet, Samuel, Saul and his companion descended from the shrine and returned to Samuel's home. There, he took Saul to the roof-garden of his home and spoke to him privately. V. 26. Saul and his companion slept on the roof-garden. At dawn the next morning Samuel called to Saul, "Awaken! I shall escort you a distance on your way home." Samuel, Saul and his companion left the house together. When they reached the outskirts of the city, Samuel requested that Saul ask his companion to walk on ahead by himself. "You remain with me here so I can instruct you and transmit the instructions I have received in your behalf through the Eternal God of Israel's inspiration."

I SAMUEL CHAPTER 10

V. 1   These verses describe Samuel's procedure and instructions after Saul's companion went ahead by himself in v. 27. Samuel took a flask of oil and symbolically poured some on Saul's head to anoint him as the king of Israel. "I hereby anoint you in the name of the Eternal and consecrate you to become dedicated as the ruler and custodian of the people of Israel, the Eternal God's patrimony. From the moment you are inaugurated as Israel's king, you shall cease being concerned with your personal needs and devote your life to the progress of the nation. It is through the evolution and development of Israel that the Eternal God of Israel shall advance His Master Plan for humanity (Gen. 12:1.3)."

V. 2   Samuel gave Saul three symbols-signs to prove to his doubting mind that though Samuel had selected him for the highest position in the nation, (I Sam. 9:20), his choice has the confirmation of the Eternal God of Israel. "When the following three incidents come to pass, this shall be your evidence of His confirmation: 1 ... As you take leave of me today, at this very moment two men are in the vicinity of Rachel's tomb in the territory of Benjamin (Gen. 35:19.20, 48:7, Joshua 18:13, Jud. 20:10, Jer. 31:14). When you shall meet them, they shall be at Tzelzach. It is they that will inform you of the return of your father's asses, after he had abandoned all hope of their return because he had become anxious for your safety."

Vs. 3.6   2 ... "When you shall reach the terebinth of Tabor, you will

I SAMUEL CHAPTER 10

meet three men on their way to visit the shrine at Beth-el (Gen. 28:17, 35:7). One shall be carrying three kids, one shall be carrying three loaves of bread and one will be carrying a bottle of wine."

V. 4. "The three men will greet you and present you with two loaves of bread, to express their loyalty to your dedication and leadership. You are obliged to accept their token of homage."

V. 5. 3 ... "When you will reach the shrine of God-at Kiriat-jearim, where the Ark is now housed in the House of God. (it is here in Gibeath Elohim that the Philistines have garrisoned their soldiers to anticipate any organized rebellion of Israel). On your way home to Gibeath Saul-Gibeath Benjamin (I Sam. 11:4, 13:2), you will meet a company of prophets. They shall be returning from the shrine by the accompaniment of lyres, timbrels, flutes and harps in order to express their exultation for having been in the presence of the Eternal God of Israel."

V. 6. "You too shall become overwhelmed by their ecstacy and will join them. Your exultation will elevate you into a higher sphere of existence."

V. 7 "When these three incidents shall have come to pass, you will have the assurance that the Eternal God has confirmed you as the chosen leader of Israel. I hereby authorize you to exercise your leadership in accord with your God given intelligence. Your efforts must at all times conform with the Eternal God's Master Plan for Israel. Take advantage of this important moment in your life as the chosen man of God, to become the man of the hour."

V. 8 V. 8, is Samuel's reply to Saul at Michmash, where he mobilized his army for war with the Philistines (I Sam. 13:3.4). "You are to go down to Gilgal and wait for me for seven days (or) until I come to you and instruct you what you are to do next." This verse is out of context here because it refers to the war with the Philistines, described in chapter 13. Chronologically this war took place after Saul's appointment as king was ratified in (I Sam. 10:17.24), and the inauguration of Saul which followed the war with the Ammonites (I Sam. 11:1.11,14.15, and chapter 12:) which is a verbatum record of Samuel's discourse at the inaugural of Saul as king of Israel.

V. 9 As Saul took leave of Samuel, he spontaneously felt the change in his life. The impact of Samuel's charge came upon him as he began to grasp the meaning and the authenticity of his authority indicated in the symbols established in vs. 2.7.

Vs. 10.11 When Saul and his companion were about to enter their home town in Gibeah, a company of prophets were descending from Gibeath-Elohim-Kiriath-jearim where the Ark of God was housed. The experience of v. 9, and the scene which confronted him stimulated his spritual consciousness. Here were a group of prophets devoted to the Eternal's

I SAMUEL CHAPTER 10

cause of implementing the spirit of God into the everyday life of humanity. Saul visualized the realization of his hopeful plans. He now feels responsible for the welfare of Israel and its historic evolution. V. 11. The townspeople who knew Saul from birth turned to each other for verification, "Is this indeed Saul the son of Kish who has joined the prophetic school of Samuel?"

Vs. 12.13 One of the natives raised the question, "Was there ever a prophet in the genealogy of Kish?" *Umi abihem* "You all know who is responsible for this prophetic development. For prophecy is not included in one's inheritance. It is one of dedication, self discipline and devotion to the cause of Israel."

It is here in this area that Samuel devoted a lifetime in establishing a school for competent young men, to become teachers and leaders to replace the corrupt priesthood. Samuel was the motivating spirit that established the prophetic school in Israel. He was succeeded by Elijah and every recognized prophet in the history of Israel. Saul entered the shrine to offer his gratitude for all that has come to pass since that day when he obeyed his father's command to seek his lost asses.

V. 14 Returning from the shrine he met his uncle Ner, he inquired of Saul and his companion, "Where have you been?" Saul replied, "We went in search of father's asses, when we were unable to find them we went to the home of Samuel for advice."

Vs. 15.16 Whereupon Saul's uncle Ner asked him, "So what did Samuel tell you?" Saul replied, "He told us that the asses were already found." Saul gave no other information that transpired between Samuel and himself (I Sam. 9:27).

Vs. 17.19 Samuel summoned the tribes of Israel to appear before the Eternal at Mitzpah, for the purpose of ratifying their choice for the king of Israel in accord with their request made in (I Sam. 8:5). As Israel's representatives assembled, Samuel reviewed their past rebelliousness going back to the time of the Exodus to this day. "Despite your ongoing knowledge that the Eternal God of Israel has directed your destiny and has protected you from your enemies and natural calamities, you have failed in your recognition of the Eternal God as the only Source of your blessings. You have directed your plea to the Eternal through me, that you be granted the opportunity to choose a king. The Eternal has granted your request." Samuel instructed the assembly to classify themselves into groups which shall identify each tribe and its respective family groupings.

Vs. 20.22 When the tribes were polled by lot, the tribe of Benjamin was their choice. Samuel then polled the tribe of Benjamin by its respective families. This resulted in choosing the family of the Matrites (renowned for their military ability (Is. 10:21). When this family was polled Saul won the nomination. As Saul's name was announced, he was not among his family. Saul had closeted himself among the baggage of his families

I SAMUEL CHAPTER 10

possessions. His modesty created his embarrasment, that he was chosen to supersede the elders of his family groupings.

Vs. 23.24 It took some persuasion to encourage Saul to take his appointed place in his family grouping. There he stood head and shoulders above all those present. Samuel presented Saul as the official choice of the House of Israel, who had also received the confirmation of the Eternal God of Israel. Samuel gratifyingly added. "There is none like him, I commend you upon your selection." Spontaneously, at this moment the assembly shouted, "long live the King."

Vs. 25.26 Samuel went into great detail as he enlarged upon the laws of the Torah, under which the land of Israel must function. "The laws of the Torah shall form the basis of the monarchy, the constitution under which it must ever function." Samuel defined the laws and responsibilities of Israel's king to the nation. The welfare of its people have the highest priority of the king's charge. Samuel defined the responsibility of the elders in uniting the people behind the king. Samuel then inscribed these laws into a book and placed it before the Ark of God. Upon the conclusion of all the ceremonies, Samuel dismissed the assembly and each tribe returned to their homes. V. 26. Saul returned to his home in Gibeah (I Sam. 11:5). With him went a loyal bodyguard who were motivated spontaneously to swear allegiance to his monarchy.

V. 27 A small group of doubters were outspoken in their challenge to Saul, "How can this man help us?" They proved their opposition by their antagonistic attitude, they brought no gift or even a symbol of faith in Saul's potential leadership. Though Saul made a mental note of this minority, for the moment he considered it strategic to ignore their presence, lest it become the nucleus of an opposing force before he will be installed as the king of Israel.

I SAMUEL CHAPTER 11

Vs. 1.4 Reviewing the political situation in Israel, Saul has been chosen as king of Israel and the laws under which he will function have been defined (I Sam. 10:24.26). Saul was authorized by Samuel to use his initiative even before he is inaugurated officially as king (I Sam. 10:7). Saul is to be prepared to react to the fluid ever changing circumstances existing in the Holyland. Saul returned to his home with a voluntary bodyguard and at this point in time is back on the farm.

Vs. 1.2 Ammonite arrogance goes back to (Judges 11:12.28). Two factors have now converged to inspire Ammon to annex this Trans-jordanian territory. 1 ... The Philistine desire to absorb the Holyland and remove Israel as a force of contention. 2 ... Ammon is aware of the animosity between the tribes occupying the territory west of the Jordan River

I SAMUEL CHAPTER 11

and those east of the Jordan River. It has grave doubts that if it annexed the territory of Jabesh-gilead, that their kinsmen would come to their assistance. It would have been advantageous for Ammon if Israel were a united force to contain Philistine expansion. Since king Nahash has reservations on this point, he has devised a plan to grant Jabesh-gilead a peace treaty on the condition that every able-bodied man incapacitate his right eye, which would handicap them in military action. It would also create an embarrasment to Israel as a nation. How will they react to his strategy? King Nahash therefore agreed to give the citizens of Jabesh-gilead seven days to give him their reply.

Vs. 3.4   The elders of Jabesh-gilead agreed to send messengers to the tribes living west of the Jordan in order to test their loyalty. In the event they fail them, they will have no other alternative but to submit to this barbaric condition.

V. 4. The messengers of Jabesh-gilead went directly to Gibeat-Saul. It is obvious that they are aware of all the details described above as to the political situation in the Holyland. Since they were under Ammonite siege for some time they may not have been included in the tribes that ratified Saul's election as King. Does this threat also apply to Reuben and Gad? The mournful scene described in this verse as the messengers conveyed their sad situation, rekindled their blood ties with the Trans-jordanian tribes.

Vs. 5.6   Saul's return from his agricultural chores brought him into contact with this mournful scene. When he learned all the details about the situation in Jabesh-gilead, Saul was overcome by a sense of anguish for his brethren. Spontaneously Saul reviewed the historic background of this ongoing friendly enemy (Judges 11:12.28). Saul's anger grew as the details exposed Ammon's bestiality. Saul was determined to take action in the name of God's concept of justice.

V. 7   Saul slaughtered two oxen and divided them into parts, he sent them by special messenger to every community in Israel. With this symbol went the warning, this is a call to arms. "Should any tribe fail to report for duty, this is the action that will be taken upon your livestock. This action is taken with the authority of Samuel and the power vested in me as your chosen King, in the name of the Eternal God of Israel."

V. 8   Saul mobilized in Bezek-Ras Ibzik, which is in the territory of Manasseh west of the Jordan River. Bezek is 12 miles west of Jabesh-gilead. Saul's call to arms brought forth 330,000 men, 30,000 came from Judah. Judah's loyalty to the cause of Israel has never been in doubt. Judah therefore insists that the record establish its outstanding contribution to the national cause. This attitude of Judah goes back to (Gen. 38:). It's thread of consistent loyalty began in (Gen. 43:1.5).

Vs. 9.10   Samuel and Saul addressed the messengers of Jabesh-gilead. "Go back at once and inform your kinsmen that our strategy

I SAMUEL CHAPTER 11

is geared to a showdown with the Ammonites by the noon hour tomorrow." The messengers returned at once and delivered their hopeful message. Their joy was unbounding.

V. 10. Confident of their position, the tribe of Manasseh sent their reply to king Nahash. "Tomorrow being the seventh day of our truce, we shall comply with your conditions in v. 2, do with us as you please but let us live in peace."

V. 11   Saul divided his forces into three groupings. He then marched his forces under the cover of darkness from Bezek to the eastern side of el Ghor, he then crossed the Wadi ez Zoeyig leading up to Jabesh-gilead. He arrived in the Ammonite camp before dawn. Saul gave them no chance to awaken to the danger they were facing. The united forces of Israel kept up the pressure to high noon, when the remnant of the Ammonite forces ran for safety. The pursuit was so complete that no two men of the Ammonites could be seen retreating together. Saul's spontaneous and sincere response secured the loyalty of Jabesh-gilead as proven in (I Sam. 31:11; II Sam. 2:9).

Vs. 12.14   This verse confirms Samuel's cooperation throughout this action. The effect of a united people inspired the punishment of the minority opposition to Saul's choice as king recorded in (I Sam. 10:27). V. 13. Saul's instinctive natural reply, "No one shall be put to death on this day! For this is the day that the Eternal God of Israel brought victory to us." Saul's leadership ability is confirmed by his silence to the opposition at his confirmation and now that he has the popular consensus and the authority to make his power felt, he ignored this minority opposition.

Vs. 14. Saul's appointment at Mitzpah (10:24) was de jure. Samuel issued an order to those in his presence, that they announce an assembly to gather at Gilgal, to inaugurate Saul as their de facto king.

V. 15   All of Israel as a united nation assembled at Gilgal, which was out of reach of Philistine domination. It is here that they inaugurated Saul as the king of Israel before the official shrine of the Eternal God of Israel. They offered sacrifices for their well-being and rejoiced over their ability to unite for this great moment in Israel's history. The Ark was still under the surveillance of the Philistines at Kiriath-jearim.

I SAMUEL CHAPTER 12

Vs. 1.3   Samuel addressed the assembly of Israel, "I have yielded to your request (I Sam. 8:5) and I have helped you establish the monarchy. This is the moment for me to step down and relinquish my office as your leader, to the king of your choice." V. 2. "From now on the king will be your leader. From the early days of my youth to this day, I have striven to unite Israel as a nation. This herculean task has caused me to

I SAMUEL CHAPTER 12

grow old before my time. In accord with your request my sons too shall step down. They shall no longer retard your progress by their inequalities. They are now one of you and may be judged by your king on their merits." V. 3. "I hereby testify in the presence of the Eternal and in the presence of His anointed. In all the years of my public service, whose ass have I taken to make my rounds among you? I traveled at my own expense. Whose ox have I taken for my personal use? Have I defrauded any of you or robbed anyone by the fiction of law? Have I ever accepted a bribe or pressured any of you for a fee or a gratuity? If you have a just claim, come forward and I will repay you." (Ex. 23:8, Deut. 16:19, 28:33).

Vs. 4.5   The assembly responded in unison. "You have not defrauded us. You have not robbed us. You have not taken anything from anyone." V. 5. "May the Eternal and His anointed (Saul) become my witness this day that you bear no personal claim against me for misconduct by malfeasance or misfeasance while I served my people on a voluntary basis." Saul testified, "I testify as the anointed of God, king of Israel, that we hold no claim against Samuel."

Vs. 6.7   Samuel is about to review with this generation a record of Israel's past history. "It was the Eternal God's law of genetic progression that brought forth and inspired Moses and Aaron to bring about the Exodus from Egypt."
V. 7. "Stand in awe as I review with you and recite chapter and verse of the historic record. I shall reason with you and establish the long list of righteous acts performed and inspired by the Eternal God of Israel to your grandparents and parents."

V. 8   Samuel goes back to the day Jacob entered Egypt as an invited guest (Gen. 46:1.4). He touched upon the record which led to the oppression (Ex. 2:23.25). He reminded them how Moses and Aaron became inspired by the Eternal to redeem Israel from Egypt (Ex. 3:6.22, 4:). It is they that were endowed with all kindnesses of the Eternal and all the marvelous miracles, which forged Israel into a nation, a civilization, a people dedicated to introduce God to an idolatrous world. *Vayoshivum* How Israel was returned to the Holyland under the leadership of Joshua (1:1.11). (See historic record in the introduction to Joshua establishing the authenticity that the Holyland was Semitic territory from the time of Shem).

V. 9   "When your forefathers rebelled against the disciplines of the Eternal's Torah, He turned them over to Sisera (Judges 4:2) of Hazor and then unto the Philistines (Jud. 13:) and unto Moab (Jud. 3:12). Each one of these enemies of Israel oppressed Israel in turn and made war upon them."

V. 10   "When your forefathers recognized the source of their problems they fully grasped the reason for their misery, was

I SAMUEL CHAPTER 12

their deviation from the Eternal's laws. They then repented and cried for help to the only Source, from whence cometh Israel's help."

V. 11 "Israel's repentance brought forth leaders inspired by the Eternal; Jerubaal-Gideon, who helped Israel against the Midianites (Jud. 6:8). Bedan-Barak from Naphtali who waged war against the oppression of Jabin of Hazor, (Jud. 4:1.10). There was also Jephtah, who came to the fore in behalf of his people against the Ammonites (Jud. 11:), and Samuel. This was inserted in the 6th century when the book of Samuel was finalized. All these inspired leaders came to the rescue of Israel and created a semblance of security and Israel prospered."

V. 12 Coming closer to their generation, Samuel reviewed the record of Nahash the king of Ammon. "It was his plan to bring the war into your midst to displace you from the east; while the Philistines pressured you from the west. It was this development that made you realize something I have been striving for all the days of my life; a central government under the guidance of the Eternal God of Israel. Your rejection of my concept of a king was brought home to me *lo*, we shall not be at the mercy of our enemies like our ancestors. We want a king like all national kings."

Vs. 13.15 "Now you have been granted your request of a king. Remember! Both you and your king are subject to the disciplines and the laws of the King of Kings. He shall demand disciplines from both of you. Should you challenge His authority, you shall be chastised even as your forefathers were in their time. History will repeat itself in your own generation to discipline you and your leaders."

Vs. 16.17 Everything Samuel included in his oration to this point was in keeping and consistent with his dedication to the cause of Israel throughout his lifetime. Verses 16.17, record for history Samuel's resentment and deeply fractured ego; that he has been superseded and rejected as a leader. These verses mar a beautiful lifetime-record free from any blemish. They contradict his own confirmation in (I Sam. 10:24). He worked all of his life to centralize the government in one authorized personality. Why was it necessary to spoil this great moment which climaxed his greatest achievement? This miracle was uncalled for. It served but one purpose to spoil this moment of greatness in Israel's new beginning. Samuel is bent on proving his overpowering greatness; even to the extent of challenging the ability of the king to produce such unseasonal phenomena as thunder, lightening and rain in the normally rainless season. Samuel's desire is to introduce this as an evil omen to interdict the assemblies great hope for a new beginning. Once again a great leader failed *lehakdisheni leenei bnei yisrael*, (Num. 20:12, I Sam. 8:19.22). See T.E.T.

Vs. 18.20 Samuel's desire to introduce fear into the ranks of Israel at this joyous moment in their history had the desired effect. V. 19. Their primitive mentality stood in awe of Samuel's ability

I SAMUEL CHAPTER 12

to intercede in their behalf. They pleaded with him that he pray in their behalf to be forgiven for their sins and for the transgression of having requested a king as their ruler. Samuel has indeed won a pyrrhic victory. He has introduced a dimension which will plague Israel for centuries. V. 20. Samuel regrets that he has overplayed his hand. He strove to console the assembly that he can forgive them for having chosen a king during his lifetime. "However, you can correct this wrong by remaining loyal to the Eternal's disciplines. Observe them sincerely with all your heart."

Vs. 21.22 The greatness of Samuel came to the surface as he strove to assuage the feelings of his assembly in the capacity of the Eternal's true prophet in Israel. The Eternal God of Israel is morally bound (Ex. 19:3.8) never to forsake Israel as his *Am segulah* genetic treasure until Israel rises by its own efforts to reach a plateau in its lifestyle which will conform with His Master Plan-the Torah. Universal civilization must first be conceived in the hearts of Israel's people which ever includes every human being who resolves to live by Torah disciplines. This is the route humanity must travel before they reach that day in human history when all of humanity recognize the Eternal God as One. His name becomes One to unite them, to strive for the Eternal's concept of the BROTHERHOOD of man (Ex. 32:11.14, 31.33, 34:7.10, Num. 14:15.21).

V. 23 Once again Samuel strives to appease the assembly, that it is his duty to pray in their behalf. Were he to fail it would be a sin against the Eternal God of Israel (Gen. 6:3, Ex. 34:6). Samuel vowed to continue to teach, even as he has in the past before Israel chose a ruler to lead it in war and in peace. He shall continue to help all those striving to reach for the Eternal's righteous path. (Deut. 12:28).

Vs. 24.25 "Every blessing in your lives is contingent upon your devotion, your sincerity in revering the Eternal and his law. Serve him faithfully with all your heart and recognize all the blessings he has showered upon you in the past. Should you deviate from the path outlined for your contentment and persist in wrongdoing, both you and your king will come to an end."

I SAMUEL CHAPTER 13

Vs. 1.2 Saul was chosen and ratified at Mitzpah. One year later he was inaugurated at Gilgal. Saul has been king of Israel at this point for two years. After the war with Ammon, Saul chose a standing army of 3000 men. Two thousand were with Saul at Michmash a strategic pass in Mount-Bethel. Saul could not be at Geba because a Philistine garrison was stationed there (I Sam. 10:5). 1000 men were with Saul's son Jonathan at Gibeat Benjamin. All the other men who fought at Jabesh-gilead were discharged; they returned to their homes in order to maintain the economy of the

I SAMUEL CHAPTER 13

Holyland. They were subject to recall in the event of an emergency. From this verse we can assume the age of Saul, that he was between 40-50 years of age.

Vs. 3.4 Jonathan initiated the war of independence by the assassination of the chief Philistine officer in Geba, Kiriat-jearim (I Samuel 10:5). As the news spread to Philistine military circles, Saul mobilized his full complement of soldiers and stationed them at Michmash. He in turn was scheduled for a meeting with Samuel at Gilgal (I Samuel 10:8 belongs here). Rashi too confirms this conclusion. There, Saul waited for the agreed seven days while preparing for war with the Philistines. However, in accord with Samuel's instructions he was to confirm the final plans.

Vs. 5.6 While Saul was being handicapped from springing into immediate action, the Philistines mobilized numberless chariots, multitudes of horsemen and myriads of soldiers. They encamped at Bethaven and their first move was to capture the pass at Michmash. Israel's retreat came about because they were waiting for instructions from Saul who was waiting for Samuel's confirmation of his strategy. As the Philistines entered the pass at Michmash, Saul's men scampered throughout the mountainous area and hid in caves, thickets, pits and behind large rocks. Whatever would offer them shelter.

Vs. 7.8 Some escaped to Gad and Gilead in Trans-jordan while some made their way to Saul at Gilgal. This waiting and procrastination had a tremendous debilitating effect upon these soldiers who came for the purpose of advancing the war of independence. Many of the soldiers left Saul and went home.

Vs. 9.10 Saul's distress motivated him to offer the sacrifices before he would spring into action. Soon after Saul offered the sacrifices Samuel arrived. Saul went out to greet him and extended his blessings for his presence.

Vs. 11.12 Samuel challenged Saul for having usurped his prerogative in offering the sacrifices himself. Saul replied, "I recognized the dangers I created for being obliged to wait for your coming. My army challenged my reasons for waiting and began to disperse for their homes. Here I waited for you and less than 10 miles away the enemy was ready to crush me and my forces at Michmash. I therefore forced myself to entreat the Eternal by my sacrifices in behalf of all my forces before I would enter into battle."

Vs. 13.14 Samuel reprimanded Saul. "You have acted foolishly for not having observed the testimonials of the Eternal upon which your monarchy must be rooted. Had you observed His commandments your dynasty would have lasted forever. Your blunder has robbed you of the potential implied in your leadership, the endurance of your

I SAMUEL CHAPTER 13

kingdom. The Eternal is now obliged to seek a man who can follow the commandments of the Eternal in order to lead Israel His people." Where was Samuel during these critical days? He had seven days after Saul informed him of the critical developments. Samuel knew every step Saul was taking. He should have been with Saul during this period to help him make the vital decisions. Saul broke no commandment. At this time in Israel's history everyone offered sacrifices locally. The abruptnesss of Samuel's charges, the finality of his decision robbed Samuel of the sympathy of history (I Sam. 12:16.19). Samuel's action now was not spontaneous; it has been brewing from the day Israel's elders asked for a king to lead them. Samuel has introduced a dimension that makes the critical difference in the heart of a prophet, a king or the common man. There ever must be sympathy and consideration for leaders that are obliged to take action in an ever fluid situation. Samuel's conduct is not in the spirit of (Gen. 6:3, Ex. 34:6). Without this ingredient in human life there can be no progress.

Vs. 15.16 Samuel returned to Gibeat-Benjamin. Before he left he offered no advice to Saul as he had agreed to do. He left Saul to depend upon his own resources. Saul polled the men that had remained with him and discovered there were but 600 men left from the multitudes that answered his call to arms in v. 4.

V. 16. Saul joined Jonathan at Geba-Gibeat-Benjamin, the Philistine forces were upon the opposite side of the mountain at Michmash.

V. 17.18 From Michmash the Philistines launched three separate columns of raiders to create havoc in the communities of Benjamin. One column operated on the Ophrah Road leading to Shual, one column headed for Beth-horon and one column headed for the border road that overlooks the valley of Zeboim.

V. 19 The text describes the critical situation which Saul inherited. The Philistine occupation of the Holyland was so complete that no arms were permitted to be owned by anyone. When Israel returned from their encounter with the Ammonites, all these arms were confiscated by the Philistines. Every blacksmith was banned from Israel's territory for fear they would create a sword or a spear.

Vs. 20.21 When an Israelite farmer desired to forge a tool they were obliged to go to Philistine blacksmiths who charged exorbitant prices for their labor. They charged a *pim*-2/3 of a silver shekel for forging a mattocks, a colter, a plowshare, a three pronged pitchfork, an axe or for setting an oxgoad.

Vs. 22.23 The text informs us that when Israel's troops reported for duty no sword or spear was available; only Saul and Jonathan owned a sword and a spear. The men were obliged to enter the battle with slings, bows and staves; armaments which were primitive even for their time. There is a deep ravine between Michmash and Geba. The raiding

I SAMUEL CHAPTER 13

parties having established their control of the countryside, the Philistine garrison boldly marched from their hidden position in the mountainous pass at Michmash in order to observe any Israeli action at Geba from this advanced position.

I SAMUEL CHAPTER 14

Vs. 1.2   Jonathan tired of idling his time in his mountainous position at Gebah, while Saul was biding his time on the outskirts of Gibeah-Geba with his 600 troops. (Jonathan's contingent were 1000 men (I Sam. 13:2). Jonathan and his arms-bearer left their troops for an effort to cross the steep ravine and to rise upon the Philistine side at Michmash to inspect the Philistine position. Jonathan did not tell his father of his inspiring initiative.

V. 3   When Samuel left Saul (I Sam. 13:10.14), devoid of any spiritual guidance, Saul obviously sent for Ahijah, the kohen, who was a son of Ahitub, the brother of Ichabod, the son of Phinehas (I Sam. 4:21) the son of Eli who was the High priest at Shiloh. Ahijah was wearing an ephod and suspended from it were the *Urim Vethumim*. See T.E.T. on (Ex. 28:13.30) for the meaning of its symbolism. We may conclude that the Ark was here this day since Jonathan dispatched the garrison of Philistines at Kiriat-jearim (I Sam. 13:3), Israel was free to move the Ark at will. No one was aware that Jonathan and his arms-bearer left the camp.

Vs. 4.5   The text describes the difficult terrain between Geba and Michmash. Both of these areas are about equal in elevation. Between these areas there were two mountainous crags, one was called Bozez and the other was called Seneh. Running down to the valley floor were steep ravines with streams emerging from the mountainous surface. Jonathan and his companion descended from Geba on the south side and planned to scale the steep cliff to the north, Michmash.

V. 6   In vs. 1.5, the text has described in very vivid details the action Jonathan is about to initiate. Had he consulted with his father and the officers in the army of his plan, they most certainly would have rejected it as impossible. Therefore, Jonathan who was wearied of the inaction, has calculated after having taken into consideration Israel's handicaps, a lack of armaments, a limited number of men, a head-on action would sacrifice great numbers of lives to Philistine superiority. Jonathan has therefore concluded that this action must be won by strategy and not by numbers. There is another factor, in these mountainous crags are the men who were displaced at Michmash and are in hiding throughout this steep ravine. Can Jonathan release this potential force in a strategic position on the north side of the mountain to encircle the enemy with Saul's forces who are waiting to spring into action on the north side? (I Sam. 13:6). Jonathan therefore has concluded,

I SAMUEL CHAPTER 14

"If it is the intention of the Eternal God of Israel to help us out of this situation, it will come to pass with few in numbers as with a multitude."

V. 7 — Jonathan's companion assured him that he will stay with him to the end of the action, no matter how it turns out. "I am with you whole heartedly."

Vs. 8.10. Jonathan explained his plan of action to his arms-bearer in great detail. "We shall descend into the ravine and rise upon the cliff to the north and there expose ourselves so the Philistines can see us. Should they say to us, wait! halt! we shall come and get you, we shall remain in our fixed position until the sentries reach us. However, should they ask us to come up to them, we shall agree to do so. This shall be our indication that the Eternal will grant us the capability to succeed in our plan."

Vs. 11.12 — They scaled the steep cliff and exposed themselves. At once the sentries shouted, "The Hebrews are coming out of the caves where they were hiding (I Sam. 13:6). Come up to us, we will teach you a lesson." Jonathan said to his arms-bearer, "This conforms with my conditions. It is a sign, an inspiration that we shall succeed. Follow me!"

Vs. 13.15 — Both men rose to the position of the sentries and engaged them in hand to hand combat. Jonathan attacked them and the arms-bearer dispatched them.

V. 14. The combat took place in a limited area and the sentries were close together. Jonathan's attack was sudden and deliberate as they dispatched about 20 men.

V. 15. Jonathan's split second timing, the surprise attack, the daring action, that these treacherous mountains can be scaled, was the signal for those in hiding to enter the fray. The effect of a multitude became a reality as the soldiers emerged to scale the cliffs and help create the terror of an earthquake. This daring act of Jonathan and his arms-bearer created the panic in the Michmash pass as men tumbled off the hills to escape the onslaught which kept building up in their fear stricken minds.

Vs. 16.19 — Saul's scouts manning the watchtower observed the pandemonium mounting in the Philistine camp as the multitudes of soldiers scampered over each other in all directions. V. 17. Saul's experience spontaneously evaluated the situation and succeeded to analyze it. He ordered a head count to determine if any of his men initiated the action. The count completed it was discovered that only Jonathan and his arms-bearer were missing.

V. 18.19. Saul requested that Ahijah bring the Ark to his position. The dangerous situation which was developing required that he remain on the spot. Before Saul could state his request of Ahijah, the liquidity of the situation jelled before his very eyes. He therefore said to Ahijah, "Stay your hand! This is no time for prayer or consultation, this is a time for action."

I SAMUEL CHAPTER 14

Vs. 20.23 Saul gave the order for battle formation and they marched to the area of Michmash pass. There they observed the confusion as the Philistines were locked in hand to hand fighting with their own forces. V. 21. Many Hebrews who were loyal to the Philistines were impressed into the army as they were considered as natives. When this pandemonium broke loose they fought against the Philistines.

Vs. 22.23 Confirms for the record the participation of those hiding in these hills, whose release was part of Jonathan's strategy (I Sam. 13:6). Saul arrived at Michmash pass and pursued the fleeing Philistines beyond Beth-aven. It was the Eternal's inspiration that stimulated Jonathan's initiative which brought victory to Israel that day.

V. 24 Saul urged his troops to take advantage of this great moment with its advantage for victory. Was it necessary for him to create stress to an already exhausted army? To drive home his command, Saul placed an interdiction upon any man that would eat that day before eventide.

Vs. 25.27 While in pursuit of the enemy, the soldiers came upon a stack of beehives. The honey was flowing to the ground, yet, no soldier who heard the oath taken by Saul dared touch it. Jonathan who was not present when his father uttered a curse, dipped his stick into the honey and tasted it. Jonathan's eyes expressed the *lift* it gave him after his weary pursuit over long hours without food. His eyes dimmed by fatigue expressed his gratification and contentment as the honey touched his lips.

V. 28 One of the soldiers informed Jonathan of Saul's curse which obligated every man to abstain from food and water for the duration of that day. This added handicap resulted in their tremendous fatigue and exhaustion.

Vs. 29.30 Jonathan replied, "My father has brought unnecessary stress upon his soldiers. He handicapped the national welfare. See for yourselves how my whole being felt the effect of my tasting a bit of honey. Had the troops eaten from the abundance of the booty that was available to them, the defeat of the Philistines would have reached much greater proportions." This experience can be compared to Joshua's instructions recorded in (Joshua 1:7).

Vs. 31.32 Despite the exhaustion of the troops they pursued the Philistines to Ajalon, a distance of about 18 miles to the Philistine border.

V. 32. Jonathan recognized the fatigue of his soldiers and gave the order to desist from the pursuit at eventide. Spontaneously they gathered sheep, cows and calves from the abundant booty and began to slaughter the animals in a manner which did not conform with the law stated in (Lev. 19:26). Also as booty they

I SAMUEL CHAPTER 14

were obligated to offer these animals as peace offerings, requiring the blood to be separated and used for sprinkling ceremoniously to express their gratitude.

V. 33 — Saul reprimanded this procedure and ordered a large stone to be rolled into place to function as an altar in the same manner as at Gilgal. This would also conform with the law which required that the blood be separated from the meat before it is eaten. (Lev. 19:26, I Sam. 13:9) See T.E.T.

Vs. 34.35 — Saul issued an order to be enforced among the troops in the field that those desiring to eat meat shall have the animal slaughtered upon this stone-altar and then they may eat it at a place of their choice. This was the first altar built by Saul officially as king of Israel in order to offer sacrifices to the Eternal God of Israel.

V. 36 — Saul proposed a plan to be carried out at night and to last unto the next morning. His plan calls for the complete annihilation of this whole contingent that retreated from Michmash. Saul is concerned whether the soldiers are up to it physically. The soldiers replied, "We are ready to follow you to the last detail. It is obvious that Saul has rearmed his troops with the arms captured in the combat. Ahijah interjected, "Before you activate your plan, we must be sure that it conforms with God's concept of justice. Let us seek confirmation from the *Urim Vethumim*."

Vs. 37.38 — Saul stated the question, "Shall we take this action? Does it conform with our goals? Can we succeed in overpowering the enemy?" Saul received no confirmation to his queries.

V. 38. Saul ordered the officers to come forward, to examine their conscience, to establish facts, if to their knowledge they observed any transgression in their ranks. Saul has concluded that if any transgression took place it must have happened this very day. For without the Eternal's inspiration, we could not have mounted this tremendous victory.

V. 39 — "I want to make it perfectly clear, though we are indebted to my beloved son for having activated the Eternal's inspiration which brought about this great victory, should he be declared guilty of any wrongdoing, he shall bear the maximum penalty of death if found guilty." Saul received no answer from all those present.

Vs. 40.42 — Saul ordered that they draw lots. Saul and Jonathan appeared on one lot and all those present were represented on the other lot. The officers agreed. It never occurred to Saul that his interdiction could possibly be the source of the wrongdoing.

V. 41. Saul addressed the assembly in the presence of the *Urim Vethumim* and Ahijah the kohen. "O Eternal God of Israel, show us Thy perfect guidance. If this iniquity was due to me or my son Jonathan show us *thumim* and if it was in the ranks of the soldiers show us *urim*." The troops were cleared.

I SAMUEL CHAPTER 14

V. 42. "Let us now determine who was the guilty one between Jonathan and me." Jonathan was indicated by *thumim*."

Vs. 43.44 Saul said to Jonathan, "What did you do?" Jonathan replied, "I tasted a bit of honey with the tip of my stick. I am obviously guilty of your curse. If it is your verdict that I die, I am ready though I transgressed your vow unwittingly."

V. 44. Saul answered, "It is for us to establish guilt, however, it is God Who determines the justice of our acts. If it be God's judgment that you die because of your sin, so shall it be."

V. 45 Saul's verdict activated the troops sense of justice as they spoke up in unity. They challenged Saul to justify his right to utter a curse as a deterrent for transgression. A curse strives for a final solution, man has no right to take an oath in God's name to challenge His concept of justice, (Lev. 27:29). When a judge who is God's representative upon earth orders the verdict of death *moth umath* it is because the criminal act has forfeited the life which God had granted him. He must be executed in order to discharge his obligation to God his Creator and his obligation to society. "What was Jonathan's crime?" He carried forth the will of the Eternal God of Israel to advance His concept of justice. Not a hair of his head shall be touched. He has risked his life for our wellbeing in order to advance the Eternal's promise to save His *am segulah*."

Vs. 46 The Eternal's concept of justice not only saved the life of Jonathan but the countless Philistine lives, for Saul's decision to annihilate the remnant of the Philistine forces was altered and permitted the soldiers to return to their homes. Israel's troops acting as a court of justice nullified Saul's irrational vow (Jud. 11:33.40).

Vs. 47.51 Saul turned his attention to securing his monarchy. He then concentrated his effort to remove every existing and potential enemy of Israel. He made war against the following and was successful in every encounter: Moabites, Ammonites, Edomites, Philistines and Zobah.

Vs. 48.49 Saul was triumphant in defeating the Amalekite plunderers. Saul's sons were, Jonathan, Ishvi, Malkishua and Eshbaal-Ishbosheth. His daughters were Merab and Michal. (I Chron. 8:33, I Sam. 31:2).

V. 50.51. Saul's wife was Ahinoam, the daughter of Ahimaaz. The name of his army commander was Abiner-Abner, the son of Ner. Kish, Saul's father and Abner's father, were brothers and their father was Abiel.

V. 52 Saul's heroic efforts concentrated in building the finest army of his time. He was ever on the lookout for military talent from the rank and file of his soldiers. For throughout his reign he fought with the Philistines who never lost their ambitious desire to displace Israel in the Holyland.

I SAMUEL CHAPTER 15

Can twentieth century man grasp the full meaning of this chapter with its instructions to exterminate the Amalekites completely to a man, including their possessions by a people who have been nurtured by the concept of mercy? "Just as the Eternal God is merciful, thou shalt be merciful." Every law in the Torah strives for the development of human relations geared to the Eternal's standards of mercy. Every human being from the beginning of time has the potential for good which is positive and the potential for evil which is negative. This is rooted in physical natural law. Since man and woman are born free, we have the choice to choose our lifestyle. We therefore must go back and examine the history, the evolution of Amalek. How did they develop the reputation of a people whose very name stands for barbarity-versus civilization.

The Amalekites were a warlike, nomadic people in the southwest of the Holyland. Its inveterate hostility to civilization is traced and documented over centuries. Every evil force which has survived into modern times is idiomatically called a progenitor of Amalek. Every generation over the centuries has felt its evil, striving to exterminate civilization. Therefore, the Torah speaks to all of humanity in (Ex. 17:14.16, Deut. 25:17.19), "Make My message clear. I shall blot out the veneration of force and violence for which Amalek ever stands as a prototype in the annals of human history. Exercise your greatest effort to destroy humanity's greatest enemy, the forces of war."

Israel strives to rise to the standards demanded by the Torah, to become The Eternal God's People. Every tragedy in Israel's history is considered the direct effect of Amalekite mores inbred in the genetic process and reenforced by its environment.

In (Gen. 14:7) we find Abraham involved in defending the territorial rights of Amalek. In (Gen. 36:12) we learn that Elifaz, the eldest son of Esau married a concubine and she gave birth to a son whom she named Amalek. Timnah his mother was obviously an Amalekite.

From the following texts we can observe their conduct over the centuries: (Ex. 17:8.16, Num. 13:29, 14:45, Deut. 25:17.19, Judges 3:13, 6:3, 33, 10:12, 7:12, I Sam. 14:48, 15: 30: I Chron. 4:42.43). In various periods of history, we find the Amalekites as mercenaries as far east as Trans-Jordan and as far west as the Red Sea on the roads leading to Egypt. From Havila in the Arabian desert to Arad in Judah. In the 7th century, Hezekiah's time, we trace their survival. Their influence has survived into the 20th century, identified as the Nazi Holocaust which cost civilization 12 million dead. The side effects will take centuries to surface in the lives of destroyed human beings who go through their lives as shadows of a once great promising period. 20th century civilization has lulled itself to sleep in a drug oriented society believing that barbarism has been wiped off the face of the earth. With this historical background let us strive to grasp the prophet Samuel's instructions to king Saul and through his failure, the failure of civilization to take the Amalekites in our societies as a serious menace to human survival.

I SAMUEL CHAPTER 15

V. 1   Samuel said to Saul, "You are the testimonial proof that every bit of advice I have given you has been in the name of the Eternal. It was in accord with the Eternal's inspiration that I anointed you king of His people Israel. Therefore, be attentive to the Eternal's command which I now bring you!"

V. 2   "The time has now come to exact punishment upon the Amalekites for all the enmity which they have demonstrated toward Israel from the days of the Exodus, through the centuries of Judges to this very day."

V. 3   "You are hereby instructed to destroy them completely. Spare no one identified as sympathetic with their mores. This includes oxen, sheep, camels and asses." Their possessions are the result of plunder, murder and every criminal advantage. You may not benefit in any way from their material possessions (Lev. 27:28.29, Deut. 13:16.19)." Saul is to obliterate the very memory of Amalek.

Vs. 4.6   Saul issued a call to arms throughout the Holyland. He enrolled his army at Telaim (Joshua 15:24). Saul mustered 200,000 infantry, plus 10,000 men from the tribe of Judah (I Sam. 11:8). V. 5. Saul advanced his forces close to the territory now occupied by Amalek (Arad) and there waited in the valley for all his conditions for action to be met.

V. 6.   Saul then notified the Kenites who were living in the vicinity of Arad (Jud. 1:16). Saul advised them to evacuate their homes for fear they may become exposed to his attack upon the Amalekites. Saul is sensitive to their kinship with Israel which goes back to (Ex. 3:1, 4:18, 18: Num. 10:29.32). Jael is the heroine in the Shirath Devorah (Judges 5:24).

V. 7   Saul attacked the Amalekites and destroyed every vestige of their communities which stretched from Havilah, in the southern tip of the Arabian desert going north toward Shur on the road to Egypt. This whole stretch borders the eastern coast of the Red Sea.

V. 8   Saul succeeded in capturing Agag the king of the Amalekites. Why he spared him is not given in the text. The Talmud Yoma 22b concludes that Saul's conscience had reservations on Samuel's instructions. A symptom which shall prolong the agony of civilization for centuries. Saul did not succeed in destroying every vestige of Amalek. They continued to carry on intermittent warfare with Israel as recorded in (I Sam. 27:8, 30:1, II Sam. 8:12).

V. 9   Saul acceded to the pleadings of his troops to spare Agag and the choicest specimens of the livestock. They did destroy everything that they considered did not conform with standards of excellence. In v.21, Saul will plead that the reason for choosing these excellent specimens of livestock was to offer them as sacrifices.

I SAMUEL CHAPTER 15

Vs. 10.11   The Eternal perturbed Samuel's conscience. Samuel's distress goes back to that day when he anointed Saul (I Sam. 10:1). The series of events recorded in (I Sam. 10:24, 11:14, 12:17.19, 13:8.14, 14:3, 18.19, 15:1) disturbed him all that night. Samuel is faced with the dilemma of activating the Eternal's *nichamti*, "I too regret having confirmed Saul as king of Israel, for he has not carried out My commands." *Vayichar lishmuel*, The Eternal's confirmation of Samuel's conflict has amplified his distress. Samuel prayed *vayazek el Adonai* for the resolution and courage to replace Saul who was his choice. Samuel recognized Saul's dedication to the cause of Israel. Samuel acknowledged his ability to lead men in the field. Samuel must concede Israel's improved political and military situation. Saul has crimped the Philistine dream of expanding from the Mediterranean to the Euphrates.

V.12   Early the next morning Samuel went to see Saul in Gibeat Saul. Samuel was informed that Saul went to Mount Carmel (Joshua 15:55) in Mount Judah, for the purpose of building a memorial to Israel's victory over the Amalekites. From there Saul was planning to go to Gilgal to offer sacrifices for their victory. This information became the charge which denoted Samuel's resolution. It spontaneously resolved the root cause of his distress and his determination to understand the Eternal's *nichamti* regret for having chosen Saul as king of Israel. It was equal to *vayinachem Adonai* (Gen. 6:6, Ex. 32:14, II Sam. 24:16). Samuel now fully grasps the Eternal's charges against Saul. He cannot carry out instructions. The change in Saul's conduct to discharge his implicit instructions of the Eternal, has created the *nichamti* change in the Eternal's original confirmation of Saul as king of Israel Samuel's dilemma and stress are exactly parallel to that experienced by Moses (Ex. 32:11, Deut. 9:18).

Vs. 13.16   When Samuel arrived at Gilgal, Saul greeted him, "Blessed art thou of the Eternal. I have fulfilled your instructions in the name of the Eternal."

V. 14. Samuel challenged Saul. "How do you account for the bleating of sheep and the lowing of oxen that I hear?"

V. 15. Saul replied, "These were set aside by the troops as choice specimens for sacrifices unto the Eternal your God. All the other livestock we have destroyed."

V. 16. Samuel is overcome by Saul's reasoning for modifying his instructions. "Hold your excuses Saul! I will tell you how the Eternal construes your weakness in permitting your soldiers to override and modify His instructions."

V. 17   "You may claim modesty in your dealings with your troops and therefore permitted them to contradict the Eternal's concept of mercy in history. How do you justify your position as king of Israel? You were anointed to lead, not to follow the popular concept of right and wrong."

I SAMUEL CHAPTER 15

V. 18 "The Eternal has sent you on a mission. He has waited for centuries, patiently waiting for the Amalekites to change their lifestyle from marauding, pilfering, robbing, brigandage and selling their souls to create chaos in normal societies and communities. Your instructions were to utterly destroy this barbaric element; to free humanity from this recessive genetic aberration of mental and moral instability."

V. 19 "Why did you disobey the Eternal, Whose natural law, moral law and ethical disciplines are based upon truth? His conclusions are never arbitrary. His decrees are based upon His long suffering patience (Gen. 6:3) that their retrogression has multiplied by procreation over the centuries. It was the Eternal's judgment that the time has come to remove every trace of their being from the face of the earth. To give mankind a fresh start to build a new world order unhandicapped by the biological, genetic, and the environmental poison which ever strives to destroy every vestige of good which has taken millenia to develop. What was your motive in defying the Eternal's will when you permitted yourself to become enticed by the booty? You should never have permitted it to enter your mind that you were justified in condoning it under the concept of mercy. The purpose of this war was not for plunder but for principles."

Vs. 20.21 Saul strove to defend his conduct. "I did obey the Eternal and carried forth my mission. I captured Agog, the infamous leader of this iniquitous society and exterminated the rest of the Amalekite communities." V. 21. "Even the intent of the soldiers was noble. They selected the best of Amalekite animal husbandry for the purpose of offering sacrifices to the Eternal your God."

V. 22 Saul's irrational defense brought forth Samuel's reply. "What delight does the Eternal take from mankind's sacrifices? It is obedience to his commands that he desires. Obedience to the Eternal God's concepts are far worthier than sacrifices. Compliance with the Eternal's natural law, ethical law and moral law are far better than the offerings of fatted rams."

V. 23 "Rebellion against the Eternal's statutes, is like the iniquity of divination. Defiance of His laws is a sin against man and God. Rebellion against the Eternal's disciplines are regressive factors that degenerate truth. The Eternal's established law demands the evolution of the Universe and all that exists therein. His law supersedes the supernatural concepts of divination. Because you have rejected the instructions of the Eternal, He has rejected you from being king of Israel."

V. 24 Saul replied to Samuel, "I recognize my sin for having transgressed your instructions in the name of the Eternal God of Israel. I plead that what I did was not with the intent of

I SAMUEL CHAPTER 15

transgressing the Eternal's instructions but out of fear of opposing the will of my soldiers."

Vs. 25.26 Saul pleaded with Samuel that he pardon his trespass by appearing with him in the presence of all the people who have assembled to offer sacrifices in behalf of their victory over the Amalekites. V. 26. Samuel rejected Saul's request out of hand. "I shall not appear with you in public in order to give the impression that our relationship has the blessings of the Eternal. Since you have rejected the Eternal's command, He has repudiated you as having the competence to rule Israel."

V. 27 As Samuel turned to leave Saul, Saul took hold of his robe in order to express his anguish. Saul fully recognized his embarrasment and the effect it will have upon the nation if he appeared in public without Samuel. Saul's desperate plea is expressed by the tension in his hands which tore Samuel's garment.

V. 28 Samuel spontaneously recognized this symbol as the Eternal's confirmation, that He has rejected Saul from being king of Israel. Samuel recognized this symbol which shall grant him the right to choose Saul's successor.

V. 29 "The Glory of Israel, is the Eternal God of Israel, He is ever consistent *lo yeshaker* in his verdict. *Noseh avon* He has weighed in the balance of His long suffering patience Saul's commitment to carrying out His implicit instructions at this moment in Israel's history by removing Amalek from the record of history. Since Saul failed to become the man of the *hour* He, Who is *Adonai* responsible for human history is governed by His own law to continue His search for a leader of Israel who can carry forth the Eternal's Master Plan for mankind. *Lo yinachem* He may not regret His verdict."

Vs. 30.31 Saul's repentant *hatathi* is the highest rank a human being can reach as a sincere repentant. It challenges our sympathy and demands our empathy with Saul's predicament. By training he is a farmer. By devotion a dedicated Israelite in the tradition of the centuries striving to rise upon the ladder of evolution. His conduct is subject to the environment of his period in history. He has been catapulted into a most difficult position. He lacks the experiential background of greatness required to rise to the demand of the hour. Saul *kabdeni na* pleads that Samuel grant him the honor of appearing with him in public, not to embarrass him by going it alone. This scene touches the very heart strings of every human being. "It is true that I have sinned. Do not embarrass me by not joining me before the elders of our people. Return with me to the services that I may worship the Eternal thy God." V. 31. Samuel joined Saul and they prayed together with the elders and the assemblage of Israel.

I SAMUEL CHAPTER 15

Vs. 32.34   Samuel requested that Agag the king of the Amalekites be brought before him. Humbled in chains, Agag felt the seriousness of this tragic moment in his life as he is being called before the bar of justice. Agag anticpates the end as he exposes his feelings, "Alas I feel the bitterness of death upon me."

V. 33. "As the champion of the Eternal, I have now become the only one to carry out His verdict. Just as your sword bereaved women of their husbands and sons, so shall your mother be bereaved." Samuel slew Agag in the hope that with him shall die symbolically every enemy of humanity.

V. 34. Samuel departed for Ramah, Saul went back to his home in Gibeah. Samuel never again came to see Saul.

V. 35   *Velo yasaf Shmuel lirot et Shaul ad yom moto* Samuel lived a life of regret; for he never put Saul out his sight (mind) until the day that he died. Samuel mourned for Saul because he had chosen him to be king of Israel. To understand why Samuel mourned we have to examine his every contact with Saul in its proper sequence. (I Sam. 9:15.17, 24, 27, 10:17.24, 11:14.15, 12:13.20, 10:17, I Sam. 10:8, belongs in 13:8, this led to Samuel's continued resentment which surfaced in 13:10.14). Samuel exposed his resentment for Saul's rulership as the peoples popular choice. He promised Saul his moral support and to guide him every step of the way until Saul gains the experience demanded as the ruler of Israel. (I Sam. 13:4) Samuel is well aware of Israel's mobilization for war against the Philistines. Saul went to Gilgal for his rendezvous with Samuel instead of defending his stronghold at Michmash. Samuel is well aware of the situation he created, by failing to give Saul his counsel and moral support to solve the tremendous odds against Israel's ability to succeed. (I Sam. 13:15.23) is the evidence that Samuel knew all the facts in advance of this action. (I Sam. 14:1.23) Samuel played no part in Jonathan's successful action.

Samuel's sudden appearance after a lapse of much time to instruct Saul (I Sam. 15:1.3), are to a man confused by the antagonism of his sponsor which has penetrated into the rank and file of the populace. Yet, despite all these handicaps it is Saul that put the fear of the Eternal into the hearts of all of Israel's enemies in the Holyland, including the Philistines and the Ammonites.

If we translate v. 35, that Saul did not see Samuel until his dying day, this would contradict (I Sam. 19:24), (Deut. 5:19) *Kol gadol velo yasaf.* In light of all these facts, we must recognize the meaning of this verse 35, Samuel mourned over his dealings with Saul. He could not forgive himself for his arbitrary conduct. *Vadonai niham* The Eternal looked at the record and was comforted that it was His inspiration that granted Samuel the intuition, the foresight to anoint Saul as king of Israel.

I SAMUEL CHAPTER 16

Vs. 1.2 From the text of this verse we must conclude the passing of a considerable amount of time between the experience described in v. 35 and Saul's problems described in (I Sam. 16:14.23). Yet, Samuel regrets his inability to resolve his arbitrary conclusion to reject Saul. As a prophet Samuel has failed to sympathize and empathize with Saul's traumatic depression. Samuel has failed Saul even as Phinehas the High Priest had failed to nullify Jephtah's irrational vow (Judges 11:35). Samuel failed to recognize the instructions given to Joshua in (Joshua 1:5.7). His overzealousness led to the experience described in (Joshua 7:6.13 see commentary on these verses).

Saul on the other hand because of his inferiority complex cannot find the courage to confront Samuel openly for having rejected him as the recognized king of Israel. On the other hand Samuel's prophetic mental capacity and dedication gives him the capacity to confront the Eternal in his soliloquy with the Eternal described in this verse.

The Eternal reprimanded Samuel, "How long do you intend to grieve over the injustice you are perpetrating upon Saul?" Samuel replied, "I have rejected Saul because I have resolved to replace him." The Eternal Who has the capability to penetrate Samuel's motive as "He Who tests the thoughts and motives of the human mind" (Jeremiah 11:20). The Eternal strives to reconcile Samuel's embryonic inspiration which has obviously been gestating in his mind even before his confrontation with Saul in (I Sam. 13:10.14). The Eternal imposes His mandate upon Samuel, "Samuel you cannot continue to grieve. Since you have rejected Saul, you must choose another to succeed him. I authorize you to go to Yishai-Jesse in Bethlehem with whom you have already been negotiating for a successor to Saul." Samuel replied, "If I do that I may jeopardize my life." The Eternal Who has the capacity to examine the heart and the mind (Jer. 17:10, 20:12) to reward each man according to his conduct assured Samuel that Saul will never raise his hand against Samuel.

V. 3 The Eternal inspired Samuel with the procedure described in vs. 3.13, Samuel is to assure Jesse and the elders of Bethlehem that he has not come to incite rebellion against Saul. His sole purpose is to celebrate by offering a peace offering to the Eternal. "I shall then inspire you with the ability to choose one of Jesse's sons to become the anointed ruler of Israel upon the demise of Saul."

Vs. 4.5 When Samuel arrived in Bethlehem, he was approached by the elders of the city to explain the meaning of his surprise visit.

They feared some new national calamity. Samuel allayed their fears, "My mission is directed on a peaceful errand. I have come to invite you to participate in a special offering to the Eternal. Therefore purify yourselves and come prepared for this special occasion." V. 5. Samuel then went directly to the home of Jesse to invite his whole family to the special sacrificial service and to supervise the preparations in accord with (Ex. 19:14).

I SAMUEL CHAPTER 16

Vs. 6.7 — Jesse assembled his sons and presented Eliab the eldest. Samuel was impressed by his stature and personality. V. 7. The Eternal reminded Samuel of his previous experience (I Sam. 9:19) when he was attracted to the tall stately personality of Saul. "My standards are based upon the inner sincerity of a human being which is the basic contributing factor that determines character (Jer. 17:10, 20:12). I have rejected this one (Eliab) because of his irascible quick temper (I Sam. 17:28)."

Vs. 8.11 — Jesse then introduced Abinadab, he then brought forth Shammah and four more of his sons for a total of seven sons. Samuel was not motivated to choose any of them. V. 11. "Are these, all of your sons" inquired Samuel? Jesse replied, "I have still another, the youngest who is attending to our flocks of sheep." "Send for him!" commanded Samuel, "for we shall not sit down to celebrate our feast until he will arrive."

V. 12 — Upon the arrival of Jesse's son David, Samuel was impressed with his ruddy complexion. He was attracted to his beautiful sparkling eyes and his handsome appearance. Samuel responded spontaneously to the Eternal's inspiration, "Arise to anoint this one for he is My choice." Though Samuel chose David from among his brothers, the purpose of his selection was unknown to any of them but Jesse, *bekerev ehab*.

V. 13 — The anointing ceremony described here was in the privacy of Samuel and David. Samuel used the same phrase *vatitzlach ruach Adonai al David* (I Sam. 10:10) that he used for Saul. See commentary for its full meaning. In this incident with David, it must have a different connotation. David was but 18 years old at his selection. 12 years shall pass by before he becomes king of all Israel. That David had special qualifications, we recognize retrospectively from the record of his life's history. The feeling of excellence created by his being chosen, gave David the sensitivity to become responsible for his every effort in his daily routine. Samuel went back to Ramah, while David returned to his flocks; a routine which demands the implementation of natural faculties; to dream dreams and to weave thoughts in an environment unrestricted by space. This was the background that exercised David's fertile imagination.

V. 14 — In (I Sam. 15:35) we have documented the reasons for Samuel's regret which occupied every day and night of his life to his demise. Samuel now records for the record of history the effect of his arbitrary action. Saul who had exposed his life to every danger for his people could not earn the recognition of his sponsor, Samuel. The pressures of daily national problems plus the heartache of being unable to receive Samuel's recognition brought on the condition which in its final stages became a depressive psychosis. Saul's fits of unreasoning rages climaxed in homicidal violence. This was the direct result of Samuel's inability to modify his excesses. Samuel failed to guide Saul; the modest and humble personality who cannot find

I SAMUEL CHAPTER 16

the courage to face Samuel on his own terms. Had Saul gone to Samuel when he was in complete control of his faculties instead of in (I Sam. 19:24), Israel's history would have followed the Eternal's Master Plan inscribed in the Torah. *Ruach Adonai* the spirit of the Eternal manifests itself in every human being who lives by the Eternal's Natural Law, Moral Law, Ethical Law. This is the formula by which to succeed as we exercise our faculties in our daily lives; normal living manifests itself in contentment and tranquility. It is not the Eternal that fractures our lives but our personal conduct in our daily human relations in the give and take of living. Samuel who wrote these verses claims that *uviatatu* the periodic ill temper of fright and fear of Saul was from the Eternal. Fright and fear can be activated only when we short circuit the Eternal God's Law, to create the tragedies which effect our lives. See commentary in T.E.T. on (Ex. 33:18.19).

Vs. 15.16 Saul's courtiers recognized the progressive deterioration of his condition. He has mentally departed from observing the *ruach Elohim* the law of the God of justice. "It is this impasse that is *mevaatecha* terrifying you." V. 16. The courtiers requested permission to find one who can play the harp. "The pleasant atmosphere and tranquility created by the Eternal's law of harmony will help you overcome your depressive moments."

V. 17 Saul authorized his courtiers to find a competent musician who can not only play his instrument well but has the competence to be a *menagen* one whose natural ability is endowed with the intuitive skill of composing and improvisation. "When you find this individual, bring him before me for my approval."

V. 18 One of Saul's courtiers recalled an experience with one of Jesses's sons, the Bethlehemite. "He plays skillfully on the harp, he also has gained a reputation as a man of valor in combatting wild animals in the field who periodically attack his flock of sheep. He also has the skill of expressing himself articulately and to coin a phrase. He has a most pleasing personality and is a God fearing man, ever conscious of observing the Eternal's law."

Vs. 19.20 Saul sent messengers to Jesse and requested the pressence of his youngest son David who is in charge of his sheep, Jesse loaded an ass with bread, an earthen jug of wine and a kid to be presented to Saul as a gift in keeping with the custom of the period.

Vs. 21.22 David presented his gift and then came before Saul. Saul took a strong liking for David. He was impressed by his personality and was reasonably sure that he qualified in accord with the recommendations described in v.18. Saul appointed him as his armor bearer to attend to his every need.

V. 22. Saul requested formal approval from David's father, Jesse, that he remain in his service. "I am impressed with him as a promising young man."

I SAMUEL CHAPTER 16

V. 23 — Whenever Saul felt depressed by Samuel's last statement (I Sam. 15:28) he could not reconcile *ruach Elohim* his depressive condition with God's concept of justice. David's playing on the harp helped Saul to regain his normal equilibrium.

Before we try to explain chapter 17, we must find the answer to (I Sam. 17:55.57). I have spent a considerable amount of time in analyzing every shred of evidence contained in the text itself without reading into it or out of it facts which simply do not exist. The theory advanced by scholars that chapter 17 consists of two accounts which were harmonized by the last compiler of the book of Samuel. This theory simply does not stand up. The discrepancy must have been clear to the compiler even as it is in our own time. I have therefore set myself the task of unscrambling this enigma before I can go ahead with the book of Samuel. I shall now set before my readers the chronology of the events described in I Samuel, chapters 16, 17, 18:1.2. Chapter 17:1.11, describes the mobilization of the Philistines and the Israelites. It describes their positions and the threat made by their giant protagonist Goliath. (I Sam. 17:12.14) introduces David and tells us how he happened to be on the military scene.

The scene described in 16:14.20 took place after the war and is the result of the scene described in 18:1. Verse 17:15, informs us that at this time, David only came to Saul in Gibeah when requested and then returned home to Bethlehem.

It was at this point in time that Saul decided to appoint David his armor-bearer 16:21. Saul therefore requested consent from David's father Jesse 16:22. 18:2, confirms his acceptance and from that day David remained in Gibeah and was on call at all times 16:23, resulting in Saul's peace of mind because of these arrangements. Sometime after the experiences described in (I Sam. 17:55.58, 16:14.23, 18:2.3) Samuel initiated the experience recorded in (I Sam. 16:1.13). Verse 13, harmonizes in all its details with all the events that began to unfold beginning with (I Sam. 18:3.30).

We must never assume that events in our personal or national life grow in a vacuum. David came to Samuel's attention as he came to Nob with Goliath's head and armaments as proof of Israel's great victory. The historic facts about the tribe of Judah are well documented beginning with (Gen. 44:14.34) see The Eternal Torah, (Joshua 14:6.15, 15:) (Judges 3:9.11). Every action recorded in Samuel involved the tribe of Judah by an independent force. All the traditions of Israel over centuries points to Judah's dedication to Israel. From the moment Israel entered the Holyland it became an established entity. It was in this atmosphere and from this genetic background that David's development grew.

When Saul made his inquiry of Abner in 17:57.58, he did not know who David was. He had never seen him before he offered his services to Saul in 17:32.

Eliab's conversation with David in (I Sam. 17:28.29), is but another bit of proof that Samuel's anointing of David did not take place until David's confrontations with Saul began to unfold itself.

I SAMUEL CHAPTER 17

Vs. 1.3 Once again the Philistines mount an attempt to force their authority up to Beit Nettif South West of Jerusalem, deep into Judah's territory. For this purpose the Philistines mobilized their forces at Socoh, or Shocoh, the modern Schuweike. From this ideal position they could control the valley leading down to the Wadi-es-Sunt, which flows into the Wadi-es-Samt or as it is called The Valley of the Acacias. The Philistines encamped at Ephes-dammim between Azekah and Socoh.

V. 2. Israel's forces encamped on the heights of Beit Nettif and their camp extended down to the valley of Elah, reaching to the Wadi-es-Sur. Here Saul made his stand to defend Philistine intentions to overrun Judah's territoy. This valley is between Jerusalem and Jaffa.

V. 3. Both armies stood opposite each other in battle array on high ground separated by the deep ravine cut by the mountain streams over centuries.

Vs. 4.11 In accord with ancient and Bedouin warfare, Goliath a Philistine champion stepped forward. He was six and one half cubits tall (9'6"). Vs. 5.7. Describes in detail the magnitude of his armor and his armaments. Vs. 8.9. The giant braggart challenged the slaves of Saul to choose one who shall represent Israel. Whoever succeeds in dispatching the other shall be considered the victor of the engagement.

Vs. 10.11. "I defy Israel to choose one who shall engage me in combat." Goliath's challenge created consternation in the ranks of Israel. Who would volunteer to challenge this freak, this giant? It was an embarrassment for Israel that no one came forward to challenge the taunting giant as he heaped invective upon Israel's forces.

Vs. 12.15 The text now introduces David and the reason he went to the battlefield. David was the son of Jesse, who was now advanced in years and retired from active service. However, he was active as an Elder in Ephrath which is the ancient name for Bethlehem. The text reports that at one time he had eight sons; though (I Sam. 16:10 and I Chron. 2:13.15) report only seven. V. 13. Tells us that David's brothers Eliab, Abinadab and Shamah were in Saul's army. V. 14. David was the youngest who tended his father's sheep in Bethlehem. The three brothers older than David were followers of Saul's but not in the service. V. 15. Is out of context here. It belongs to (I Sam. 18:1) see introduction to chapter 17.

Vs. 16.18 Every morning for a period of forty days the Philistine giant Goliath pronounced his challenge described in v.10. V. 17. The text now describes the errand which brought David to the battlefield as the armies were waiting to be activated. Jesse instructed David to deliver an ephah of parched corn and 10 loaves of bread to his three brothers in the army.

I SAMUEL CHAPTER 17

V. 18. He also was to deliver 10 cakes of cheese to the officers of their command. (Each tribe was responsible for its food and armaments). "Report back to me as to their welfare, and to confirm their safety to me, you are to bring back *arubatham* a symbol, a tangible item or coin."

Vs. 19.24 Confirms that Saul's army which included David's brothers were still encamped in the vicinity of Elah. V. 20. David arose at dawn and left on his father's mission to the battlefield at Elah. He arrived at the camp when the soldiers stood for morning muster. V. 21. The same activity was going on in the Philistine camp and both armies were being lined up in battle array. V. 22. David left his parcels of food with the commissary and hastened to greet his brothers. V. 23. While David was talking with his brothers, Goliath stepped forward in front of the battle lines and made his daily challenge as described in v.10. David overheard the harangue.
V. 24. He observed the terrible effect it had upon the morale of the soldiers.

Vs. 25.27 David felt challenged as he overheard *arubatham* their evaluation of the situation. "It is the Philistines intention to destroy Israel." David also learned from them, "The man that will succeed to destroy this braggart will be rewarded by the king with great riches. He will also become eligible to marry his daughter. He who succeeds in accomplishing this valorous act will become free of all taxes."

V. 26. David's provocation inspired him to ask these men to repeat the details of the reward. Enthusiastically David challenged, "Who does he think he is to taunt the ranks of the army of the living God." V. 27. The men repeated the details of the promised reward.

V. 28 Eliab, David's oldest brother overheard David as he expressed his indignation, "Who does this uncircumcized Philistine think he is to challenge the army of the living God?" Eliab's wrath rose in anger as he challenged David. "What was your purpose to come down to Elah? Whom did you leave in charge with the sheep in the wilderness? I am well aware of your impudence and impertinence; your purpose of coming here was to observe the war."

V. 29 David tried to defend himself, "What have I done now, to call forth your anger against me? Can't I express my thoughts on the situation? I do have an opinion." This experience is but another self evident proof that the scene described in (I Sam. 16:3.13) did not take place until after the war and described in (I Sam. 18:1).

V. 30 Undismayed by his brother's reprimand, David pursued his interest in the current event and Goliath's challenge to the integrity of Israel. He turned to yet another group of soldiers

I SAMUEL CHAPTER 17

and asked them to explain the reward being offered to him who shall challenge the giant Goliath. They repeated verbatum the details as recorded in v.25.

Vs. 31.33 — David's remarks made in v.26, were reported to Saul and David soon found himself in the presence of king Saul.
V. 32. David addressed king Saul, "I see no reason for depression or to resign our fate because of this Philistine challenge. I, your humble servant will take up his challenge."
V. 33. Saul replied to David, "How can you a mere boy challenge this veteran warrior, whose experience goes back to his youth?"

Vs. 34.35 — David replied to Saul, "You may consider me as but a boy, however, I have had numerous brushes with danger while I was in the field with the sheep of my father. One time a lion helped himself to one of my sheep. Another time a bear attacked my flock."
V. 35. "In both these cases I went after the lion and grabbed him by his beard and dislodged the sheep from his mouth and when he attacked me I killed him. In my experience with the bear I seized his chin and dislodged the sheep from his mouth and then killed the bear outright."

Vs. 36.37 — "Just as I succeeded to kill the lion and the bear, I shall dispatch this uncircumcized Philistine. He has defied and taunted the ranks of the living God; this must not go by unchallenged." V. 37. "I feel most confident that the Eternal, who saved me from the lion and the bear, He will protect me and save me from this Philistine giant." Saul was impressed with David's courage. "Go! And may the Eternal be with you to protect you."

Vs. 38.40 — Saul dressed David in his garments; a coat of mail, a copper helmet. He then girded his garments with a sword. David had no experience with these weighty garments and therefore refused to be encumbered by them. He removed them from his body. He then picked up his staff and went down to the Wadi-sur and selected five smooth stones from the stream. These he placed in his shepherd's sack. He took hold of his slingshot and marched toward the Philistine giant.

Vs. 41.42 — The Philistine came closer to David, preceded by his shield bearer. He then caught sight of David, he sized him up and expressed his scorn. It was below his dignity, a man of war endowed with superhuman strength to enter combat with a mere youth with the flush of boyhood upon his face. Goliath burst forth his contempt upon the Israelites for this was no challenger worthy of his competence.

Vs. 43.45 — The Philistine challenged David, "Do you think me a dog that you come toward me with a stick?" The Philistine cursed David in the name of his gods.

I SAMUEL CHAPTER 17

V. 44. "Come closer and I will give your body to the birds of the heavens and to the beasts of the field."

V. 45. David replied, "You come at me with a sword, a spear and a javelin. I shall challenge you in the name of the Eternal God, Who is the Master, the Host of the Universe. It is He Who is the God of the army of Israel that you are defying."

V. 46 "This is the very day that the Eternal will deliver you into my hands. I will slay you and remove your head. It is the carcasses of your Philistine hordes that I shall distribute to the birds of the heavens and the beasts of the field. I shall establish for history that Israel's God is the God of justice."

V. 47 "This whole assembly shall become witnesses and give testimony that the Eternal God of Israel, will grant Israel salvation without a sword and without a spear. The Eternal God of history is the Force, that ever fights on the side of justice. (Ex. 14:14) He is the God of war that shall deliver you into the hands of Israel."

Vs. 48.49 Goliath the Philistine strode toward David and David hastened simultaneously to establish his battle line, to face the Philistine squarely and establish his target. V. 49. David reached into his pouch for a stone, set it into his sling and aimed to hit the Philistine in the forehead between the eyes which was not protected by his copper helmet. David's perfect aim drove the stone into Goliath's skull; he lost his balance and fell forward on his face.

Vs. 50.51 David overpowered this powerful braggart with his slingshot (Jud. 20:16). He smote Goliath even though he had no sword.
V. 51. David ran toward the dead giant, drew his sword from its sheath and slew him by cutting off his head. The Philistine soldiers observing their dead hero fled from the scene of battle.

Vs. 52.53 Stimulated by the scene, Saul gave the signal for the war cry and the order to pursue the enemy. They pursued the Philistines to Gai-Gath and then continued on to Ekron. The mortally wounded spread across the roads to Saaraim and the roads leading to Gath and Ekron. V. 53. Returning from their pursuit, the Israelite soldiers plundered the Philistine Camp at Socoh.

V. 54 The action described in this verse took place after David had made his presence before Saul in v.58. David took Goliath's head and went up to Nob (Jerusalem was out of bounds at this time) where the House of God stood. Here was the prophetic school of Samuel and the seat of the kohanim. David's outgoing personality took advantage of this victorious moment to display Israel's victory in all of the surrounding communities. David deposited the sword in the Mishkan as a memento. Not

I SAMUEL CHAPTER 17

realizing that one day he will retrieve it (I Sam. 21:10). One day this barbarous experience shall repeat itself (I Sam. 31:10) as Saul became the victim of this common ancient practice of barbarism.

David proceeded to his home in Bethlehem and there he deposited the rest of his baggage which probably was Goliath's war garments and his armaments. It was David's heroic act described in vs. 31.54 and his presence in Nob that brought him to the attention of Samuel.

Vs. 55.58   This verse should follow v.40. When Saul observed David's courageous and optimistic stance as he walked fearlessly toward Goliath, he turned to Abner his army commander. "Abner! Whose son is that boy?" Abner replied, "By your life I swear that I do not know." V. 56. Saul requested that Abner find out who the *elem* young man is. Who is his father? David's stature grew as Saul observed his self confident posture in combat.

V. 57. Abner retrieved David from the ranks of Israel's soldiers and brought him to Saul. As David made his presence before king Saul, he held securely the head of his victim Goliath.

V. 58. Saul asked David, "Who is your father?" David replied, "My father is your humble servant Jesse of Bethlehem in Judah."

I SAMUEL CHAPTER 18

V. 1   By the time David finished his conversation with king Saul, Jonathan the son of Saul was overwhelmed by David's personality and his tenacious perseverance in the presence of his elders. Spontaneously, Jonathan became attached to David. His instinctive love was selfless. It required no proof or evidence. Jonathan loved him as himself. Jonathan is the hero of the battle fought at Michmash and rcorded in Chapter 14. Sometime after the war with the Philistines Saul's depression developed into the scene described in (I Sam. 16:14.20). The text in (I Sam 17:15) applies to this point in time as David came before Saul only on request and returned to his father's sheep in Bethlehem.

V. 2   Jonathan recognized the tremendous effect of David's musical talents. He recognized the peace and harmony that David's presence created upon Saul's depressed and easily provoked soul. It was at this time that Saul appointed David as his armor bearer (I Sam. 16:21). This verse belongs here. Both Jonathan and Saul developed a tremendous respect and affection for David. Saul then requested that Jesse give his permission for David to remain with Saul on a full time basis. David became a permanent resident in Gibeah. Saul took him into his service the day Jesse gave his consent and did not permit him to return home to his father's house. The effect of this new arrangement is described in (I Sam. 16:23). David was on call on a moments notice to play and appease Saul from his depressive and psychotic delusions.

I SAMUEL CHAPTER 18

V. 3 Now that David became a permanent resident in Gibeah, Jonathan and David made a pact. Jonathan prophetically recognized David's personality as being of great promise. Jonathan is knowledgeable of the root reasons for his father's depressions, they are rooted in Samuel's rejection.

Vs. 4.5 David who came in the garments of a shepherd is now to be presented by Jonathan with his princely tunic, his sword, his bow and his belt. This is in keeping with ancient palatial custom.

V. 5. David went out as an appointed officer and emissary of king Saul as described in vs.13.16. He was successful in every mission that Saul commissioned him. David's personality had a tremendous impact upon his troops and the courtiers surrounding king Saul.

Vs. 6.7 When the soldiers returned from the war with the Philistines, the women from the surrounding towns came forth to greet Saul with singing and dancing. They celebrated his victory with timbrels, recitation and shouting for joy. They recited prose by the accompaniment of a three stringed instrument.

V. 7. The women danced as they sang, "Saul had slain thousands, and David his tens of thousands." It became a national hymn. Its popularity spread into Philistia (I Sam. 21:12).

V. 8 This experience added stress to an already vexed man. It was Saul that fought every war of his time successfully; yet David who was only involved in this one combat is the one that is singled out. "How could people forget so quickly? It seems that all David lacks is the crown of kingship."

Vs. 9.10 This public demonstration created apprehension in the mind of Saul. He became envious of David's good fortune and from that day as he overheard David's public acclaim, Saul viewed David with suspicion. Saul brooded over this incident; it disturbed his tranquility. It obviously disturbed his sleep for on the morrow his courtiers reported an evil spirit unhinged his mental equilibrium. With every passing hour he sank ever deeper into a depressed mood. He now transferred his enmity from Samuel to David. David was pressed into service in moments like this to create a normal and tranquil atmosphere by creating soothing tunes to appease his king. Saul sat as was his normal custom with his spear in hand that served him as his kingly sceptre. Saul's tantrum was the result of *vayitnabeh* he visualized in the depression of his soul the effect of Samuel's last words to him (I Sam. 15:28). Saul pondered the Eternal's desire to wrest the kingdom from him. Saul viewed the future and concluded that it is David that is destined to occupy his throne.

V. 11 Saul activated his inner thoughts to pin David against the wall with his spear. He raised his hand with the intention of

I SAMUEL CHAPTER 18

plunging the spear into David and pin him to the wall. David's quick reflex action anticipated the worst in Saul's moments of ecstatic frenzy, as he escaped Saul's threatening gesture twice. However, Saul was spared from enacting this tragic scene by the murmerings of his *yetzer hatov* as his *Zelem Elohim* came to the fore and caused him to relent from this dastardly act.

V. 12 When Saul reviewed his conduct of v.11, he concluded that the Eternal's protective custody has been removed from him and has been transferred to David who shall be his successor. This new dimension created fear in the heart of Saul as he began to stand in awe of David's presence of mind, his sensitivity, to react to the slightest motion that may challenge his safety. Saul's vexation is a perfect example of the evolution of evil thought as described in (Gen. 4:7). Saul's evil thoughts created the anger which opened wide the door for sinister thoughts to ensnare him. Saul's fear of God's law of justice granted him the self control to desist from throwing the spear.

V. 13 In Saul's saner moments he fully realized he fabricated his fears. However, the seed of hate that he planted in his heart has created his conflict. David's ability, his popularity with the public can be a tremendous asset to his government. Saul therefore appointed David as a captain over 1000 men. This act removed David's presence from his daily sight in order to remove him from his mind. However, the seed of evil reminded Saul, that as a captain he shall be exposed to many dangers. This could lead to his death. No court of justice could convict him for killing him.

V. 14 David was successful in every assignment given him by Saul. David was responsive to the Eternal's inspiration and was attentive to the Eternal's Natural Law, Moral Law and Ethical Law. This was the secret of his success.

Vs. 15.16 Saul's successes are enviable. His inferiority complex reenforced by Samuel, who denigrated his accomplishments have left a void which he cannot satisfy because of his envy of David's ability. His seed of hate has rooted and has created hostility that has blacked out his Godly image. Saul cannot reconcile the fact that all of Israel in general and the tribe of Judah in particular recognize David's executive ability. He is envious of their desire to reciprocate by their expression of respect and affection. Saul's mental block fails to grasp the glory which should be his because he has had the foresight to catapult David to play an important part in his government.

V. 17 Saul is knowledgeable of the rumor made in his name by the soldiers (I Sam. 17:25) in his army. He offers to honor the pledge they made in his name for the important part David played in defeating the Philistines. "I will give my elder daughter Merab to you in marriage on the condition that you become involved in directing the wars we

I SAMUEL CHAPTER 18

are obliged to wage with our enemies in the name of the Eternal." History has kept alive Saul's inner conflict and challenges his motive in offering David his daughter in marriage. He is ever opening wider the door for his evil thoughts. Should David marry his daughter and tragedy overtake him, she too will become the victim of her father's insane hatred.

V. 18   David replied to Saul's offer and reward, "Who am I but a humble shepherd? What is my potential as a soldier of fortune? My life as a soldier is ever in potential danger. My family genealogy has a humble origin (Ruth-Boaz, Jud. 12:8, Ruth 4:13.22) in Israel, I hardly deserve this high honor of becoming the son-in-law of the king of Israel."

V. 19   While king Saul was promising David to marry Merab, she had become engaged to Adriel a native of Abel-meholah, a town in the Jordan valley near Beth-shean (Jud. 7:22). The prophet Elishah was born in this town (I Kings 19:16). This experience permits us a view of his personal life to round out the picture of Saul.

Vs. 20.21   Simultaneously with the discovery that Merab was promised to Adriel, it was made known that Michal, Saul's younger daughter loved David. King Saul was pleased that Michal will become the bait to endanger David's life in his military activities with the Philistines. Saul remarked, "It is your destiny to be engaged twice."

Vs. 22.24   Saul is perceptive that David may have reason to challenge Saul's sincerity because of the switch of Merab to Michal. He therefore has requested that it be made known secretly, "The king is fond of you; all the courtiers love you. We urge you to take advantage of this opportunity to become king Saul's son-in-law." David replied to them, "I consider it a great honor; in light of the fact that I am a poor man with insignificant achievement." David's reply was reported to the king.

Vs. 25.27   Once again Saul conveyed his message of intent through his courtiers. "I have no desire to receive a dowry from David. I recognize his humble financial position. I am willing to accept in leu of a dowry, David's proof of dedication and loyalty to me by substituting his ability to obtain 100 Philistine foreskins." David's youth and inexperience excited his sense of adventure, he accepted the challenge. He activated his plan at once as he mobilized his 1000 men. In his great zeal he delivered 200 foreskins. Saul had no alternative, he gave Michal to David as his wife.

Vs. 28.30   David's feat has heightened Saul's awe. In his saner moments he envied David for having been blessed with the Eternal's protective custody in everything that he undertook. David's successes enhanced Michal's love for David. Saul recognized that David has won an ally in marrying Michal; she will never permit any harm to come to him because of her love.

I SAMUEL CHAPTER 18

Saul's fear of David grew with every passing day. Everytime the Philistines mounted an action against Israel, David anticipated it and took preemptive action. His successes won the recognition of Saul's army commanders. His fame grew and was soon recognized as a national figure. With every stride forward that David took, Saul enlarged his enmity toward him. Saul instinctively visualized David as the man Samuel had in mind when he said, "The Eternal God of Israel will give your throne to the man that He considers to be better than you." Saul feared David and envied him his divine protection, which endowed him with qualities vital to create and enhance Israel's history.

I SAMUEL CHAPTER 19

V. 1 (I Sam. 16:21, 18:1,3,4) Jonathan's love for David grew from admiration to the point where he loved him more than he loved himself. Jonathan stands ready to make any personal sacrifice to enhance David's welfare. Saul's admiration and affection were displaced and became absorbed by envy, jealousy and hate. In the beginning Saul recognized his envy and charged it to his personal insecurity (I Sam. 13:14,15:28). Periodically he emerged fom his psychotic depressive moments that created his delusions. He then regretted his schizophrenic desire to kill David. He then modified his plans to create dangerous assignments which could lead David into a death trap (I Sam. 18:25). Saul stoops to utilize his own daughters to activate his subtle desires to kill David. Saul has now opened wide the door. He has destroyed every iota of his human tranquility. Saul's resolution to kill David has torn to shreds his well ordered human soul. Saul now enlists his own son Jonathan and everyone of his courtiers to ally themselves with him for the purpose of killing David outright.

Vs. 2.3 Jonathan warns David, "My father Saul is desirous of killing you. Absent yourself from your normal duties tomorrow morning. Instead go into hiding in the field where my father takes his daily stroll. I will engage him in conversation close to your hiding place, that you may be able to overhear the contents of our discussion; I intend to speak to him in your behalf. Pending the result of our talking, I shall then inform you what you shall do."

Vs. 4.6 Jonathan reviewed and evaluated with his father Saul all that David had already accomplished in behalf of Israel: David's combat with Goliath and his successful campaigns to contain the Philistines. "Every one of these victories gave you reason to rejoice because they reflected glory upon the administration of your government. Why should you stoop and bring shame upon yourself by spilling innocent blood? Killing David will not solve your personal problems." Saul was receptive to Jonathan's plea. He took an oath, "I swear that as the Eternal liveth (Deut. 19:10) I shall not be the cause of David's death."

I SAMUEL CHAPTER 19

V. 7 Jonathan reviewed with David the details of his conversation with his father and Jonathan advised him to return to Saul's service as if nothing had happened. *Vayaveh* calls our attention to the fact that David was reluctant to return to the king's service. David had sat closer to Saul than any person in the realm. David has felt the impact of Saul's disturbed mind and has perceived the confusion and derangement of his perplexed soul. Despite all these alarming facts David permitted Jonathan to bring him back to Saul's service in order to reciprocate his affection for Jonathan and to prove his discernment of Jonathan's problem.

V. 8 Soon after David's return to Saul the Philistines attempted to invade Israel's territory and declare war upon Israel. David was called to create the strategy in the field and to take command of his army. His dedicated devotion to Israel's cause, his ability to create strategy and to lead his men, routed the Philistines as they disbanded in disarray and confusion.

V. 9 What is the meaning of "an evil spirit from the Eternal God came upon Saul?" Saul ignored his *yetzer hatov* the built in potential for good that creates the tranquility of a well ordered soul. Saul has bypassed his *ruach Adonai* good judgment that every success contributed by David is in harmony with the Eternal's direction in history. Saul has ignored his reason for being chosen as king of Israel. He was chosen because of his ability to destroy the Philistine enemy of history, that is bent upon retarding Israel's development in the Holyland. David's conquests are Saul's victories. Saul's seed of hate has created the mental block that has short-circuited his *ruach Adonai*. Saul has jammed the Eternal's message to his heart to recognize His law, His standards of truth in the direction of human history. The evil spirit of the Eternal, is the result of Saul's brooding over his failure to complete the deed fixed in his mind (I Sam. 18:11). Saul was sitting in his normal position; spear in hand on the ready to respond to his evil inclination *yetzer hara* which is building to a crescendo. David too, is sitting in his normal position and playing his instrument, while striving to tranquilize Saul's distressed soul. David's heart is palpitating while striving to fathom Saul's studied concentration to strike David at the precise instant that he must pluck the exact string with his hand. It is the *ruach Adonai* direction and inspiration of the Eternal that gives David the capability to fulfill both demands, the harmony of his tune and the demand to survive.

V. 10 David's instincts for survival have been honed and sharpened by (I Sam. 17:34.37) his lifetime experiences. David anticipates Saul's action created by his evil inclination to pin him to the wall with his spear. When Saul lifted his spear and aimed, at that very split second David made good his escape as the spear pierced the wall behind his empty seat. David fled that very night, resolved never to return under any circumstances.

I SAMUEL CHAPTER 19

V. 11 David fled to his home. He explained his situation to Michal. Saul sent messengers to guard his home all that night, to grant David the opportunity to bid his wife farewell before he will leave in the morning. The soldiers had strict orders to kill David on sight. It was Michal who was knowledgeable of her father's orders that warned David and insisted he escape at once, "For in the morning you shall be a dead man."

V. 12 While the guards waited at the front door, Michal helped David escape through a rear window. David tiptoed *vayelech* away from the house; he then changed his gait *vayivrach* as he ran to put distance between him and his pursuers in order to make good *vayimalet* his escape. We are indebted to David for having recorded his experience in (Ps. 59).

V. 13 Michal took one of her figurines and placed it in the bed and camouflaged it to appear as if David was confined by illness in his bed. There is no need to explain that at this point in Israel's history it was a common practice to possess a household idol. It will yet take centuries before this symbol of superstition and fortune telling will disappear from Jewish homes. It has never disappeared from most homes into the 20th century.

V. 14.17 When David failed to leave his home in the morning the guards returned to Saul. He ordered that they return, to enter the house and take him by force. Michal explained that David was ill and confined to bed and invited them to see for themselves. Saul then ordered that he be taken with his bed and to kill him at once. They then discovered the camouflage. From the text we learn that Saul joined the posse to make sure that his orders will be carried out. Observing the hoax and deception, Saul challenged his daughter Michal, "Why did you deceive me? How could you permit my enemy to escape?" Michal replied to her father, "David threatened to kill me if I did not help him to escape the guards."

V. 18.20 David made good his escape. He went directly to the home of Samuel in Ramah. He gave Samuel a detailed account of Saul's attempts upon his life. Samuel invited David to join him for his regular attendance at his prophetic school in Naioth-Ramah. When Saul learned of David's whereabouts he sent soldiers to capture David. The ecstatic atmosphere at Naioth overcame their reason to disturb the sanctity of the moment. They therefore joined the exercises.

Vs. 21.22 When Saul dispatched a second and a third contingent, they too came under the spell of prophetic inspiration and the atmosphere of spiritual ecstacy. (I Sam. 10:5) Saul was determined to enforce his orders; he therefore went to Naioth himself. On his way to Naioth he arrived at the well, known as the cistern of Secu. He inquired

I SAMUEL CHAPTER 19

as to the whereabouts of Samuel and David. He was informed they were both at Naioth.

Vs. 23.24 From the moment Saul was approaching Naioth in Ramah, he started to recall his experience recorded in (I Sam. 10:5.6). He felt the spirit of the peaceful atmosphere; his fears disappeared, he was able to sort out his reason; he felt the tranquility of a well ordered mind deeply within himself. Saul completely forgot the reason for his coming to Naioth.

Saul joined the assembly at Samuel's prophetic school. He removed his kingly cloak to humble himself as an equal to the rest of the assembly. Saul then joined them in the recitation of psalms and hymns to heighten their spirituality in the service of the Eternal God. While the congregation continued in their fervent prayer, Saul became ecstatic as if in a trance as he saw Samuel. *Vayipol arom* Saul divested himself of every reservation as he shared his agony with Samuel. For a full 24 hour period Saul reviewed the torture of his soul. He reminded Samuel of that terrible scene in (I Sam. 15:24.28). To fully understand and empathize with Saul, read the summation of (I Sam. 15:35 and Samuel's traumatic guilt in 16:1.3).

History can only conjecture what actually took place between Saul and Samuel this 24 hour period as both men bared their souls in search for the Eternal God's concept of justice as they strove to honor His concept of truth. Only the capriciousness of humanity can pass off Samuel and Saul's experience by saying, "Is Saul too among the prophets?"

I SAMUEL CHAPTER 20

When David returned safely from the following experiences (I Sam. 18:27.28, 19:8) Saul resigned himself to the reality that David's ability to escape the dangers of war had an element of the supernatural. He therefore resolved to enlist his son Jonathan and his courtiers to the fulfillment of his diabolical plan (I Sam. 19:1). Jonathan's loyalty to David is rooted to the justice of his cause, it is bound by a covenant (I Sam. 18:1,3.5) and the reality that David possessed qualities which can enhance the kingdom of Israel. Jonathan therefore made Saul's threat known to David and followed up his sincere effort by lecturing his father Saul. Saul recognized Jonathan's plea in this moment of his serenity (I Sam. 19:4.7) and resulted in Saul's oath not to harm David.

The details described in (I Sam. 19:9.24) are completely unknown to Jonathan. While Saul was involved in his denouement with Samuel in v. 24, David escaped Saul's trap and returned for a moment of truth with Jonathan. This is the moment when Jonathan is filled in by David with the details for the first time.

Vs. 1.4 David fled from Naioth in Ramah and went to the home of

I SAMUEL CHAPTER 20

Jonathan in Gibeah. He poured out the bitterness which pervaded his heart. "What have I done! What is my crime! How have I offended your father! That he is desirous of killing me?"

V. 2. Jonathan defended his position. "Heaven forbid that my father should desecrate his oath (I Sam. 19:6). You shall not die! It cannot be! My father always shares his confidences with me."

V. 3. David validated his reply by an oath and proceeded to give Jonathan the details of his experiences, "Death is but one step away whenever I am in the presence of your father. It should be obvious to you why he did not tell you. He knew you would be grieved and aggravated."

V. 4. Jonathan is convinced from the record of David's dangerous experiences that his father's schizophrenic condition has deteriorated to the point of no return. Jonathan replied to David, "How can I help you? Tell me! Command me! And I will do it."

Vs. 5.7 From the details of David's request of Jonathan, we get a glimpse of Samuel's instructions to David at Naioth. "That he is to return to Saul's service. He is to make every contribution toward the orderly function of Israel's government during this trying period in Saul's life. Samuel has no desire that Saul abdicate his throne. Events must take its natural course." David's presence is vital for the nation's wellbeing. "You are advised to take every precaution to survive until that day when you will become the king of Israel." David's request now becomes reasonable and conforms with our understanding of Samuel's instructions given to David at Naioth. David replied, "Tomorrow is the celebration of the new moon. I am normally expected to be present at the king's festive table. I would like to absent myself until the festivities are over on the second day of the festival. I will return on the third day under the following conditions: If your father notes my absence, you are to tell him that you gave me permission to return to Bethlehem for the annual family sacrifices there." V. 7. "Should your father be gracious in his reply, this will be your proof that he forgives both of us for the breach of his authority. However, should he become angered and distressed, this will confirm his intentions to pursue me and harm me."

V. 8 "Remember! It is you (Jonathan) that initiated a covenant with me (I Sam. 18:3.4). I therefore trust you implicitly to evaluate the intentions of your father. However, if it be your intention to give me a favorable reply in order to bring me back to your father as you did once before (I Sam. 19:7), when he desecrated his oath to you, and I endangered my life then because of my faith in your evaluation. I therefore give you permission to kill me yourself, now, but do not return me to your father that he kill me."

Vs. 9.10 Jonathan was startled by David's challenge, "How can you entertain the idea that I did not take into consideration your exposure to danger without warning you?"

I SAMUEL CHAPTER 20

V. 10. David replied, "Is there anyone I can trust better than you to perceive the effect of your father's acrimonious answer? Or, is there anyone but you who can discern my constant fears?"

Vs. 11.13 Jonathan suggested they leave (his home) and go out into the field where no one can eavesdrop on their conversation. When they reached the outskirts of Gibeah, Jonathan said to David, "I hereby swear by the Eternal God of Israel, that on the morrow when I sound out my father's intentions, and the reply is favorable to you, I most certainly will report it to you. However, should my father intend to harm you, may the Eternal God of Israel punish me if I do not convey the news to you personally, that I may bid you farewell, that you go in peace with my blessings that you ever be in the custody of the Eternal God of Israel even as my father was in the past."

V. 14 David has already confided in Jonathan of his anointment by Samuel, to succeed Saul. Jonathan fears the moment, should David be forced to flee and he becomes entrapped by the irrational problems of his father. He, like David fears that he may not survive the extra dangers; while striving to remain loyal to his father's excesses. The pressures of his dramatic conclusions to face the realities of history inspire Jonathan to say to David, *velo im odenu chai*, "Our covenant applies not only during our lifetime if we are capable of surviving the existing dangers, but becomes an obligation to include our posterity to fulfill its intent." *Velo amuth*, "You, too, are to take every precaution that I do not die, even as I shall help you to survive this day."

Vs. 15.17 Jonathan cautions David about the future, "When the time comes for you to even the score with all your present enemies, you are to remain faithful to my posterity to infinity." Jonathan amended his original oath and covenant to bind David's posterity to their covenant. This reciprocal covenant binds them both to their respective families. Jonathan recognizes David's potential for greatness, he disregards his own future and is desirous to build his immortality upon his great love for David. During these soul-searching days, he recognized his father's jealousy as cruel as the grave, while his love for David burned with the flame of the Eternal God. Jonathan therefore caused David to swear again that their affections never waned nor lagged during these trying years, their love is to infinity for it shall survive even after their death in the hearts of their posterity.

V. 18 Jonathan now turned to his plan to ascertain the criteria upon which will be based David's decision either to return to Saul's service or to leave it forever because of the threat to his life. "Tomorrow is the first day of the festival celebrating the new moon—new month. Your absence will be noted because your seat will be vacant. Many of the courtiers will read into this fact many innuendos."

V. 19 Jonathan is instructing David that when he leaves him he may

I SAMUEL CHAPTER 20

go into hiding in a place of his own choice. "However, on the third evening from tonight which will mark the end of the festival, you are to return to the stone of Ezel (where you have hidden before (I Sam. 19:2)) and where we are at this moment as we are formulating our plans."

Vs. 20.22　　Jonathan continued to tell David, "That on the third day which is a regular working day I shall return here and pretend that I am shooting at a target. I will shoot three arrows to the side of the stone of Ezel. If the arrows fall short of the stone of Ezel, this will be your signal that you are to return to the king despite his hostility. However, if the arrows fall beyond the stone of Ezel, you are to take this signal as your alarm to escape because the situation is dangerous and the king will probably send a posse to search for you."

Vs. 23.25　　As Jonathan is about to take leave of David, he returned to the subject of their reciprocal oath in vs. 14.17, "The Eternal is our witness that neither of us may transgress its intent to infinity." Vs. 24.25. David hid in the field as agreed that very evening. On the morrow, the first day of the festival the king sat in his usual place by the wall. Jonathan relinquished his normal seat to his uncle Avner, in anticipation of any controversy arising during the meal. David's seat remained vacant.

V. 26　　King Saul made no comment publicly because of David's absence. It was assumed that he was not fit ritually to participate in the special sacrifice. This verse confirms our explanation that Samuel ordered David to return to the king with Saul's personal assurance to Samuel that no harm would come to him. David's reservations now are the normal precautions of a prudent man. David does not expect miracles in human relations. Particularly after his almost fatal experiences.

Vs. 27.29　　When David failed to come to the festival on the second day of the two-day festival, the king turned to Jonathan, "Do you know why David did not take his regular seat at the table either yesterday or today?"

Vs. 28.29.　Jonathan replied, "David requested that I give him permission to go to Bethlehem, in answer to an invitation from his elder brother for a family reunion."

V. 30　　Saul flew into a rage against Jonathan. "You son of a perverse rebellious woman," he shouted (an expression of derision). "I know that you are receptive to the cause of the son of Jesse. I know that you favor him against your own self-interest. Your conduct is a disgrace to the mother who bore you."

V. 31　　"Mind you! As long as the son of Jesse remains alive, your potential of becoming the king of Israel shall remain

I SAMUEL CHAPTER 20

Vs. 32.33 — uncertain. Since you gave him permission to go, you go and bring him back for I have condemned him to die."

Vs. 32.33 — Saul brandished his spear in an effort to strike Jonathan. Jonathan now had the evidence that his father's schizophrenia to kill David was fixed in his heart, his psyche and in his soul. Saul has bypassed his *Zelem Elohim*; every fibre in his body is feeding on his psychosis (I Sam. 18:11, 19:10).

Vs. 34.40 — Jonathan rose from the table on the second festive day; he ate no food because he grieved over David's destiny and because his father had humiliated him. In the morning of the third day Jonathan took a young boy with him to give David the prearranged signal (I. Sam. 20:19.22). As Jonathan shot his three arrows he added emphasis to his inanimate arrows. "Quick! Hurry! Don't stop! Jonathan shouted to make sure that David got the message. The boy had no concept of Jonathan's gameplan. The field being clear with none present Jonathan looked forward to spending a moment of farewell with David. He therefore gave the lad the gear and he requested that he return them back to his home.

V. 41 — David waited in his hiding place; he allowed enough time to elapse for the boy to get back to town. He then emerged from his hiding place toward the south of the stone of Ezel. As David came face to face with Jonathan, he fell upon his face and bowed three times in gratitude to Jonathan's cooperation. David rose and embraced Jonathan, they kissed each other and wept in their embrace. David's weeping exceeded Jonathan's weeping for he now fully realized that Saul's die has been cast. David fully grasped the implications of Saul's decision; he shall become an outcast as he runs from place to place to save his life.

V. 42 — Jonathan said to David, "Go in peace, ever remember our oath in the name of the Eternal. It is He that shall testify against us if either of us fails to keep our oath taken between you and me and between our posterity forever."

I SAMUEL CHAPTER 21

Vs. 1.2 — David took leave of Jonathan and went directly to Nob, while Jonathan returned to Gibeah. Upon David's arrival in Nob, he went directly to Ahimelech the kohen who was in charge of the Mishkan which was functioning here since the destruction of the Mishkan in Shiloh. The *Urim Vetumim* were here but the Ark was still at Kiriat-Jearim (I Sam. 7:1.2). Ahimelech was awed by David's presence and hastened to be of service to him. However, he was surprised that he was traveling without a retinue that usually accompanied him on government business.

Vs. 3.5 — David informed Ahimelech, "I am traveling on a special

I SAMUEL CHAPTER 21

mission for king Saul which is highly classified. I have sent my men ahead where I shall meet them."

V. 4. David is desirous of obtaining a supply of food from Ahimelech. "Would you have about five loaves of bread or any other food supplies which you could spare?"

V. 5. Ahimelech replied, "The only bread I have is the sanctified Showbread which only the kohanim may eat" (Lev. 24:5.9). Ahimelech interjected, "In an instance of emergency any layman who is ritually clean may eat this bread. If your men can conform with these requirements, they too may eat it."

Vs. 6.7   David assured Ahimelech, "My men have been away from home for these past three days, also their clothing and implements were fresh when we started on this mission. They therefore would conform with the requirements of ritual purity. The effect of this sanctified bread in their knapsacks would certainly inspire them to maintain this required high standard." V. 7. Ahimelech gave David the Showbread though he had no other to replace it. He urged David to take it because he has an obligation to feed his hungry men.

Vs. 8.10   The text interrupts to tell us that Doeg the Edomite (so called because his residence was formerly in Edom), Saul's chief of the shepherds was there simultaneously with David. This was a tragic coincident which will cost Ahimelech his life.

Vs. 9.10.   Doeg witnessed Ahimelech's gracious response to David's request for supplies of food and was present as David accepted Goliath's sword which David had deposited here as a memorial.

Vs. 11.12   David took his supplies and left at once to see Achish the king-governor of Gath. After his brush with Doeg, he concluded he must leave Israel in order to escape Saul's jurisdiction. David recognized the hazards of being in Philistia and remembered the experience recorded in (Gen. 37:24). When he calculated the odds he concluded he would be safer in Gath than in Israel. When the citizens of Gath saw David they recognized him as the king of Israel. They quoted the popular tune recorded in (I Sam. 18:6.7).

Vs. 13.16   These comments gave David reason to fear for his safety. He spontaneously feigned insanity as he spoke in a muddled speech in a babel of confused language. He pretended to write upon the doors of the city gates while permitting his saliva to drool down to his beard. He made irrational statements while writing with his spittle. When Achish was notified of David's presence, he rebuked them for their error. "What you are looking at is a raving mad man. Why do you bring him to my attention? Do I lack mad men and lunatics that you bring him here to entertain me and taunt me with my personal problems?" Sometime after this experience David wrote (Ps. 34:) in which he describes the usefulness of his mad act.

I SAMUEL CHAPTER 22

V. 1 David managed his escape from Gath in Philistia and went to the rocky fortress in Adullam about 12 miles southeast of Bethlehem (Joshua 15:35, 12:15, I Chron. 11:15.16). When David arrived here he notified his kinsmen of his whereabouts. He warned them to take precautions in the event Saul decides to pursue him here. David's kinsmen came to see him in Adullam and they agreed upon a defensive action.

V. 2 David's notoriety in the Holyland attracted many sympathizers who empathized with his predicament. All those whose lives had become complicated because of debt or other personal involvements and who desired a fresh start flocked to David's assistance. They volunteered to join his cause, to help him to defend himself as a fugitive of Saul's persecution. These volunteers gave David a force of about 400 men.

Vs. 3.5 David recognized the potential danger to his parents who may become a pawn in Saul's pursuit of David, he therefore gained the cooperation of the king of Moab, that they stay in his territory under his jurisdiction for their safety and comfort. The king of Moab was sympathetic to David because of his genealogy which goes back to Ruth the Moabitess. David's parents and family remained in Mitzpeh Moab during the whole period that he was in the cave at Adullam.

The prophet Gad, a student of Samuel's prophetic school knew of David's anointment as king of Israel. He came to David in Adullam and advised him not to confine himself to Adullam, that he expand his field of operations to gain the sympathy of the whole country. David accepted his advice and went to the forest of Hereth near Beth-shemesh.

Vs. 6.10 Saul is knowledgeable of David's position that he now has a troop of soldiers sympathetic to his cause. While in Gibeah, Saul was holding court under his favorite tamarisk tree as much of his information was being put together regarding David's progress in defending himself. Saul spontaneously took his courtiers to task, "You sons of Benjamin, why have you conspired against me? I suppose you too anticipate important appointments from the son of Jesse and the rewards of fields and vineyards from his government. Is this the reason for not informing me of the pact with my own son (Jonathan)? Is there anyone here concerned with my welfare, to tell me of an ambush set against me by my own son to day?"

Doeg the Edomite spoke up, "I saw the son of Jesse when he came to the Mishkan in Nob to see Ahimelech the son of Ahitub. I overheard him counseling David in the name of the Eternal. He also supplied him with food and gave him the sword which belonged to Goliaath the Philistine."

Vs. 11.13 Saul issued an order for Ahimelech and his associate kohanim to come to Gibeah. When they arrived he challenged them. "Why have you conspired against me by counseling the son

I SAMUEL CHAPTER 22

of Jesse, by giving him food and a sword that he may create an ambush against me?"

Vs. 14.16 — Ahimelech defended himself, "Everything I did for David was in the name of the king. He is the most esteemed in your kingdom. Everything I did for him was to help you. I have done no wrong that you should accuse me of rebelling against you. I had no information that David was no longer in your service nor that he did not speak in your name." Saul disregarded Ahimelech's defense. He issued his verdict that Ahimelech was to die.

Vs. 17.19 — Saul issued an order to his guards to kill Ahimelech. They demurred from this dastardly act to kill the servants of the Eternal whom they recognized as innocent of any wrongdoing against Saul. King Saul then turned to Doeg the Edomite who obeyed Saul's command at once. Doeg slew Ahimelech and 85 men that were active in the priesthood at Nob in the Mishkan. Doeg put the whole city of Nob to the sword. He showed no mercy to any man, woman or child. He slew their infants, oxen, asses and sheep.

Vs. 20.23 — Abiathar the son of Ahimelech managed to escape the massacre at Nob. He fled to the forest of Hereth and reported the details of the massacre. David felt the weight of his own guilt in this whole episode. It was a tragic oversight on his part that he took no precautions against Doeg the Edomite. He should have anticipated that he would report his presence at Nob to king Saul. This sad and tragic experience has become a black page in Israel's history and David analyzed it in (Ps. 52), "You could have pleaded my cause with Saul in behalf of Ahimelech. You had the opportunity to erase this tragedy from the mind of Saul. Instead you employed your tongue for falsehood and evil. Truth and righteousness have no domain in your heart." David concluded his lament by recognizing Doeg's preoccupation to save himself; this has brought tragedy to others. David pleaded with Abiathar that he stay with him. David vowed, "Whoever seeks your life must also seek mine. Fear not, I hold myself responsible for your life."

I SAMUEL CHAPTER 23

Vs. 1.2 — (I Sam. 22:18.20) informs us that when Abiathar the son of Ahimelech escaped from Saul's massacre of the kohanim, he took his father's ephod and the *Urim Vetumim* with him and joined David in the forest of Hereth. When David was notified that the Philistines are pillaging the threshing fields in Keilah, three miles south of Adullam in the territory of Judah, David consulted with Abiathar in the name of the Eternal, should he expose his dangerous position in order to help his Judean brethren? Abiathar confirmed David's spontaneous desire, that he most certainly should respond to their appeal for help.

I SAMUEL CHAPTER 23

Vs. 3.6   David's men shared their fears with David, "We are in fear of our lives here in the territory of our brethren; if we go to Keilah we create the chance of double jeopardy by confronting both the Philistines and Saul's forces." David recognized the rationale of his men. He once again consulted with Abiathar and confronted the *Urim Vetumim* with his problem. David was encouraged to develop his strategy to confront the Philistines frontally. They would succeed in defeating the Philistines and retrieve the crops which they pilfered. They were assured that Saul's forces would be no obstacle. David led his men to Keilah and routed the Philistines from the threshing floor, pursued them to their own villages close to Israel's border, retrieved their crops and in turn confiscated their livestock and returned to Keilah.

Vs. 7.9   In the above action David's intelligence came from the men in the field. Now that Saul was notified of the action against the Philistines instead of being gratified he ordered the pursuit of David and his men. Saul concluded that Keilah is a walled city; if he blockades the entrance and surrounds the wall David could not possibly escape. Saul's vengeance bypassed the welfare of Judah as he concluded that, "God has created the conditions for me to destroy David." When David learned of Saul's intentions to make him the quarry, he once again consulted with Abiathar.

Vs. 10.12   When David approached the *Urim Vetumim*, he prayed, "O Eternal God of Israel, Saul will not hesitate to destroy Keilah even as he laid Nob and its habitants waste. Assuming that this will be his strategy, will the people of Keilah surrender me to Saul, despite the fact that we came to their help when only their crops were pilfered? When Saul threatens to destroy Keilah, will they ignore our kindness and turn us over to Saul in order to save their lives?" The Eternal inspired David to recognize, that if he stands and fights, Saul will most certainly destroy everything that moves to satisfy his vengeance. David's prudence recognized the reality, he decided to leave Keilah in order to avoid a genocidal war.

V. 13   David's force has grown to 600 men (I Sam. 22:2, 25:13, 27:2, 30:10). They decided to leave Keilah at once and they leaked the information to Saul's forces via the underground. When Saul was informed that David and his troops have taken to the open road, Saul called off his mobilization.

Vs. 14.15   David's strategy is that of a fugitive. He is aware of Saul's desire to box him into a corner. Therefore, David took every precaution to stay in the open. He went to the rocky formations with their caves in the wilderness of Judah, he then went to the hill country of Judah and then to the wilderness of Ziph, which is about four miles southeast of Hebron. It then stretches northeast toward the Dead Sea. Saul made every effort to reach David but God's concept of justice prevailed as Saul's men

I SAMUEL CHAPTER 23

kept David informed. He was therefore a step or two ahead of his posses. David finally settled down in Horshah-Khoreisa, a ruin about 2 miles south of the community of Ziph.

Vs. 16.18   Jonathan came to visit David in Horshah, to assure him of his utmost faith in his destiny to become the king of Israel.
Jonathan reaffirmed his dedication to David's cause and assured him Saul will never find him. "Fear not my father's constant pursuit to satisfy his evil desire to harm you. When you become king of Israel I shall dedicate my services to you and become your viceroy. My father is aware of my position; I am consecrated to your destiny to become king of Israel." At this point in time there are no secrets in Israel of David's anointment to become king of Israel upon the demise of Saul. Jonathan has assured David he has no claim upon the throne of Saul, he has no intention of succeeding his father. This was Jonathan's reason to come to Horshah to renew his covenant and to make his position clear to David. His oath now was taken *lifne Adonai* in the presence of the *Urim Vetumim*. For a clear understanding and full meaning of the *Urim Vetumim* see T.E.T. on (Ex. 28:13.30). David is determined to remain at Horshah because of Jonathan's position.

Vs. 19.23   The indigenous desert people in the wilderness of Ziph (not Judeans) came to Saul in Gibeah and reported David's hiding place in Horshah, at the hill of Hachilah south of Jeshimon. They offered Saul their help to capture David. Saul thanked them for their compassion and blessed them. Saul urged them to confirm David's camping grounds and to record his daily movements. "For he is a crafty fellow. When you have noted all these details send me the information, I will then ferret him out from among the clans of Judah." David has recorded this experience in (Ps. 54:5). "Strangers have risen up against me, impudent men seek my soul. They have no concept of God nor His desire to introduce justice among men."

Vs. 24.28   The Ziphites left ahead of Saul's posse, David was in the wilderness of Maon, in the lowlands south of the wastelands.
While here he was tipped off regarding Saul's mission and his plans. Saul did not find him because David had entered the rocky areas around Maon in order to be on high ground. While David was climbing up on one side of the mountain, Saul was descending. Saul's every effort to encircle David failed. While in the pursuit of David and his men, Saul was notified that the Philistines are beginning to invade Israel's territory. Saul ended the pursuit of his imaginary enemy to face the real enemy the Philistines. History has recognized the propitious moment of this incident by naming this mountainous crag, the Rock of Separation. David has evaluated Saul's folly in (Ps. 116). David reminds us how Saul dissipated his capabilities to pursue a phantom that destroyed his every waking and slumbering moment, until his life became but a bad dream. Only death could put an end to his pursuits.

I SAMUEL CHAPTER 24

V. 1   David left the vicinity of Ziph and went to the western shore of the Dead Sea into the mountainous area of En-gedi. In (Gen. 14:7, II Chron. 20:2) it was called Hazezon Tamar, it is the modern Wadi el Hasasa. This cavernous area is where the Ibex, wild goats make their home. Rising from the road on the shore of the Dead Sea there are many natural sweet water springs and therefore the shepherds graze their sheep in this area. David and his men chose this area for its excellent shelter.

Vs. 2.4   When Saul completed his defensive action against the Philistines (I Sam. 23:27.28) he was notified that David was at En-gedi. Saul mobilized 3000 handpicked men and resumed his search for David. Arriving at En-gedi Saul entered one of the caves used as a sheepcote for the purpose of relieving himself. Coming in from the light, Saul was unable to see anyone in the rear of the cavernus cave. In the rear of this cave sat David and some of his men.

V. 5   David's men had no difficulty in recognizing Saul as he entered. They whispered to David, "This is the day that the Eternal promised to deliver your enemy into your hands, you can now do with him as you please." David spontaneously rose and stealthily cut the corner of Saul's cloak (I Sam. 15:27.28).

V. 6   Belongs after vs. 7.8. After David vented his inner feelings which pervaded his heart in the words he spoke to his men in vs. 7.8, David reproached himself for having reawakened in his conscience that terrible scene which he witnessed in the lives of Saul and Samuel that began with (I Sam. 15:24.31, 16:1.2, 19:23.24) and ended with that frontal confrontation which shall be interred in their graves. David's remorse recognized and empathized with Saul's schizophrenia as the result of Samuel's excesses. From this verse emerges a human being who possesses a dimension of greatness which sets him apart from all the human beings of his time. Though Saul will kill David on sight despite the fact that he already knows that he is the anointed of God, David's national pride and dedication to Torah principles, disciplines his conduct. David has risen another step upon the ladder of evolution as he reaches for (Isaiah's vision 42:6) Israel's goal, "Is to become a light unto the nations."

Vs. 7.8   David replied to his men, "Saul is the anointed king of Israel by the authority of the Eternal (I Sam. 10:1) God of Israel. I recognize him as my king as long as he lives. God forbids me from entertaining even the thought of harming him." David rebuked his men and stayed their impulse to kill Saul. Saul left the cave ignorant of the fact that David spared his life.

Vs. 9.10   David arose from his hiding place and walked out of the cave. From this high point he called down to Saul, "My lord and king!" As the king turned to look for the individual whose

I SAMUEL CHAPTER 24

voice he heard, David bowed low in homage with his face to the ground. David challenged Saul, "Why do you listen to your evil inclination that David desires to harm you?"

Vs. 11.12 David said to Saul, "See for yourself my dedication to you and to the Eternal's Torah. I was challenged today with the opportunity to kill you. My loyalty to you and to Him, in Whose name you were anointed prevailed as my good inclination inspired me to show you mercy and compassion. See, my father, observe the corner of your cloak in my hand. Though I had the opportunity to kill you, I did not. Should this not convince you of my loyalty? I have never rebelled against you nor have I ever conspired against you. As the anointed of the Eternal God of Israel, I recognized your authority and never transgressed against you. Yet, you are determined to kill me."

Vs. 13.14 "I rest my case with the Eternal God. May His standard of justice prevail between you and me. Should you decide to kill me, may the Eternal God of Israel avenge my death in accord with His law. I, hereby vow that I shall never raise my hand against you to do you any harm." V. 14. "Wicked and vengeful deeds sprout from hearts that encourage man's evil inclination to grow into evil deeds, while those that cultivate their inclination for righteousness become incapable of evil (Gen. 4:7). I vow that I shall never harm you."

Vs. 15.16 Sarcastically and ironically David raised the question and gave the answer. "It should have been below the dignity of the king of Israel to pursue me whose life is compared to a dead dog. Why does the exulted king of Israel chase after me whose life can be compared to a flea? For I fly whither I can to save my life."
V. 16. "I place my faith in the Eternal to vindicate me when He weighs the evidence, as He examines *bochen kelayoth valev* (Jer. 11:20) our motives. May His verdict vindicate me against you."

V. 17 When David concluded his plea to Saul, Saul asked, "Is this your voice my son?" The eloquence of David's spontaneous and sincere generosity touched the soul of Saul the shepherd, who followed his flock with sensitivity and thoughtfulness to their needs (I Sam. 11:4.6). Saul wept as a sincere repentant as he recognized the root cause of his misery. It is these experiences (I Sam. 15:27.28, 35, 16:1.2, 19:22.24) that have overwhelmed him. Saul had neither the guidance or the experience to cope with his personal problems when left to his own devices.

Vs. 18.19 The accolade Saul is conferring upon David is the exact expression David's progenitor used in (Gen. 38:26) "David, you are more righteous and just than I, for in all your dealings with me you were generous and endowed me with kindness while I repaid you with evil and hostility. The Eternal recognized my transgression and gave you the

I SAMUEL CHAPTER 24

opportunity to repay my iniquity by killing me, yet, you refused to be the instrument of my destruction."

Vs. 20.21 "You have cornered your enemy and you were determined to let him go unharmed. I am certain the Eternal will reward you generously for what you have done for me today. I now know that you shall succeed me as king of Israel. You have proven yourself worthy that Israel's kingdom shall remain in your hands (I Sam. 12:14)."

Vs. 22.23 "I desire that you take an oath this day that you shall not kill my descendants in the manner of ancient succeeding kings, that my name continue in the annals of history (I Sam. 20:15).

V. 23. David swore to Saul in accord with his request and in accord with his covenant with Jonathan. Saul went home to Gibeah and David and his men went up to their cave in En-gedi.

I SAMUEL CHAPTER 25

The prophet Samuel died after a long and useful life. See introduction to chapter eight for details. From the time that Samuel entered the Mishkan to serve under Eli, he devoted his life completely to the cause of Israel. All of Israel united to eulogize his memory in gratitude for a dedicated life devoted to unite the loose confederation of Hebrew tribes into a united central government. This resulted in mounting a united action to free Israel from Philistine subjugation in the west and containing the Ammonites in the east.

Samuel followed Moses' direction and chose both Saul and David during his lifetime to insure the continuity of a central authority. Samuel founded a school for the development of prophets who shall dedicate their lives to the spiritual development of Israel. Samuel's experience recorded in (I Sam. 2:12.17, 22.36) led him to refine the excesses of the priesthood (I Sam. 15:22.23). He devoted every day of his life to establish courts of justice. We are indebted to him for documenting the record of the period of the *Judges*. He recorded their failures and searched for the dedicated minority that will fight back the avalanche of ignorance which led to assimilation. Samuel was buried in his own homestead, in a grave prepared by him during his lifetime in Ramah. The effectiveness of Samuel's leadership is highlighted by binding the rising hope of David's leadership simultaneously with the burial of his master Samuel. Only a comma separates their continuity.

V. 1 David has survived the psychopathic machinations of Saul because he was a realist. He was endowed with the capability to analyze every given situation. He then honed its details to insure his success. Despite Saul's momentary change of heart described in chapter 24, David recognized the reality of his position. Saul stood in awe of Samuel during his lifetime. Now, with the demise of Samuel, David concluded that Saul will reverse his promise (I Sam. 24:17.23) and continue his schizophrenic game to corner and capture his quarry David. David therefore

I SAMUEL CHAPTER 25

chose to go to Midbar Paran, south of Kadesh-barnea, north of the Sinai Peninsula, in order to stay out of Saul's reach. This vast expanse of open territory gave David the room to maneuver in any critical action that Saul may mount against him.

Vs. 2.3 David's inner feelings at this moment in his life are described in Psalm 13, which he composed while in the wilderness of Paran. While in this area he became exposed to the flocks of sheep and goats belonging to a man by the name of Nabal. Nabal was a wealthy man whose home was in Maon and his agricultural operations were in nearby Carmel in Judah. Nabal was a descendant of Caleb. We are informed that he owned 3000 sheep and 1000 goats. The time frame for the following narrative is sheep shearing time in the spring. Nabal's wife was Abigail a beautiful woman with outstanding personal qualities and respected for her comprehension and insight. Nabal was really his nickname because of his cantankerous character. He was quarrelsome and a difficult tyrant to his employees and a despot in his human relations. Though Nabal came from a noble family, his conduct is recorded as unusual and history has deliberately misspelled his name.

V. 4 From this narrative we learn of David's dependence upon the generosity of his kinsmen to support him in gratitude for his policing the area against marauding and pilfering. David has extended a protective canopy over the large holdings of Nabal, though he refused to recognize him or his valuable services. All of Israel are aware that David has been chosen to become the king of Israel upon the demise of Saul, yet, Nabal completely ignored his national status or even his genealogy. He belittled the importance of David's father Jesse. With the above background, we can understand David's indignation. David has recorded his experience in Psalm 14.

Vs. 5.8 When David learned of Nabal's festival at sheep shearing time, a festive moment in agricultural history which is celebrated by generosity to the poor, the needy, and gifts to family and friends. In this manner the farmers expressed their gratitude for their prosperity. At this festive moment he was not invited to participate nor was he remembered for the services he rendered to Nabal during the past year. David therefore dispatched ten of his young men to subtly remind him of his oversight. David instructed them in their manner of approach and his message to Nabal, "In the name of David we have come to wish you peace on this happy occasion. *Ko lechai* May your prosperity continue throughout your lifetime. May you and your families and all that is yours continue to live in peace. We have come to remind you at this happy moment of the services we extended to your shepherds that were grazing and pasturing your sheep in the Wilderness of Paran and its environs. We made sure that wild animals did not attack your flocks, we discouraged marauders from pilfering. We protected your shepherds from any possible harm. You can verify these facts by asking your shepherds that were in our area to confirm our claim. Since you have overlooked either to invite us to

I SAMUEL CHAPTER 25

your festival at Carmel or to express your recognition for our services, David requests that you share your prosperity with us at this important moment of thanksgiving. We will be grateful for whatever you will give us as an expression of gratitude for our services."

Vs. 9.11   When David's men delivered the message to Nabal, Nabal replied, "Who is David? Who is Jesse? These days there are many slaves that break away from their masters. Do you expect me to take the food and water which I prepared for my employees and give it to those that I do not even know?" The text reflects upon an attitude which was not uncommon throughout the period of the *Judges* and continued into the end of this generation. It also informs us that there were many wealthy Israelites in the eleventh century. Nabal is but an example of those who ignored every collective effort to establish national unity. Nabal is not even conscious of the local or national leaders to whom they are indebted for their safety in a sea of enemies.

Vs. 12.13   David's men returned and reported Nabal's antagonistic reply. David chose 400 of his soldiers and left 200 men behind to guard the camp. Though David preferred to arouse Nabal's sense of communal responsibility on a voluntary basis, he is now intent upon reminding Nabal of his moral obligation to pay for the protective shelter they extended to him, to his men and to his property during their wanderings in the unpoliced areas surrounding the wilderness. Since Nabal was adamant in his greedy reply and his refusal to recognize his obligation, David intends to remind him by force.

Vs. 14.17   One of Nabal's men who was present at David's presentation and Nabal's arrogant reply to David's men, anticipated a reaction to Nabal's insolence. He therefore came to Abigail, Nabal's wife to express his outrage at Nabal's conduct. He confirmed David's claim and he elaborated upon his protective services. "They not only kept marauders and wild animals from attacking our flocks but they never demanded or took anything for their efforts. They protected us both day and night like a protective wall they shielded us from danger." This man cautioned Abigail, "Should David decide to avenge Nabal's outrageous conduct, he could cause much harm to every member of your household and to the whole community. Obviously I tried to remind Nabal of his moral obligation but to no avail. You know I am sure how incorrigible Nabal can be. He would not listen to any of us."

Vs. 18.19   Abigail recognized the consistency of the man's plea. She busied herself at once in preparing a generous reciprocal reward for David and his men. Abigail's gift included: 200 loaves of bread, two bottles of wine, five dressed sheep, five bushels of parched corn, 100 cakes of raisins and 200 cakes of pressed figs. Abigail instructed her

I SAMUEL CHAPTER 25

help to go ahead and she will follow. Abigail did not tell Nabal of her response to David's plea. As Abigail and her people were coming down one trail from the mountain, David and his men were coming down the mountain on another trail. At a given point both trails converged and it appeared that David was coming toward her. David was obviously going to rise upon the same trail from which she had just emerged on his way to Carmel.

Vs. 20.22 These verses should follow v. 13. When David mobilized his soldiers for action against Nabal, he reviewed out loud to his men the effect of Nabal's reply. "It was foolish for us to protect this man's property in the wilderness. Is his arrogant reply his way of rewarding us with evil for our good deed?" In his moment of anger David uttered an oath of condemnation against Nabal. What inflamed David's resentment of Nabal was, "How could a man of substance and wealth be so ignorant of national affairs or his tribal genealogy?"

Vs. 23.24 When Abigail's people came face to face with David and his men, Abigail dismounted from her donkey and walked forward to prostrate herself before David. "I assume the blame for my husband's *belial* boorish conduct. Nabal is insensitive to the feelings of others. He is disloyal to the Eternal God, the Source of his blessings. He ignores those that are hungry and is foolishly complacent when he denies the thirsty, his water (Is. 32:5.6).

Vs. 25.26 Abigail continued her plea, "I did not see your men when they made their presentation to Nabal. When I learned of Nabal's conduct, I hastened at once to correct the unfairness of Nabal's conduct. I am here to restrain you from any harm that you could inflict upon Nabal and his household for his boorish conduct. I am grateful to the Eternal for having inspired me to act at once to keep you from avenging yourself. May your enemies be condemned before the Eternal even as Nabal stands convicted this day before the Eternal God for the animosity Nabal has shown to you my lord and for the contempt he has expressed to your men."

Vs. 27.29 "Pray accept my modest gift for the great service that you and the men who follow your leadership have bestowed upon us. It has indeed enriched our wellbeing. Pardon my boldness, any act of violence would be a blot upon your conscience, for you are destined by the Eternal to build a dynasty faithful to the Eternal God's standards of justice. You who are to become dedicated to fight the battles of the Eternal God of Israel must avoid the spilling of innocent blood. Turn away from your intentions to avenge yourself upon Nabal. May no evil act be charged against you, that it may disturb your conscience and your peace. I pray that he (Saul) that is intent upon pursuing you to take your life, shall be deterred from his goal. May the Eternal God keep you bound (safe) in the bundle of life (good health, mentally and physically). May your security ever remain in God's care because of your

I SAMUEL CHAPTER 25

virtuous desire to fling your enemies away from you, even as you succeeded by the hollow of your sling." (Goliath)

Vs. 30.31 "When the day comes that you assume the throne, let not this action which you have planned become a stumbling block upon your past record. Take not the law into your hands my lord to spill innocent blood for vengeance belongs to the Eternal God. Should you heed my plea my lord, *ulehoshia adoni lo* and reject your desire for vengeance, your self control shall prove your salvation and a sign of great courage. When that day comes remember your maid for having kept you from your evil determination."

Vs. 32.35 David replied to Abigail, "Praised be the Eternal God of Israel who granted me the merit to meet you. I bless your prudence that has earned my eternal blessings. I am grateful to you for having restrained me from causing you any harm. Had you not come to intercept me, not a single male would have survived my hand before daybreak tomorrow." David accepted Abigail's gift and then said to her, "Go up to your home safely. I have heeded your plea. Your decision to confront me was providential."

Vs. 36.39 Abigail came home to her husband in the midst of a feast. Nabal was in a merry mood and high from much wine. She waited until the next day to describe her experience with David. When she told Nabal the details of her experience and the generous gift which she bestowed upon David, Nabal had a heart attack. Nabal's heart turned dead like a stone, he probably suffered a stroke. Three factors came together to create the final shock of Nabal's life. His will had been thwarted, Abigail's generous gift and the possible tragedy which his incorrigible character could have brought upon his household to destroy all that he had achieved in a lifetime. About ten days later Nabal died as a result of his stroke. When David was informed of Nabal's death he offered a prayer of gratitude, that Nabal died as a result of his own lifestyle, a just punishment for his intransigence and greed. David was grateful to the Eternal God of history, "Who intervened in my behalf and sent me His *malach*-Abigail, to redirect my desire for vengeance." Some time passed by and David remembered Abigail's plea in v.31, "Remember your maid Abigail." David sent messengers to propose marriage to Abigail.

Vs. 40.44 When David's messengers came to bring Abigail to him, she responded spontaneously and offered to perform any menial task when she would marry David. Abigail obviously a wealthy woman recognized the years which shall pass by, that she may have to conform to the life of David's fugitive existence before he can achieve the promise of becoming the king of Israel. However, when she looked back upon years of living with the incorrigible Nabal, even "washing the feet of David's servants" will be acceptable to her. Abigail hastened to join David's messengers. She mounted her donkey while her five maids in attendance followed her to make

I SAMUEL CHAPTER 25

a new life as David's wife. David was already married to Ahinoam from Jezreel in Judah. Abigail became David's second wife.

V. 44. In (I Sam. 18:20) Michal the daughter of Saul became David's wife. In one of king Saul's moments of distress he gave Michal to Palti the son of Laish from Gallim (Is. 10:30). (See Addendum, page 277 for all the details regarding Michal and David).

I SAMUEL CHAPTER 26

V. 1 Once again the Ziphites came to Gibeah to report David's whereabouts to Saul (I Sam. 23:14.21). This time they reported that David is in the Wilderness of Judah, in the Hills of Hachilah. We may conclude that David's reason for coming north from the Wilderness of Paran is to be closer to Maon and Carmel (I Sam. 25:40.42).

Vs. 2.5 Despite Saul's goodwill expressed in (I Sam. 24:17.23) Saul responded to his evil inclination and mobilized his special force of 3000 men to search for David in the Wilderness of Judah, in the Hills of Hachilah. These hills face Hajeshimon-the wasteland on the west bank of the Dead Sea. Saul did not go into the forest but made his camp close to the main roadside. When David learned of Saul's presence in the area, he sent scouts to confirm the information. Having validated the information that Saul was in the area David rose upon one of the high hills to observe the layout of Saul's camp by moon light. David took note of Saul's position by the camp fire, that Abner the son of Ner was sleeping close to Saul and the troops slept in a circle around them.

Vs. 6.11 When David returned from reconnoitering Saul's military camp his men questioned him and he reported to Ahimelech the Hittite, a soldier of fortune in David's force and to Abishai the son of Zeruiah the brother of Joab. David asked for a volunteer to join him to go into Saul's camp. Abishai volunteered to go with David. They both went down to Saul's camp and observed Saul fast asleep inside the barricade, his spear was stuck in the ground close to his head. Abner and the troops were sleeping around Saul. Abishai asked David for permission to go down and thrust his spear at Saul. He assured David only one thrust wil accomplish his desire to pin Saul to the ground under him. "This is your opportunity to eliminate your enemy." David warned Abishai against any violent act against the anointed of God. "The time will come for him to die. I am forbidden by the Eternal's moral law to raise my hand against him. Let us take his spear and his water jug and be on our way."

V. 12 David did not trust Abishai with this sensitive feat, he feared Abishai lacked the restraint to activate his thought. David took Saul's spear and his jug of water and left as stealthily as they came.

I SAMUEL CHAPTER 26

Vs. 13.16   David crossed over to another mountain peak. Having established a reasonable distance from Saul's camp, he shouted across the canyon to awaken the troops and then directed his call to Abner. Abner shouted back, "Who are you?" David answered, "You, who was chosen to guard the king, where were you when one of our men came to strike the king? You deserve to die because of your negligence to duty. Look about for the proof. Where is the king's spear and his jug of water?"

Vs. 17.20   Saul recognized David's voice as it pierced the darkness of night. "Is that you my son?" David replied, "Yes, why do you persist in pursuing me? What is my guilt? Had the Eternal proffered charges against me, I would be given the opportunity to defend myself and clear myself by an offering for my innocence. However, if you pursue me because of men who have instigated you against me to drive me out of the Holyland, my rightful heritage, to force me to worship other gods, may these men be cursed before the Eternal (I Sam. 24:10). If I am to die let me die in the Holyland where those responsible for my demise will be held accountable by Israel's standards of justice in accord with Torah law. Why does the king of Israel stoop to pursue a single flea as if he were pursuing a partridge in the hills?" David has reference to the 3000 men who have been diverted from their normal duties to police the country.

V. 21   Saul replied to David, "Come back to me my son! I recognize my sin. I shall cease my effort to harm you. I recognize your dedication to my welfare, that my life is sacred and precious to you. I have erred and acted foolishly."

Vs. 22.23   David replied to Saul, "Here is the spear of your majesty. Send one of your men to retrieve it. May the Eternal render His reward to each of us in accord with His ability to recognize our righteousness and the sincerity of our faith and dedication. Though the Eternal challenged me this day (by giving me the opportunity) to strike you down, I dared not raise my hand against the anointed of the Eternal God of Israel."

Vs. 24.25   "It is my fervent prayer that the Eternal shall enlarge His protective custody over my life as a reciprocal reward for my disciplined evaluation of your life this day. May the Eternal deliver me from every dangerous situation."

V. 25. Saul answered David, "May you be blessed my son David. You shall achieve, and you shall prevail." David then went his way, and Saul returned home to Gibeah.

I SAMUEL CHAPTER 27

Vs. 1.4   David the realist recognized the odds of escaping Saul's pursuit are getting slimmer with every passing day. David has

I SAMUEL CHAPTER 27

become firm in his resolution to leave Israel and become out of bounds to Saul's reach. David completed his negotiations with Achish the son of Maoch, the king-governor of Gath a province of the Philistines. His men took their families with them and David took his two wives Ahinoam the Jezreelite and Abigail the former wife of the late Nabal the Carmelite and migrated to Gath. When Saul heard of David's flight to Gath, he resigned himself to the fact that David is out of bounds for him. This psychological fact should have been therapy for Saul's psychopathic condition.

Vs. 5.7   Arriving in Gath, David thanked Achish for his asylum. David soon realized that it would be more advantageous not to expose himself in this capital city of Philistia. He therefore requested and was granted permission to occupy the community of Ziklag. Ziklag is 11 miles southeast of Gaza. In (Joshua 15:31) Ziklag is part of the Judean heritage now in Philistine hands. David remained in Ziklag one year and four months.

Vs. 8.9   Geshuri, Girzi and Amalek are three distinct roaming tribesmen who roamed the Negeb area between Shur and the eastern border line of Egypt. This has been their lifestyle going back to the beginning of time. They were available at a price to anyone that hired them. At this point in history they were pilfering the Judean families in their allotted territory. The Geshuri in this verse have no relationship with the Geshurites established north of Havoth-jair. The Girzites in this verse have no connection with Gezer recorded in (Joshua 10:33, 12:12, 13:2, 19:5). We have met the Amalekites trying to do their thing in (Ex. 17:8.16, Num. 13:29, Jud. 6:3, I Sam. 15:1.3). What David is doing conforms with Israel's goal commanded in these verses. It also gave him the opportunity to take for himself and the men that fought with him the booty vital for their sustenance. He did not take any captives but shared his booty with Achish his host.

Vs. 10.12   When Achish inquired of David where they made their raid, David replied, "In the Negeb of Judah and in the Negeb of the Jerahmeelites and the Negeb of the Kenites. These tribes were identified with Israel going back to Jethro. Jethro's descendants who converted to Israel are now living in Arad in the territory of Judah. This convinced Achish of David's loyalty. There is another reason for David tearing out every root and branch of these marauding and pilfering tribesmen. Shur is the ancient transport route from Beer-sheba to Egypt. It is also called Darb el Shur. David's purpose is to clear this corridor for all time and not for the simple reason of booty. These tribes were the *shosim* in (Jud. 2:16). Achish was convinced of David's loyalty because his activity was in the area of the Judean Negeb.

I SAMUEL CHAPTER 28

Vs. 1.2 (I Sam. 14:52) Established Saul's capability to control Philistine aggression. The Philistines have now reevaluated their position in light of Saul's problems. Saul has dissipated his priorities by pursuing a phantom enemy. This enemy who was to succeed Saul is now in their hands and resigned to his fate. They have also discerned that Saul's psychological handicap has affected the morale of Israel's soldiers. This then is the propitious moment to administer a decisive blow to Israel. As a formality Achish says to David, "I anticipate that you and your men will join us in this action against Israel." David answered Achish flippantly, in an ambiguous manner, "Obviously you know what your servant will do." Achish is pleased with David's reply. "In that case I will appoint you as my body guard for life."

V. 3 This verse is introduced at this point to explain Saul's position on a law of the Torah (Lev. 19:31). Do not invoke the dead through oracles; creating the illusion of getting answers to questions. To become ensnared and enslaved by oracles is to lose our independence and freedom of action. *Tumah*, is moral and mental subjection. *Kedushah*, is moral and spiritual elevation which leads to *reach nichoach*- contentment and peace. See T.E.T. for an enlargement of this subject (Lev. 20:27, Deut. 18:9.22). During Saul's lifetime he strove to abolish the practice of necromancy, spiritualism and all its ramifications. Samuel is dead. There is no doubt about this fact, he was eulogized by multitudes who witnessed the burial of Samuel. They were present as he was lowered into a grave he chose during his lifetime in his own homestead in Ramah. This verse is contrasted with v.7, to describe the extent of Saul's loneliness, the depression which occupied every breath that he took.

V. 4 The Philistines mobilized for war and marched on to Shunem and pitched their camp. Saul countered by camping at Gilboah. This was Israel's final choice for the battle (I Sam. 31:1). Therefore (I Sam. 29:1) should be the first order of the Philistines at Aphek and Israel countered this by mobilizing at Ayin in Jezreel. The Philistines went to Jezreel to counter Israel's action (I Sam. 29:11). It was at this point that Israel went to Gilboa and the Philistines went to Shunem, where the battle took place.

Vs. 5.6 Saul looked down from Mount Gilboa into the camp of the Philistines at Shunem, he is terrified at the sight. He has lost courage, he is afraid. Images of fright and panic emerge from his strife ridden soul. The reason v.3 precedes this verse is to establish the reality of Saul's hallucination. Samuel the representative of the Eternal God upon earth is dead. Saul has recapitulated the details of the experience to prove it. Saul has visions of the priests of Nob pointing their finger at him and charging him with their murder. Saul recollects David's challenge to his integrity (I Sam. 24:12,23, 26:21.25). Saul is surrounded by his valorous soldiers awaiting his order. Saul lacks the courage to issue an order. He desires the assurance of a miracle. Samuel

I SAMUEL CHAPTER 28

is dead, the Kohanim are dead, the *Urim Vetumin* are with Abitathar (I Sam. 22:18.23) who fears Saul's presence. Saul thinks back to that day in Ramah (I Sam. 9:9.10, 19:23.24). Saul has no one to turn to, to bolster his courage, to assuage his fear, to calm his trembling heart. Saul's desire to live is gone, he has lost his spirit. V. 6. Saul prayed to the Eternal, he felt no response, he could dream no dreams nor visualize a solution. Abiathar rejected him, the prophets at Ramah ignored his pleas.

Vs. 7.8 Clearly describes Saul's mental condition as he requested the services of a woman that can divine a ghost. Saul is informed there is a woman in En-dor who has the ability to consult ghosts. V. 8. Saul changed his princely garments and disguised himself. He then set out under cover of darkness with two men from Israel's camp at Gilboa. The distance from Gilboa to En-dor is about four miles. The route they were obliged to take was treacherous because they had to avoid the Philistine camp at Shunem. Arriving at the home of the woman, the witch of Endor, Saul requested that she divine for him the medium of a ghost, the personality that I shall name for you.

V. 9 The woman called Saul's attention to the king's decree against necromancy and all other manner of witchcraft. She reminded him that those reported divining a ghost and found guilty became subject to the death penalty. "What you are requesting could become a trap for me."

V. 10 Saul took an oath in the name of the Eternal God, that she will not be punished for her service to him. Saul's inconsistent oath is a desecration of (Ex. 20:7) a basic commandment of the Torah. He is vowing to desecrate a moral and ethical discipline. By perjuring himself, Saul exposed himself to the severest penalty: death. The Eternal holds each individual responsible for a false oath. A false oath is the abomination that destroys all human development. Saul's first misstep in this matter was to request the services of witchcraft. His second desecration was to take a false oath. He thereby activated the daemonic process in the dark recesses of his subconscious. Saul's guilty conscience is fuelling the process of his neurosis. When Saul divested himself of his Zelem Elohim, his godly image, his capacity for intelligence, he permitted the daemonic virus to feed on his neurosis.

Vs. 11.12 The woman having agreed to divine a ghost for her visitor now asked Saul whose ghost he desired her to bring forth. When Saul asked for Samuel, the woman shrieked out loud, she was now certain that he is Saul for only he would be interested in divining the spirit of Samuel. She now sees clearly the trap the king had ensnared her into. The woman challenged Saul, "Why did you deceive me?"

Vs. 13.14 The woman's shriek as she recognized Saul, served her purpose that she recognized her ghost. It also set the mood for her seance. The woman's ecstatic outburst warmed to Saul's

I SAMUEL CHAPTER 28

possessed soul in the necromantic state. Her clairvoyance proceeded to develop by intuitive perception the special relationship between her guest the king and Samuel the apparition. It has been public knowledge that Saul could not put Samuel out of his mind (I Sam. 15:35, 16:1) neither could Samuel forgive himself for having been the cause of Saul's neurosis and depression. Saul is impressed with the woman's intuitive comprehension of his problem. He now begins to feed the *fraud* with questions of reality. Saul asked, "What do you see in your traumatic experience that caused you so much anguish?" The woman replied, "I see a godlike human being coming up from the earth." Saul desired confirmation of her apparition, "What does he look like?" The woman replied, "It is an old man that I see covered with a robe (I Sam. 15:27)." Saul is satisfied that the woman is possessed of genuine occult powers as she heightened her perception to prove her clairvoyance. Saul is deeply impressed by the genuineness of her apparition. Saul prostrated himself with his face to the ground as he visulaized Samuel's presence.

V. 15 Saul anticipated Samuel's anger for disturbing his rest in the grave as he once again conjures up that terrible scene (I Sam. 15:26.30). Saul recalls a thought which has incubated in his mind during his distressful days and nights that Samuel is angered because he had called him before the bar of justice. Saul is quick to change the mood and the subject. "Samuel! I need your help! The Philistines are encamped against me. I have prayed for guidance to the Eternal God of Israel. He has turned away from me. The prophets whom you have inspired to guide the leaders of Israel have rejected me. They refuse to analyze my terrible dreams. I am terribly in need of your help in these crisis filled days."

Vs. 16.18 Samuel replied to Saul, "Since you are aware that the Eternal has forsaken you because you have disregarded His instructions, the Eternal has decided that you go it on your own. He has become your adversary because you modified His decision in the war of the Amalekites. It was at that moment that I was instructed that the Eternal rent the monarchy from your leadership and gave it to David. I can now tell you, your crisis did not begin this day. It was a long time in its coming before the Eternal forsook you completely. Your second blunder was the tragic destruction of the Kohanim in Nob. It was at that moment that the prophets rejected you. Your third misstep occurred when David remonstrated with you and you did not honor your promise (I Sam. 24:17.23, 26:21). It was at that moment that the Eternal abandoned you because you failed to challenge your conscience, you refused to examine your conduct. What have you done to awaken the Eternal's mercy? The Eternal is no adversary. Satan is a human creation."

V. 19 "Now as to your immediate problem. Because of your malfeasance in office as the leader of Israel, the nation shall be

I SAMUEL CHAPTER 28

defeated by the Philistines. Tomorrow, you and your sons shall join me in the grave."

Vs. 20.25   Saul was terrified by Samuel's prediction. He fell to the ground in a complete faint because he had not eaten for 24 hours. It was at this critical moment that the woman ceased being a fraud and recognized the reality of Saul's condition. She pleaded with Saul that he calm his terror stricken mind as he emerged from his soliloquy with Samuel. The woman urged Saul to partake of some food which he continued to reject. She therefore said to Saul, "I have listened to you and heeded your request, even though my conduct was punishable by death. Now, you listen to me and be attentive to my advice. I shall place some food before you that you regain your strength to return to your responsibilities." Saul refused, the two companions who came with him urged him and he listened to them. He rose from the ground and sat on the bed. The woman hastily slaughtered a calf, baked some unleavened cakes and set the prepared food before Saul and his companions and they ate. They then returned to camp Gilboa that very night.

Sadya, Hai Gaon, Nachmanidies, agree the witch had no special powers. Saul came knowing his fate. The spirit of Samuel was with Saul every day of his life as king of Israel. Saul volunteered the leads which gave the sorceress the clues to pursue her medium.

Rabbi Samuel ben Hofni Gaon, Maimonidies, Ralbag, Ibn Ezra, confirm the procedure as a fraud.

Maimonidies ... Concludes that after having examined all the literature on the subjects of: Ghosts, Mantics, Mediums, Horoscope, Supersitition, Fortune Telling, Spiritualism, Astrology, Divination, Teraphim, Incantations, Soothsayers, Sorcery, Magic, Witchcraft, Snake Charmers, Good luck-Bad luck symbols, Mediums, Intoxicating Drugs, Ecstacy, Necromancy, Divine Powers.

Maimonidies concludes "All these mediums are lies and falsehood. These are the mediums through which the ancient world was led astray. These are the mediums through which the modern world is being led astray. In 1300 BCE. the Torah concluded (Num. 23:23) "There is no enchantment in Jacob, neither is there any divination in Israel."

"Whoever believes in these Torah forbidden practices are the fools, the retarded whose minds are impaired. What the Torah has forbidden are not words of wisdom but methods of confusion and vanity. The Jewish prophets saw these methods and procedures as falsifying the name of God."

Isaiah 29:4, Jeremiah 27:9:10, 8.9, Ezekiel 12:24,13:6.9,17, 21:26, 22:28, Isaiah 57:3, II Kings 21:6, 2 Chronicles 33:6, Micah 3:11.

Recognizing the above enumerated practices existing in human societies to which the Hebrews became exposed in ancient civilization, the Torah established the *Urim Vetummim* and the prophetic personalities whose allegiance is to the Divinely inspired laws of the Torah (Ex. 28:30). Rashbam ... reminds us that the *Urim Vetummim* were not to be used as an Oracle. The High Priest wore the *Urim Vetummim* when critical questions arose which begged for honest answers,

I SAMUEL CHAPTER 28

that basic to this symbol was the unity of Israel. The Kohen Gadol's counsel must reflect at all times *Urim*, the light of the Eternal God, the *Zelem Elohim* given in the spirit of *Vetummim* in perfect justice to all mankind.

For additional information on the above subject, see The Eternal Torah on: Lev. 19:26,31.32, 20:1.6 ... Deut. 13:13.19, 18:9.15, 19:14.

I SAMUEL CHAPTER 29

Vs. 1.2   This verse is a continuation of (I Sam. 28:2) the Philistines camped at Aphek and Israel camped at Ain-Jalud in Jezreel. The Philistines were organized in accord with their numerical units and the rear guard was represented by Achish and his commitment to the Philistine forces. In this group David and his men were represented.

Vs. 3.5   When the Philistine generals saw David and his men as they passed in review, they challenged Achish's good judgment in permitting David to join their forces. Achish defended his position, "He has been with me for more than a year (I Sam. 27:7) ever since he defected from Israel. I trust him implicitly." The Philistine generals are determined that David and his men shall not march into battle with them, "Lest he become an adversary and turn upon us in battle. How else can he appease his Eternal God but with the heads of our soldiers. Remember! He is the David of whom it is popularly related, "Saul has slain thousands; David, his tens of thousands."

Vs. 6.11   Achish summoned David and reported the conclusion of the Philistine generals. Achish took an oath in the name of the Eternal God of Israel, to assure David of his faith in him. "Go back to Ziklag in peace and let us not displease the lords of Philistia." David's charmed life is reflected in this turn of events (I Sam. 28:1.2). David is elated that he has been discharged from his terrible guilt of becoming an adversary of his kinsmen. However, he played his part as he challenged Achish to state his reasons for being disqualified. "You are as acceptable to me as the angel of God. I have no reason to doubt your loyalty to me. However, I cannot risk the displeasure of the generals." Vs. 10.11. Achish advised David that he plan with his men to stay the night and leave for Ziklag the next morning. David arose at dawn and left for Ziklag and the Philistine army left Aphek for Jezreel.

I SAMUEL CHAPTER 30

Vs. 1.2   Three days after they were discharged from the Philistine army, David and his men arrived in Ziklag, a distance of about 80 miles. Arriving in Ziklag they were faced with a terrible disaster. An Amalekite group had raided Ziklag, they destroyed the city by fire and carried off the women and children. At this moment they had no idea

I SAMUEL CHAPTER 30

whether they were killed or carried off as captives to be sold in the slave market in Egypt. This could not have been the same group recorded in (I Sam. 27:8.9).

Vs. 3.6 When David and his men evaluated the loss of their families, their tragedy came home to them. David's two wives Ahinoam and Abigail were included in the missing. The bitterness of their experience emerged as they wept and recognized their dereliction in not leaving some of the men behind to guard their families. They blamed David for his commitment to Achish to join him in the Philistine war. A war which raised tremendous soul searching for them. The indignation of David's men rose to the point that they charged him with this tragedy and threatened to stone him.

Vs. 7.10 David consulted with Abiathar the son of Ahimelech in front of the *Urim Vetummim*. The question David put, "Shall he pursue the search for the raiders? What are the chances of his finding them? Will he succeed if he does catch up with them?" David received Abiathar's confirmation through the *Urim Vetummim*, that he will succeed in all these three areas for in reality they form but one question, is it advisable. David mobilized his men and marched to Besor, the Wadi esh-Sheirah, which flows from Gaza into the Mediterranean Sea. From this verse we gather they started out the same day they returned from Aphek, a journey of about 80 miles. Many of the men were exhausted as they arrived at Besor which is about 25 miles from Ziklag. Obviously drained by their mental anguish and depressed because of their tragedy, David and his men agreed to excuse about 200 of their men to remain here to recuperate from their traumatic experience.

Vs. 11.12 David took 400 of his men and journeyed from Besor in search of the marauders. While traveling they came upon an Egyptian young man who was left behind by his master because he was too ill to go on. David revived the young man with food and drink, they also gave him part of a pressed fig cake and two cakes of raisins. After he ate and drank water he revived himself from his dehydration for he had not eaten for 72 hours.

Vs. 13.15 David then questioned the young man, "To whom do you belong and where are you from?" The Egyptian replied, "I am an Egyptian slave of an Amalekite. My master abandoned me when I took sick three days ago. We had been on a raiding mission in the negeb-south. We began with the Cherethites on the Mediterranean coast and we raided some Judean settlements in the territory of Caleb. We then went north to Ziklag and raided it and then destroyed it by fire." David asked the youth if he could lead them to this Amalekite group? The Egyptian replied, "I will take you there if you take an oath not to kill me or to return me to my master."

Vs. 16.17 The young Egyptian led David and his men down to the Amalekite camp. They were spread all over the ground feasting on the spoils which they had taken from the

I SAMUEL CHAPTER 30

Cherethites-Greeks-Philistines and from the Judeans. David and his men rested that night in the area of the Amalekite raiders. At dawn the next morning they attacked them all that day until eventide. Of all that made up this large group only about 400 escaped on their camels.

Vs. 18.20 David and his men succeeded in liberating their families including David's two wives. They recovered most of their personal chattels. They then created a division between the flocks of sheep and herds which represented their personal property and the flocks and herds which they gained by this Amalekite raid. David's men triumphantly announced as they drove them ahead of their line of march, "This is David's spoil."

Vs. 21.22 Returning to Besor, they greeted the men that they left behind. The ruffians in David's group who returned from their action chided those that were left behind, "You shall not receive any part of the booty which we have recovered from the Amalekites. Take your wives and children and be on your way." They refused to recognize their rightful title to the property which originally belonged to them.

Vs. 23.25 David rejected this greedy interpretation. "We must recognize our collective good fortune, that the Eternal God protected us from harm, returned us safely and reunited us with our families. Who could agree with your egotistic self-interest in this matter? He that remains in camp protecting our personal property is as actively involved as those that take part in battle. They are entitled to their equal share." David established this ruling as a precedent for all future time.

Vs. 26.31 When David returned to Ziklag, he sent gifts to the elders of Judah and to his friends. "This gift he announced is from the spoil taken from the enemies of the Eternal God." David sent gifts to Beth-el, Ramoth in the negeb, Jattir, Aroer, Shiphmoth, Eshtemoa, Racal, the cities of Jerachmeel, the Kenites in Arad, Hormah, Bor-ashan, Athach, Hebron, and to all the places where David and his men wandered in the Negeb of Judah during Saul's traumatic pursuit of David and his men. What comes through to us in the 20th century is the development of a charismatic personality endowed with an abundance of natural ability. At this stage we see his skill in military leadership, his poetic and musical talents. His genuine idealism that has its roots in Torah disciplines. David's relationship with Jonathan, (I Sam. 18:1,3.5, 20:8,17,41.42, 23:16.18). David's statesmanship and his unlimited dedication to Saul the anointed of God and his speeches to Saul in (I Sam. 24:9.23, 26:17.25). David's ability to negotiate (I Sam. 29:6.9). David's gratitude to people who helped him during these trying years as expressed by the above abundance and generosity comes directly from his heart which created the momentum of goodwill, the spontaneous ability to create graciousness and recognition in the sight of both man and God.

I SAMUEL CHAPTER 31

Vs. 1.3 When Saul returned from the witch of En-dor, the battle was already in progress. The pressure was intensive, it became a rout with many casualties right from the start of the action. What was lacking was the key to Israel's failure, no leadership from the top. The rank and file in the army felt this traumatic experience. The Philistines searched for and found the positions controlled by Saul and his capable sons. Saul is a completely disoriented man and the Philistines know it. Their intention is to destroy every vestige of those responsible for governing Israel. The archers therefore concentrated upon Saul's position.

Vs. 4.6 These verses confirm Saul's exhaustion both mentally and physically. His neurosis has drained every desire to survive.
He therefore commanded his armor-bearer to kill him. Saul pleads with him, "Better that you do it than the Philistines, who shall gloat over their heroic feat." The armor-bearer is terrified by the very thought of killing his king the anointed of the Eternal God of Israel. Saul summed up his courage and fell upon his sword. The spontaneous reaction of the armor-bearer as he witnessed his king's lifeless body swoon to the ground was to join him in death as he was proud to serve him in life. Israel's tragedy was enlarged as Saul's three sons, Jonathan, Abinadab and Malkishua, who fought valiantly died the same day with their father the king.

V. 7 The residents who lived in the towns north of Jezreel fled before the Philistine onslaught. The Philistines did not penetrate into Trans-Jordan. Jabesh and Mahanaim remained in Israel's possession (v.12, II Sam. 2:8). The Philistines resettled every community that was evacuated by Israel. Two centuries have elapsed since the Philistines entered the Holyland en masse almost simultaneously with Joshua's entry into the Holyland. They succeeded in uniting their communities under five serens-governors or kings. During these centuries they never lost sight of their goal to conquer all of the territory west of the Jordan. They are now well on their way to achieve their goal. Israel's defeat is the result of a lack of leadership and the dissipation of their physical and moral vitality. Israel's Manifest Destiny is rooted in a united nation under the Eternal God of Israel and governed by the disciplines inscribed in the Torah. When Israel will unite internally under the demands inscribed in the Torah, then and only then will the Messianic dream spread its canopy of peace to all of humanity.

Vs. 8.10 The day after the battle, the Philistines returned to strip the dead of their clothes, to retrieve armaments left behind and any and all possessions of value. It was at this time they discovered the bodies of king Saul and his three sons that fell in the battle at Gilboa. They cut off the head of Saul, stripped his armor and sent his head to their houses of worship where it remained on display to express their complete victory over Israel. The bodies of king Saul and his sons were hung upon the outerside of the wall surrounding the city of Beth-shan.

I SAMUEL CHAPTER 31

Vs. 11.13 When the inhabitants of Jabesh-gilead learned of the desecration of Saul's body and the hanging of the bodies of Saul's three sons on the wall of Beth-shan, they organized a military force to retrieve the bodies. They started their journey at sunset, traveled all that night as they crossed the Jordan River westward and recovered the bodies of Saul, Jonathan, Abinadab and Malkishua from the wall of Beth-shan east of Gilboa. They took their bodies back to Jabesh and cremated them because the bodies had become decomposed. They then gathered their remains and buried them under the tamarisk tree in Jabesh. They observed seven days of mourning for the loss of these noble personalities and fasted to honor their memory. The tribes in Jabesh thereby expressed their gratitude to Israel's first king who came to their defense against the Amonites in (I Sam. 11:11, II Sam. 1.12).

Though 3000 years have passed by since the death of king Saul, we the readers in the 20th century must empathize with this noble human being. In the course of writing this commentary, my sympathy for Saul grew with every passage that I analyzed, dissected and weighed its merits. Saul's victories for Israel are heroic. Our sympathy for him grows as we observe his inner conflict. Saul's virtues, his generalship are marks of a noble human being. His modesty led him to believe he was inadequate for the great task of uniting the nation. We must challenge Samuel's lack of guidance as he had originally promised to follow the lessons of Moses: (Ex. 33:15.16, Num. 20:12, Deut. 3:28, 31:3, Joshua 1:7,10.13, Num. 27:16.20).

The scenes described in (I Sam. 13:14, 15:24.31,35, 19:24,28:15.19), win our deepest sympathy for Saul. Samuel who had dedicated his life to unite the nation failed in his guidance to the man he chose to achieve this herculean task.

I offer my gratitude to the Eternal God of Israel, for having granted me the inspiration and the impetus to create a commentary upon this difficult book to assist both student and scholar to recapture the early history of Israel.

Completed this 26th day of Elul 5741.

David Lieberman

ADDENDUM OF THE HISTORIC RECORD
of
MICHAL ... The daughter of king Saul and the wife of David

I Samuel 14.49	Establishes the genealogy of Merab and Michal as king Saul's daughters.
I Sam. 18:17.19	Describes king Saul's desire to give Merab to David though she was already bethrothed to Adriel of Mehola.
I Sam. 18:20.29	King Saul's motives for giving Michal to David and the conditions for his dowry.
I Sam. 25:44	King Saul took Michal from David and gave her to Paltiel son of Laish from Galim in Benjamin, about the time when David fled from Gibeah. David never divorced her.

When David was anointed by the prohpet Samuel, he was 18 years old. This was after his victory over Goliath. David's marriage to Michal and their separation took place within the framework of less than two years.

II Sam. 3:5	Ithream's mother was Eglah. I reject the effort made in Sanhedrin 19b, 21a, that Eglah is synonymous with Michal. David married Michal when he was about 19 years of age.
II Sam. 3:13.16	About two years later Michal became a pawn of history when she was given to Paltiel. Michal and Paltiel lived happily together is quite clear though they too had no children.
II Sam. 6:23	King David was 36 years old when he took Michal from Paltiel and brought her to Hebron. The description of Paltiel in Erubin 96a, is unworthy of the sages.
II Sam. 5:4.5	King David was about 35-36 years old at the unification of Israel.
II Sam. 6:20.23	Establishes for the record Michal's animosity toward David for having taken her from Paltiel and the happy life she lead with him though childless. From the record it is quite clear

that she never bore a child in her lifetime.

II Sam. 21:8	Merab had five sons with Adriel. The text is in error to call her Michal. San. 19b, explains this idiosyncracy that upon the death of Merab, Michal adopted and raised Merab's children.

Two ancient Hebrew MSS. on the book of Samuel read 'Merab' correctly.

THE ETERNAL TORAH

SAMUEL TWO
SHMUEL BETH

TABLE OF CONTENTS FOR THE BOOK OF II SAMUEL
can be used as a synopsis to summarize the whole book of II Samuel

CHAPTER 1
Pages 285.287

David is informed of King Saul's death and the demise of his sons, Jonathan, Abinadab and Malkishua. Vs. 17.27, David's lamentation as he mourned their tragic death.

CHAPTER 2
Pages 288.291

David returns to Hebron and is anointed as king of Judah. Vs. 5.7, King David pays tribute to the people of Jabesh-gilead for honoring the memory of King Saul and his heroic sons. He solicits their loyalty to his government.
Vs. 8.10, Abner counters by establishing Ish-bosheth as king of the other tribes of Israel in Mahanaim, east of the Jordan.
Vs. 11.32, David ruled in Hebron over the tribe of Judah for seven years and six months. The rest of the chapter is devoted to describe the friction between Abner and Joab, the son of Zeruiah, King David's sister, resulting in a fratricidal war.

CHAPTER 3
Pages 291.296

Vs. 1.5, record the names of King David's wives and the sons they bore while he ruled in Hebron.
Vs. 6.11, Abner's premeditated conflict with Ish-bosheth.
Vs. 12.21, Abner negotiates with David and lays the groundwork for a united kingdom under David.
Vs. 22.30, Joab intercepts Abner and kills him to avenge his brother Asahel's death in Gibeon.
Vs. 31.39, King David is hard put to express his distress and sorrow as he eulogizes Abner's death and curses the treachery of Joab.

CHAPTER 4
Pages 296.298

Without Abner, Ish-bosheth becomes a non entity. This feeling filters down to the lower ranks and leads to his assassination, by Baanah and Rechav.

CHAPTER 5
Pages 298.300

Vs. 1.5, Abner's groundwork comes to fruition as David is anointed as king of a united Israel.
Vs. 6.10, King David lays siege to Jerusalem and captures it from the Jebusites. The expansion of the Milo, is indicative of his ability to rule.
V. 11.12, Hiram, King of Phoenicia, expresses his confidence in King David's government by building a palace for him.
Vs. 13.18, King David expanded his family by adding wives and concubines. Listed here are the names of the sons born to him in Jerusalem.
Vs. 19.25, records Philistine reaction to the unification of Israel's government. They mobilized at Rephaim and were defeated by King David's army.

TABLE OF CONTENTS: II SAMUEL

CHAPTER 6
Pages 300.303

King David strives to consolidate the spiritual life of Israel by bringing the Ark of the Covenant from Baalah-Kiriat-jearim to his newly built Tabernacle in Jerusalem. The incident of Perez-uzzah. Michal's rebuke to David as he rejoiced in his effort to enrich Israel's spiritual national life.

CHAPTER 7
Pages 303.308

King David shares his inspiration with the prophet Nathan, that he is desirous to build a Temple.

Vs. 8.17, the prophet Nathan outlines the nation's priorities, before King David can fulfill his noble inspiration. In v.16, Nathan rewards King David for his effort in taking full possession of the pockets of resistance by promising that his dynasty shall be established forever.

Vs. 18.29, King David's soliloquy before the Ark of the Covenant in gratitude for the promise of an ongoing dynasty.

CHAPTER 8
Pages 308.311

Vs. 1.14, King David activated the prophet Nathan's instructions by expanding the Holyland to its maximum territorial promise.

Vs. 15.18, King David organized his government upon the principles outlined in the Torah, the pursuit of justice and righteous living.

CHAPTER 9
Pages 311.312

In keeping with his resolution, king David strives to redeem his vow to Jonathan. He adopted his son Mephibosheth and restored all of king Saul's landholdings to Mephibosheth.

CHAPTER 10
Pages 312.314

Vs. 1.5, King David conveyed his message of sympathy to Hanan, upon the demise of his father the king of Ammon. Their infamous conduct leads to war. Vs. 6.19, Ammon hired mercenaries to defend themselves against any attack by Israel. The text describes the strategy used by Joab, the successful conclusion of the war with Ammon and their indemnity to David's government.

CHAPTER 11
Pages 314.316

King David is determined to capture the city of Rabbah and its satelite communities. The incident of Bath-sheba, its tragic consequences ending in the death of Uriah the Hittite.

CHAPTER 12
Pages 316.319

Vs. 1.13, the prophet Nathan challenges king David's transgression with Bath-sheba. Vs. 14.23, King David's distress and prayer for the recovery of Bath-sheba's child. Vs. 24.25, the birth of Solomon and the reconciliation with the prophet Nathan, as he called him "beloved of God." Vs. 26.31, describes the conclusion of the war with Ammon.

TABLE OF CONTENTS: II SAMUEL

CHAPTER 13 Pages 319.322	The rape of Tamar by her brother Amnon. Absolom's revenge. Absalom flees to the home of his father-in-law Talmai, king of Geshur.
CHAPTER 14 Pages 323.325	Vs. 1.20, Joab intervenes to bring Absalom back to Jerusalem. He engaged the service of the woman from Tekoa. Vs. 21.24, King David orders Joab to bring back Absalom to Jerusalem and place him under house arrest in his home. Vs. 25.27, describe Absalom's personality. Recorded here are his three sons and one daughter called Tamar. Vs. 28.32, two years have past and Absalom is determined to enlist Joab's offices to intercede in his behalf. Vs. 33, King David is reconciled with Absalom.
CHAPTER 15 Pages 325.329	Vs. 1.12, Absalom plans and initiates rebellion against his father. Vs. 13.37, King David goes into exile with his retinue of loyal followers.
CHAPTER 16 Pages 329.331	Ziba double crosses Mephibosheth, as he supplies king David with his vital necessities of food. Vs. 5.14, Shimei the son of Gera, takes advantage of king David's distress at Bachurim. Vs. 15.23, Ahithophel advises Absalom to take possession publicly of his fathers concubines to establish his irrevocaable decision to capture the crown.
CHAPTER 17 Pages 331.334	Vs. 1.14, Ahithophel's advice for military action against David and his retinue is countered by Hushai. Vs. 15.22, King David is notified of Absalom's plan to attack him. V.23, Ahithophel's embarrassment led to his suicide. Vs. 24.26, King David arrived at Mahanaim about the same time that Absalom arrived with his soldiers led by Amasa at Gilead. Vs. 27.29, Shobi the son of Nahash, the brother of Hanun king of Ammon, Machir son of Amiel from Lo-debar and Barzillai the Gileadite from Roglim, came spontaneously to supply king David with their vital necessities.
CHAPTER 18 Pages 334.336	King David organized his army for action. By unanimous consent David was ordered to stay behind. He therefore ordered them to deal gently with Absalom. Vs. 6.15, the battle shaped up and spread to the forest of Ephraim. It was here that Absalom met his end. Vs. 16.18, having accomplished his goal Joab called off the pursuit. Absalom was interred at Yad Absalom. Vs. 19.32, describes the sensitivity of Ahimaaz the son of Zadok in his effort to convey the sad news to king David and his reaction when finally notified of Absalom's death.

TABLE OF CONTENTS: II SAMUEL

CHAPTER 19
Pages 336.340

Vs. 1.5, King David's mourning over Absalom creates a pall of gloom and guilt over king David's soldiers. Vs. 6.8, Joab confronts king David for mourning the death of Absalom. Joab demands that king David recognize the loyalty of his followers by accepting their sympathy. Vs. 9.16, King David initiates an effort beginning with Judah to close ranks for a new beginning as he plans to return to Jerusalem. Vs. 17.31, Shimei seeks king David's pardon. Ziba, is in the forefront of the reception. Mephibosheth's noble character in his showdown with Ziba in the presence of king David. Vs. 32.41, King David expresses his gratitude to Barzilai as his son Chimhan returns with king David to Jerusalem. Vs. 42.44, the age old animosity surfaces as the ten northern tribes vie with the tribe of Judah, to escort their king back to Jerusalem.

CHAPTER 20
Pages 341.343

Vs. 1.3, Sheba the son of Bichri, incites discension at this sensitive moment. King David returns to his palace. His first order was to separate himself from his concubines. Vs. 4.12, King David activates his desire to replace Joab as he appoints Amasa and charges him to pursue Sheba ben Bichri. The conflict is resolved as Joab kills Amasa. Vs. 13.26, Joab assumes command of the troops and pursues Sheba ben Bichri, to Abel-maacah. King David reorganizes his government.

CHAPTER 21
Pages 343.346

Vs. 1.9, King David is confronted by three consecutive years of draught and famine. The appeasement of the Nethinim-Gibeonites. Vs. 10.14, the reinterrment of the bodies of king Saul, his sons and his descendants who paid with their lives to appease the Gibeonites. Vs. 15.17, the war with the Philistines recorded here belongs to (2 Sam. 5:17.21). Vs. 18.22, to (2 Sam. 5:22.25).

CHAPTER 22
Pages 347.353

Vs. 1.51, King David's Song of Thanksgiving.

CHAPTER 23
pages 353.357

Vs. 1.7, Excerpts from the memoirs of king David, not included in the Book of Psalms.

CHAPTER 24
Pages 357.360

Vs. 1.9, King David orders a census to be taken Vs. 10.17, King David regrets his reason for the census and the method of taking it. Both do not conform to Torah law. The prophet Gad rebukes king David for his egotistic conduct. The prophet gives his king the opportunity to choose the method of his punishment. Vs. 18.25, upon the inspiration of the prophet Gad, king David purchases an altar site from Aravnah the Jebusite and thereby stays his punishment of the plague.

PREFACE TO THE BOOK OF II SAMUEL

Every scholar in history vies to enlarge upon King David's accomplishments and to treat his indulgences with sympathy and compassion. To help the reader grasp the grandeur of David the king, David the charismatic military leder and David the Psalmist, I shall summarize his life as it unfolded itself in the Book of Samuel.

(ISam.17:17.20,26,28.58), introduce David as a teen age shepherd. He volunteered to endanger his life for his king (Saul) and his people to become the man of the hour. (ISam.16:16.22), David's genius as a musician with the ability to write poetry and verse are recognized. From this moment David's star rises (ISam.18:1.5,14.16), as he proves his executive ability as a leader of men. It was in this interim period that the Prophet Samuel anointed him as king Saul's successor (ISam.16:13.)

The following events (ISam.18:28, 19:10, 20:1,41.42 21:7,10.11, 24:10.23, 25:32, 26:11.25, IISam.1:23.24, 2:4) took place in the 12 year period which elapsed from the day of his anointment, to the day he became king of Judah. David's Ode, "How have the mighty fallen?" led to the conclusion, they lacked the ability to defend themselves. He wrote Psalms and set them to music to create the dedication and the rhythm to teach the use of the newly invented brass bow. Two years later (IISam.5:15), he united the country and ruled from Hebron. At about the age of 37, David established his capital in Jerusalem and ruled there for 33 years. (IISam.8:1), King David destroyed the Philistine dream of expansion to the Euphrates.

(IISam.6:, 7.8.17,18.29) King David brought the Ark to Jerusalem in the hope that he will build The House in the name of the Eternal God of Israel, in order to unify the spirituality of Israel by a Central Sanctuary. The Prophet Nathan reminded his king of his priority to fulfill the mitzvah of *vehorashtem et haaretz*, to establish the security of the Holyland to its maximum perimeter as prescribed in the Torah. The Prophet Nathan consoled king David by promising him a Dynasty that shall endure to infinity. King David pours out his frustration before the Eternal.

As a dedicated soldier of the Eternal, David fulfilled his priority as recorded in chapters 8,9,10. From this high point in his career, chapters 11 through 20, represent the stress created by his lifestyle which led to his exile from Jerusalem. From this low point king David is inspired by (Gen.6.3, Ex.34:6.7) and rises once again. He expresses his innermost gratitude in chapter 22. This was the moment to build the Temple, the dream closest to his heart. Instead king David bypassed the opportunity as he became enticed by his ego to expand the Holyland into an Empire (IISam.24:). Every future event described in the Books of Kings are tied to this moment in the history of Israel.

David Lieberman

II SAMUEL CHAPTER 1

V. 1   When David returned from his encounter with the Amalekites described in (I Sam.30:17.19) he was completely unaware of Saul's death and the tragic outcome of the war with the Philistines. The action described in (I Sam.30:26.31) took place immediately upon David's return to Ziklag.

V. 2   Upon the third day after David's return to Ziklag a young man came to David in Ziklag and reported the death of king Saul and his son Jonathan. The text now contrasts a similar experience which is recorded in (I Sam.4:12), there, tradition established the personality as Saul and it described his *madav* torn clothes and soil upon his head to express his deep mourning for the national tragedy he is about to report. In this verse the text uses the term *begadav* to describe the treacherous deception as he flung himself to the ground to convey his loyalty to David as Saul's successor.

Vs. 3.4   David said to the young man, "Where are you coming from?" The young man answered, "I have just escaped from the camp of Israel." David pursued his inquiry, "What was the situation on the battlefield when you left? Tell me the details!" The young man described the scene how the troops fled from the battlefield. He told of the many soldiers slain by the Philistine onslaught, that both king Saul and his son Jonathan died in the combat.

Vs. 5.10   David challenged the young man reporting the news, "How do you know that Saul and his son are dead?" The young man replied, "I was present on Mount Gilboa and observed Saul leaning on his spear. It was clear to me that he was wounded by the Philistine archers. He was also aware that their horsemen were closing in on him to kill him. At that very instant he observed my presence and called to me. When I responded, he asked me to identify myself. I told him that I was an Amalekite. King Saul then requested that I kill him, for he was in agony from his wound, that the shudder of death was overtaking him. I then proceeded to honor his request that I kill him in order to put him out of his misery. It was clear to me that he could not survive after his spear had penetrated his body. I then took the crown from his head and his identifying armlet from his arm and brought them here to you my lord."

Vs. 11.12   David rent his clothes spontaneously. The men present at the hearing who observed his reaction rent their clothes to express their grief upon the national calamity, the death of king Saul and his son Jonathan. They wailed and wept in unison. To express their grief they fasted unto the evening of that day. They felt the impact of the tragedy which had overtaken the people of the Eternal and mourned with the House of Israel for all those slain in the battle.

Vs.13.16   The scene described in these verses took place after the full impact of the disaster had been assimilated and David

II SAMUEL CHAPTER 1

confirmed the truth of the young man's report. David now turned to the young man and questioned him in the manner of a judge in order to establish the extent of his implication in the death of Saul. "Where are you from?" The young man replied, "I am the son of a resident alien, an Amalekite." David challenged the young man's insolence, "How did you dare to raise your hand with the intent to kill the anointed of the Eternal God of Israel?" David issued his verdict as he called upon one of his attendant soldiers to kill him. As the soldier was about to strike the young man down, David verbalized his decree, "Your own mouth gave me the testimony which condemned you to death when you stated, 'I killed king Saul the Eternal's anointed in order to put him out of his misery.'"

Vs.17.18 David composed the following lamentation to commemorate the noble lives of Saul and his son Jonathan. Both the words and the tempo were to teach and inspire the discipline of archery in the ranks of Judah. This lamentation was composed to remember the heroic stand of all those who lost their lives on the mountain of Gilboa, because they were deficient in the skills vital for the defense of Israel. This Ode was inscribed in the Book of Yashar, which is mentioned only here and in (Joshua 10:13). Since scholars have never been able to prove the existence of a book called *Yashar*, we must conclude that *Yashar* is a noun and refers to the heroic record of Israel's righteous personalities recorded in the books which have become known to all of humanity as the Bible. David made his historic debut in (I Sam.17:12.58), from the record we can observe Jacob's prophetic evaluation of Judah stated in [Gen.49:8.12 and Moses' appraisal given in Deut.33:7] beginning to unfold itself See T.E.T. on the above mentioned verses.

V.19 "How have the mighty fallen?" With all the advantages of the hills of Gilboa, the pride of Israel's courageous and fearless heroes have fallen (I Sam. 14:1.16, 47.48). David's concern with finding the answers to his question repeats itself in vs.25,27. David concluded that Israel's weakness lies in their inability to match Philistine archery which is capable of inflicting the enemy from a distance and to adjust its fighting position to the need of the moment. "It is now obvious to me how the mighty have fallen."

V.20 "Do not publish this information in Gath, lest it become common knowledge in Ashkelon and all the principal cities of Philistia." This defect in Israel's capability will inspire the women of Philistia to encourage their men to greater military activity and to exult over their prowess to remove Israel from the Holyland (I Sam.18:6.7).

V.21 David utters a curse upon Mount Gilboa. "May no dew or rain descend upon you. May your fields become incapable of offering tithes to assuage your guilt, for having permitted the leather and wood shields of Israel's soldiers to become ineffective against the skill

II SAMUEL CHAPTER 1

of Philistine archers, as if they were not treated with oil." The impact of Philistine arrows penetrated the porosity of Israel's shields. (They had no metal shields I Sam.13:19.22). Saul too, shared the common fate of every soldier; though he was anointed by the sacred oil; for his weapons were inadequate to protect him. This is David's conclusion, "How the heroic soldiers of Israel had fallen."

V.22 "Despite Philistine superiority in arms, the bow of Jonathan never failed to draw the blood of his enemies. Nor did the sword of Saul return empty after it penetrated the source of Philistine presumptuousness."

V.23 "Saul and Jonathan, who had endeared themselves to everyone during their lifetime, shall continue in death as in life to bind their beloved memories to the immortal history of Israel. May Jonathan receive his reward for remaining loyal and dedicated to the wellbeing of his father, for the threat of death could not challenge his singleness of purpose to remain united in death even as in life. May history recognize their loyalty and dedication. Swifter than eagles and mightier than lions were Saul and Jonathan as they responded to the cause of Israel."

V.24 "Lament ye daughters of Israel over Saul's tragic death. It was he that deterred the Philistine and Ammonite enemy from pillaging the countryside. It was his protective custody that enabled you to live securely in order to wear your crimson finery and to display your jewels of gold to enhance your apparel (I Sam.14:47.48)."

V.25 "Women of Israel! Fathom the reason for Saul's death. How were these mighty warriors felled in the midst of battle? How did he, that rose from the valley of despair (I Sam.14:6,45,13:8.18) to victory, only to be slain upon the heights of Gilboa?"

V.26 "I grieve for you my brother Jonathan. My love for you shall persist long after your death. You have endeared yourself to me by your sincerity that originated from the depth of your soul. My love for you is the reciprocal recognition of your dedication and observance of *veahafta* to advance the brotherhood of man through the unity of the Eternal God (Deut.6:4.9,7:13). My love for you was on a higher level than the passing love of man for woman."

V.27 David persists in his original question. "How were these mighty men of war slain? *Vayovdu* they were slain because *kley milchamah* their weapons of war were inadequate for their defense."

II SAMUEL CHAPTER 2

V.1 Sometime after David discharged his moral obligation to mourn for his brother Jonathan and for king Saul, David began an analysis of his national position. At this moment in time he is dependent upon Philistine permission for any plan he may desire to undertake in order to translate the full meaning of his having been anointed to succeed king Saul. Twelve years have passed by since that day in (I Sam.16:12.13) David's life when he was anointed at the age of 18. Saul's pursuit to destroy him as his future successor has honed his experience. He is now a recognized leader with a nucleus of a military force. During Saul's lifetime David refrained from taking any position that would challenge Saul's authority. During these five years, David has dreamed dreams to implement his political and military experience. He recognized his dedication to the cause of Israel must ever be his contribution to unite Israel in order to fulfill its manifest destiny in the Holyland. Yet, because of his entanglements with the Philistines and their powerful control of all the territory east of Philistia to the Jordan River, he may not mount an organized effort to expel them from their new found hegemony. In light of the above analysis, David met with Abiathar and took counsel with him as he laid before him his plan for rebuilding Israel's political fortunes. David is desirous of negotiating with the Elders of the tribe of Judah, and to establish his government in the ancient city of Hebron. Its historic ties reach back to Abraham, Isaac and Jacob. Hebron is strategically situated 20 miles south of Jerusalem. Even at this early date David recognizes the future importance of occupying Jerusalem. Abiathar consulted with the authority of the *Urim Vethummim* and officially confirmed David's plans.

Vs.2.3 David negotiated with the Elders of the tribe of Judah and informed them of his intentions to establish his government in Hebron. V.4, establishes their agreement to recognize him as the king of Judah and confirms his choice of making Hebron his seat of government. David must now request and receive permission from Achish, one of the five governors kings of Philistia, with whom he has a treaty. V.2, confirms the fact that he received king Achish's consent to become king of Judah. But another example of David's charmed personality. It was the Finger of the Eternal God of history moving the pieces on the human chessboard. David left Ziklag with his whole household, which included his two wives Ahinoam the Jezreelitess and Abigail the former wife of the late Nabal, the Carmelite. David severed his connections completely with the city of Ziklag. This is confirmed by the fact that his move included all the men that have become identified with his political and military plans, to defend their national rights and to become the recognized ruler of Israel in accord with the full meaning of his anointment by the prophet Samuel
(I Sam.16:13). David's followers took their families from Ziklag in Philistia and settled them in the towns and villages surrounding Hebron.

V.4 Soon after David's arrival in Hebron, the Elders of Judah

II SAMUEL CHAPTER 2

officially anointed and installed David as the recognized king of Judah. It is inconceivable that David did not know the details recorded in (I Sam.31:11.13). Chapter one records every detail of David's grief. *Vayagidu le David lemor* David was informed that Abner, who was Saul's military captain, a cousin of Saul (his father Kish and Abner's father Ner were brothers), "He had made good his escape from the tragedy at Gilboa and has organized a small force to harass and oppose Philistine rule. Abner is now negotiating with the tribes of Trans-Jordan to enlarge his ability to regain control of Saul's original hegemony." It is David's control of Judah that gave Abner the courage to carry on his clandestine effort against Philistine occupation of the Holyland.

V.5 The above information prompted David to cement his loyalty with the tribes in Trans-Jordan. As king of Judah, David sent messengers to the Elders of Jabesh-gilead, to express his personal and national gratitude for having risked their lives to retrieve the bodies of king Saul and his three valiant sons (I Sam.31:11.13). "Your pious act of burying them with full honors and respect was befitting the anointed sovereign of Israel. You have earned the Eternal's recognition for the highest form of faithfulness and mercy."

Vs.6.7. David is aware of the strong ties between the tribes of Gilead and the house of Saul (I Sam.11:1.15), he therefore promised them not only recognition but a generous reward for their heroic deed. "None can be more certain that king Saul is dead than you who paid him your last respect as your sovereign king. I now request that you recognize me as the rightful heir to Saul's throne. I have been anointed by the prophet Samuel to succeed Saul. I have also been anointed by the tribe of Judah to govern as their king. Prove your loyalty to me by your valiant conduct even as you did to king Saul. I shall reciprocate your loyalty by generously rewarding you for your dedication by spreading my protective custody over you in times of distress."

Vs.8.11 After about five years of relentless effort to remove Philistine authority from many of Israel's communities, Abner took the initiative to crown Ish-bosheth, the last remaining son of Saul. He did not participate in any military effort because of a physical disability. Ish-bosheth is also known as Eshbaal in (I Chron.8:33, 9:39). Abner took Ish-bosheth to Mahanaim in Trans-Jordan, where he would be out of Philistine reach. Abner proved his statesmanship as well as his military capability by having turned around Israel's political condition as occupied territory of the Philistines. He was the rightful head of his government while Ish-bosheth was but the puppet king. Abner succeeded in rallying the following tribes to his cause: Reuben, Gad, the eastern branch of Manasseh and the tribe of Asher, who were the principal inhabitants of the plain of Esdraelon and the tribe of Benjamin. Abner now succeeded to establish a numerical majority for his government as the

II SAMUEL CHAPTER 2

rightful heir to Saul's dynasty. The Philistines looked on passively as Israel dissipated its national strength. The Philistines counted on David's loyalty. It anticipated the hope that David and Abner's goals shall come into conflict, they will then step in and take over handily the remains of their unsuccessful development. Ish-bosheth was 40 years old when he assumed the throne of Israel. He succeeded to reign for two years over the above recorded tribes while David ruled over the tribe of Judah in Hebron for seven years and six months.

V.12 Some time after Ish-bosheth was crowned by Abner in Mahanaim, Abner felt secure enough to move his seat of government to Gibeon, north of Jerusalem. Abner recognized this point in time to challenge David's ability to defend himself against his numerical majority.

V.13 The text now introduces the beginning of a fratricidal war which conformed with Philistine calculations. The principal characters on both sides of this political intrigue are blood relations of the ruling powers. Abner is the cousin of his puppet king Ish-bosheth. Joab is the son of Zeruiah, David's sister. Both of these men have grandiose political ambitions for themselves in the potential unification of Israel. David recognized Abner's tremendous potential as a dedicated statesman. From the record (I Sam.24:5,26:6.12) we observe David's fear of Joab and Abishai, they were eager to kill Saul.

Vs.14.18 In keeping with ancient military mores practiced by the indigenous population of the Holyland, Abner suggested a military match to Abner, to create the atmosphere for war as the lives of the combatants are snuffed out and become a challenge for revenge. From the term *vyisachaku* we observe how far Israel has strayed from Torah disciplines. Playfully they chose 12 men from each army, knowing full well that the results would be bloodshed and the beginning of a fratricidal war. Looking back from the 20th century, we observe the breach of the oral law recorded in (Gen.4:9.12,9:5.) and the written law in (Ex.20:13). In the course of this first engagement Abner and his army were routed by David's army which was well trained and led by Joab and his two brothers Abishai and Asahel, he was reputed to be as fleet on foot as a roe-deer (of the genus Careolus).

Vs.19.21 Consistent with Joab and Abishai's temperament, Asahel pursued Abner in order to destroy the real force behind the puppet Ish-bosheth. Asahel was relentless in his pursuit. Abner is reluctant to attack Asahel for he recognized the implications should he kill Asahel. Abner challenged Asahel to confirm his identity as he closed in on Abner. Validating his identity, Abner suggested that Asahel satisfy his ego by attacking one of his men and take his armor as a war memento. Asahel was adamant and refused to yield.

V.22 Abner pleaded with Asahel that he cease his pursuit, "Lest I

II SAMUEL CHAPTER 2

be forced to defend myself and strike you down. Should I kill you I shall become answerable to your brothers; this could set off a continuous vendetta with consequences to infinity."

V.23 Asahel was unyielding and ignored Abner's appeal. Abner then struck Asahel in the groin with the handle of his spear. It was his intention to wound him. However, Asahel's speed was his undoing as his body and Abner's spear were traveling in opposite directions. It caught Asahel under his fifth rib, in the area where the liver and the gall are suspended. Joab and Abishai's troops pursued Abner to avenge their brother's death. When they came to the spot where Asahel's body lay dead they froze in their tracks as they paused to mourn his death.

Vs.24.26 Joab and Abishai pursued Abner unto sunset of that day. When Abner reached the hill of Ammah which faces Giah leading to the wilderness of Gibeon, Abner regrouped his retreating troops and was determined to make a stand upon the hill. From the hill he called unto Joab, "Must the sword devour forever? Should you pursue me unrelentingly, you must anticipate the bitter feelings which your conduct will create in pursuing a policy of fratricide. I challenge you to call off your pursuit."

V.27 Joab replied, "Had you not spoken, we would have pursued you all through the night to morning of the next day. You, Abner, must assume your share of the guilt for the tragedy of this day. For when we met this morning it was as brothers until you initiated your challenge in v. 14. Were it not for your challenge, your desire for combat, every man that lost his life in this action would have returned home in peace to his family."

Vs.28.29 Joab blew the horn to signal the end of the pursuit of Abner. Abner ordered his troops to follow him as they marched all that night to the Arabah, the lowlands leading to the Jordan River. They crossed at Bithron and returned to Mahanaim.

Vs.30.32 Joab assembled his troops in order to call the roll. They recorded the loss of 19 troops plus Asahel. The text records the loss of 360 men in Abner's army as the result of his challenge to initiate the war of fratricide. Joab's men carried Asahel's body back to Bethlehem and laid him to rest in the family tomb. Joab then marched all that night and arrived in Hebron at dawn.

II SAMUEL CHAPTER 3

V.1 The ongoing vendetta between Abner of the House of Saul and Joab, the son of Zeruiah, David's sister, was a personal feud between these two protagonists. Their hostility goes back to the lifetime of Saul. The incident described in (II Sam.2:12.32) concluded with

II SAMUEL CHAPTER 3

the death of Asahel; Joab and Abishai's brother. It was the beginnng of *aruchah* an ongoing battle for personal interests which cost 360 lives of Abner's men and 20 of Joab's force. It must be clearly understood that Joab's vendetta was contrary to David's goal. It was a divisive effort which highlights the distance Israel has strayed from its constitution, the Torah, which outlines Israel's place in history and its manifest destiny to become "A light unto the nations of the world."

David's fortunes waxed stronger because his goals were directed to the one central theme, a united nation under the Eternal God of Israel. Abner dissipated his tremendous potential by feuding with Joab and following his own self interest. He stood ready to join any side that would grant him the greatest gain. David recognized his ability and was anxious to harness his potential capabilities for the welfare of the nation.

Vs.2.5   From these verses we learn that although David came to Hebron with two wives, he took unto himself four more wives for a total of six. Each of them bore David a son. Ahinoam bore Amnon, Abigail bore Chileab, Maacah bore Absalom, Haggith bore Adonijah, Abital bore Shephatiah, Eglah bore Ithream. (Contrary to some sources Eglah is not Michal. See Addenda on page 277 for detailed proof of this conclusion). See T.E.T. on (Gen.22:24, Deut.3:14) for the genealogy of the Maacatites and Talmai king of Geshur.

Vs.6.7   Under the guise of devotion to Ish-bosheth, Abner reached out to establish the meaning of his position in the government, that he is the rightful successor to Saul. After the death of king Saul, Rizpah the daughter of Aiah, was prepared to spend her widowhood in the palace of Ish-bosheth at Mahanaim. Because she was forbidden in marriage to another king (San.18a, laws of kings, Rambam ch.2,hal.2). Ish-bosheth reprimanded Abner for following the Near East custom that the marriage of a former king's wife bestowed legitimacy even to the aspirant to the throne (II Sam.12:8,16:21, I Kings 2:13.22). Ish-bosheth suspected Abner of intimacy with his father's concubine Rizpah.

V.8   Abner resented the accusation of Ish-bosheth. "You treat me as if I were the underdog in your government. Every day of my active life, I have served the House of Saul with utmost loyalty. Have I betrayed your cause? Even this very day I defended your interests at the risk of my life and you have the temerity to reproach me over a woman."

Vs.9.11   Abner took an oath, "Since you (Ish-bosheth) minimize the importance of my position in your government, I shall transfer my loyalty to David. I shall assist him in establishing his kingdom over a united country from Dan to Beer-sheba." Ish-bosheth kept his peace, for he now fully recognizes that Abner's arrogance was predicated upon a well thought-out plan of action. Only Abner's arrogant anger was

II SAMUEL CHAPTER 3

spontaneous. V.9, clarifies Abner's conclusion that he had made a mistake by crowning Ish-bosheth. Abner the strategist, Abner the statesman, recognized David's Divine destiny (I Sam. 24:21,25:30,26:25). Abner the statesman comprehends that he has made the wrong move because he placed his self interest above the welfare of a united Israel.

V.12   Abner implemented his bold stroke *tachtav* as he sent messengers to David at once. This move is Abner's last minute perception, his ego has overplayed its hand. Abner's message, *lemi arets* "It is I that controls the politcal power of the country, that desires to make a treaty with you. I have the ability to choose who shall govern Israel." David's sensitivity most certainly saw through Abner's *lemi arets*, even as David had the self control to overrule his ego in his dealings with Abigail in (I Sam.25:30, and his shrewd reply to Achish in 28:2). David ignored Abner's arrogance because he perceived Abner's cooperation would remove him as an enemy, an opposing force. Abner's copartnership could signal the loyalty of a whole new constituency for his government and would bring nearer the day for Israel's Manifest Destiny, "To become a light unto the nations of the world."

V.13   David agreed to accept Abner's offer to help him consolidate the political loyalty of the house of Saul, into David's camp. However, David made but one condition to test Abner's king-making capability, "Bring back to me Michal the daughter of Saul." David demanded that Abner prove himself by bringing Michal back to him or else forget about his plan of consolidating their forces. This was David's psychological reason to remove the insult imposed on him when Michal's father king Saul took her from him and gave her to Paltiel (I Sam.25:44). See addenda on page 277 for an enlargement on the legal, personal and historical ramifications concerning Michal.

Vs.14.15   David reinforced the demand made to Abner by sending a formal message to Ish-bosheth requesting the return of Michal. "Go back into the record to confirm my demand. I jeopardized my life to fulfill the demand made by your father king Saul that I earn my dowry as a precondition before he would grant me the right to marry Michal (I Sam.18:25,25:44)." David's pressure upon Abner and Abner's coercion upon Ish-bosheth produced the distress which initiated the order that Abner become the executioner of taking Michal by force from Paltiel to fulfill David's threat in v.13.

V.16   The text records the tragic scene as Abner took Michal by force from Paltiel. History records the details; how Paltiel wept all the way to Bachurim, to express his shattered feelings and great love for Michal, although she never bore a child to him or to David. Abner finally ordered Paltiel to go back to his home and reconcile himself to the *fate accompli*, that Michal as the daughter of king Saul must fulfill her position

II SAMUEL CHAPTER 3

in society as a pawn of history. Only then did Paltiel reconcile himself with his fate and return home to Gallim north of Jerusalem. The ramifications of this incident can be ignored by any other society where such actions are daily occurrences. In Israel we are concerned with the moral, ethical and legal ramifications in the life of one human being, the injustice involved continues to activate our conscience to demand justice for this injustice. In the Addenda on p. 277 I shall present every shred of evidence from the record and may the guilt fall where it belongs.

Vs.17.19 — The conference alluded to here was held before Abner's messengers met with David in v.12. Abner addressed the Elders of Israel, "You have expressed a desire in the past to offer David the opportunity to become your king. I recommend that this is the moment for you to implement your desire by action." From vs. 17.18, we learn that when king Saul died the northern tribes were ready to recognize David as the anointed successor to Saul. It was Abner's vigorous opposition that insisted that Ish-bosheth was the rightful successor to Saul. Abner's quote, "I will deliver My people Israel from the hands of the Philistines and all of its enemies through My servant David," is a complete fabrication. Abner invented it to convince the Elders that their original desire to recognize David's anointment by Samuel was authentic. Having succeeded with the northern tribes, Abner made a special plea to the tribe of Benjamin. He feared their opposition to unseat Ish-bosheth. Abner is now ready to inform David that he has won the unanimous consent of Benjamin and all the northern tribes.

Vs.20.21 — Abner chose 20 representative personalities of Israel, to escort Michal as he would make her presentation to David. David gave a banquet in their honor. Abner disclosed the results of his discussions with the various tribes. At the conclusion of the banquet Abner said to David, "I shall now rally the official representatives of Israel to come to Hebron for the purpose of ratifying our treaty with you. As my king you may then exercise your full potential in ruling over a united nation." David dismissed Abner and his representatives, he offered them his blessings that they go in peace.

Vs.22.23 — Before David met with Abner's messengers, he sent Joab on a military mission because he anticipated his violent opposition to Abner. V.22, reports Joab's return with abundant plunder to indicate the success of his mission. Fortuitously Joab returned after Abner had already left. When Joab learned of Abner's visit and that he had been permitted to leave peacefully, Joab's treacherous imagination tried to reestablish the picture and the substance of the negotiations.

Vs.24.25 — Joab's bitter hatred of Abner magnified and augmented his arrogant attack upon his sovereign. Joab challenged David's judgment for permitting Abner to come to Hebron and leave

II SAMUEL CHAPTER 3

peacefully. Joab's presumptuousness calculated that any negotiations with Abner indicated that his important position in David's government would be challenged. Joab reprimanded David, "How could you be so naive? To permit the clever Abner to come here in order to establish your coming and going, is to anticipate your future plans. Your dealings with him are contrary to your self interest."

Vs.26.27   Joab took his leave from David's presence determined to nip in the bud any plan that may jeopardize his position in David's government. Joab is determined to exercise his right for vengeance against Abner on the premise of Asahel's death (II Sam.2:19.23). Joab sent messengers to overtake Abner and to recall him to Hebron in the name of David. Abner was intercepted at the cistern of Sirah or Ain Sarah. When Abner arrived at the city gate, Joab requested a word with him *basheli* in private. When Abner yielded to Joab's request, Joab stabbed him in the groin. Centuries have come and gone since the Torah established disciplines to expose the barbarity of the law of the jungle and the survival of the fittest. See commentary in T.E.T. on the following verses (Gen.9:5.6, Ex.21:14, Num.35:16.21, Deut.19:2.7). Man persists in ignoring his zelem Elohim.

Vs.28.30   When Abner's death was reported to David, David issued a public statement. "I had no complicity in the death of Abner."

David reiterated in a public statement, that all of his negotiations with Abner were in good faith and based upon his desire to unite the country through the cooperation of Abner. "My kingdom shall forever be innocent before the Eternal God of Israel. I had no part in the killing of Abner. He who killed Abner and shed his blood did so as an act of treason against my efforts to unite the country to pursue peace in our borders. May the guilt of this beastly act fall upon the head of Joab and his father's house." David's frustration at the hands of Joab and Abishai climax his bitter feelings as David curses them and their posterity in this agonizing moment of his distress (Gen.49:5.7). To utter a curse in moments of tragedy is to lose self control over the self which activates reflexive psychological misery upon the curser and the one being cursed. David's intentions were noble; for he was pained and grieved as he calculated the tremendous setback of this tragic incident. However, his means of expressing his bitterness were ignoble. Joab's guilt should have been tried by a court of justice and penalized in accord with the evidence. David's curse was vain, it ended in a vendetta in (I Kings 2:5.6) when David instructed Solomon to kill Joab. The text corrects the record that both Joab and Abishai were equally guilty for killing Abner because Abner had killed Asahel their brother at the battle in Gibeon.

Vs.31.32   David issued an order to Joab and all his courtiers to declare and implement a period of mourning by rending their clothes and to gird their bodies in accord with the ancient custom of wearing sackcloth. They were ordered to express their sorrow before the bier of Abner. To express his deep feelings of tragedy publicly, David followed the bier which bore Abner to his last resting place as he was buried in Hebron. David

II SAMUEL CHAPTER 3

wept at the graveside of Abner as he intoned Abner's sentiments, "Shall the sword devour forever? Knowest thou that it will be bitterness in the end." All those present were deeply moved by the depth of David's sorrow. They too recognized Israel's National tragedy.

Vs. 33.35   King David lamented Abner's loss, "Should Abner have died the death of a wicked man? Your hands were not bound, nor were your feet placed in fetters. You met your end at the hands of scheming treacherous men." David's lament and deep distress acquitted David of any complicity in the eyes of all those present at the graveside. When David returned from the cemetery he was served food in accord with the custom of mourning. David vowed that he would not eat, that he would fast unto sunset.

Vs.36.37   Observing David's distress over the loss of Abner, the northern tribes including Benjamin were motivated to recognize his sincerity. They reviewed the details of the tragedy and acknowledged that David stood to gain from Abner's cooperation. He had the following, the ability to influence the nation to recognize David as the chosen leader of a united Israel. Abner's strategy of crowning Ish-bosheth only delayed unification by two years, as he satisfied his ego trip. However, he was negotiable in recognizing his error and was flexible enough to reverse himself. David weighed the facts before he agreed to have Abner play an important role in uniting the nation. David perceived Abner's underpinnings were rooted in his dedication to his people. Despite Joab and Abishai's courage in war, David recognized their intransigence and therefore never trusted them.

Vs 38.39   David addressed his retinue as he lamented the death of Abner, "This day a great man has fallen in Israel. He deserves to be recognized as a prince among men." David has been king of Judah for about seven years at this point in time. He admits publicly that the sons of Zeruiah represent a divisive influence which shall use every barbaric method of violence, even fratricide to gain their ends. "I shall bide my time when the Eternal God of Israel will create the circumstances to avenge the death of Abner (I Kings 2:1.6, Ex.34:6.7).

II SAMUEL CHAPTER 4

V.1   When Ish-bosheth, the son of Saul was informed of Abner's murder in Hebron and all the honors that were bestowed upon him as he was laid to rest as a national hero, consternation and terror overcame him. Ish-bosheth took a sounding of his loyal subjects in order to determine their reaction to these circumstances. After he evaluated their position he lost heart; he recognized his inability to govern without a consensus.

Vs.2.3   The tyranny, the cruel exercise of power described in (II Sam. 2:30.32, 3:24.27) expose the acceptance in the ranks

II SAMUEL CHAPTER 4

of Israel of the murderous habits inherited from the indigenous population. The incident described in this chapter is in keeping with the accepted mores of the day. There were two company commanders in the army of Ish-bosheth, Baanah and Rechab, they were the sons of Rimon from the town of Beeroth in the territory of Benjamin. In accord with (Josh.9:17) they were Amorites-Gibeonites who were granted citizenships on the condition they would observe the Seven Laws of Noah. Many of the original Gibeonites were employed in the city of Nob. When king Saul murdered the kohanim in Nob (I Sam. 22:18.21,31:7),they fled to Gitaim-Gath in Philistia.

V.4 Baanah and Rechab planned to assassinate Ish-bosheth. Their motive was to remove the last descendant of Saul, who is eligible to reign as king. They calculated that by removing Ish-bosheth, David would be enabled to become king of a united Israel. They anticipated that David would reward them for their loyalty. V.4, describes Baanah and Rechab's conclusions. The only other living descendant of Saul, was Mephibosheth the son of Jonathan. However, he was ineligible because when Saul and Jonathan were killed at Gilboa in Jezreel, he was but five years old then. His governess was carrying him as they fled from the Philistine invasion; in her haste to leave she dropped Mephibosheth; this resulted in maiming his legs. This made him ineligible to become king. He was 12 years old at this time.

Vs.5.8 Rechab and Baanah arrived in Mahanaim and went directly to the home of Ish-bosheth, arriving there when he was taking his midday siesta and when the armed guard is relaxed. Their pretense for entering was to purchase wheat from the king's granary. They entered the king's room, stabbed him in the groin, they then cut off his head and concealed it in their sacks of wheat. From Mahanaim they traveled all that afternoon through the Arabah and continued to travel all that night until they arrived in Hebron at David's headquarters. Coming before David, they said, "Here is the head of your enemy Ish-bosheth, the son of Saul, who sought to kill you. This day the Eternal has avenged all the wrongs of Saul and his posterity."

Vs.9.10 David replied to Rechab and Baanah, "I ever put my faith in the Eternal. It is He that redeemed my soul from every dangerous situation. I never depend upon man to keep me safe from danger. When I was told by an eye witness that he killed Saul, he incriminated himself in order to earn a reward. I killed him on the spot in order to express my grief. This was my spontaneous means of rewarding him for his evil tidings."

Vs.11.12 "Your evidence condemns you to die as evil and wicked men. You dared to kill an innocent and righteous man while he was relaxing on his own bed. I am duty bound to remove the likes of you from the face of the earth." David gave an order that they be executed, to sever their hands and feet which were the instruments of their treachery and to

II SAMUEL CHAPTER 4

hang them by the pool of Hebron to publicize this treasonous and barbarous act. David issued an order to inter the head of Ish-bosheth in the plot of Abner his cousin.

II SAMUEL CHAPTER 5

Vs.1.3 The ten tribes of Israel chose representatives and came to Hebron for the purpose of finalizing their treaty with David and the tribe of Judah. "We recognize you as one of our own. Your background satisfies the specifications laid down in the Torah (Deut.17:14.15). Your genealogy validates you as a native son of Israel. *Asher yivchar Adonai* your credentials establish your worthiness to be chosen by the Eternal God of Israel. You have proven your ability and your dedication to lead Israel by the law of the Torah in war as in peace (I Sam.17:32, 18:15.16, 24:10.16, 17.21, 25:28.31). As a shepherd concerned with the welfare of his whole flock, you shall rule over us." V.3, reiterates the unanimity that prevailed in the hearts of the Elders and in the minds of all the representatives that came to Hebron to anoint David for the third time (I Sam.16:13,II Sam.2.4). For the details of their Covenant see T.E.T. (Deut.17:14.20,ISam.10:25).

Vs.4.5 David was 18 years old when he was anointed by Samuel. He was 30 years old when he became king of Judah. He reigned for seven years and six months in Hebron. David then reigned over a united Israel for 33 years. For a total of 40 years from 1004-965 BCE.

Vs.6.8 As the recognized anointed king of all Israel, David is obliged to consolidate his position in order to spread his authority to the northern tribes and to exercise the utmost control over the tribe of Benjamin and all those communities which made up the backbone of Saul's forces. David therefore reviewed the past history recorded in (Jud.1:8.21,19:11.12,and Joshua 10:) see details of our commentary on these texts for the efforts made in the past to occupy Jerusalem. We of the 20th century are indeed fortunate to be able to round out the archaeological picture of this impregnable fortress which goes back to the second millenium BCE. All the above information confirms the reasons that the Jebusites felt secure in their citadel. It is this piece of territory that literally divides the Holyland in half. It separates the north from the south. All the above historic and geographic facts lead David to one conclusion. This is the time, Jerusalem is the place to prove his leadership to the ten tribes who have just pledged their loyalty to him. This is the time to make it known to the Philistines in the west with whom he is still on good terms and the Ammonites in the east, that it is his intention to rule authoritatively. He desires to live in peace with those that want peace and to challenge by war those that will challenge his intentions. David initiated negotiations with the Jebusites at this time. However, the military action described here took place at a much later time. The Jebusites replied to David, "You will never succeed in getting into

II SAMUEL CHAPTER 5

the citadel! Even the blind and the lame in our community have the ability to turn you back from entering this fortress." David accepted the challenge. David too is knowledgeable that he cannot storm the citadel frontally. Having examined the past historic and geographic record, he knew of the gutter which runs from the spring of Gihon to the top of the hill on which the fortress of Zion stood (II Chron.32:30). In 1867 when this water channel or gutter as it is called was discovered by Warren, it confirmed to history David's conclusions. It was this shaft that supplied the Jebusites with their water needs to the fortress. David offered a reward to him that will succeed to penetrate into the citadel through this channel and destroy the *'lame and the blind'* that are defending it.

Vs.9.10   David occupied the stronghold, renamed it the city of David. He then fortified the north side which was vulnerable by filling it in. This is known to this day as the Millo. In Solomon's time (I Kings 9:24,11:27) he continued to fill in this area and built homes on it. In (II Chron. 32:5) Hezekiah 728-698 BCE refortified the Millo, to the north of Mount Zion. It was David's intentions to integrate the Jebusites in accord with (Ex.23:27.30) that they live in peace with Israel. He therefore gave them the option to establish the city of Jebus upon Mount Moriah. David's ability to lead Israel in accord with Torah law, gave the Israelites the confirmation that the Eternal God of the Universe endowed him with every ingredient for success. When David transferred his capital from Hebron to Jerusalem, he removed the last physical barrier that divided Israel.

Vs.11.12   Hiram I, in this verse is Avibaal-Abibalus. The Hiram that succeeded him became king upon his demise at the age of 19. He ruled for 34 years from 969-936 BCE. David ruled from 1004-965. Solomon 965-928 BCE. The Phoenicians trace their origin back to Shem. In addition to their genetic background, they had many other things in common, their language, their geographic contiguity with Israel, their trade relations with Israel go back to Israel's arrival in Egypt in 1523 BCE. See comm. T.E.T. on the following texts (Gen.49:13, Deut.33:18.19,22,Ex.1:7 and the addenda on pp.553,261). David's conrtrol of the Holyland created the potential for an overland route to India and the Orient, Tzor-Phoenicia, anticipated the potential. Hiram is therefore desirous to cement their relations with the new king. Their mutual common competitor on the Mediterannean coast is Philistia. Philistia is also their common enemy. Hiram's spontaneous recognition of David's kingdom represents his faith in David's leadership. Hiram's faith in David presents him with an offer to build him a palace. The above information is the full meaning of v.10, "For the Eternal God the Master of the Universe was with him." David recognized that he is but the *malach Adonai* the instrument through whom Israel can fulfill its Manifest Destiny to become a light unto the nations of the world.

Vs.13:16   When David established his capital in Jerusalem, he took several wives and concubines. These were in addition to those

II SAMUEL CHAPTER 5

recorded in (II Sam.3:2.5). V.14, lists the names of the sons born to these women in Jerusalem: Shammua, Shobab, Nathan, Solomon, Elishua, Nepheg, Japhia, Elishama, Eliada, and Eliphelet.

Vs.17.21   The war recorded here with the Philistines took place while David's capital was still in Hebron. When the Philistines evaluated the meaning of a united Israel under David, their first effort was to capture him personally. David therefore went down to his old fortress in Adullam, in the wilderness of Ziph about four miles southeast of Hebron. Here in the *metzudah* the fastness, the fortress stronghold of the mountainous wasteland, he organized his strategy and evaluated the Philistine mobilization in the valley of Rephaim. Here David took counsel with the Elders, his military officers and with the Kohen, to establish their cause and their strategy. Having established their goal and their capability to defeat the enemy, David anticipated that the Philistines would move southward to Bethlehem and then to Hebron. Before the Philistines could wheel into position for battle, David's army hit them like an avalanche of waters breaking through a dam. This sudden force forced them to retreat. In their haste they abandoned their images and good luck charms which were to assure their victory. David named this battlefield Baal-perazim, the shattering of the idolatrous images as he gave orders to the army to destroy them.

Vs.22.25   Once again the Philistines made an attempt to probe David's strength in the field of battle and encamped in the valley of Rephaim northwest of Jerusalem. David followed his normal procedure to take counsel *Badonai* with the Kohen Gadol, to establish the moral right of his position and the reasons for going to war. The *Urim Vetummim* were not to be used as an oracle. This symbolic breast plate worn by the Kohen was to remind the Kohen and Israel's leaders that their plans must take into consideration the interests and welfare of each and every tribe in Israel. Having established the justice of his position, David consulted with his military staff, to determine their strategy. The concensus was to create a surrounding tactic to encircle the Philistines and force them to retreat from the valley of Rephaim. The actual battle took place between Gibeon and Gezer. From v.24, we observe David's sensitivity to the natural surroundings. Here must have been at this point in time a forest of balsam trees. David's strategy utilized the natural rhythm of marching feet as its echo is magnified through the trees to give him the signal for his attack. David followed the inspiration of the Eternal; once again he routed the Philistines from Geba all the way to Gezer.

II SAMUEL CHAPTER 6

Vs.1.5   In (II Sam. 5:17) David's mobilization was from the *metzudah* in Adullam. This is the meaning of, "And David mobilized once again." David chose 30,000 men that were picked for the

II SAMUEL CHAPTER 6

sole purpose of bringing the Ark from Baalah (Josh.15:9) which is the same as Kiriat-jearim. The Ark has been here since its return by the Philistines after the destruction of the Mishkan-Tabernacle at Shiloh in 1050 BCE. by the Philistines (I Sam. 6:1.21,7:1, I Chron. 13:6). In this Ark of God were kept the shattered first Tablets containing the Ten Commandments, together with the second set of Tablets and a copy of the Torah, that was placed into the Ark when it was completed by Joshua, the Leviim, and the Nesiim (Ex. 32:7.19,34:1, Deut. 31:24.26). Enclosing these sacred objects were the Cherubim, symbolizing the brotherhood that man can attain as he marches through history under the inspiration of The Eternal God of The Universe, the Lord of Hosts (Ex.25.10.22). The Ark of the Covenant demonstrates the tangential connection between the Eternal God and man. Inscribed in the Torah are the disciplines and ideals for which mankind must strive to attain the perfection of human relations. See comm. in T.E.T. on (Gen.3:24). The instructions given in the Torah are emphatic, that the Ark was to be carried by the staves which were permanently attached. The choice of placing the Ark upon a new wagon was respectful, however, it exposed the ignorance of the law as stated in the Torah. The Ark was placed on a new wagon and conveyed from the home of Abinadab on the hill of Kiriat-jearim. (It is doubtful that Abinadab was still living at this point in time). Therefore, Uzzah walked alongside of the Ark and his brother Achio led the cart on its way to Jerusalem.

V.5, describes the elaborate instrumentation which supplied the musical rhythm as David and the House of Israel danced and rejoiced at this important new beginning as a united nation under the Eternal God of Israel.

Vs.6.8   When the wagon bearing the Ark arrived in the area where the threshing floor of Nachon stood, the oxen hitched to the wagon stumbled causing the Ark to vibrate. Uzzah who was walking alongside the Ark, reached out spontaneously to steady the Ark to keep it from falling. At that precise split second, Uzzah recognized his error for having permitted the Ark to be carried on a wagon instead of by the staves attached to the Ark for this sole purpose. (Uzzah, a Levi, was recognized for his worthiness (I Sam.6:20.21) by all of Israel. It was here in the House of Abinadab, the home of Uzzah and his brother Achio, that the Ark stood these past 55 years. It is the 10th year of David's reign as king.) The awesome thought of his transgression that he had violated the discipline *kevalah eth hakodesh vametu (Num.4:20)*, sent shock waves of terror through his conscience; creating an acute vascular lesion of the brain, a form of apoplectic paralysis. To paraphrase Torath Kohanim on (Lev.10:1.3) "Uzzah's soul was burned while the rest of his body remained untouched, a stroke." The Torah strives to teach human beings to conceive with the mind, that the Holy and sacred Ark, is the tangible symbol of God's Presence. The laws and disciplines inscribed in the sacred Ark are equal to the soul that grants mankind the capacity to discern the force that determines his

II SAMUEL CHAPTER 6

humanity. Without this concept of the Ark's sacredness, those that view it only with their eyes as an object, do so because their souls are already dead.

Contained in this Ark is the Covenant made with Noah, that committed every human being down the centuries to infinity (Gen.9:8.11, 17:3.4, 26:3.5, 28:10.15, Joshua1:8.9, Is.59:21). The Eternal's revelations contained in this Ark are humanity's immortal potential which link the generations to infinity.

V.8, Uzzah's indiscretion cost him his life as he died beside the Ark of God. David was distressed; not with the Eternal God, but with Uzzah, who should have known the disciplines demanded by law, quoted above. David is grieved by the quality of Levitic leadership. He recognized this *Peretz-Uzzah* as a national calamity. David perceived this tragedy as a warning to him as king of Israel. He must assume the spiritual and cultural direction of the nation as the first order of business. Only from Israel's dedication to spiritual and moral vigilance can emerge not only the safety of its Leviim, its spiritual teachers, but the moral force dedicated to resist the enemies of mankind.

Vs.9.11 David recognized the serious implications of this tragedy that shall require self examination of the whole nation before he can determine his next step. One thing is certain, neither he nor the nation are worthy enough at this moment to celebrate. Before the lessons of this experience are resolved and assimilated, Israel must rise unto a new plateau, before the Ark of God is brought to Jerusalem. David therefore placed the Ark of the Eternal in the home of Obed-edom, a Levite of the family of Korach now living in the Levitic city of Gath-rimmon (I Chron.15:18,24,26:4, Joshua 21:24).

The Ark remained here for three months while David consulted with his own conscience. What shall be his first step? When David was informed that Obed-edom and his whole community had prospered because of their resolution to rededicate themselves to the disciplines demanded of them as teachers in Israel, David was pleased. He recognized their formula for a new plateau harmonized with his plans for the consecration of the House of Israel to Torah disciplines. In this mood of searching the inner meaning of *Peretz-Uzzah* David composed Psalms 24 and 132.

Vs.12.16 David is pleased by the report made in v.11. He therefore announced his intention to bring the Ark from the home of Obed-edom to Jerusalem. David gathered a representative assemblage of Israel and went to Gath-rimmon. They carried the Ark of God by the attached staves in accord with the procedure required by law. David strove to create a spiritual atmosphere and therefore ordered the cortege to pause after they had made six paces and the kohanim offered sacrifices of thanksgiving in the anticipated hope their effort shall be completed without incident. David removed his princely garments and donned a Levitic ephod. He led the dancing and whirling to express his delight for a successful journey to Jerusalem and a new

II SAMUEL CHAPTER 6

beginning. With shouts of joy and with the blast of the shofar they entered the City of David carrying the Ark of the Eternal God. Michal who observed the scene from her home expressed her animosity for David publicly as she denigrated his joy by dancing and whirling before the Ark of God. For the record, Michal's scorn for David began when she was taken from the home of Paltiel (II Sam.3:14.16,20).

Vs.17.19   David brought the Ark of the Eternal into the special tent prepared for its reception. Here they offered burnt offerings and peace offerings in gratitude for this momentous juncture in Israel's history. David blessed the multitudinous assembly in the name of the Eternal, the Supreme Master of the Universe. Every man and woman present were presented with a loaf of bread, a cake and a cake of raisins. The festivities ended as the assemblage were discharged and returned to their homes.

Vs.20.22   As David entered his home with the intention of blessing his family, Michal confronted him for naively dancing and exposing himself in dance with everyone. Michal accused him, "You cavorted in the sight of the lowly slave girls." David replied, "I danced before the Eternal God of Israel to express my gratitude for having been chosen over all the members of your father's family. My outer joy was an expression of my inner feelings of thankfulness for having reached this day. I shall continue to humble myself in order to gain the loyalty of every slave girl that you denigrated this day."

V.23   The seed of hate has its own chemistry; for it poisons its genetic potential. Michal was barren all her life. She did not conceive a child at any point in her lifetime. At this high point in David's career we must recognize the injustice done to Michal when she was taken from Paltiel (II Sam.3:13.16). From the text we must conclude they lived happily together though she bore him no child.

II SAMUEL CHAPTER 7

The chronology of the events described in chapters 5,6,7, embraced a period of about 16 to 20 years. Both encounters with the Philistines described in (II Sam.5:17.25) took place while David's capital was in the city of Hebron. Then followed the acquisition of Jerusalem (II Sam. 5:6.10) and the fortification of the Millo, as David filled it in. It is from this project that it received its name. It was here that he built homes for his expanding retinue that shall help him build a strong central government. (II Sam. 8:15.18) records the appointment of Joab as the General of the army *Sar-hazaba*, Jehoshaphat became the *mazkir*, the historian or keeper of records. Shavsha kept the records of the army as David established universal conscription (II Sam.6:1). This position was handed down from father to son. Benaiah the son of Jehoiada was appointed as commander in

II SAMUEL CHAPTER 7

chief of the Cherethites and Pelethites. These mercenaries of Greek origin became the nucleus of David's standing army.

It was at this point that Ahimelech the son of Abiathar was appointed kohen to serve in Jerusalem, in the Mishkan which was being built in anticipation of bringing the Ark of the Covenant to Jerusalem, described in (II Sam. 6:2.19). David also appointed Zadok, as the kohen in Gibeon, he was active in the Levitical choirs which were established by Samuel. There he composed hymns in the tradition of Samuel, to elevate the service at the Mishkan upon a higher plateau while retaining the sacrificial service as described in the Torah. In keeping with David's desire to establish Jerusalem as the center of Israel's religious life, Zadok became the royal Psalmist. From this school came Asaph, Heman, and Jeduthun the sons of Korach, who left an indelible impression upon the Book of Psalms.

Poetry as an international art form had its early beginnings in this renaissance of Israel's history. David took his inspiration from Moses as he presided as a judge to insure justice for all (Ps.122:3,5). Hushai the Arki and Ahithophel of the Judean city of Gilo were appointed as confidential advisers to the king. It was during this period devoted to establishing a strong central government that Hiram offered to build a palace for David (II Sam.5:11.12,13:16). It was also in this interim period that Solomon was born in Jerusalem.

From the above details we can conclude that chapter seven records the activities which took place at the end of the second decade of David's rule, about 984 BCE.

Solomon was anointed during his father's lifetime in 967 BCE. He ruled on his own from 965-928 BCE.

Vs.1.3 Some time after David was already settled in the palace built for him by Hiram, king of Phoenicia, David confided his innermost thoughts to the prophet Nathan his confidant of long standing. David's keen observation of the religious practices prevalent in the Holyland leads him to the conclusion that just as a strong central government is vital for the security of the nation, so it is of the utmost importance to establish a Central Sanctuary which shall elevate the spiritual life of the nation. David took his theme from (Deut.16:21.22) which exposes the primitive mentality of his generation. David observed the idolatrous heathen customs which have perpetuated themselves into the mores of his people. These practices deny the freedom of action to solve daily problems as man aborts his *Zelem Elohim*, his God-given intelligence. Man can serve the Eternal God by observing His law in his everyday life. David equates the effect of his luxurious palatial home upon the morale of the people of Israel, who have completely forgotten about the Ark of God and the importance of its guidelines to help Israel speed the process of civlization. "I am dwelling in a house of cedar, while the Ark of the Eternal God

II SAMUEL CHAPTER 7

abides in a tent!" David is desirous of building a Central Sanctuary, from which shall emanate the standards of Holyness-perfection, that shall inspire dedication to the nation and Israel's place in history. David's desire harmonizes with the prophet Nathan's goals for the people of Israel. He has long recognized David's dedication and faith in the guidelines of the Eternal God of Israel. Nathan therefore said to David, "Go and fulfill your desire for the Eternal God looks with favor upon your sincere desire."

Vs.4.7   Nathan took his leave of David and concentrated upon David's plans to build a House in the name of God. That very night Nathan was inspired by the Eternal to examine the details of this new project. Nathan is directed to look into the guidelines of the Torah (Ex.20:24.25,25:8.9,Deut.12:1.19). Having examined the details inscribed in these texts, Nathan is inspired to deliver the following message to David. "In accord with Israel's primitive past experience from the time of the Exodus, God's Presence has dwelt in a humble tent (Ex.33:9.11,40:1.3) and then in a formal Tabernacle. In the interim of these 350 years, has the Eternal reproached Israel's tribal leaders, Nesiim, for not having built a House for the Ark of the Covenant? Examining the historic record (Deut.12:9) there is much land to be conquered in accord with the specifics outlined in (Num.34:1.15), for the territory which shall encompass the Holyland, therefore yours is the task to fulfill the demand of *vehorashtem* inheriting and taking possession of Israel's rightful inheritance. When you have established the basis for the security of your dynasty upon a solid foundation, as each community recognizes your central authority, then and only then shall the people of Israel be ready to accept your advanced evolutionary development."

Vs.8.11   Nathan came before David and reviewed his accomplishments from the day he was anointed to become king of Israel. "The Eternal elevated you from the pasture-land, where you proved your excellence in caring for your father's sheep. He inspired you to create the circumstances to defeat Israel's enemies. Your accomplishments succeeded because of your dedication to the Eternal's guidance. As the Eternal's instrument, *malach*, you have succeeded in uniting the Eternal's Chosen People in the Holyland. For your dedication you have earned the gratitude of Israel and the recognition of other nations and peoples. You must recognize that yours is the task to create in Israel the pride and dedication to defend themselves against every tyranny which confronted Israel in the period of the Judges."

What the prophet Nathan has demonstrated in these verses is the knowledge of Israel's past history as recorded in the Torah. Nathan's prophetic capability has given him the capacity to anticipate wars which David will have to lead before the time becomes propitious for building a House in the name of the Eternal God. "When that time has been reached the Eternal will credit your dedication to the national welfare that you had made it possible for your posterity to live in peace (I Kings5:1,15.20, I Chron.22:5.12, Ps.30:1.13)." This was the

II SAMUEL CHAPTER 7

prophet Nathan's subtle message to David that he concentrate upon winning the security vital for his posterity to live in peace.

Vs.12.14 Vs.4.16 are the sum and substance of the prophet Nathan's visionary inspiration he shared with David. Having made his point that David will not build the House of God, Nathan consoled David as he elaborated on the future. "Your noble thoughts to build a House which shall bear the Eternal's name will come to fruition after you have accomplished your life's work, to win security for Israel in the Holyland. I now confirm the Eternal's promise that your dynasty shall withstand the vicissitudes of time. Your successor shall build the House of God that shall bear His name forever. As long as he recognizes the Eternal God of Israel as his Father, the Eternal will treat him as a son. As a son he shall be obliged to walk in the Eternal's prescribed path for living as outlined in the Eternal's Torah. As a Father, the Eternal will chastise him when he defaults from the guidelines inscribed in the Torah, (Ps.89:27.38). Though he be the king of Israel, the Eternal will chastise him with the same disciplinary rod used to afflict every human being who ignores the Eternal's Natural Law, Moral Law, Ethical Law. As a Father the Eternal will wait patiently (Gen.6:3,Ex.34:6.7) for his repentance and resolution to try again." Nathan is sensitive to David's hurt, that he shall not build God's house, from which shall emanate the Eternal's Presence, he therefore assured David, "Your dynasty and its succession of kings shall ever be securely rooted to your reward for having dedicated your whole life in the service of the Eternal your God."

Vs.15.16 The "Messianic" hope that David's inspiring legacy shall reverberate throughout Israel's history and regenerate dedicated leaders in Israel to keep alive the Eternal's goal for all of humanity has become David's reward as recorded in the following texts (I Kings 8:17,9:4,15:4, II Kings 8:19, Ps.89:).

Vs.17.19 When the prophet Nathan concluded his message to David and his sensitive effort to assuage David's disappointment and frustration, David entered the Mishkan and sat humbly in the Presence of the Eternal's Ark, to express his gratitude for the Eternal's promise expressed by the prophet Nathan in vs.4.16. "What am I, O Eternal God, that you have singled me out from all the members of the tribe of Judah? (Gen.49:8.12, Deut.33:7. See T.E.T. on these verses.) You have endowed me with the highest honor in the possession of Israel. (Gen.32:11) I humble myself before Thee O God, for all the kindness You have bestowed upon me and for the great promise for my future posterity (I Chron.17:16.27). May my blessings become an example to all in Israel, of Your generosity to those that dedicate themselves to become copartners in Your management of civilization."

Vs.20.22 "Words fail me to express my gratitude. In light of Your ability to penetrate my innermost thoughts (Ps.139:16), You

II SAMUEL CHAPTER 7

have observed my genetic development from the time I was but an embryo. You have recorded my effort to walk in Your Light. Your recognition through the prophet Samuel endowed me with the inspiration to succeed in my every endeavor. V.21, "It was Your inspiration that challenged my potential to enlarge my latent ability (Deut.11:18.25, see T.E.T.) in order to inspire me to teach these truths to my posterity. V.22, Who in the pantheon of man-made gods can compare with the Eternal God of Israel? For it is the Eternal that directs the paths of history. Who is like unto Thee O God Whose almighty natural forces are programmed to demand justice in return for the miracle of daily living." See T.E.T. (Deut.4:34.35).

Vs.23.24   *Umi keamcha Yisrael*, "Who is like Your people Israel? Only one people amongst all of humanity chose *asher halchu Elohim* to follow the leadership of the Eternal God as they went down to Egypt (Gen.46:2.3). When they became oppressed by the tyrants of Egypt, it was You the Eternal God of Israel that remained sensitive and concerned with Israel's prayerful plea (Ex.3:7.10) for Your help. Egyptian tyranny penetrated the firmament to Your abode when Israel was denied its human rights, *asher halchu Elohim*. It was You the Eternal God of Israel, Who sent Moses and Aaron to emancipate them (Ex.4:16,7:1) *lifdoth lo leam* in order to elevate Israel to become Your people. *Velasum lo leshem*, It was You the Eternal God of Israel that charged Israel (Ex.19:5.8) to become Your *am segulah* genetic treasure, to introduce genetic progression into the lifestyle of humanity. When Israel was challenged to accept Your Natural Law, Moral Law and Ethical Law (Ex.19:5.8) Israel's response was spontaneous, as they replied, "All that the Eternal requests of us we shall dedicate ourselves to uphold."

Velaasot lachem hagedulah venaraoth learzecha, "You the Eternal God of Israel have indeed honored Your promise and returned Israel to the Holyland (Gen.15:16, I Chron.17:21) by driving out the tyrannical elements and their idolatrous regressive practices. *Mipnei amcha asher paditha mimizraim*, David muses as he repeats all the wonderful things that You, O Eternal God, made possible, in order to establish the people You redeemed from Egyptian bondage, as You poured forth your wrath upon the *goyim velohav* degenerate people who challenged Your authority (Gen.6:3) to demand that they repent from their barbaric, degenerate and debauched practices. David testifies for the record of history, "You, O God of justice, have established Your people Israel as Your very own people forever."

Vs.17.24   Represents David's gratitude for having been chosen to become the instrument of the Eternal God of Israel, to bring about the unification of Israel as a united nation that accords with the promise of the Eternal God of Israel. David now turns to the promise made by the prophet Nathan in vs. 12.14.

Vs.25.29   "O Eternal God of Israel, I pray that You will fulfill the

II SAMUEL CHAPTER 7

promise made to Your humble servant and to my house forever. May Your name become glorified in the hearts of my posterity even as it has been in mine all the days of my life. May they succeed in making known to all of humanity that the Eternal God of Israel is the Master of the Universe. As the God who guarantees every human being his human rights, You demand *zedakah umishpat* (Gen.18:19) in the life of every human being. In this spirit do I pray, that my posterity become inspired to dedicate their lives to maintain the values engraved in your Torah in order to merit Your blessings and deserving of Your promise."

II SAMUEL CHAPTER 8

V.1   David appreciated Nathan's introspection and evaluation of the national situation. He fully grasped the intent of the prophet Nathan's soliloquy with the Eternal God of Israel described in chapter seven. David concentrated upon Nathan's message and perceived that the contents of his message paralleled the instructions given by Moses in the name of the Eternal in (Num.33:55.56, Deut.9:4.6,11:23.25,18:9.15, Joshua 1:1.9 see T.E.T. on these verses). Israel's failure to fulfill the *mitzvah* of *vehorashtem* brought about the dark age in the period of the Judges and the chaos in Saul's time. David perceived that Nathan's message was not intended to denigrate his desire to build a House in the name of God but to emphasize the priority incumbent upon every generation of Israel *vehorashtem eth haarets* to take possession of the Holyland. This is the moment for David to engrave his name in Israel's history as the one who has won the peace for Israel by the creation of safe borders. David comprehends Nathan's intent, that building the Temple now, would imply that Israel has already achieved the first step of *vehorashtem eth haarets*.

See chronology to chapter seven that David is now about 55-59 years of age, he is at the height of his powers. His government and international reputation are fully established. His inspired leadership has won the respect of a united nation.

Having resolved his disappointment, he turned to the task ahead. The first step in securing safe borders begins with destroying the Philistine dream of conquering the Holyland. He repossessed Gath and its surrounding towns and villages. This strategic action decontrolled *metheg haamah* the rest of the four Philistine municipalities from its central government. David literally bridled their ability to govern themselves and to unite for any future expansion. The essence of David's strategy was to inform Philistia, "We shall tolerate your presence in the Holyland as long as you keep the peace."

V.2   Having secured his western border, David decided to settle a personal matter and at the same time to serve notice on Moab that he intends to establish his eastern border to encompass the territory to the Euphrates River which conforms with (Num.34:). When

II SAMUEL CHAPTER 8

David was a fugitive from Saul's tyranny (I Sam.22:3.5) he had entrusted his parents in the custody of the government of Moab, where they would be safe from the treachery of king Saul. Rashi quotes a *midrash*, tradition, that when David was advised to leave the Cave of Adullam, his parents were murdered by the Moabites. Only one of his brothers escaped. David's decision charges Moab as having violated their kinship (Deut.2:9) and having violated their promise to protect his parents from any harm.

To settle his personal score, he classified those that were directly involved with the killing of his parents and those that could have protected them and stood passively by as they were executed. On the national score David decreed to permit them to occupy their territory as long as they keep the peace and honor the tax which he levied against them as their share for his military protection and government.

Vs.3.8 — Hadadezer the son of Rehob, the king of Zobah, an Assyrian province north of Damascus formed an alliance with the Arameans of Damascus for the purpose of establishing his hegemony to the Euphrates River. Hadadezer's action conflicted with Israel's destiny. The text describes in great detail (I Chron.18:3.8) David's victory. The description here of the battle and the details given in (II Sam.10:16.19) are probably connected with the events at that time. V.6 describes David's army of occupation to secure his authority and to levy their tribute for the government of Israel. The timing of David's strategy conformed with the Eternal's guidance inspired through the prophet Nathan. The odds in equipment and men against Israel's force were overcome by David's strategy. The text recognizes this and therefore records, David succeeded in his every undertaking. V.7, David took the golden dress shields used by Hadadezer's retinue and brought them back to Jerusalem. This was added to the building material that David was accumulating for the day when Israel shall have fulfilled the *mitzvah* of *horashtem* and become worthy to build the Temple in the name of the Eternal God of Israel.

V.8. From the towns of Betah and Berothai, David captured a vast amount of copper which was set aside for the building of the Temple.

Vs.9.12 — When Toi, the king of Hamath, which was north of Zobah, heard of David's victory over Hadadezer, his perpetual enemy, he sent his son Joram with gifts of silver, gold and copper to express his gratitude. David added this gift together with all the booty he had amassed to become dedicated to the Eternal God's Temple. Some of the treasure that had already been dedicated came from the following campaigns with Edom, Moab, Ammon, Philistines, Amalekites, and now Hadadezer, the son of Rehob, the king of Zobah.

Vs.13.14 — David won the gratitude of multitudes when he returned from his war with Edom in the area of the Dead Sea. He stationed a military garrison there in order to exact tribute from them and

II SAMUEL CHAPTER 8

to insure his control over the territory. (II Kings 14:7), corrects the error in this verse which reads Aram instead of Edom.

Vs.15.18 David reigned over a united Israel. His government was firmly established and dedicated to pursue justice in accord with Israel's Constitution, the Torah. Joab, the son of Zeruiah, was the commander of Israel's army; Jehoshaphat, the son of Ahilud, was the recorder; Zadok, the son of Ahitub, and Ahimelech, the son of Abiathar, were the kohanim; Seraiah was the scribe; Benaiah, the son of Jehoiada, was the commander of the Cherethites and Pelethites and David's sons were 'kohanim.' (I Kings 4:5, I Chron. 18:17) define the meaning of the word 'kohanim' as used here to mean that David's sons occupied important positions in the government. This information confirms our conclusion that David was between the ages of 55-59 at this point in time.

The unique personality of David which has come down to us in the record of the Book of Samuel, is essentially the evaluation, by others, of his tangible accomplishments. To penetrate into the innermost thoughts that motivated this unusual personality, we must study the Psalms written by this dedicated individual. His whole life was devoted to the cause of his people.

Psalm 60 was written by David in this period of time and reflects his innermost thoughts. David begins his Psalm by comparing Israel's Manifest Destiny to a rose. When Israel observes the disciplines of the Torah, it becomes worthy to receive the Eternal's protective custody. Israel's dedication enables it to withstand the storms of history. A rose is protected by its thorns from being mishandled. However, it's thorns cannot protect it against the powerful winds of time.

(Psalm 60:3) David reminds history, that in the period of the Judges, when Israel adopted the mores of the indigenous neighbors in the Holyland and each person opted to do his or her own thing, Israel became defenseless against the winds and storms of time. The Eternal removed His protective custody to awaken, to stir, Israel's consciousness to return to His disciplines.

(Psalm 60:4) The inner discord and dissension created anarchy in the ranks of Israel. This was the signal for Israel's enemies to overwhelm it. The effect was like an earthquake. "I now pray that you heal its breaches." David is inspired by (Ex.32:31.34) as he pleads Israel's cause. He feels the command of the Eternal directing his effort to lead his people back upon the righteous path.

(Psalm 60:5) "Help me to redirect Israel's understanding of our victories over our former enemies, as but a new beginning to return to Your guidelines inscribed in Your Torah. Permit not these victories to go to our heads like the wine of bewilderment."

(Psalm 60:6) "You have granted me the sign of victory; now endow me with the ability to choose my next move in the direction of moral truth, that I may not

II SAMUEL CHAPTER 8

follow the logical and *'common'* meaning of military victory." David looked back into the record of Israel's charismatic leaders from Joshua to Saul who were endowed with the *'banner'* of victory, yet, they were incapable of adorning *'koshet'* or shaping its victories to conform with the Eternal's Master Plan for Civilization." (Zechariah 9:16.17)

(Psalm 60:8) David is striving for the Eternal's guidance to redirect the human heart from, "To the victor belong the spoils," to read "To the victor is the challenge to offer peace to his former enemies."

II SAMUEL CHAPTER 9

Vs.1.3 Consistent with David's conclusions in Psalm 60, David is desirous of keeping faith with the vow made to Jonathan (I Sam.20:15.17). David begins to implement his good fortune by extending his blessings close to home. David initiated an inquiry, "Is there anyone still living of the original members of the House of Saul?" David is informed there is a faithful servant of Saul, who is still living on his estate in Gibeah, and his name is Ziba. Radak establishes the identity of Ziba as a Canaanite. When Ziba was ordered to come before David, he identified himself. David questioned him, "Is there anyone left of the House of Saul? I am desirous of honoring my vow made to Jonathan." Ziba replied, "Yes, there is a son of Jonathan who is handicapped because of an accident recorded in (II Sam.4:4)."

Vs.4.8 David continued his inquiry of Ziba, "Where can I find Jonathan's son Mephibosheth?" Ziba replied, "He is living at the home of Machir, the son of Amiel, in Lo-Debar, in the area of Mahanaim." He is considered a man of substance and wealth, as recorded in (II Sam.17:27).

David sent for Mephibosheth; he came before David and prostrated himself. He then identified himself. David then addressed him, "Be not afraid and have no fear; my purpose of bringing you here is to honor a vow made to your father Jonathan. I hereby go on record that I shall restore all the landholdings of your grandfather king Saul; in addition, I am desirous that you honor me by taking your meals with me at your pleasure." Mephibosheth prostrated himself once again as he acknowledged David's respect and loyalty to the memory of his father, Jonathan. "What am I, but your humble servant, who likens himself to a dead dog; I am overwhelmed that you show me such concern."

Vs.9.10 David summoned Ziba and elevated him to become Mephibosheth's trusted steward, "I hereby transfer title to all the landholdings which originally belonged to all the members of king Saul's family, to become the sole possession of Mephibosheth. I further charge you, your 15 sons and your 20 day workers (slaves) to manage and work the land, to harvest its crops and market its produce, in order to earn an income

II SAMUEL CHAPTER 9

for Mephibosheth. Mephibosheth shall be my honored guest for the duration of his life."

Vs.11.13   Ziba replied to David, "I shall do as you instruct me; I recognize and respect your decision to elevate Mephibosheth to his royal station by residing in your home in Jerusalem." V.12, should read, Mephibosheth had a young son by the name of Mica; "He, too, shall join his father at my table as one of the king's sons." David's concern for Mephibosheth and his family made it possible for the House of Saul to continue for several generations as recorded in (I Chron.8:34). V.13, confirms that Mephibosheth and his family lived in Jerusalem and took their meals as part of David's family, because David recognized his handicap on both of his legs.

II SAMUEL CHAPTER 10

Vs.1.2   *Vayehi acahare chen*, And it came to pass after David had evaluated the lessons contained in (Ps.60:4.6, Deut.23:4.9, Ps.23:3), *nafshi yeshovev* "My soul must ever be responsive to the Eternal's direction." By honoring his vow to Jonathan, he has responded to the Eternal's direction. David has reviewed the political situation and has recognized the genetic retrogression of Ammon, Moab and Edom. Past experience informed him that he cannot destroy them nor may he absorb them. He therefore is inspired to make a gesture to civilize them. History has proven him right. Ammon and Moab will continue to be a thorn in the side of Israel's body politic until Nebuchadnezzar will destroy their fortresses and assimilate them into his empire in the 6th century BCE. In keeping with his inspiration, David sent messengers to Hanun to convey Israel's condolences upon the demise of his father Nahash. This is David's effort to redirect history in keeping with the Eternal's Master Plan for civilization. This gesture was intended to indicate his desire for a new beginning in the spirit of (Deut.2:17.19).

Vs.3.5   Ammonite officialdom challenged David's intentions as they said to Hanun, "So you think that David's gesture to comfort you is sincere? This is his way of coming here in peace in order to explore our cities and then attack us." Hanan was influenced by the thinking of his officials and strove to give his reply in no uncertain terms. Hanan ordered one side of the messengers' beards to be clipped, and they also cut away one side of their outer garments to expose their buttocks. He then discharged them to become an object of ridicule. When David was informed of this incident he sent a message that they remain in Jericho until their beards will once again be restored.

Vs.6.8   The Ammonites soon realized their evil conduct demanded a reply. They therefore hired 10,000 Arameans from Beth Rehob, 10,000 Arameans from Zobah, 10,000 Maacatites and

II SAMUEL CHAPTER 10

12,000 men from the king of Tob. For the geographic position of these communities that supplied mercenaries see T.E.T. on the following texts (Deut.3:14, Jud.11:3.5, I Chron.19:6.7). We also learn that the Ammonites paid 1000 talents of silver for the mercenaries. When David was informed of this activity, he mobilized his full complement of soldiers under the leadership of Joab. The Ammonite plan was to challenge Joab's army at the entrance of the city of Rabbah, while the mercenaries remained in the field on the ready to surround the Israelites as they attacked the city.

Vs.9.10   Joab scrutinized the military situation; he concluded that the Ammonites were leaning heavily upon their fortified city as a natural advantage. He therefore assigned a portion of his military force under the leadership of his brother Abishai, to police the Ammonite army, to make sure they will not get beyond the city gates in order to keep them from joining the main battle which he will wage against the mercenaries.

Vs.11.12   Joab made it quite clear to Abishai, "Should the battle go in favor of the mercenaries, Abishai was to come to his aid. Should the Ammonites break out and overcome your holding action, I will come to your assistance. Be firm and resolute for the sake of Israel. Inspire your men to resolve there be no captives from our ranks as we dedicate our lives to the Eternal God of Israel. With faith in our cause, we shall do our best and accept the Eternal's verdict with grace."

Vs.13.14   Joab launched his attack against the mercenaries and made his determined resolution felt in the impact of his army's attack. This spark of Joab's faith penetrated the self-preservation instinct of the mercenaries as they fled from the impact of Joab's army. When the Ammonites observed the retreat of their hired allies, they too retreated into their fortified city of Rabbah. Joab recognized the reality of the situation and returned to Jerusalem to plan for another day.

Vs.15.19   The Ammonites accepted their rout and once again regrouped under the leadership of Shovach, Hadadezer's commander whom we encountered in (II Sam.8:3); their hegemony was on the eastern side of the Euphrates. Hadadezer mobilized the Aramean mercenaries from the western side of the Euphrates and encamped at Helam. When David's intelligence reported this move, he mobilized the full complement of his army and crossed the Jordan eastward prepared for action at Helam. Shovach ordered the Arameans into battle and met their *Waterloo* as they fled the force of Israel's attack. 700 Aramean charioteers and 40,000 horsemen lost their lives, including Shovach, the commander-in-chief of Hadadezer's forces. (I Chron.19:16.19, II Sam. 8:3.10) describe some of the details of the ongoing action initiated by the Ammonites and their allies. V. 19, Hadadezer's vassal states on the western side of the Euphrates River, sued for peace and followed the example set by king Toi.

II SAMUEL CHAPTER 10

In (II Sam. 8:6.10) the Arameans were restrained from coming to Ammon's assistance because David left a garrison of soldiers to restrain their military actions and to exact tribute from them to cover the cost.

II SAMUEL CHAPTER 11

V.1   A year had gone by since the two wars with Ammon and Hadadezer, recorded in (II Sam.10:6,15.16). It is now the month of March, when ancient kings planned their military campaigns in the spring of the year as winter-sown crops are being readied for harvest. The pasture is fertile; an army can live off the soil. During these winter months David's military had planned this campaign in order to cut Ammon down to size to secure Israel's eastern borders. David and Joab are aware of the difficulties in capturing their capital city of Rabbah, they therefore intend to besiege Rabbah and to take control of all the vassal communities in the Ammonite feudal system that are under king Hanan's control. This action will bridle their ability to organize for future expansion.

Vs.2.3   From the details we may conclude that David no longer takes part in the military campaigns. David arose from his afternoon siesta and took a stroll upon the palace roof garden. From this vantage point he observed a beautiful woman bathing in her home. Stimulated by the scene, he made an inquiry in order to identify her. He is advised, "She is Bathsheba, the daughter of Eliam and the wife of Uriah the Hittite, a convert to Israel (II Sam.23:34.39). She is also the granddaughter of Ahitophel.

Vs.4.6   David sent messengers to invite her to his chambers. She consented and accepted his invitation. David was overcome by her beauty. The text is intent upon confirming that Bathsheba had just purified herself after her period; to establish the fact that she was not pregnant. After David had lain with her, Bathsheba returned to her home. When she conceived she sent word to David, "I am pregnant." David dispatched a message to Joab at the battle front, "Send Uriah the Hittite to me."

Vs.7.9   Uriah arrived at the palace and the king asked him to report on the progress at the front. David then ordered Uriah, "Go home, bathe and relax from your long journey." When Uriah left the palace a gift was sent to him from the king. However, Uriah did not go to his home but slept with the palace guard.

Vs.10.13   Upon investigation, David confirmed his fears that Uriah did not sleep in his home. David sought him out and reproached him, "You have just returned from your arduous duties of the military campaign and no doubt are fatigued by the journey from Trans-Jordan to Jerusalem. You should go home for some rest." Uriah replied, "The Ark of the Eternal (I Sam.14:18,4:3, II Sam.15:24), the tribe of Judah, Joab and the whole

II SAMUEL CHAPTER 11

army of Israel are encamped in the open field. Shall I go home in a mood of festivity to relax with my wife?" Uriah took an oath, "That neither his conscience nor his sensitivity to the feelings of his comrades in arms will permit him to indulge himself with such comfort." From the details, David is convinced that Uriah is aware that he has been cuckolded (from the practice of the cuckoo that lays its eggs in other birds nests to be hatched by them). David once again suggests to Uriah, "Stay here today and tomorrow; I shall then discharge you to return to the battle front." Uriah stayed in Jerusalem that day and once again slept with the guard. On the morrow Uriah was summoned to the palace, he was invited to dine with the king. They ate and drank together and Uriah permitted himself to become intoxicated so that he forgot the complications of his personal life. Despite Uriah's inebriation, he was consistent in his personal discipline. He did not go home to do the thing that would have come natural to most men. From these details there emerges a human being who is a convert to Israel because he recognized the advanced disciplines, morals and ethics demanded by Israel's Torah. Uriah is dedicated to his God and to his people. He has won recognition as a good soldier and has endangered his life in their behalf. He strives to be loyal to his king, though it may cost him his life.

Vs.14.17 Reviewing David's biography from the day he made his debut in history (I Sam.16:11.13), we observe his enchanted life. He has proved his ability to overcome the most formidable obstacles, to succeed and rise to the top of his every undertaking. From diversity he has risen to the highest honor of the nation. Sitting in his palace, he has permitted his conscience to relax. His digression has entrapped him (Gen.6:3) to mar a lifetime of excellence. Uriah's greatness of character shines as the midday sun. He exercises restraint while David's indulgence like his ancestor Judah (Gen.38:26) has ensnared him. Yet, he fails to admit that Uriah's sense of justice deserves the highest recognition for his moral standards. David ignored his *Zelem Elohim*, conscience, as he put into writing the letter that will condemn him in the annals of history as he orders the assassination of Uriah. "Place Uriah in the front line where he will be exposed to the greatest danger. Instruct the men to retreat, abandoning Uriah to the direct arrows of the Ammonites." Uriah's death included those that remained loyal to his position. The nobility of Uriah cannot be overemphasized as he delivered David's letter intact to Joab, though David was already suspect in his thoughts.

Vs.18.21 Joab sent a detailed report of the battle to David and coached the messenger to anticipate the king's anger for having permitted Uriah and his men to come close to the city wall where they became exposed to the random missiles and arrows catapulted from the city wall in the manner of (Jud.9:52.57).

Vs.22.25 Joab's messenger delivered his report to David. In it he described casually how Uriah and some of his men were struck by the Ammonite archers from the top of the wall.

II SAMUEL CHAPTER 11

David gave his reply orally to Joab's messenger, "Do not be distressed about this matter; the sword always takes its toll. Press on with your attack upon the city of Rabbah and destroy it! Comfort Joab over the death of Uriah. These are indeed the fortunes of war."

Vs.26.27   Bathsheba lamented over the death of *baalah*, her legal husband, and mourned the tragic loss of *ishah*, the man she loved. After the formal period of mourning, David brought Bathsheba to the palace in order to console her and to alleviate her embarrassment. Bathsheba became David's wife and then bore him a son.

The following texts in Talmud Babli: (Kid.43a, San.56a, 107a, Sab.56a, Ket.9b) are an effort to exonerate king David. We must reject their conclusions as unworthy of their sacred memory.

II SAMUEL CHAPTER 12

Vs.1.4   The Eternal God, the Master of the Universe, holds every living creature accountable for its life (Gen.4:9.11, 9:5.6) and the lives of others. This Eternal God of justice and history demands justice in behalf of all His creatures, be they of high or low station in the eyes of human society. It is this Eternal God of Israel that sent the prophet Nathan to David after Bathsheba's child was born. Nathan's parable in these verses is to immortalize Israel's concern with the evolution of justice in the human heart by holding their king and all future kings responsible for their misdeeds. David listened attentively as Nathan unfolded the extent of the oppression which this rich man in his parable exercised over the poor man. Nathan aptly points out his selfishness as he ignored God's law by denying the poor man his human rights.

Vs.5.6   As Nathan's parable unfolded, it kindled David's wrath as he became incensed with the conduct of the rich man. Spontaneously he shouted, "Such a man deserves to die! He should be fined and forced to pay *shevuataim* four times the value demanded by Torah law (Ex.21:37). This rich man has no heart, no pity or compassion for the poor."

Vs.7.9   The prophet Nathan waited for David to finish his condemnation of the rich man in his parable. "That rich man in my parable is you! (Gen.4:6.7) As the exemplary head of the nation of Israel, you pursued your animal desires in order to satisfy your passion. You exercised your authority to demand that which the law forbids all human beings, you then opened wide the door to all the implications that led to putting Uriah to the sword and then taking possession of his wife. I shall now speak in the name of the Eternal God of Israel."

"It was the Eternal that inspired the prophet Samuel to anoint you (I

II SAMUEL CHAPTER 12

Sam.16:12.13) as the king of Israel. He guided your every step and protected you from the treachery of king Saul. He then created the climate for you to succeed Ishbosheth and to inherit legally all of his property and social rights. It was the Eternal's direction in history that made possible the unification of the state under your sovereignty. Had you observed scrupulously the Eternal God's law, your example would have inspired your posterity to become dedicated and deserving of His ongoing promise to become the symbol of renown (Gen.22:17.18) to inspire all of humanity to live by His Master Plan, the Torah."

Nathan continued his charge to David, "I now declare you guilty of transgressing three basic commandments of the Torah (Ex.20:14.16). You are guilty of putting Uriah to the sword as you implicated the Ammonites to become your accomplices to this treacherous deed. You committed adultery and then took Bathsheba as your wife."

Vs.10.12 The prophet Nathan continued his charge to king David, "The immediate effect of the transgressions you were sworn to uphold (Deut.17:14.20) have already surfaced in the intrigue prevalent in the lives of your posterity as they will vie for the crown of Israel. The example of treachery shall continue to surface and may never depart from your House." (II Sam.13:28) records the murder of Amnon. (II Sam.18:14) records the death of Absalom as a rebel; and (I Kings2:25) the execution of Adonijahu. "Your son Absalom, (II Sam.18:14) will rise against you to create calamity within your own household as he will take possession of your wives publicly. You transgressed in the privacy of your palace; they shall be shameless as they implement their treachery in broad daylight.

While David was involved in enlarging his harem and satisfying the needs of his many children by enlarging the effectiveness of his government, Nathan penetrated the trappings of government and the social intrigue as it chose sides before it will surface in the open.

Vs.13.15 David said to the prophet Nathan, "I recognize my transgression of the Eternal's guidelines for history." Nathan sympathized with David's predicament, (Gen.6:3.6, Ex.34:6.7) see T.E.T. Nathan is quick to assure him, "You will not die but live to see the effect of your disobedience." The Eternal reflects upon the human condition and laments through His grief; how humanity frustrates its own happiness for it lacks the dedication to discipline its split personality, the *yezer tov* and *yezer ra*, the conflict between animalistic passions and the drive for humanity's place in the evolutionary process. David's infraction of the Eternal's Torah law has made a shambles of his life's work as it shattered the crown of civilization.

The sigh of the prophet's *efes* has survived the centuries. "Though you have sinned against yourself, your misdeed shall stand as a charge against you; you have aided and abetted the enemies of the Eternal God of Israel. I regret to inform you that Bathsheba's child will die, to give testimony to all of mankind, that the

II SAMUEL CHAPTER 12

sovereign of Israel must be held accountable for his transgression." Nathan having discharged his message, departed for his home.

Vs.16.19   Soon after Nathan's departure, the child that Uriah's wife Bathsheba had born to David became critically ill. David closeted himself in the privacy of the palace to entreat Israel's God of justice in behalf of the child. David fasted and rested on the bare ground in order to deprive himself of any comfort. The senior members of his household pleaded with him that he rise and partake of food with them but he refused. On the seventh day of his ordeal in doing penance, the child died. The members of his household refrained from telling him, for fear of its effect upon him. Observing the whispering all about him, he concluded the bad news and asked the senior members of his household to confirm or deny that the child is dead.

Vs.20.23   David's period of prayer and penance was done in the hope of averting Nathan's prophetic decree. Now that it had come to pass, he became reconciled to the first step of Nathan's verdict. The king rose from the ground, bathed, anointed himself and changed his clothes. He went directly to the House of the Eternal, the Mishkan, and prostrated himself before the Ark of God. He then returned to the palace and asked for food and he ate. When challenged for his procedure, David replied, "As long as the child was alive, there was hope for his recovery. I therefore prayed that I could reverse the decree. Now that the child is dead I accept my grief graciously. I can only go to join him; he can no longer return to me."

Vs.24.25   David went to Bathsheba to console her grief, to resolve their past errors, and to strive for a new beginning. In the course of time, Bathsheba conceived and bore David a son. David named him Shlomo, in the hope that his birth should indicate a new era of peace for Israel. David announced the birth of his son to the prophet Nathan. When Nathan congratulated king David, he blessed the child and named him Jedidiah, the beloved of the Eternal God.

Vs.26.31   Joab is confident of his victory over the Ammonites. He notified David to come to the scene of battle with the reserves of the army, that the victory of Rabbah be credited to David. To confirm his optimism he assured David that he has already captured the outer city which contains the water supply for the inner city. The Jabbok-Vadi-Zarka is the key to the victory. David came with the reserves and gave the siege the *coup de grace*. The crown mentioned in the text was normally worn by the idol Milkam. It weighed more than 55 to 60 pounds of solid gold and in it were set semi-precious stones. It is facetious to conclude that David actually wore it, particularly after the scenes described in chapter 12, which set a mood of reservation in anticipation of Nathan's evaluation and verdict of things to come. In keeping with David's past practice of occupation, he set the people to work to continue to contribute to the gross national product of the nation. David's sole

II SAMUEL CHAPTER 12

reason for this siege was to destroy the intransigent Ammonite government which had been a thorn in the side of Israel's body politic for 300 years. Having accomplished this, he secured his position there by establishing his control. Then David, and his troops who fought in the war, returned to Jerusalem.

II SAMUEL CHAPTER 13

The following eight chapters are devoted to recording the effect of David's personal transgression (Deut.17:17, Ex.20:14.16) as charged by the prophet Nathan in (II Sam.12:7.12). King David has failed in becoming a moral example for his family and the nation by accepting the polygamous practices of his time and environment. These practices are a reinforcement of pagan licentiousness. The effectiveness of this *'license'* can be felt in the 20th century as we accept the banal practices of our environment, by doing our own thing while ignoring Torah disciplines. The prophet Nathan's admonition to king David echoes down the centuries as he reminded the king, "You are going to be told what you are doing; for the long-range effect is cumulative." Violent images are stored in the brain; when they are retrieved, depends upon circumstances that we set into motion. The lust of Amnon led to the revenge of Absalom. From fratricide to anarchy and rebellion is but a matter of degree.

Vs.1.2 These verses describe the circumstances which robbed king David's remaining years of tranquility. Amnon was the son of Ahinoam, the Jezreelite. He was king David's oldest son. Absalom and his older sister Tamar, were children of Maacah, the daughter of Talmai, the king of Geshur. See the following texts in T.E.T. for their genealogy (II Sam.3:2.5, Gen.22:24, Deut.3:14). Amnon became infatuated with Tamar's moral rectitude and her beautiful personality. The text is precise and intent upon highlighting the fact that despite the permissiveness of the times in her environment, Tamar was meticulous in her modesty and moral behavior. Though her younger brother Absalom was already married, she chose to remain a virgin in a sea of licentiousness. Tamar's unadorned elegance became a challenge to Amnon. He became obsessed with the idea of seducing her, even though he knew that in accord with Torah law (Lev.18:9, 6.18) see T.E.T., he could never marry her. Amnon cultivated a distorted form of lust outside of the context of love. The adultery which he committed in his heart created the depression which made him sick.

Vs.3.14 Amnon's continuous brooding over his obsession overpowered his common sense and logic. Jonadab is a friend to anyone who is willing to share personal confidences. As a cousin, he subtly evoked anxiety in his desire to share Amnon's most intimate thoughts which are the source of his anguish. Amnon had no reservations. He bluntly told Jonadab, "I am in love with Tamar." Jonadab concluded Amnon's desires were sexual. Despite this *chacham* intelligent conclusion, he opened the door for

II SAMUEL CHAPTER 13

Amnon by suggesting a plan by which he could fulfill his desire. "Pretend you are sick. When your father comes to visit you, make a request that he order your sister, Tamar, to come to your home and prepare some food for you which will help you recover from your illness." Amnon followed Jonadab's instructions; he took to his bed and his father, the king, came to visit him. Amnon made his request, and the king sent a message to Tamar and conveyed Amnon's desire. Conforming to the king's order, Tamar went to Amnon's home. Tamar busied herself and kneaded some cakes which she fried in oil, while Amnon looked on and admired her from his bed. Tamar handed the cakes to Amnon's household help that they serve them to Amnon. Amnon refused to eat them unless his servants left the room and Tamar would serve him personally. Tamar accommodated him and came close to his bed to serve him. At this point he addressed Tamar, "Come lie with me!" Tamar did not take him seriously. She enumerated the restraining prohibitions in Israel's law and tradition against such wanton behavior. Tamar challenged Amnon to ever remember their blood ties and his princely position. Observing Amnon's insistence, Tamar charged him, "Are you just another scoundrel in Israel? Should you fulfill your desire, I shall be disgraced." Tamar played for time as she suggested, "Speak to the king. He shall recognize your desire to marry me, and he then will not refuse me to you." Despite all of Tamar's efforts, Amnon overpowered her and proceeded to seduce her.

Vs.15.17   These verses express Amnon's disgust with himself for having permitted his lust to overcome Tamar's pleas in her consistent desire to remain a virgin. Tamar's struggle to reject Amnon's approach triggered his violent withdrawal and revulsion for Tamar. Amnon recognized his erotic behavior, and he hated himself for having exposed his innermost thoughts to become labeled as a scoundrel. Amnon's deceitful conduct has unfrocked him of his princely position. Amnon's loathing for himself is natural; his despicable conduct awakened his conscience to recognize his self-created exile when he rejected Tamar's plea to prove his maturity by self-control. Amnon saw clearly, now that the fever had left his blood, that "He who circumvents moral law is responsible for his own destruction."

Amnon's great love-desire for Tamar turned to hate and loathing as he shouted, "Get out of my life." Tamar pleaded with him, "Should you force this shame upon me by sending me away in this moment of my distress, you will be compounding my shame and embarrassment." Amnon ignored Tamar's plea. He summoned his attendant and commanded him, "Get this woman out of my presence and prevent her from coming back into this house."

Vs.18.22   The text subtly tells us that anyone could identify Tamar as a princess by the noble garment she was wearing to conform with her position. From the moment the attendant closed the door behind her, her identity would become public knowledge to compound her embarrassment. Tamar resolved to express her grief publicly; she rent her

II SAMUEL CHAPTER 13

princely dress and placed soil upon her head; she raised her hands above her head and bemoaned her fate publicly on her way home. Absalom observed her distress and questioned her, "Was your brother Amnon responsible for this?" He counseled her not to brood over this matter at this moment. "Since Amnon is your brother, we must be discreet and avoid any public scandal." Tamar remained under the custody of her brother Absalom, where she meditated silently over her wretched condition. She bemoaned the abandonment of the ideals she had set for her life. When king David learned of this incident, he felt trapped in light of his own indulgences. Once again he failed to call his son to task for his despicable conduct. David's failure to reprimand and discipline his children was the momentum that heaped many sorrows upon him in the last decade of his life. Absalom avoided any conversation on the above described episode; his hatred for Amnon never left his thoughts as he brooded over the despicable violation of his sister Tamar.

Vs.23.27 Two years have passed by since the seduction of Tamar. Though the tragic experience had become history, Absalom never forgot as he bided his time. He is now ready to activate his revenge. Absalom is planning a sheep-shearing festival at his residence in Baal-hazor, in the territory near Ephraim. He invited all the king's sons (II Sam.3:2.5, 5:13.16). He then perfunctorily went through the motions of inviting king David and his retinue. David tactfully declined, "No, my son, we must not all come; it could become a burden to you." Absalom urged his father to come, but he turned him down and abruptly bid him farewell. As a last thought, Absalom addressed his father, "Since you will not come, permit my brother Amnon to come with us." King David was startled by Absalom's request, for it recalled a bad dream that stirred his memory. The king replied, "Why do you want him to join you?" Absalom pressed his invitation and urged his father to consent to Amnon's presence as a substitute for his father's absence. King David ceased his opposition and consented to Absalom's request.

Vs.28.29 Absalom now has all of his principals in place. His last step is to instruct his men in the details of his premeditated plan: "Observe the moment when Amnon is merry and under the influence of wine, I will give you the signal to kill him. Do not fear, for it is I who is assuming the responsibility for your action. Be brave and resolute in your determination to complete the task." When Absalom's men implemented his instructions and had assassinated Amnon, all of David's other sons fled from the scene. They feared for their lives as they were outnumbered by Absalom's men.

Vs.30.33 The tragic news reached king David even while his sons were fleeing from Absalom's wrath. It was reported that all of the king's sons had been assassinated, that not one had survived the terror. David rent his garments and lay on the ground to express his grief. Observing the king's torment, all of his courtiers followed their king's procedure, to express their sympathy with king David's distress. Once again, Jonadab's *wise*

II SAMUEL CHAPTER 13

counsel came to the fore. "My sovereign, you have been misinformed. Only Amnon is dead, for Absalom has bided his time and made his resolution on the very day that Amnon had violated his sister, Tamar." From vs. 3 and 33, we may conclude why Jonadab was called a *chacham*; he was wise and sagacious in extracting the confidential thoughts of those whom he befriended. Had he not counseled Amnon, he might still be alive. From v.33, we can conclude that Jonadab was also privy to Absalom's innermost motives. He now strives to assuage and to pacify king David to be grateful, "That only Amnon is dead; Absalom was justified in avenging his sister's seduction. Be comforted that justice has been served."

V.34 Absalom fled the scene of the assassination as he feared the repercussions for his criminal act. He now perceived that his murderous action will be misconstrued, that he deliberately eliminated Amnon, who was the heir-apparent to the throne of king David. David's other sons anticipated Absalom's premeditated refuge would be at the home of his father-in-law, Talmai, in Geshur, the territory of the Maacatites. Talmai had already broken the long tradition of their kinship with Israel (II Sam.10:6.8). Absalom therefore felt secure in this sanctuary that will protect him from the storm of vengeance. David's sons therefore took a roundabout road on their way back to Jerusalem, in order to avoid a confrontation with Absalom and his assassins. The lookout in v.34 was confused when he observed a group coming from an entirely different direction; from the side of the mountain instead of the main road.

Vs.35.36 Jonadab went to great lengths to comfort king David, that only Amnon is dead. "Here are your other sons to confirm the correctness of my information. I was privy to Absalom's *simah* (in v.32), for Absalom shared his resolution with me on that fatal day of Tamar's seduction." When David's other sons made their appearance before their father, the king, they spontaneously broke into weeping to express their dire distress. The courtiers present were overcome by this scene and joined in lamenting the death of Amnon.

Vs.37.39 Absalom had fled to his premeditated hideout, the home of Talmai, the son of Amihud, the king of Geshur. Here Absalom stayed for three years with the father (grandfather) of his mother Maacah (II Sam.3:3). David mourned the loss of Amnon; he could not put him out of his mind. David did toy with the idea of retribution against Absalom and at the same time settling the military score with the king of Geshur. After the lapse of a year or so he resolved to resign himself to the reality of the situation. His great love for his children was more important than any military victory or revenge against his own kin.

II SAMUEL CHAPTER 14

Vs.1.3   Joab the son of Zeruiah, has proven his dedication to king David and the national cause of Israel. He has been close enough to his sovereign to perceive his thoughts from day to day. Joab recognized the long thread of yearning that bound his king with the life of Absalom. Yet he desists from forgiving him for his crime against Amnon. Joab therefore takes the initiative to create the environment and the demand for Absalom's return to Jerusalem. Joab exposed his sensitivity and understanding that the subject must become urgent through a third party. Joab therefore sent a message to *ishah chachamah*, an intelligent woman, who has the ability to put into words her perceptions of a difficult situation. Joab described the details which led Absalom to murder Amnon, in order to give her the background of facts upon which she will build her presentation to the king. Joab suggested that she appear as a mourner by wearing garments to create the desired mood, down to the most minute details of her cosmetics and anointment. She is coached by Joab to express her long-time grief over a departed one. Tekoah is about 12 miles southeast of Jerusalem. Tekoah is in the territory of Judah and became the birthplace of the prophet Amos, who will come to the fore in the 8th century BCE.

Vs.4.7   The woman from Tekoah came before king David, prostrated herself and appealed to him for counsel. The king agreed to hear her distressing problem. "I am a widow; before my husband died, I gave birth to two sons. One day they came to blows while in the solitude of a distant field. One of them was killed. My clan are now demanding that I surrender the guilty one that he may be punished for his crime. They demand the death penalty though this would sever the genetic continuity of my husband's immortality." The basis of her pleas was taken from (Gen.4:13.16).

Vs.8.11   King David sympathetically instructed the woman from Tekoah, "Go home, I will issue my verdict in your behalf."
The woman enjoined the king, "Place the guilt upon me and my family for having created an atmosphere to induce such conduct. Your Majesty and your government must not assume the guilt which is solely our own." King David comforted the woman, "Should anyone take you to task in this matter, report it to me. I will make sure that he will not burden you with any guilt in this matter." The woman once again interjected, "In the name of the Eternal, your God Who demands justice in the life of every human being, I plead that you intercept those who are demanding the death penalty of my only remaining son, that he survive as our only heir." King David assured her, "I vow it in the name of the living Eternal God, not a hair of his head will suffer any injury."

Vs.12.17   Having received the verdict in vs.8.11, the woman from Tekoah begged the king's indulgence, that she may plead (for Absalom) an analogous situation. "I have reservations in accepting your assurances to save my son from his avengers. Your verdict in my

II SAMUEL CHAPTER 14

son's case contradicts your conclusions in your own son's case. By refusing to pardon Absalom, you have denied God's people, Israel, of their heir apparent. In light of human experience, that each of us must die, for human life is as unstable as water, for when we pour it on the ground it is absorbed by the soil and cannot be retrieved. Death robs us of the ability to correct our errors. God will not punish you for bringing your son Absalom back to Jerusalem from his exile. Forgive my impertinence for having challenged your integrity. I am frightened by public opinion that may dispute your consistency. Though I came for the sole purpose of pleading in my own cause, I took the liberty to plead with you to reassess your decree in your own son's case. Accept my humble plea for mercy, even as your sense of justice has seen fit to protect me from those desiring to destroy my immortality. I express my gratitude for the comfort you have given me. I recognize your Majesty as the angel of God, ever striving for the ability to discern tyranny from mercy, virtue from violence. May the Eternal, your God, ever be with you to inspire your efforts with excellence."

Vs.18.20 King David exposed his receptivity to the plea of the woman from Tekoah. "You have graciously revealed your innermost thoughts to me. I now challenge your motives for coming before me with your hypothetical case in order to defy my sense of mercy in behalf of my son Absalom. Tell me! Withhold nothing from me! Was Joab the motivating vehicle that animated you to come before me?" The woman replied, "Your question truly establishes the proof that you are indeed an angel of God, for no one can conceal the events of the nation without you becoming privy to the information. Every word I have uttered before you is the result of Joab's inspiration."

Vs.21.24 King David addressed Joab, "I am indebted to you for challenging my obstinacy in this matter with Absalom. I am ready to reverse my decree that it harmonize with your plea. Go! Bring back Absalom." Joab prostrated himself before his king to express his gratitude for having recognized the justice of his request. Joab went to Geshur and brought Absalom back to Jerusalem. Absalom went directly to his former home in order to accord with the king's instructions. King David made it known that he was not yet ready to come face to face with Absalom, nor to grant him an outright pardon for his crime. King David's mitigating sentence from exile in Geshur to house arrest in Jerusalem indicates his prophetic conclusions, that this wound shall fester to disturb his peace.

Vs.25.27 The text in these verses describes the extraordinary beauty and perfection of Absalom's physique that won the admiration and popularity in his public relations. This popularity and public acclaim fed his ego. He had concluded in his heart that none of his brothers were as fit as he to succeed his father as king of Israel. It was this egotistical individual that was confined for two years to his home in Jerusalem after his father commuted his sentence. Here he brooded and planned anarchy and rebellion

II SAMUEL CHAPTER 14

against his father. The text reports that he had three sons and one daughter whom he named Tamar. There is no record of the sons' names. It is therefore concluded that they died young while their father was in Geshur (II Sam.18:18).

Vs.28.29 For two years Absalom was under house arrest in his home. He had begun to conclude that this may become his fate for the rest of his life. Here he rationalized the futility of his life that has removed him from the day to day events in the development of the nation. From the text we must discern that Joab's motive for bringing back Absalom to Jerusalem was rooted in his desire to assuage the grief of his king. It was his sincere wish that they become reconciled for a new beginning. Absalom, having had the time to evaluate every facet of his situation, is determined to have the meaning of his retention resolved. Joab is the logical person to represent his cause. Therefore, Absalom sent a message to Joab, requesting his presence. Joab did not reply. From Joab's refusal, we may conclude the completeness of Absalom's internment. The members of the official government were restrained from communicating with him. This created the public impression that king David had no intention of modifying his verdict for Absalom's criminal act. It also sheds light upon king David's closeness with Amnon his oldest son. Twice did Absalom request Joab's presence and twice he ignored his message. Joab's firm refusal to answer Absalom's request signaled the firmness of king David's edict for Absalom's isolation.

Vs.30.33 Absalom is determined to break out of his isolation by creating an emergency that would bring Joab to his home. From this verse we learn that Joab's fields were adjacent to Absalom's property. In his desperation, Absalom instructed his help to set Joab's barley field on fire. Alarmed at this reckless and irrational act, Joab came at once to Absalom's home, to demand an explanation for his wanton conduct. Absalom replied, "Twice I sent messages to your home and you ignored them. I would like you to speak to the king in my behalf. What was the purpose of bringing me here from Geshur? Had I remained there I would have enjoyed my freedom. I demand an audience with the king. I desire that he adjudicate this matter; if I am guilty of death, let him enforce his verdict!" Joab went to the king and delivered Absalom's message. King David responded by summoning Absalom to come before him. Absalom came and prostrated himself before his father, the king. David recognized this as a moment for mercy and reconciliation. He ordered him to rise and kissed him to indicate his forgiveness.

II SAMUEL CHAPTER 15

The time frame for this chapter is toward the end of king David's reign. Rumors fill the national airwaves that king David has determined to set aside all the sons that were born to him in Hebron (II Sam.3:2.5), to deny them their legal

II SAMUEL CHAPTER 15

rights of succession in favor of Solomon who was born in Jerusalem to his mother Bathsheba. The dissension and discord created by king David, his indulgence with Bathsheba, were but the sparks which ignited the intrigue smoldering in the suppressed body politic of the nation. Solomon was the youngest of those born in Jerusalem (II Sam.5:13.16). Chapters 11 through 14 are but the exposed details of the scenario. Joab, David's field marshal, and Ahithophel, king David's infallible counselor, are opposed to bypassing Absalom. While Ahithophel headed Absalom's conspiracy, Joab remained loyal to his king. Adonijah, the son of Haggith, had contempt for the egotistical Absalom. Against this background, we must judge Joab's conduct so vividly described in chapter 14. It was during the two years of Absalom's house arrest in Jerusalem that Joab was meticulous in making any public contact with Absalom. From the details in (II Sam.14:28.33) we may conclude the public conflagration was Joab's inspiration to bring back Absalom into the mainstream of king David's court.

Vs.1.6 Against this background we may better understand the underpinnings of Absalom's next move as he provided himself with a chariot, horses and 50 runners to create the pomp and circumstance that he is the chosen successor of his father, king David. Vs.2.6 are his effort to create the popular demand that will acclaim his renown for his moral concern with justice and the establishment of good government. What Absalom was doing publicly in Jerusalem, Ahithophel was duplicating clandestinely among the tribal leaders whose loyalties to king David were cemented only by the prosperity which they were enjoying after three centuries of chaos. This was the preoccupation of Absalom from the moment he was pardoned by his father; to win the hearts and minds of the people of Israel, to establish his popularity in the nation in order to create a demand that he succeed his father.

Vs.7.9 The numerical figure in v.7, of forty years indicates this was the 37th year of king David's reign. This also corresponds to the fourth year of Absalom's return to Jerusalem. (Absalom is about age 30). Absalom's demagoguery has already planted the seeds of superiority, by his method of shaking hands, he has created the spirit of hail fellow well met, he has augmented his intimacy and recognition. Absalom and his counselors have concluded that all the indicators of his deception are fully in place; he feels secure with the loyalties of the people of Israel. Against this background, Absalom requested and was granted permission to go to Hebron to honor a vow he claimed to have made six years before while still in Geshur. Though his father, king David, is aware of Absalom's intentions and his reason for going to Hebron is to activate his rebellion, king David honored his request and said to him, "Go in peace." From these three words spoken by a dedicated father to his son, king David has given history the ability to penetrate into the sensitivity of a great human being. King David has rationalized all the available facts which have surfaced in his heart, in his mind and from the various opinions that have manifested themselves as evidence during these past seven years since Amnon was assassinated by his brother Absalom. King David is deeply pained

II SAMUEL CHAPTER 15

that there is no single example recorded in the life of Absalom, to confirm that he became involved in the day to day problems of government as a potential heir-apparent to king David. His father recognized his potential, yet, he failed to capitalize on his natural ability, in the manner of Jonathan, the son of Saul. Every day since his father had become reconciled with Absalom were spent in planning this rebellion. Was it necessary for Absalom to go to Hebron to honor his alleged vow? The main Central Sanctuary has been in Jerusalem for almost the past 30 years. These facts outweigh his father's love for Absalom to convince him that he is a loser. Every bit of historic record connected with his life are involved with subterfuge (II Sam.13:22.27, 37.38, 14:1.4, 18.20, 23, 28, 33).

King David has resolved never to condemn his son to be killed for his treasonous conduct (II Sam.18:5). King David stands ready to accept the Eternal's verdict as the God of history, if it be His decree that Absalom become the king of Israel, he will accept His judgment as just, in light of all his own transgressions. King David's, "Go in peace and succeed in whatever you do, if it conforms with the Eternal God of history," is the prayer of a tender, loving father.

Vs.10.12   Absalom sent representatives throughout the Holyland to deliver the following message, "When you hear the blast of the shofar originating in Hebron, this will be your signal that Absalom has been anointed king of Israel." To lend the official approval to his ceremony, Absalom had invited 200 prominent personalities to lend prestige to his gathering as he proclaimed to them it bore the authority of king David. He did not inform them that they were to witness the crowning of Absalom. The conspiracy gained dignity and the official stamp of approval as Ahithophel, David's trusted counselor from Gilo, made his presence felt.

Vs.13.16   When David was notified that all the details were in place for the crowning of Absalom as king of Israel, David instructed his courtiers and all the members of his family that he plans to leave Jerusalem and go into exile. David's decision to abandon Jerusalem was based upon several factors. He had no plan to defend himself against Absalom in the city which he built with so much love and effort. David is desirous of avoiding any bloodshed of its inhabitants. However, should Absalom strive to make war upon him, he shall stand and fight in the field without exposing any civilians. To challenge Absalom's respect for his father, David left his concubines in the palace that it be occupied in his absence (II Sam.16:21). King David had no illusions of receiving any consideration at the hands of Absalom. He placed his faith in the hands of the Eternal God. He is confident of his past record in having advanced the national welfare. A half century has passed since that day when he was anointed by the prophet Samuel. Every moment of his life has been devoted to the national interest. Though king David recognized Absalom's rebellion as the Eternal's punishing rod for his own transgressions in failing to become a moral example, he has never lost his hope and faith that this, too, shall pass. This is the

II SAMUEL CHAPTER 15

spirit of all his followers who stand ready to follow him to the ends of the earth, because of his dedication to truth.

Vs.17.18 When king David reached the last house before leaving Jerusalem, he stood in a fixed position to express his personal gratitude to each and every man and woman dedicated to his cause. In the line of march were his faithful Cherethites and Pelethites, and the six hundred Gittites that had joined him in fleeing from Saul's pursuit (I Sam. 23:13).

Vs.19.22 Ittai was a Philistine who had defected and joined king David in his war with the Philistines. He was recognized for his loyalty as a leader of his Gittite troops. V.20. King David pleaded with Ittai, "Since you joined us but recently, why should you exile yourself in my behalf?" Transfer your loyalty to Absalom or return to your own people. You have demonstrated your dedication to me in the past, and for this I express my gratitude. Feel free to do what is best for your own welfare. Take your kinsmen who have served me faithfully and return to your own people." Ittai replied to king David, "I hereby take an oath, that as long as you live, I shall follow you to the ends of the earth enduring the dangers of death equally with the blessings I have enjoyed in the past." David accepted Ittai's rededication and ordered him, his men and their families to march on. In (II Sam.18:2) we find Ittai is in the forefront of David's defense.

Vs.23.29 We now learn that king David had urged the civilian population to remain loyal to their government and to carry on for the sake of the national welfare. These people have now lined the wayside to bid their charismatic king farewell. There faith never waned that he would return to his original glory. For the moment, they mourned the exile of their benefactor. As the king led his followers across the Kidron Valley in order to reach the road by the wilderness, Zadok, Abiathar and the Leviim appeared with the Ark of the Covenant of God, to pray for their welfare and safety from all dangers. David approached Zadok and Abiathar, "Take the Ark of God back to Jerusalem! If the Eternal God of Israel accepts my prayers and repentance, I shall be gratified to see the Ark of God once again in its abode in Jerusalem. However, should my plea be rejected, I am ready to accept His verdict. It is in the interest of the nation that I order you to retrun. You, Zadok, and your son Ahimaaz, and you, Abiathar, and your son Jonathan, are obliged to serve the people of Israel. Inspire them never to lose faith in the Eternal God of Israel. I shall remain in the steppes of the wilderness until you order me to return to Jerusalem."

Vs.30.31 King David crossed the wadi Kidron and rose to the Mount of Olives to take one last look at the city of Jerusalem from this high point. The king walked barefoot, weeping as he traveled; enshrouded by his guilt for having brought about this calamity upon his people.

II SAMUEL CHAPTER 15

It was in this setting and in this mood that king David composed Psalm 3:5, "I weep as I call to the Eternal, feeling confident that He has heard my plea from this mountain which faces His Sanctuary."

It was here that king David was informed that Ahithophel, his counselor, had joined the conspiracy with Absalom. David prayed that the Eternal confound his counsel.

Vs.32.37   When king David reached the highest point on the Mount of Olives, where all those in the king's retinue had planned to prostrate themselves facing the Tabernacle in Jerusalem, Hushai, the Archite (Josh.16:2) was already there to greet him. There he stood with a torn robe, and earth upon his head to express his grief for the exile of his king. Hushai had come to join his sovereign. King David expressed his gratitude to Hushai for his loyalty and said to him, "If you march with me, your advanced age will become a burden to me. However, should you go back to Jerusalem, your long experience in offering me years of wise counsel can now be of infinitely more service to me by nullifying Ahithophel's counsel against me (II Sam.17:5.7, 14.16). There in Jerusalem you will have the cooperation of Zadok and Abiathar and their sons Ahimaaz and Jonathan; they can relay your message to me." Hushai recognized king David's practical advice; he returned to Jerusalem just as Absalom and his followers were entering the city.

II SAMUEL CHAPTER 16

Vs.1.4   Soon after king David departed the summit of the Mount of Olives, Ziba, the employee of Mephibosheth, the son of Jonathan, came toward king David with a gift of a pair of saddled asses carrying 200 loaves of bread, 100 cakes of dried raisins, 100 cakes of dried figs and a large jar of wine. The term *kaaitz* is to inform us that these fruits were dried in the summer sun. King David asked Ziba, "What are you doing with all these?" Ziba replied, "I have brought the asses for the women in your family to ride upon, the bread and the fruit are for your retinue and the wine is for those that may become faint and exhausted while traveling in the wilderness." King David is concerned with the question, "By whose authority have you brought all this for our comfort and welfare, and where is *ben adonecha*, Mephibosheth, the son of Jonathan?" Ziba replied, "He has remained in Jerusalem in the hope that when the rebellion is over, he shall be restored to his grandfather's throne." Ziba is implying that he has brought this gift on his own initiative. King David replied to Ziba, "Since Mephibosheth has joined the rebellion against me, it is obvious that everything that originally belonged to Mephibosheth is now yours." Ziba acknowledged the king's generosity for recognizing him as the rightful heir as he prostrated himself before the king. To

II SAMUEL CHAPTER 16

understand these four verses, how Ziba deceived Mephibosheth, see (II Sam. 9:1.13, 19:18, 25.31).

Vs.5.8 As king David was approaching the community of Bahurim, which is east of Mount Scopus, a member of the tribe of Benjamin by the name of Shimei, the son of Gera, approached him, hurling insults at the king. He threw stones at the king and his courtiers and shouted, "Get out, you criminal, you villain! You are being punished for the crimes that you committed against the family of Saul whose throne you seized (II Sam. 3:23.28, 4:5.12, 11:24.25)." Shimei's intent is to humiliate king David even if it costs him his life.

Vs.9.14 Abishai, the son of Zeruiah, came forward to protect the king's honor (I Sam.26:8, II Sam.19:22), and he made an effort to punish Shimei for abusing the king. King David restrained him and said, "There is no need for you to punish Shimei. He is expressing his convictions in order to punish me for my past transgressions. Can we really determine what is motivating him to do this, any more than you can determine what motivates you to punish him in my behalf? How can I blame Shimei for striving to avenge the house of Saul, when my own son of whom I have a right to expect kindness and consideration desires to kill me? This is hardly the moment when I can yield to my chagrin and mortification, to shed the blood of another to assuage my misery and bitterness. There will come a time when I will calmly evaluate the full meaning of Shimei's conduct (I Kings 2:8). May the Eternal God, Who can penetrate *beeni*, the bitterness of my tears which feeds the pain in my heart, reverse the abuse of Shimei to become the momentum and the fountain of my future blessings." King David is resolved to express his humility by accepting Shimei's physical and verbal abuse as Shimei walked alongside of his retinue and threw soil and stones at random in order to expose his implacability, his venom, and his hatred toward king David. King David and his followers ignored Shimei's abuse as they continued on to Bahurim. Here they rested from their physical and mental exhaustion.

Vs.15.19 While king David and his retinue were resting in Bahurim, Absalom, Ahithophel and his followers arrived at the palace in Jerusalem. Hushai went directly to Absalom and pronounced his position, "Long live the king!" Surprised by Hushai's conduct, Absalom challenged his sincerity, "Is this the extent of your loyalty to an old friend?" Hushai replied to Absalom, "My loyalty is with him, whom the Eternal has chosen to become king of Israel. As the successor to your father, I will serve you even as I had served him."

Vs.20.23 Absalom turned to Ahithophel for advice, "What shall be our first move?" Ahithophel instructed Absalom, "Take possession of your father's concubines that are in the palace, in order to convince the populace that you shall never retreat or be reconciled

II SAMUEL CHAPTER 16

from your determination to become king of Israel." King David had hoped that this would become a stumbling block to Absalom. When he accepted the advice from the 'oracle-Ahithophel' that he follow the ancient immoral practice of violating the wives of the king, Absalom proved that he was but a puppet. From this desecration, to accepting Ahithophel's advice to kill his father, became a minor decision. What motivated Ahithophel, the *oracle*, to advise Absalom to desecrate a law which has been the accepted norm for 300 years? Israel's fidelity and reason for becoming a nation rests upon the observance of (Lev.18:8,28.29). Israel's exemplary dedication to these sexual laws are to become a *'light'* that shall inspire the genetic progression and development of civilization. "It is I, the Eternal God of justice that demands it as a condition for Israel's continuity." The moral depravity of ancient and modern sexual debauchery and licentiousness defy not only Torah law but denigrate scientific knowledge of biology and embryology which has given us all the proof vital to expose sexual perversion as the root of human retrogression in the scheme of evolution. It is the licentious practice of incest that creates the psychological *satans* which become rooted in the human heart to overshadow the light of God, making murder and war possible. For a more complete analysis of this subject, see T.E.T. (Lev.18:1.30). Israel's national life rises or falls if it cannot balance the equation: Natural law, Moral law....sexual demand, perversion. Ahithophel's advice was a desecration of human rights. Torah law is the demand which may never be ignored. Civilization rises or falls in just proportion as individuals observe its statutes.

II SAMUEL CHAPTER 17

Vs.1.6   Ahithophel is ready for the second step of his plan to attack king David and his retinue. He therefore requested permission to draft a force of 12,000 men and insisted that they act at once, that very evening, before king David and his followers refresh themselves from their long trek from Jerusalem. From the text in chapter 16 we have observed the weary, disheartened king, the discouragement in his rank and file retinue; they have had no opportunity to plan their next step. It is this weakness that Ahithophel is desirous of capitalizing upon by throwing fresh troops into the campaign to create panic among the civilians. While they are scampering for safety, they will concentrate upon seeking out king David and kill him. He is willing to return the rest of his followers to Jerusalem. Ahithophel assured Absalom, "Once we dispose of king David, even his staunch followers will accept your majesty as a *fait accompli* and will be ready to transfer their loyalty to you peacefully."

Though Absalom recognized the momentum implied in Ahithophel's plan, he is not quite ready to ignore his conscience, his Zelem Elohim, by consenting to kill his father. From the details in the text, we may conclude that Hushai was excluded from the conference. Absalom satisfied his disturbed conscience by

II SAMUEL CHAPTER 17

requesting that Hushai the Archite be consulted for a second opinion. Absalom summoned Hushai and repeated verbatim the full details of Ahithophel's strategy and plan for the capture of king David and to remove him completely as an obstacle to Absalom's government.

Vs.7.10   Hushai responded to Absalom, "Though I normally respect Ahithophel's wisdom, this time, I disagree with him fully for the following reasons: You must ever be mindful of your father the king and his loyal and courageous men who are skilled and accustomed by long experience to fighting and adopting to every difficult situation. Should you take them by surprise, they will recognize the odds and will strike back like a desperate bear in the field that has been robbed of its whelps. You must also take into consideration as an intrepid warrior, he will be spending the night surrounded by his troops. Therefore, dismiss from your mind that you can single out king David and isolate him from his troops and his retinue. You must come prepared to stand and fight and suffer many casualties. No matter how heroic your soldiers, they shall recognize the skill of your father's forces and soon become disheartened. When the news of this panic becomes known, it will unloosen an avalanche of public opinion against you. For your war with your father is a civil war; the casualties will involve members of our immediate families." Hushai is ever mindful in recognizing the reality of king David's position. The only way he can help him is by gaining time for him.

Vs.11.14   Hushai, having negated Ahithophel's plan, is now ready to propose his own strategy. "In light of the reasons I have advanced, you must plan a much larger force. An army which shall represent every tribe in the Holyland, from Dan to Beer-sheba. To inspire your cause, you, as the king, must lead your army in the field of battle." Hushai is feeding Absalom's ego as he described the potential victory by the weight of sheer numbers that will overcome the handicap of experience. "Should your father withdraw into a city, you will have the capability of combing the city until you will succeed in ferreting out king David from his hiding place. Not a pebble willl escape their search until they accomplish their goal." Absalom recognized the many advantages of Hushai's strategy; it transferred the responsibility of removing his father from the national scene from his own conscience to that of the nation.

Vs.15.17   Hushai is concerned with the probability, should Absalom reverse himself and decide to follow Ahithophel's plan, he therefore contacted Zadok and Abiathar and described both plans to them. Hushai ordered them to send the following message to king David, "Do not spend the night at the ford of the wilderness. Cross the Jordan at once, for you are in danger of being attacked by a very large force. V.17 informs us that Jonathan and Ahimaaz did not go back to Jerusalem (II Sam.15:35.37) for fear they would be intercepted; they therefore stationed themselves at the Spring of En-rogel, which is identified with the modern Bir Eyyub. Here the maids come

II SAMUEL CHAPTER 17

to wash their clothes. Abiathar and Zadok gave their message to one of their trustworthy maids and she relayed it casually to Jonathan and Ahimaaz.

Vs.18.20 Despite the precautions, Jonathan and Ahimaaz were observed waiting at the spring of En-rogel. They concluded their detection when a young man spontaneously started to run toward Jerusalem as he recognized them. Anticipating a search for their whereabouts, they went to Bahurim, to the home of a reliable person and hid there in a cistern normally used to collect rainwater. The woman of the house casually, while going about her chores, placed a cover over the cistern and camouflaged it by spreading groats over the cover; that it appear as being dehydrated by the sun. Jonathan and Ahimaaz's suspicion proved correct, for shortly after they hid in the cistern, Absalom's men came in search for them. They questioned the woman of the house as to their whereabouts. She told them, "They have gone in the direction of the Jordan, (*michal hamaim* is a contraction from *yachol*) with the intention of crossing the Jordan when the current will slacken." Absalom's men searched the area and did not find them. They returned to Jerusalem.

Vs.21.23 Jonathan and Ahimaaz came up from their hiding place and delivered their message to king David. "Cross the Jordan this very night, in order to frustrate Ahithophel's plan to take you by surprise." King David gave the order to evacuate the camp at once. They crossed the Jordan before dawn. When the sun rose and spread its morning light every last one of David's camp had already made their escape eastward toward Mahanaim. When Ahithophel was notified that David had succeeded in crossing the Jordan, he concluded that Absalom's cause was doomed. His plans for taking possession of David's concubines by Absalom and his counsel to kill king David are now public knowledge. He can now be held for treason. Rather than wait to be tried and disgraced, Ahithophel saddled his ass and secretly left Jerusalem for his home in Gilo. There he set his personal affairs in order and hanged himself. He was buried in his ancestral tomb.

Vs.24.29 Before Absalom arrived at the western shore of the Jordan, king David was already settled in Mahanaim. Here he made his plans to stand and fight for his personal life and for the life of the nation. In anticipation of the civil war ahead, Absalom appointed Amasa, the son of Ithra and Abigail. Abigail was the daughter of Nahash and Zeruiah. Zeruiah was also the mother of Joab. Amasa led Absalom's forces and encamped on the eastern shore of the Jordan in Gilead, while Joab, who led king David's forces, encamped further northeast at Mahanaim.

When David came to Mahanaim, Shobi, the son of Nahash, the former king of Ammon, came from their capital city of Rabbath-ammon, and joining him were Machir, the son of Ammiel (II Sam.9:4) from Lo-debar, and Barzillai, from Rogelim in the territory of Gilead (II Sam.19:32.40). Shobi was appointed

II SAMUEL CHAPTER 17

governor in Ammon after king David defeated them (II Sam.12:26.31). These three named individuals came to David in Mahanaim and presented him with couches for sleeping and sitting, and earthenware utensils for their comfort. They also presented wheat, barley, flour, parched grain, beans, lentils, honey, curds, a flock of sheep and cheese. These thoughtful leaders anticipated the needs of king David, his troops, and his courtiers, who had become weary from their long trek and had become hungry, faint, and thirsty while traveling in the wilderness.

II SAMUEL CHAPTER 18

Vs.1.4 When king David arrived in Mahanaim, thousands volunteered to join him. He reviewed the volunteers and organized them into companies in anticipation of the day he will be called upon to mobilize them for combat. He appointed captains over each group of 1000 soldiers and captains over each 100 soldiers. King David organized his command by placing Joab at the head of one third of his force. Abishai, the brother of Joab, whose mother was Zeruiah, controlled another third, and Ittai, the Gittite, over one third of his army. David had planned to assume the over-all command and lead his forces into combat. Joab, Abishai and Ittai rejected his heroic gesture. "Should we become exposed to a rout, and even if half of us are sacrificed, we are expendable. Your leadership is worth more than the 10,000 men that comprise our augmented army. It is far better that you remain in Mahanaim and assume the over-all responsibility of our supply system and direct our strategy in the field." King David replied, "I will follow your advice and do whatever you think best to accomplish our goal." It was at this time and in this mood that king David wrote Psalm 20, "The Eternal God of Israel will answer you in the day of trouble; the Eternal God of Jacob will raise you on high. He will send you your help and enable you to reach your goals. Out of the Sanctuary He will strengthen you from Zion. Some put their faith in chariots, others in horses, but as for us, we place our faith and trust in the Eternal God of justice."

Vs.5.8 King David stood at attention at the city gate and bade the officers and their soldiers Godspeed as they left Mahanaim. He instructed each of his generals, "Deal gently with my boy Absalom, for my sake." This order was given in the presence of all the soldiers. They traveled south toward the area of Succoth. From the moment they contacted Absalom's army, they went on the offensive and forced his army to retreat into the pasture land east of the Jordan River. This pasture land was used traditionally by the tribe of Ephraim, whose territory began on the western shore of the Jordan (Baba Kama 80b, also cited in Rambam's Laws of Civil Damages 5:3). The pressure of king David's army forced Absalom to retreat across the Jordan westward and head for the forest of Ephraim. Here the armies were locked in hand-to-hand fighting. V.7 reports the loss of 20,000 men in Absalom's army.

II SAMUEL CHAPTER 18

V.8 clarifies the reason for this great loss of life; most of the casualties were the result of the natural obstacles in the forest, swamps, falling trees, and wild beasts.

Vs.9.13 Absalom was riding a mule as he retreated with his army into the forest, his hair became entangled in the branch of a terebinth tree which forced his head to become locked in the brambles, while his mule sped on. Absalom remained suspended between heaven and earth. One of Joab's soldiers came upon the scene and reported it to him. Joab challenged him, "Why didn't you kill him? Had you killed him, I would have owed you ten shekels of silver and a belt for your sword." The soldier responded to Joab, "I would not kill king David's son even if I already had received 1000 shekels of silver. Besides, I heard king David's charge to you, Abishai, and Ittai, 'Be kind to my son, Absalom.' Had I killed him you would have refused to defend me before the king. It would have become public knowledge that I killed Absalom and that I lied to protect you."

Vs.14.18 Joab replied, "Seeing that I cannot depend upon you, I shall do it myself." Joab took three darts and drove them through Absalom's chest; which pinned him against the terebinth tree. The arms bearers that supplied Joab with the darts closed in on Absalom and killed him outright in order to remove him from his painful end. Joab sounded the horn to cease the pursuit. They removed Absalom's body from the tree, placed it into a pit in the forest, and covered it with a heap of stones. Some time later Absalom's body was reinterred into the mausoleum which he had built during his lifetime. Absalom was survived by a daughter (II Sam.14:27) who became the favorite queen of Rehoboam and the mother of the heir-apparent, Abijam. In this mausoleum, which is known to this day as Yad Absalom, in the Kidron valley of Jerusalem, Absalom probably laid to rest his three sons who died prematurely.

Vs.19.23 Ahimaaz, the son of Zadok, the high priest, requested permission from Joab that he be the one to carry the message to king David, that the rebellion was over. Joab restrained him, "You shall not be the one to report the death of Absalom!" Joab called a Cushite from the ranks, "Go! Report to king David what you have seen." The Cushite ran off to fulfill his mission. Ahimaaz once again pleaded with Joab for permission to deliver the news. Joab said to Ahimaaz, "Why should you be the one to deliver the bad news that the king's son is dead?" Ahimaaz replied, "If you try to restrain me I will speed the news to him anyway." Ahimaaz overtook the Cushite and ran ahead of him.

Vs.24.32 King David was sitting between the inner and outer gate of the city of Mahanaim. Here he sat waiting anxiously for news of the combat. Above him on the wall stood the watchman in the watchtower on the ready to relay the news to king David. Suddenly he called out, "I see a single runner." Shortly thereafter, the watchman reported, "I see a

II SAMUEL CHAPTER 18

second messenger." King David concluded both of these runners are bringing reports of the war. The watchman announced, "I recognize the first messenger as Ahimaaz, the son of Zadok." The king replied, "He must be bringing good news." Coming closer to king David, Ahimaaz shouted as he prostrated himself before the king, "All is well! Praised be your God for having delivered those that rebelled against you." When the king inquired, "Is my son safe?" Ahimaaz replied, "I saw a large crowd just as I was being dispatched by your servant Joab, after he had already sent off another courier. I therefore do not know the meaning of the crowd around Joab." King David ordered Ahimaaz to step aside to permit the second courier to deliver his message. The Cushite came before king David and reported, "Your highness, you have been vindicated this day in your war with those that rebelled against you." King David asked the Cushite, "Is Absalom safe?" The Cushite replied, "May all your enemies fare as that young man has fared at the hands of your defenders."

II SAMUEL CHAPTER 19

V.1   Provoked and shaken by the news that Absalom was dead, king David rose from his seat between the gates of the city of Mahanaim and went up to the watchtower on the wall of the city gates and wept, bemoaning the death of Absalom. "My son, my son Absalom!" He wailed out loud, "Would that I had died instead of you! O Absalom, my son, my son." Each time he pronounced his son's name, his personal guilt in Absalom's conduct engraved itself upon his conscience and amplified the pain in his heart. It was in this moment of *'truth'* that king David perceived through the veil of his tears, that he had not maximized his genetic potential for greatness. His personal life failed to follow the disciplines demanded by the Eternal God of history. "O my son, my son, I have failed you and the nation, when I failed to come face to face with my Zelem Elohim, my Godly image. I failed to inspire you by my example to overcome the moral and physical obstacles that retarded me from becoming a light unto my children and the nation." Absalom's death had pierced the veil of his mental block when it shocked him to recognize the consistency, the logical connection of the Eternal God's disciplines inscribed in the Torah. It is these laws that govern the lives of every human being; be they of low or high station. The higher we rise upon the social and national ladder, the greater the demand that we harmonize our personal lives with the disciplines of the Eternal's natural law, moral law and ethical law. Through king David's tears, he is forced to admit his arbitrary conduct in his relations with Absalom. It was he as judge and as executioner who implemented the Eternal's decree (II Sam. 18:1.2) as he sent forth his organized forces to deal with Absalom's rebellion.

Vs.2.5 The impact of king David's depression weighed heavily upon Joab. He now fully comprehended the full implications of king

II SAMUEL CHAPTER 19

David's admonition, "Deal kindly with my boy, Absalom." Joab's victory has been turned to sorrow. His humble soldiers who offered their lives for this victory feel the weight of their guilt for having participated in this action that brought on the grief of their king. Their sympathy for king David at this moment is the reason for their embarrassment. They returned to Mahanaim feeling like cowards who escaped their responsibility. Like thieves caught in the act, they returned to their homes stealthily; for fear that public opinion will point its finger at them and charge them, "You are responsible for the grief of king David." King David covered his face to stifle his weeping, yet, it electrified the nation and it became a crescendo as each individual repeated sympathetically with their king, "My son, Absalom, Absalom, my son."

Vs.6.7   Joab stood at the pinnacle of his life. Yet, his victory has been turned to ashes. Joab the realist, the man who had the courage to kill Abner (II Sam.3:27) when he interfered with his leadership. He is the same personality that also pleaded Absalom's cause (II Sam.14:1.33). It was he and none other who was responsible for his reconciliation with his father. Only he has the ability to see clearly the justice of his criminal act by becoming the executioner of Absalom. He is pained by the guilt and embarrassment that now weighs so heavily upon the conscience of his soldiers, who fought so valiantly for their king and the welfare of the nation. No other individual in the nation of Israel has the temerity and courage to put the king in his place and to charge him with the pall of sadness he has created in the Holyland by his conduct. Joab came before king David and bluntly charged him, "This day you have humiliated all your followers who have endangered their lives to save your life, the lives of your sons and daughters, the lives of your wives and your concubines. Your example of expressing your grief publicly has encouraged those who expressed their animosity toward you by joining Absalom's rebellion against you. Conversely, your conduct has shown contempt to those loyal to you, your kingdom and the nation. Were Absalom alive today and the rest of us dead, this would have pleased you. This should have been the day for you to observe the mitzvah of *bikerovai ekadesh* to control your grief; lest this great moment in history becomes a national tragedy. Your dedication as king of Israel is not to your rebellious son, Absalom, but to the whole nation of Israel." See T.E.T. (Lev.10:3.7).

Vs.8.9   "Arise! Go out and speak to the hearts of your people who have dedicated themselves to your cause. Should you fail to heed my plea, I take an oath, not a single man will remain with you overnight. Should you permit this to happen, it will become the greatest disaster in your whole life." King David perfunctorily made his appearance at the gate of the city of Mahanaim. As the word reached his troops, they presented themselves before their king. Those that had embraced Absalom's cause fled to their homes. There is no indication in the text or even a tradition that king David addressed his followers in accord with Joab's request. This is the retrogressive

II SAMUEL CHAPTER 19

factor in king David's personality that retarded him from becoming a model for all future kings in Israel. Reviewing the great men in Israel: Moses failed the Eternal (Num.20:12); Joshua failed the Eternal, in exceeding His law by creating an arbitrary ban (Josh.7:10.13). The Prophet Samuel failed to guide king Saul as he promised him in (I Sam. 13:8). This led to the Eternal's reprimand in (I Sam. 15:10.11). Saul failed when he executed the kohanim including the Gibeonites (I Sam. 22:11.19). King David's failures climaxed in the rebellion of Absalom and the execution of Saul's descendants (I Sam. 24:21.23, II Sam. 21:1.9). Gibeonites (I Sam.22:11.19).

Vs.10.11   King David remained in Mahanaim, while the nation's affairs remained in limbo. By design, he had decided to challenge the mood of the nation. During this interim period he reviewed the past: beginning with the first 20 years of his life which held such promise both for him and the nation; then the ten years which were spent in exile as a refugee, escaping from the wrath of king Saul. The past 35 years were devoted to fulfilling the mitzvah of *horashtem*, inheriting the full complement of land as outlined in (Num.34:) and striving to unite the nation in the Holyland. King David sees clearly that his personal failures have cancelled out his great successes. It is king David's personal failures that are occupying the minds of the people as they, too, are debating the question, "Shall they bring king David back to Jerusalem and recognize him for all that he has accomplished in the past or shall they seek new leadership for a new beginning?"

When all the facts surfaced, the ten tribes of Israel concluded, that despite all the great good that David had contributed to the welfare of the nation, they had failed to grant him the recognition for his efforts; nor have they given him the loyalty and gratitude of a united nation that he deserved. They, too, recognized their responsibility in becoming a contributory factor in Absalom's rebellion against king David. From this soul-searching period came the momentum for a national movement to reinstall king David in Jerusalem as their king and to rededicate themselves to the national welfare.

Vs.12.15   When the popular demand initiated by the ten tribes in the north and in Trans-jordan reached king David, he was deeply perturbed that the tribe of Judah, which was basically responsible for the rebellion, was not a part of the united action. Observing the inertia of the tribe of Judah, the king sent a message to the High priests Zadok and Abiathar, "Speak to the elders of Judah, prod them, 'Why should you exclude yourselves from the movement to bring king David back to Jerusalem? As my kinsmen you should be in the forefront of the movement." Zadok and Abiathar went to Amasa and delivered the king's message, "I, king David, hereby take an oath to appoint you my army commander to replace Joab when I am reinstalled in Jerusalem." Amasa took the initiative and rallied the patriotism of his kinsmen in Judah. From Amasa's call to action originated the message of the king, "Come back to Jerusalem with all your followers."

II SAMUEL CHAPTER 19

Vs.16.18   King David left Mahanaim and arrived at the eastern shore of the Jordan River, the Judites assembled at Gilgal, which was east of Jericho. Here they waited until the king arrived at the Jordan. Shimei, the son of Gera, the Benjaminite, the man who abused king David at the beginning of the rebellion (II Sam.16:5.8), now regretted his action for having become guilty of the law (Ex.22:27). He feared the king's justified punishment, and therefore came forth from Bachurim accompanied by 1000 Benjaminites. With him was Ziba, the servant of Mephibosheth from the House of Saul, his 15 sons and 20 slaves (II Sam.9:9.13, 16:1.4). Their intent is to be in the forefront of the reception that is forming to bring king David back to Jerusalem. Shimei and his followers offered their services to the king. To express their great joy that the king prevailed over his enemies, they jumped into the Jordan *vezalchu et hayarden* to create a path for the king and his retinue.

Vs.19.24   While the ferry-boat was carrying the king's family across the Jordan, Shimei flung himself at the feet of the king, "Hold me not guilty for the sin I committed on the day you left Jerusalem. I fully recognize my guilt. I have therefore come to be in the forefront of the House of Joseph to express our loyalty." Abishai, the brother of Joab, spoke up and charged Shimei for cursing the anointed of the Eternal. He turned to the king and challenged him, "Are you going to pardon Shimei in exchange for a mere confession?" King David interjected, "This is a matter which should not concern the sons of Zeruiah. Shimei's conduct involves but me and him. Your logic of challenging my compassion is inappropriate under the present circumstances (II Sam.16:10). This is hardly a day or a moment for vengeance. Not a single Israelite, no matter of his guilt will be put to death this day. My exultant joy of regaining my throne by the acclamation of a united Israel must not be marred by a single fatality. I take an oath you shall not die by my hand this day (I Kings 2:8)."

Vs.25.31   The scene described in these verses took place in Jerusalem. It is placed here because of Ziba's presence in Shimei's representation for the House of Saul. Mephibosheth came down to greet the king from his estate in Gibeah. He appeared before king David in the palace. He had not pared his toenails, or had he trimmed his beard-mustache, he had not washed his clothes, from the day king David went into exile, to this very day he had observed as a period of mourning for his benefactor. The king asked Mephibosheth, "Why didn't you come with me when I left Jerusalem?" Mephibosheth answererd the king, "I could not, because Ziba deceived me. My plan was to join you. However, being dependent upon Ziba to take me, he forsook me. I recognize you as an angel of God for all you have done for me. Despite all the evil conduct of my family, you have singled me out to honor me by including me at your table as one of your princes. Even though I have been deceived by Ziba, I have no right to appeal to you." King David interrupted, "You need not concern yourself any more. I hereby decree that Ziba

II SAMUEL CHAPTER 19

shall divide the property with you." Mephibosheth interjected, "Let him take it all! I am fully rewarded by your safe return" (II Sam.16:1.4).

Vs.32.39   Barzillai, the Gileadite from Rogelim (II Sam.17:27), who had supplied king David and all those that were with him in Mahanaim with many of their necessities, he came down to the eastern shore of the Jordan to bid his king farewell. King David urged him to come to Jerusalem, that he may reciprocate his spontaneous generosity. Barzillai, who is now 80 years of age, replied to the king, "My days are literally numbered; besides I can barely appreciate good food from bad food. I therefore would not appreciate the luxurious comfort you desire to provide for me. All foods taste alike to me, my hearing is impaired to appreciate the singing of men or women. My coming with you would only become a burden to you. I could barely cross the Jordan with you. There is no reason for you to reward me so generously. Permit me to go back to Rogelim and live out my life. I will then die in my own community and be laid to rest near the graves of my father and mother. However, if you insist on rewarding me, take my son Chimham with you and do what you think is best for his development." King David replied to Barzillai, "I shall be pleased to carry out your plans for his development and maturity. Feel free to direct me as a substitute for you in assuming your responsibility as a father."

Vs.40.44   The troops crossed the Jordan first. King David kissed Barzillai and bade him farewell as he started his journey back to Rogelim. King David and Chimham crossed the Jordan and were greeted by a representation of Judite soldiers and a large contingent from all the other tribes of Israel. From here they went to Gilgal. When they arrived in Gilgal, the men of Israel who represented the northern tribes complained to king David for having been slighted by his fellow Judites, when they desired to join in the honor of crossing with the king. The Judites replied, "As fellow Judites we felt we had a priority. Why should you let this perturb you? We gained nothing from this privilege." The Israelites replied, "Our share in king David is greater by token of the fact that we represent 10 tribes and you are but one. Why did you offend us? It was we who initiated the proposal to reinstate king David in Jerusalem." From V. 44, we may derive two conclusions: 1-that each of the tribes vied for recognition for the initiative which resulted in a united kingdom, 2-it exposed the pettiness of the average Judite, their desire to create friction in a crucial moment of history, to hurt human feelings by blurting out, *vayikesh devar ish Jehudah* harsh words which created the ripples of animosity. This is not the protoplasm out of which we can build a united nation. To unite a nation one must have the sensitvity of a king David. See vs.19.24, for an example how king David handled the crudeness of Shimei, the son of Gera. It is these thoughtless, crude hotheads that tear the fabric of unity apart among individuals, families and nations.

II SAMUEL CHAPTER 20

Vs.1.2 A scoundrel by the name of Sheba, son of Bichri, a Benjaminite, came to the reception of king David for the sole purpose of inciting dissension at the slightest provocation. When king David passively ignored the complaint of the Israelites (II Sam.19:42.44) he thereby gave them the opportunity to kindle the old animosities between Judah and the other tribes of Israel. Had king David taken their complaint seriously, in the same manner that he evaluated and controlled his anger with Shimei, son of Gera, who was also a Benjaminite, he could have allayed the smoldering embers of dissent. Once again the retrogressive factor in king David's personality surfaced (II Sam.13:38.39, 14:33, 15:7.9, 19:8.9).

Sheba's sounding of the horn was premeditated. He had no official authority to use it and (II Sam.20:16.22) substantiates this conclusion. Sheba's timing was the stimulus to ignite the spark that fanned the sleeping embers of animosity toward the Judites as he proclaimed, "We have no portion in king David's government. We have no place in the heart of (David) Jesse's son! Return ye, every man to your home in order to express your resentment for this contemptuous act."

Every representative Israelite spontaneously followed Sheba. King David made no effort to assuage the frayed feelings of the Israelites. He completely ignored their action and continued his journey to Jerusalem.

V.3 The rebellion of Absalom and now the potential rebellion of the rabble rouser Sheba, detonated king David's Zelem Elohim; his intelligence was activated to grasp the full meaning of (Gen.6:3). Human error is the result of the ongoing conflict between the physical desires of man and the Eternal's demand that we make our contribution to the evolution of history. King David is inspired to perceive that he must strive to harmonize the Eternal's basic truth; man's development must be reflected in his contribution to genetic progression. When king David arrived in Jerusalem, he implemented his resolution by separating himself from his ten concubines. He established separate homes for them and provided for them for the rest of their natural lives. Like widows of the king, they remained out of bounds.

Vs.4.6 In keeping with his promise to elevate Amasa to Joab's position, king David gave him the opportunity to prove himself, "I give you three days to mobilize an army from the tribe of Judah and report back to me in Jerusalem." When Amasa failed to appear at the appointed time, the king called in Abishai, the brother of Joab, and confided his innermost fears, "Unless we react to Sheba's treasonous act at once, it could harm us even more than the rebellion of Absalom. I therefore direct you to mobilize our regular standing soldiers who normally fight under the leadership of Joab. Pursue this rabble rouser until you find him. For he may find a fortified

II SAMUEL CHAPTER 20

city in which to hide and thereby elude our grasp, challenging us to destroy the city and its inhabitants. This is not my intention.

Vs.7.8   King David had every intention to replace Joab after the death of Absalom (II Sam.19:6.9) and Joab's crude and penetrating showdown with the king. Joab's evaluation of the political situation dictated his decision to join his brother Abishai and to lead his loyal soldiers, the Cherethites, the Pelethites and the Gittites to help nip any potential rebellion before it gathers any momentum. It is also obvious that he was aware of king David's promise to Amasa. This fact helped him to overlook the slight of placing his brother in command of this operation, because it gave him the opportunity to express his determination that Amasa shall not succeed him. Joab and Abishai led their soldiers from Jerusalem in pursuit of Sheba, the son of Bichri. Arriving at the great stone (a marker) in Gibeon, Amasa and his drafted army from Judah came toward Joab with his men.

Vs.9.13   From the following details it is quite clear that Joab's plan to kill Amasa was premeditated. The text describes how this outstanding soldier mounted his sword in such a careless manner that it fell to the ground from its scabbard. He nonchalantly stooped to retrieve his sword with his left hand. Amasa was completely distracted by this incident. Holding the sword in his left hand Joab approached Amasa, "How are you, brother?" His right hand reached for Amasa's beard as he pretended he was going to kiss him while his left hand penetrated Amasa's groin. Joab's precision found its mark as Amasa's entrails poured out of his abdomen. This is the second time (II Sam.3:26.27) we have a detailed record of his expertise with the sword and his sagacious ability to follow through on his predetermined course. V.10. One of Joab's soldiers standing close by Amasa's body called out facetiously, "He that favors Joab and he that favors king David follow Joab." The soldier was reprimanded for his levity in the presence of Amasa's dead body. Only then did the soldier remove Amasa's body from the highway to a nearby field and covered it with a garment. Having satisfied his first reason for joining Abishai, Joab gave the order for all the soldiers to fall in line; this included Amasa's Judite draftees. Joab turned to the second reason; the search for Sheba.

Vs.14.15   Sheba and his followers had gone throughout the various tribes in his effort to gain support for his rebellion until he reached Abel-beth-maacah, which is west of Dan. See T.E.T. for the historic background of this community and its inhabitants (Deut.3:14, II Chron.16:4 Abel-maim, I Kings15:20, II Kings15:29). Abel-beth-maacah, offered Sheba and his Bichrite followers asylum in their fortified city. Joab traced Sheba's migration to this community. Here they started to build a mound of earth and stones for the purpose of breaching the wall.

Vs.16.21   While Joab and Abishai's men were engaged in building their rampart for the siege of Beth-maacah, a bright woman

II SAMUEL CHAPTER 20

mounted the wall and demanded Joab's attention. When Joab approached her and identified himself, the woman said to him, "In ancient times, we of Abel-beth-maacah upheld the law given in (Deut.20:10.11). When the people of Canaan took counsel with the people of Abel, we always advised them to make peace with Israel. I, too, am one of those, who seeks the welfare of Israel. Why should you desire to kill and destroy a city in Israel?" Joab replied, "Far be it for me to kill and destroy and ruin. We are in search of Sheba the son of Bichri, who desires to create rebellion against king David. Just hand him over to us and I will withdraw from the city."

Vs.22.26   The woman assured Joab, "His head will be thrown over the wall to you." The woman consulted the leaders of the city, and they agreed to her conditions. They executed Sheba and threw his head over the wall to Joab. Joab sounded the horn. The soldiers ceased building their rampart and returned to Jerusalem. The details given in vs.23.26 are a duplication of the details given in (II Sam.8:16.18) with a slight variation. The intent in these verses is to confirm the fact that with the restoration of king David in Jerusalem, Joab was reinstated as commander-in-chief of the whole army in Israel. Benaiah, son of Jehoiada, commanded the Cherethites and the Pelethites. Adoram was in charge of the labor-gangs under the corvee for drafted labor. This was a new institution which was expanded in Solomon's time. Jehoshaphat, son of Ahilud was the recorder, Sheva was the scribe and Zadok and Abiathar were the High Priests. Ira, the Jairite of Manasseh became a minister (kohen) an honorary position in the same manner as (II Sam.8:18).

II SAMUEL CHAPTER 21

Vs.1.14   These verses deal with a famine which took place about 14 years after the death of king Saul. This was the fifth year of king David's reign in the city of Jerusalem. Chronologically its rightful place is before chapter nine. See table of contents for details.

Vs.15.22   The details recorded in these verses belong to the Hebron period and are a part of (II Sam.5:17.25) before the capital was transferred to Jerusalem. In accord with (II Sam.8:15) David reigned over a united Israel. He had already established the maximum perimeter or borders of Israel which conforms with (Num.34:1.15). Within this perimeter king David is obliged to integrate all the ethnic groups who have agreed to observe the minimal standards of The Seven Laws of Noah. In return they shall be guaranteed their basic human rights and equal protection under the law of the Torah which demands justice and righteousness for all its inhabitants.

V.1   King David is troubled and hard put to ascertain the cause of three consecutive years of drought. After every meteorological reason known at that time were investigated, the reason for

II SAMUEL CHAPTER 21

the drought still evaded them. In keeping with the mood and the moral standards of the period, king David's counselors concluded, they must probe and test their moral conduct as a community to ascertain the reason for nature's infliction (Gen.4:8.12, 9:5.6, Num.35:33.34). These laws hold every human being accountable to uphold the Eternal's Natural Law, Moral Law and Ethical Law. When we ignore the demand of these laws, this activates the critical moment where Heaven and Earth meet to deny humanity their ability to survive. From these laws king David and his counselors concluded the drought and the famine are a Divine visitation. Therefore, king David must become the *goel hadam*, the prosecutor, to demand justice for any criminal act which has become the cause that has short-circuited "The Earth's Natural Law," which in turn now demands an accounting for crimes chargeable to the nation. Upon closer investigation the indicators pointed to the massacre in Nob by king Saul recorded in (I Samuel 22:11.23). In this massacre were included 85 kohanim actively engaged in the priesthood, their wives, children and their livestock. Included were seven Gibeonite-Nethinim, actively engaged in the menial chores at the Sanctuary in Nob. These Nethinim were part of the Gibeonite community with whom Joshua had concluded a treaty because they had voluntarily conformed with the minimal standards demanded by Torah Law (Deut.20:10, Joshua 9:15,20.23). Following this massacre, king Saul reacted overzealously beyond the letter of the law to purge *bekanoto* them.

Vs.2.6   King David sent for the Gibeonites, who were Hivites. "We have searched our records and we recognize that you were aggrieved by our late king Saul. State your demands, we are desirous of satisfying your grievances in order to expiate king Saul's injustice toward your community. We do this because we are desirous of your forgiveness that you may pray in our behalf that this drought come to an end. The Gibeonites replied, "Though we are poor by your standards, we make no claim for material advantages of gold or silver, we bear no malice nor do we accuse the people of Israel for having wronged us."

King David responded, "On behalf of the people of Israel, we are desirous of satisfying your claim. State your demand." The Gibeonites answered, "We request that you surrender the seven known male survivors, who are immediate descendants of king Saul, who sought *lehashmidenu* to exterminate us. We further request your permission to impale them on a stake in Gibeah of Saul, before the House of the Eternal where the Nethinim were massacred (Num.24:4)." King David sought to appease each and every member of their community with a handnsome ransom, yet, despite their poverty they sought no financial ransom. King David pursued his effort to compensate them in any other manner than surrendering Saul's descendants to pay the maximum penalty for a crime performed by their grandparent. King David concluded his negotiations by telling them, "I will honor your request." To complete the record of the Gibeonites, many went abroad to escape Saul's persecution. In the 5th century

II SAMUEL CHAPTER 21

BCE, Ezra recruited Nethinim-who were Gibeonites (Ezra 7:7.24, 8:1.20), Nehemiah 3: reports their resettlement in Jerusalem together with other skilled personnel. (Neh.10:1.40) they were accepted in an assembly in Jerusalem to ratify a covenant obviously as converts to Judaism.

V.7   Was inserted here after king David had established the whereabouts of Mephibosheth, the son of Jonathan (II Sam.9:1.13). It is obvious the Gibeonites knew nothing about the existence of Mephibosheth because he was living in Lo-debar, close to Mahanaim, in the home of Machir, son of Ammiel (II Sam.17:27). This is the same Machir that supplied king David with his needs while in exile from his son Absalom's rebellion.

Vs.8.9   King David summoned Armoni and Mephibosheth, the two sons born to Rizpah and king Saul. She was the daughter of Aiah. He also summoned the five sons of Merab, who were adopted by their aunt Michal after the death of Merab. Merab's husband was Barzillai the Meholathite. King David surrendered these seven descendants of king Saul to the Gibeonites. They impaled them upon the hill of Gibeat Saul (I Sam.22:18.19) where the kohanim and the Gibeonites were massacred. These seven descendants of Saul died together to expiate the death of the kohanim and the Gibeonites. David gave instructions that they were to remain impaled until the rains came to indicate Israel's forgiveness in this massacre. The text established the time frame for the execution as the spring, in the beginning of the barley harvest.

King David's action in this matter raises many questions: (Deut.21:22.23, 24:16). The Torah has specifically reversed the ancient barbaric practice written into Babylonian law. In accord with Torah law, "Parents may not be charged for criminal acts of their children, nor may children be charged with the transgressions of their parents." In later centuries the sages enlarged upon this law, by banning parents or children from giving testimony as witnesses against each other. We must reject Rabbi Yochanan's comment in (Yebamoth 79a). In light of (Psalms 119:126), precisely at this critical moment when king David was obliged to uphold the Eternal's law, he has ignored the Eternal's teachings. King David's defection from Torah law at this decisive moment when he stood at the height of his political powers, causes us to ask the question, "Were the descendants of Saul considered expendable, in order to eliminate them as potential contenders to the throne of Israel?" (II Sam.6:21.23).

V.10   Rizpah, king Saul's concubine emerges from this tragedy as the noblest personality of this period. Her kindness, her love, her mercy, survive the centuries as she built a temporary shelter to protect herself from the elements. Here in her sackcloth shelter she stayed to protect the bodies of her dear ones from bird and beast; from the moment they were executed in Nisan to the month of Heshvan, when the rains

II SAMUEL CHAPTER 21

came. For six months she vigilantly challenged the callousness of her period which permitted this desecreation of Torah law (Deut.21:22.23). The Torah directs mercy even to a criminal. Once he has discharged his debt to society, his burial must be performed with the same dignity, that we stand ready to extend to the noblest individual. To permit the dead body to hang past sunset of the same day of death, is an affront to the Eternal God, in Whose image man has been created. (Gen.3:19) "Permit the evil conduct of man to disintegrate into the individual components of the soil, that the soil ever remain pure for the living." (Eccl.12:7,13.14) "Permit the soul of man to return to its Creator, in order to give an accounting for its life upon Earth."

Vs.11.14 When king David learned of Rizpah's vigilance, the consideration and respect she had extended to the House of Saul, he was touched by her noble example. Only then did king David order the remains of the seven bodies that were impaled to be buried. They also exhumed the remains of the bodies of king Saul and his three sons: Jonathan, Abinadab, Ishvi and (Malchishua-Ishbosheth), they were laid to rest in the family sepulcher of their father and grandfather Kish, in the town of Zela in the territory of Benjamin. (King Saul and his three sons' bodies were buried in Trans-jordan (I Sam.31:12.13).

Vs.15.17 The action described in these verses took place in (II Sam.5:17.21), see commentary for details. We are now given some details of the heroism of king David's loyal soldiers. In the course of this battle king David was exhausted by the military action. At this critical moment one of the giant sons of the ancient Rephaim, Ishbi-benob, who was girded in new armor and with a new special spear, (The text tells us the weight of the spear was 300 copper shekels, to express the size of this giant man), came upon David in his weakened condition and was prepared to kill him. Abishai, the son of Zeruiah, his father was an Ishmaelite, came to David's aid and killed Ishbi-benob. It was this incident and at this time that king David's officers took an oath, that he shall no longer join them in the field of battle, lest the light of Israel's king become extinguished.

Vs.18.22 The battle described in these verses is recorded in (II Sam.5:22.25) see commentary for details. In this action Sibbecai the Hushathite killed Saph, a descendant of the giant Rephaim. In another battle in the same war, Elhanan the son of Jair (I Chron.20:5) the Bethlehemite slew the brother of Goliath, the Gittite. The text describes the ferocity of this giant; his spear was as large and as treacherous as a weaver's beam. In another battle which took place in Gath, Jonathan, the son of Shimea, dispatched another giant who was a descendant of the Rephaim, who had six fingers on each hand and six toes on each foot. These four giant descendants of the Rephaim were killed by king David's men.

II SAMUEL CHAPTER 22

Chapter 22 is a biographic Ode that records the multi-faceted life of king David. I have striven to pinpoint the various experiences recorded in the book of Samuel that have inspired the text of the Ode. I have also given chapter and verse that have stimulated and animated king David's thoughts. I join the sainted Rashi, in his conclusion that this chapter was written very close to the end of David's reign. This chapter was the original version of Psalm 18. Tractate Sofrim has concluded that king David made 74 minor variations in the text before it became a part of the Book of Psalms.

King David attributes all his successes to his faith in the Eternal God of history. His faith inspired him to dedicate himself to the Eternal's Blueprint - the Torah, for the development of Israel's history. This chapter is a fitting addenda to a lifetime devoted to his God and to his people. King David confirms for the record that his successes were the result of his sensitivity to the Eternal's demand *laasot tzedakah umishpat*.

Vs.1.2   King David dedicated this Ode to the Eternal God of Israel. He expresses his gratitude for his survival and his victories over Israel's national enemies and his internal enemies. David is ever mindful to credit the Eternal for his survival of the tremendous odds he faced in Saul's psychopathic desire to kill him (I Sam.18:11.16, 25,28.29, 19:1.2,10.11, 20:30.34, 21:11, 23:14.16,24.28, 24:5.8,11.16, 26:9.10,20.21). "O Eternal God, You have been my stronghold, You have protected me at all times. You have been my liberator that rescued me from all dangers."

Vs.3.4   You, O God, are *tzuri*, the source of my security (II Sam.5:17.25, 15:15.22). *Echzeh bo* in His protective custody do I take shelter. His disciplines shielded me from harm. *Vekeren yishi*, they became the source of my power. *Misgabi umnusi*. You are my fortress into which I ever take refuge. *Moshii*, He is my savior *mechamas toshieni*, Who rescued me from the violence of my enemies.

V.4   *Mehulal ekra Adonai*, (Ex.15.11) With utmost faith do I call upon the Eternal. It is He that has protected Israel in the past. *Umeovai ivashea*. My prayers bolster my faith-self assurance, that He shall deliver me from my enemies.

Vs.5.6   *Afafuni chevleh maveth*. The portents of danger have encompassed me, *venachale belial*, the counsel of charlatans plan to destroy me (Ex.15:8, Deut.13:14, II Sam.16:5.8,21.23, 17:1.4, 20:12, Ps.124:3.4). *Hevle sheol sabuni*. The pangs of death besiege me (Gen.37:35, II Sam.18:7, 17, 19:1.3) the grave opened wide to ambush me and devour me.

V.7   *Batzar li ekra Adonai*. From the depths of my anguish, I called upon the Eternal my God. *Vayishma mehechalo koli*. My prayers penetrated the firmament to His abode. He heard my

II SAMUEL CHAPTER 22

voice. *Veshavathi beasnav*, He stood at attention as my plea pierced His conscience (Ex.2:23.25, 34:6.7) to animate His mercy.

V.8 *Vayithgaash vatirash haarets*. The Earth rocked and quaked. *Mozdei harim yirgazu*. The very foundation of the mountains trembled. *Vayithgaashu*, humanity trembled, *ki charah lo*, as the Eternal gave expression to His indignation of human corruption, anarchy and rebellion. (Gen.6:6.7, 7:4, Ex.14:21). The *Tsunami* in the Aegean Sea, that destroyed the island of Thera at the time of the Exodus had devastated Egypt. (Ex. 15:5.8, Joshua 3:14.17, II Sam. 18:8, Ps. 60:4.6). See Addendum pp. 70.77.

V.9 King David describes the great geological drama of Santorini. *Alah ashan beapo*. Smoke rose from the Eternal's nostrils, to express His anger at the shambles man is making of His world (Ex.14:24, 15:7.8), *Veesh mipiv tochel*. The flame of His anger devoured the human tyrants; like coal they nourished the flame *gehalim baaru mimenu*, that implemented the geological drama (Ex.14:19, Gen.19:24.28, I Sam.14:15) which became the Eternal's Pillar of Fire, to kindle the torchlight of hope for Israel, and a new beginning for the world.

V.10 *Vayet shamaim vayered*. The Eternal manifested His authority as He bent the heavens to descend upon the Earth, to observe at first hand the shambles man has made of his environment by war, slavery and anarchy (Gen.3:24, 6:6.7, 19:24.28, Is.43:19, Ex.20:18). *Vaaraphel tachath raglav*. Concealed and invisible from the human eye by their ignorance, the Eternal came down to Earth to introduce a new beginning.

V.11 *Vayirkav al keruv vayaaf*. The Eternal mounted a Cherub (Gen.1:2). He scanned the earth to observe the effect of His Natural Law, Moral Law and Ethical Law. *Vayera al kanfe ruach*. Yet mankind failed to grasp the Eternal's Presence in the affairs of man (Ex.33:18.23) how every living creature draws its existence from the Eternal, the Source of his intelligence-Zelem Elohim rooted in the genetic process. Therefore every living moment is an encounter with God. Yet, man confirms the Presence of God, only, after the Eternal has come down in the whirlwind, to punish man for not measuring up to his true potential (Gen.2:7, 6:3, Ps.104:3.5).

Vs.12.13 *Vayasheth choshech sevivothav sukoth*. Human ignorance concludes that God's dwelling place is like a pavilion enshrouded by darkness to conceal Him from man. *Hashrath maim avei shechakim*. Yet, it is these dark clouds that filter and distill and refine mankind's water supply so vital for every living thing (Gen.13:10, H2O). *Minoga negdo baaru gachale esh*. One day by the process of evolution, man will come to recognize these emanations from the light of God are but the atoms functioning in these dark clouds which burn like coal to fulfill the needs of every living thing upon Earth.

II SAMUEL CHAPTER 22

Vs.14.15 *Yarem min-shamaim Adonai.* The Eternal utilizes nature's powers as a man of war; they thundereth from the heavens to advance the process of civilization upon Earth (Ex.15:2.6, Judges 5:20.22, I Sam. 7:10, Ps.29:3). *Veelyon yiten kolo.* Blessed is the man who recognizes God, as the highest rung of human intelligence. *El Elyon*, he has granted Israel every victory beginning with Abraham (Gen.14:20.22) and throughout Israel's history. *Vayishlach chizim vayefizem.* The spontaneity of the Eternal's response to my call (says David) is the Source of my salvation v.4. *Barak vayehumem.* When my enemies recognize the Source of the arrows of lightning, they are confounded (Ex.8:15, Judges 5:20.22) as the battle turns into a rout.

V.16 *Vayerau afike yam, yigalu mosdoth harim.* When mankind becomes exposed *begaarath Adonai* to the rebuke of the Eternal, *minishmath ruach apo*, and feels the full force of His indignation, the cataclysmic phenomena described in vs. 8.9 is activated. The seas divide, the mountains quake and pour forth lava to destroy every living thing within reach. This is the point in time that man is given the ability to see the very foundation of the world exposed and laid bare, to teach tyrannical despots the power, the force of the Eternal God's natural powers (Gen.19:25.26).

Vs.17.18 *Yishlach mimarom yikacheni.* At every critical moment of my life, You reached down from Your abode. *Yamsheni mimayim rabim*, You drew me out from the torrents of turbulent waters that threatened my life (Ps.144:7). *Yatzileni meovai az*, You reached down to rescue me from my powerful enemies. *Misonai ki amtzu mimeni.* From foes whose collective strength was beyond my capability. King David cannot overlook the years of misery created by king Saul, the years he spent in enemy territory as a fugitive. For details see references given above in vs.1.2.

Vs.19.20 *Yekadmuni beyom edi.* At the lowest point in my life, when every calamity came home to me, the Eternal came to my rescue as He inspired men of good will and courage to sacrifice their lives in my behalf (Deut. 32:35, II Sam. 15:19.37, Ps. 17:13.14). II Sam.15:19.37, Ps.17:13.14). *Vayehi Adonai lemishan li.* The Eternal was my stay as He surrounded me with dedicated and loyal men. *Vayotzieni lamerchav*, You, O God, led me out of my straightened situation and granted me freedom to serve Thee once again. *Yechaltzeni ki chafetz bi*, You reciprocated my faith as expressed in v.3 (Ps.116:8, 118:5).

V.21 *Yigmeleni Adonai ketzidkathi.* May the Eternal reward me, commensurate with my dedication to His cause, the evolution of humanity. *Kebor yadai yashiv li*, You, O Eternal God, Who can penetrate the innermost secrets of man, reward me in accord with my sincerity; as I strive both actively and passively to fulfill your disciplines and commandments.

II SAMUEL CHAPTER 22

V.22 *Ki shamarti darchei Adonai*. I have observed the commandments of the Eternal, out of my sincere conviction. *Velo rashathi Meelohai*. When I strayed from the disciplines of the Eternal, I did so because of my humanity (Gen.6:3). I never challenged His direction and demand for righteous conduct.

V.23 *Ki chal mishpatav lenegdi*. The Eternal's laws are ever in my conscience (Deut.17:18.20). *Vechukothav lo asur mimenah*. I ever strive not to depart from the Eternal's statutes, because collectively they create harmony in the symphony of life.

Vs.24.25 *Vaeheyeh tamim imo*. I strive to be forthright and sincere with my God. *Vaeshtamrah meavoni*, in order to protect myself against impiety. *Vayashev Adonai li ketzidki*. When I transgressed the Eternal's statutes (II Sam.11:4.5, 12:5.7,12.13, Ps.51), I recognized my transgression and accepted His judgment graciously. *Kebori leneged eynav*, in accord with my Creator's conclusions and judgment, to the extent of my culpability.

Vs.26.27 *Im chasid tithchasad*. The Eternal recognizes the selfless devotion of human kindness, to reward man with an equal measure of kindness. *Im gibor tamim titamam*. To him who strives to transmit the Eternal's disciplines in human relations, the Eternal rewards him in accord with his dedication to His Divine law. *Im nabar titabar*. The Eternal rewards the upright in accord with his consecration and sincerity (I Sam. 24:5.23). *Veim ikesh litapal*. Those that are deceptive and perverse are punished in just measure of their conceit and cunning.

V.28 *Veeth-am ani toshia*. King David parallels his call to serve his God with that of Moses (I Sam.16:13, Ex.2:23, 3:6.7, Deut.26:7). Israel's cry for help had penetrated the firmament; they were denied their human rights which are guaranteed by the Eternal God. Therefore He was grieved. *Veenecha al ramim tashpil*. The Eternal resolved to humble the arrogant (Ex.10:7, 11:9).

Vs.29.30 *Ki atah neiri Adonai*, You, O Eternal, are my light, my inspiration that animates my life. You are the Source that has stimulated me to dedicate my life to my people; this has crowned me with the title, the Lamp of Israel (II Sam. 21:17, Pr.20:27). *Ki bechah arutz gedud*, You have endowed me with the capability (Ps.119:105) to pursue a troop. *Belohai adaleg shur*, You, O God, have granted me the resolution to acquire Mount Zion in behalf of my people (I Sam. 30:8, II Sam. 5:6.10). Against formidable odds and in concert with Your demand I scaled the fortress of Zion.

V.31 *Hael tamim darko*. The way of the Eternal God is perfect. *Imrath Adonai zeruphah*. The word of the Eternal has been

II SAMUEL CHAPTER 22

tested and refined in the crucible of history (Ex. 33:18.23). It is ever consistent. It harmonizes to create the sanctity-perfection in men and women's lives, in just proportion to human resolution to observe His disciplines. *Magen hu lechal hachosim bo.* He is a shield to all those that look to Him for guidance. The Eternal scans the souls of men and women in search of human beings whose perspective and dedication conform with His guidelines for human development.

V.32 *Ki mi-El mibalade Adonai.* What claim have man's pantheon of idolatrous images to be recognized as God? Only the Eternal is the God of history. It is He that created the nucleus which contains the Blueprint for all life. God pronounced His creation as good and firmly established Natural Law, Moral Law and Ethical Law, for mankind's welfare to live and prosper in just proportion as he contributes to the Eternal's plan for evolution the perfection of human relations. *Umi zur mibalade Elohenu.* Where can humanity find solace, comfort, consolation and deliverance from daily problems? Only the Eternal is the bedrock of human security because it is rooted in His law. To live by His law is to maintain health of body and mind which leads to the gateway of happiness.

V.33 *Hael mauzi chayil.* It is this Eternal God, that has endowed me with natural ability and inspiration to perceive His guidance in my everyday life. *Vayather tamim darki,* it is He that has granted me the freedom to choose my path in life. It is He that has granted me the perception to dedicate my life to His standards of excellence.

V.34 *Meshaveh raglai kaayaloth.* It is *Hazur,* my Rock, my Redeemer, my Fortress of strength, that granted me the physical ability to run as fast as a hind and the agility to evade my enemies. *Veal bamothai yaamideni.* It is He that bequeathed me through genetic progression and inspiration the ability to reach for the mountain tops (I Sam.23:14) to secure my position against those who are envious of my blessings.

V.35 *Melamed yadai lamilchamah.* The Eternal's blessings of natural ability granted me the capablity to defend myself and to teach others the art of self defense (II Sam.1:18). *Venicheth kesheth-nechushah zeroothav.* My dedication to the Eternal's direction granted me the foresight to discern the superiority of the brass bow used by our enemies. My perception encouraged me to develop the physical power to bend a bow of brass (Ps.144:1).

V.36 *Vatiten li magen yishecha.* Despite my natural ability to defend myself, I am ever dependent upon the salvation of my Eternal God, to inspire me to choose the right moment for my response (Ps.142:6.8, I Sam. 19:10.11). *Vaanothcha tarbeni.* Despite my skills, it is Your reply to my prayers that have enabled me to succeed. Your condescension to my prayers also taught me humility, to credit my glory to the Eternal God.

II SAMUEL CHAPTER 22

V.37 *Tarchiv tzaadi tachteni*, You, Who granted me the ability to walk stridently, with confidence, *velo maadu karsulai*, that my ankles or knees do not buckle beneath me by the doubt of the justness of my mission (Ps.18:37).

Vs.38.39 *Erdefah oivai veashmidem.* Continue to grant me the ability to destroy my enemies. *Velo ashuv ad kalotham.* That I do not turn back empty handed until I have destroyed them. *Vaachalem vaemchatzem velo yekumun.* Grant me the ability to obliterate them, that they may not rise against me again. *Veyiplu tachath raglai.* These verses are full of bitterness; king David has spent a lifetime girded for war against political, tribal and national enemies of Israel. He is weary of all this strife, that has denied him the privilege of building a House in the name of God (II Sam.7:1.3). Let me see them destroyed as they lay at my feet lifeless, that I can get on with building for peace.

Vs.40.41 *Vatazreni hail lamilchamah.* It is true you have girded me with strength and determination to succeed in war. *Tachria kamai tachteni*, You have granted me the ability to subdue my foes. *Veovai tatah li oref*, You created the conditions as Israel's enemies turned tail and ran for their lives. In the same spirit I pray *mesanai veatzmithem*, that you shall come to my assistance to help me to expose my personal enemies for their treasonous conduct.

Vs.42.43 *Yishu veen moshia*, I am ever grateful to those that remained loyal to my cause and did not join the opposition to help them. *El Adonai velo anem*, I am every thankful to You, O Eternal God, for having confirmed the justness of my cause, as You ignored their plea for deliverance (II Sam.15:19.37, 18:6.8). *Veeshchakem kaafar aretz.* With your help, I pounded them into the dust of the earth. *Ketit chutzoth adikem erkaem*, I trod them down until they were unidentifiable from the soil of the roadway.

V.44 *Vatefalteni merivei ami*, You have rescued me from the strife of my own brethren. To offset my heartache for having become the punishing rod of the Eternal. *Tishmereni lerosh goim*, You have rewarded me by becoming the king of many alien nations, as I fulfilled your *mitzvah* of *vehorashtem* (II Sam. 8:1.18). *Am lo yadaati yaavduni*, You have consolidated my sovereignty in my own land and over alien peoples who opposed me in taking possession of the Holyland.

Vs.45.46 *Benei nechar yithkachashu li.* Aliens have chosen to be condescending to me in gratitude for their security and human rights which are guaranteed by Torah law (Deut.33:29). *Lishmoa ozen yishamu li.* They are attentive to my direction for they respect my dedication to the Eternal's law. *Bene nechar yibolu.* Alien opposition has

II SAMUEL CHAPTER 22

withered. *Veyachgeru mimisgerotham.* Only in secret do they dare show their enmity toward the government of Israel.

Vs.47.49 *Chai Adonai ubaruch tzuri.* In contrast to v.32, king David testifies; the Eternal God liveth and blessed be the Rock. *Veyarum Elohei tzur yishi.* Exalted be He, who granted me victory. *Hael hanothen nekamoth li.* The God Who has vindicated me in the eyes of all humanity, *umorid amim tachteni.* It is He Who has decreed that I become their ruler. *Umozii meovai, umikamai terommeni.* The Eternal, Who has rescued me from Israel's national enemies, has now justified my position as His anointed king of a united Israel. *Meish chamasim hatzileni.* May this same Eternal God grant me now, in the evening of my life the continued safety from lawless men (II Sam. 3:26.30, 20:9.10).

Vs.50.51 *Al ken odecha Adonai bagoyim, uleshimcha azamer.* In gratitude for all You have done for me, O Eternal God, I shall devote my efforts to bring Your message of hope to all of humanity, to help create human beings of good will. *Migdol yeshuoth malko,* You have been a tower of victory and salvation to Israel's king. *Veoseh chesed limeshicho.* May You ever deal kindly with Israel's anointed king, *leDavid ulezaro ad olam.* Continue Your kindness and protection to David and his posterity forever. (II Sam. 7:12.16).

II SAMUEL CHAPTER 23

V.1 This is the introduction by the compiler of the book of Samuel. Vs.1.7 are among the last memoirs of king David. These verses were not included in the Book of Psalms. King David's last will and testament is given in (I Kings2:1.12). These verses are the reflections of king David, the son of Jesse, who was anointed by the inspiration of the God of Jacob-Israel, to become known in Israel's history as the sweet singer of Israel.

Vs.2.3 *Ruach Adonai diber bi,* King David proclaims for the record of history, that if we study the texts of his writings, we will conclude that his inspiration came directly from the Eternal God, Who motivated his *Zelem Elohim,* perception, and granted him the ability to observe the 'link' how every living creature draws its existence from the Eternal, the Source of all life (Sforno). *Umilotho al lelshoni* The Eternal's message animated me to transmit His direction for the evolution of Israel to become a light unto humanity (Is.42:6).

Amar Elohei Yisrael, I shall speak in the name of the God of Israel, in the same spirit as the Eternal God spoke to Abraham (Gen.18:17.19) that he inspire his posterity to become the conscience of man and in the same spirit that the Eternal God of Israel spoke to Moses (Deut.16:20) *tzedek tzedek tirdof.* The

II SAMUEL CHAPTER 23

highest demand in the life of every human being is the pursuit of justice. *Li diber Tzur Yisrael*, I am now the recipient of the same message; for the Rock of Israel has spoken to me to convey His message to my generation. Israel's God is sanctified by righteousness and justice in our everyday living. *Moshel baadam*. This ever remains the Eternal's demand for Israel's *morashah* inheritance of the Holyland, that he, who rules the land of Israel shall establish standards for justice. *Tzadik moshel yirath Elohim*. That he, who rules over men must give evidence of his reverence for God, and take his direction from His inspiration to establish justice in the land (Ps.72:).

V.4 *Ucheor boker yizrach shemesh*. Every new regime is comparable to a new day, a new beginning as mankind looks forward to a bright, sunny future. *Boker lo avoth*. It is comparable to a cloudless morning. *Minoga mimatar*, the shining sun has been sterilized by the rain. *Deshe mearetz*. The freshness of the sprouting grass is the promise of fresh growth as the blessings of the Creator become evident. To maintain this prosperous picture, it is vital that the ruler be dedicated to righteousness and justice.

V.5 *Ki lo chen bethi im El*. My reign cannot be compared with that of my predecessor (Saul) (I Sam.15:17.19,23,35). *Ki berith olam sam li*. For the Eternal has granted me an everlasting covenant (II Sam.7:8.16). A covenant in which my obligations as a ruler have been set forth. *Aruchah bakol ushemurah*. To assure the permanence of my dynasty, the Eternal has vowed to protect my posterity who shall succeed me, that they not wither as grass which has lost the Source of its nourishment. The Eternal has provided, *Ki chal yishi vechal chefetz*, for every contingency, that my aspirations shall succeed. *Ki-lo yatzmiach*. That it will not germinate, sprout, grow and flourish is remote from my mind.

Vs.6 *Uvelial kekotz munad kulaham*. Worthless rulers are compared to thorns which are soon cast away. *Ki lo beyad yikach*. So are corrupt and Godless regimes. When they are new, like fresh thorns, they can be manipulated, controlled and managed. However, when they advance in years, they become incorrigible and must be cast aside.

V.7 *Veish yiga bahem*. Incorrigible leaders are intractable and beyond redemption; it is impossible to get through to them. *Yimale barzel veetz chanith*. One must come armed and fully protected by a coat of mail, a staff and a spear. *Uvaesh sarof yisarfu bashaveth*. There is but one solution for worthless and Godless regimes, they must be destroyed by fire like brambles and thorns; to make certain that they cease as a living organism to introduce retrogression in the Eternal God's standards for righteousness and justice.

The following heroic personalities recorded in vs.8.39 have distinguished

II SAMUEL CHAPTER 23

themselves during the reign of king David. They have been singled out from the thousands who made up the army of Israel because of their special skills in warfare. Since the text of these verses are faulty, I shall insert the corrected format of the text which has been accepted by scholars down the centuries and include the source of the correction.

V.8 (I Chron.11:11) Yashbeam, the son of Chachmoni, headed the list of these same personalities who made up king David's counselors. The phrase *Basheveth tachkmoni*, is a mnemonic standing for *Yoshev rosh biyeshivath chachme hamedina*. Adino Haetzni was the chief of captains, who was responsible to Abishai v.19, and Joab was the commander in chief.

Vs.9.10 Elazar, the son of Dodo, the Ahohite. He was one of the three valiant men with David in the battle of Ephes-dammim, with the Philistines (I Sam.17:1, I Chron.11:12.13). He was also one of those involved in the mopping up operations after Goliath was slain by David. He fought on until his hand froze to his sword. Following his intrepid performance, the soldiers came to strip the slain Philistines.

Vs.11.12 Shammah, the son of Age, the Ararite from Havoth-jair, single-handedly pursued the Philistines, whenever they set upon the Israelite fields at harvest time. (I Chron.11:14) *vayithyatzvu*, credits both Elazar and Shammah for coming to the rescue of the farmers where they were growing *adashim*, lentils, '*seorim*,' barley.

Vs.13.19 The experience referred to is (II Sam.5:17.25, I Chron.15:19). Three of king David's chiefs came down to the Cave of Adullam, while a force of Philistines were in the area of Bethlehem. King David facetiously requested a drink of water from his childhood spring in Bethlehem. These three men broke through the enemy lines and brought king David the water from the cistern which is in the wall of the city. King David refused to drink water for which his men had risked their lives. Instead he poured it as a libation to God. Heading the three groups mentioned was Abishai, the brother of Joab, whose mother was Zeruiah, a sister of king David. He was second in command and responsible to Joab. However, the heroism of Yashbeam, Elazar and Shammah were unmatched.

Vs.20.23 Benaiah, the son of Jehoiada, was a most valiant man. His home was in Kabzeel (Joshua 15:21, IISam.8:18, I Chron.11:22.25). He is credited with many outstanding and daring achievements. It was he that slew two lion-hearted men who were defending the altar-hearths belonging to the king of Moab, in the city of Ataroth (see line 12 Moabite Stone). He also tracked down a lion in the snow to a pit and went down to kill it there. Confronted by a huge Egyptian, who was armed with a spear; Benaiah charged him with his staff and took the Egyptian's spear and killed him with his own spear. Of the thirty valiant men in this chapter, he was a

II SAMUEL CHAPTER 23

most outstanding soldier, though he was outranked by the first three men named. King David appointed him to head his personal body guard. He was recognized for his dependability to come through every critical situation.

Vs.24.39   The following is a list of the thirty valiant men recognized for their heroism. Heading the list was Abishai the brother of Joab. Included in the list is Asahel their younger brother whose death is reported in (II Sam. 2.23). (I Chron. 1:41.47), reports 16 additional names:

Elchanan the son of Dodo from
   Bethlehem
Shammah the Harodite
Elika the Harodite
Heletz Hapalti
Ira, the son of Ikesh the Tekoite
Abiezer the Anathothite
Mebbunai, the Hushathite
Zalmon the Ahohite
Maharai the Netophathite
Heleb, the son of Baanah, the
   Netophathite
Ittai, the son of Ribai of Gibeah of
   the tribe of Benjamin
Benaiah the Pirathonite
Hiddai of Nahale-goash
Abi-albon, the Arbathite
Amaveth, the Barhumite
Eliahba, the Shaalbonite of the sons
   of Jashen, Jonathan
Eliahba and Jonathan, the sons of
   Jashen, the Shaalbonite
Shammah, the Hararite
Ahiam, the son of Sharar the Ararite
Eliphelet, the son of Ahasbi, the son of the Maacathite
Eliam, the son of Ahithophel, the Gilonite
Hezri, the Carmelite
Paarai, the Arbite
Igal, the son of Nathan of Zobah
Bani, the Gadite
Zelek, the Ammonite
Naharai, the Beerothite,who was the armour
   bearer to Joab, the son of Zeruiah
Ira, the Ithrite
Uriah, the Hittite.

II SAMUEL CHAPTER 23

Thirty-seven in all. Three in vs.8.12, three in vs.13.23, thirty-one in vs.24.39. The constant number of those named to fill the needs of the corps was 30.

II SAMUEL CHAPTER 24

Vs.1.2 Once again the anger of the Eternal was raised against Israel. The first time was in chapter 21. In (I Chron.21:1) the text tells us the subject of this sentence is Satan, he is to entice David's ego. *Vayaseth eth David* King David's ego is anxious to create the statistic for history of his accomplishments during his reign. From v.9, we discover the motive of his ego is to draft a large army. King David issued a directive to Joab and his host to organize a census, which shall include every community in the Holyland from Dan to Beer-sheba, "That I may know the sum of the people."

Vs.3.4 Joab is justified in challenging king David's motive, "What purpose will it serve?" Although king David used the term *haam*, what he conveyed to Joab was every able-bodied man that can carry arms in war. Joab challenged king David's motive, that Israel is precluded from building an empire. It may not expand outside of the allotted perimeter outlined in (Num.34:1.15). Despite Joab's subtle reply, in a quotation given in the words of Moses, "May the Eternal your God increase the numbers of Israel a thousand fold (Deut.1:11) and may you live to see it. It should be obvious to you that our population has increaseed!" King David withstood Joab's opposition to his plan for a census.

Vs.5.9 Joab organized the census and began in Trans-jordan, then went north to Dan, westward toward Zidon-Phoenicia. They numbered the Israelites living in the city of Zor and in other communities, though occupied by aliens, it is part of the Holyland, they then traveled southward to Beer-sheba. At the end of nine months they returned to Jerusalem. Joab issued the report to king David, 800,000 valiant men that had military training and represented the northern territory of Israel and 500,00 men from the tribe of Judah. It is important to note that Judah still considered itself a separate entity. In (Chron.21:5) the number is given as 1,100,000 for the northern tribes of Israel and 470,000 in Judah. This discrepancy is corrected by pointing out that Joab at first gave *mifkad* an overall sum and then gave *mispar* a detailed breakdown of his first report.

Vs.10.12 When king David evaluated his obstinate action, he fully grasped his transgression. King David entered his *mikdash-meat*, his inner sanctuary, his heart, and confessed to himself his transgression, he then addressed the Eternal, "I have sinned greatly in what I have done; I beseech Thee, remit the guilt of Your servant David, for I have

II SAMUEL CHAPTER 24

acted foolishly." When king David arose the next morning after his confession the prophet Gad (I Sam.22:5, I Chron.29:29) had already been alerted and was commanded to appear before king David. "You are to offer him the same three choices David had pronounced in behalf of king Saul (I Sam.26:10). 'That king Saul's life will come to an end in one of three ways: "1, In the course of his lifetime he will be smitten by physical illness, 2, he will live out his allotted time span, 3, he will be swept away by the enemy in battle."

V.13 The prophet Gad came before king David and challenged his motive in conducting his census, "You cannot escape your guilt in this egotistical-satanic challenge to the Eternal's direction given in (Ex.30:12)." When the prophet Nathan pointed to David's highest priority (II Sam.7:8.11, Num.33:52.53), it was to perform the *mitzvah* of inheriting the Holyland as outlined in (Num.34:1.15). Had he issued a draft for an army at that time he would have been justified. The prophet Nathan had emphasized the Eternal's demand to create an oasis for civilization; from which shall emanate the ideas for the evolution of humanity (Is.2:1.4). David's transgression is obvious. Now was the time to build for peace. David should have consulted with the prophet Nathan, to redirect his priority, now that he had fulfilled the *mitzvah* of *vehorashtem*, to concentrate his efforts to building the Temple, instead of mobilizing for a war of expansion.

This was the time and moment to electrify the nation by the law given in (Ex.30:12.16) *lechaper al nafshotechem* to create the invincible peace of mind when one contributes to the national welfare. This *mitzvah* of contributing *'trumah Ladonai'* a half shekel on a democratic basis for the building of a House in the name of the Eternal God, would have penetrated the consciousness of the people, to pause and count their blessings in gratitude for having accomplished what Moses had set out to do for them 400 years before this time.

The Eternal did not incite David against the census which became a demand in his thinking. The Eternal's anger with David was caused by his ignoring a law which was in the Torah for 400 years, that a census must be conducted in a mood of elevation and construction. David's digression from observing the law in (E.30:12.16) is on a par with ignoring (Ex.20:17). The prophet Gad addressed king David, "Choose your own punishment for the infraction of the Eternal's law."

1..."Seven years of drought and famine." (I Chron.21:12) corrected the number to three years.
2..."Your satanic-egotistical census could invoke Israel's enemies to construe your census as a mobilization for war. Should this have been your motive, be it known you shall be pursued for three months before you once again gain control."
3..."Or you may choose three days of pestilence which will ravage the Holyland."

V.14 King David said to the prophet Gad, "I recognize my transgression and I recognize my dilemma and my distress. I

II SAMUEL CHAPTER 24

choose to let the Eternal God choose my punishment (Ex.34:6.7, Ps.6:) Whose compassion is everlasting. Let me not be beholden to the mercies of man. War would be subject to the impact of the enemy's determination. Famine would be subject to the mercy of those who control the granaries."

V.15   The infectious plague visited upon the Holyland was implemented by the Eternal's natural law. The incubation period lasted three days. The full impact of the infection struck on the third day and lasted from the morning of the third day until noon. The virulence of the infection was felt from Dan to Beer-sheba. The total loss in lives of those who could not build up an immunity was 77,000.

V.16   This verse can only be understood as a metaphor, a literary device to convey the full meaning of Israel's punishment; chargeable to king David for defaulting in his leadership as he strayed from the Etrernal's directions in history. Israel, too, was caught up in its prosperity and has strayed from its destiny (Is.2:2.4, 42:6).

There should have been a public demand for building the Temple. This was the moment for Israel to express its gratitude for all its blessings. In v.16 king David visualized through his distress that the angel of God has come to destroy Jerusalem, the city of his dreams. It was king David that advanced the concept of the Central Sanctuary when he mobilized 30,000 representative individuals to celebrate the return of the Ark of God and set it up in his newly acquired city of Jerusalem (II Sam.6:). He never relinquished his dream as he accumulated the funds and material for its construction despite the prophet Nathan's redirection (II Sam.7:1.17). *Vayinachem Adonai el haraah* king David's faith never wavered: (Ex.34:6) "I now comprehend Your mercy; that when man falters, it is Your grace that grants man the ability to rise again." King David's confession in v.17 and the Eternal's order to the *malach* were spontaneous as they converged on the threshing floor of Araunah, the very spot where the *Akedath Yizchak* (Gen.22:11.12) took place. This is the very piece of ground upon which the Temple in the name of the Eternal God shall be built.

V.17   As king David visualized the potential destruction of his dream, David addressed the Eternal, "I alone am guilty, I alone have done wrong; Why punish these poor sheep? They are innocent. I assume the blame as the king of Israel for having brought this iniquity upon Israel. Punish me and my father's household."

Vs.18.19   The prophet Gad came before king David that very day and ordered him to build an altar upon the threshing floor of Araunah. King David set forth at once to implement the prophet's instructions.

Vs.20.23   Araunah came forward to greet the king and his retinue. As

II SAMUEL CHAPTER 24

king David approached Araunah, he prostrated himself before the king and asked, "Why has the king come to his servant Araunah?" King David replied, "I have come to buy this threshing floor from you, that I may build an altar upon it to stay this plague among my people." Araunah replied to the king, "Let my lord the king take it and use it for whatever purpose he may desire, and offer up whatever he desires. You need not buy it." Araunah offered to supply king David with all that he may need to offer his sacrifice. "I give it all to you, O king, and may the Eternal, your God respond to you with favor."

Vs.24.25   King David replied to Araunah, "I cannot accept your offer as a gratuity, for I may not offer sacrifices which cost me nothing." King David bought the threshing-floor and the oxen for fifty shekels of silver. He built an altar unto the Eternal God and offered burnt offerings and peace offerings. The Eternal responded to king David's plea in behalf of the Holyland and all of its inhabitants and the plague was checked. (I Chron.21:25) informs us that king David paid 600 shekels of gold. Tractate Zebachim 116b completes the record that king David in recognizing his error, set about involving the whole House of Israel. He now fully realized that a House built in the name of the Eternal God, must be the effort of the whole House of Israel. He therefore collected 50 gold shekels from each tribe to pay for Araunah's threshing floor and all its appurtenances, accessories and the oxen.

With utmost gratitude to the Eternal God, for having granted me the capacity to explain the sacred books of Samuel to my generation, I herewith set my hand on this Eve of the Sabbath of Parshath Beshalach, the Sabbath when we recite the 'Shirath Mosheh.' The 12th day of Shebat 5742.

David Lieberman.